DATE DUE

MAR	05 1984		
MAY	8 1984		
~~JUN 06 1984~~			
11-1-93 p-ag			

DEMCO NO. 38-298

ILLUMINATED
MANUSCRIPTS

BURT FRANKLIN BIBLIOGRAPHICAL SERIES

1. Burt Franklin & G. Legman. David Ricardo and Ricardian theory. A bibliographical checklist. New York, 1949.
2. Francesco Cordasco. A Junius Bibliography. With a preliminary essay on the political background, text and identity. A contribution to 18th century constitutional and literary history. With eight appendices. New York, 1949.
3. Burt Franklin & Francesco Cordasco. Adam Smith: a bibliographical checklist. An international record of critical writings and scholarship relating to Smith and Smithian theory, 1876-1950. New York, 1950.
4. Edmund Silberner. Moses Hess: an annotated bibliography. New York, 1951.
5. Francesco Cordasco. The Bohn Libraries. A history and checklist. New York, 1951.
6. Jan M. Novotny. A Library of Public Finance and Economics.
7. Andrew George Little. Initia operum latinorum, quae saeculis XIII, XIV, XV, attribuuntur, secundum ordinem alphatbeti disposita. 13 + 275 pp. 8vo., cloth. (Manchester University Publications, n. 5 - 1905). New York: Burt Franklin, 1958.
8. John William Bradley. Dictionary of miniaturists, illuminators, calligraphers and copyists with references to their works, and notices of their patrons, compiled from sources, many hitherto inedited, from the establishment of Christianity to the 18th century. 3 volumes, lg. 8vo., cloth. (London, 1887-89) New York: Burt Franklin, 1958.
9. Frank Wadleigh Chandler. The literature of roguery. 2 vols., 8vo., cloth. (The Types of English Literature, ed. by W. A. Neilson). (Boston, 1907). New York: Burt Franklin, 1958.
10. Robert Huntington Fletcher. The Arthurian material in the chronicles, especially those of Great Britain and France, 9 + 313 pp., bibliography, 8vo., cloth ([Harvard] Notes and Studies in Philology 10, 1906) New York: Burt Franklin, 1958.
11. John Alexander Herbert. Illuminated manuscripts. 10 + 355 pp., 51 plates; index of manuscripts, scribes and illuminators; bibliography, lg. 8vo., cloth. (London, 1911). New York: Burt Franklin, 1958.

BREVIARY OF JOHN THE FEARLESS, DUKE OF BURGUNDY
FRENCH, 1404-19
Brit. Mus., Harl. 2897

ILLUMINATED MANUSCRIPTS

BY

J. A. HERBERT

Burt Franklin Bibliographical Series XI

BURT FRANKLIN
New York 25, N. Y.

Published by
BURT FRANKLIN
514 West 113th Street
New York 25, N. Y.

This work was originally published
LONDON
1911

MANUFACTURED IN THE UNITED STATES OF AMERICA
NOBLE OFFSET PRINTERS, INC., 400 LAFAYETTE ST., NEW YORK, N. Y.

TO
SIR GEORGE WARNER
MAGISTRO DISCIPULUS

PREFACE

IN the following pages an attempt is made to sketch the history of the illumination of vellum manuscripts, from classical times down to the decay and virtual disuse of the art which resulted inevitably, though not immediately, from the introduction of printing; describing the main characteristics of each of the most important periods and schools, and following the development of the successive styles so far as existing materials allow. These materials, for some sections abundant almost to excess, are for others scanty, and sometimes fail altogether; so that it is no easy task to make them tell an orderly, consecutive, and well-proportioned story. The question of proportion is always a difficult one for the author of a compendium; and I must admit that exception might be taken to my allotting so much more space to a few Classical and Early Christian manuscripts than to the vast bulk of French fifteenth century work. My defence is that the student of illumination, for whose guidance this book is intended, is sure to be already familiar with examples of the later work, and to need little more than a few hints as to what is best in it; so that a much greater degree of compression is permissible and desirable here than in discussing the earlier manuscripts, which are rare, little known, and difficult of access, yet have vital significance as marking stages in the development of the art. The references in the footnotes, and the classified bibliography and index of manu-

ILLUMINATED MANUSCRIPTS

scripts at the end, will, it is hoped, be of service to the reader who wishes to carry his studies further.

My thanks are due to the late Sir T. Brooke, Mr. H. Yates Thompson, and the Rev. E. S. Dewick, for the plate from Mr. Dewick's edition of the Metz Pontifical. I have also to thank Mr. Thompson for giving me repeated access to his splendid collection, and for leave to reproduce a page from his Hours of Jeanne de Navarre. The plate from Kraus's edition of the Codex Egberti is given by kind permission of Messrs. Herder, the publishers; those from the Codex Rossanensis and Codex Gertrudianus, by kind permission of my friend Dr. A. Haseloff. For the plate from the Peterborough Psalter I have to thank the President and Fellows of the Society of Antiquaries; for those from the "Très Riches Heures" and the "Quarante Fouquet," M. Gustave Macon, Conservateur-adjoint of the Musée Condé. I am further indebted to many other possessors or custodians of manuscripts, notably to M. Omont at Paris, Mr. Madan at Oxford, Mr. Palmer at S. Kensington, and Père van den Gheyn at Brussels. Finally, I wish to record my gratitude to three friends who have laid me under specially great obligations: Miss Evelyn Underhill, my colleague Mr. G. F. Hill, and, above all, my departmental chief, Sir George Warner, Keeper of MSS. in the British Museum. The extent of my debt to the last-named, indeed, is but faintly suggested on the dedication-page and in the footnotes.

J. A. HERBERT

1 *June,* 1911

CONTENTS

	PAGE
PREFACE, ...	vii
LIST OF PLATES, ...	xi
CHAPTER I. THE ILLUMINATION OF CLASSICAL MANUSCRIPTS, ...	1
,, II. EARLY CHRISTIAN ILLUMINATION TO THE END OF THE SIXTH CENTURY,	14
,, III. BYZANTINE ILLUMINATION, . .	36
,, IV. CELTIC ILLUMINATION, . . .	66
,, V. THE CAROLINGIAN RENAISSANCE, .	88
,, VI. OUTLINE-DRAWINGS OF THE NINTH, TENTH, AND ELEVENTH CENTURIES, ESPECIALLY IN ENGLAND,	106
,, VII. ENGLISH ILLUMINATION TO A.D. 1200,	122
,, VIII. GERMAN, FRENCH, AND FLEMISH ILLUMINATION, A.D. 900–1200, .	143
,, IX. ITALIAN ILLUMINATION BEFORE 1300,	160
,, X. ENGLISH ILLUMINATION IN THE THIRTEENTH CENTURY, . .	174
,, XI. FRENCH, FLEMISH, AND GERMAN ILLUMINATION IN THE THIRTEENTH CENTURY, ...	192
,, XII. ILLUSTRATIONS OF THE APOCALYPSE,	209

ILLUMINATED MANUSCRIPTS

			PAGE
Chapter XIII.	English Illumination in the Fourteenth and Fifteenth Centuries,	. . . .	220
,, XIV.	French Illumination in the Fourteenth Century,	.	236
,, XV.	Italian Illumination in the Fourteenth Century,	.	255
,, XVI.	French Illumination after 1400,	. . .	265
,, XVII.	The Italian Renaissance,	.	286
,, XVIII.	Flemish Illumination after 1300,	. . . .	306

Note on the various kinds of Liturgical Illuminated Manuscripts, ... 324
Select Bibliography, ... 331
Index I—Manuscripts, ... 341
 ,, II—Scribes and Illuminators, . . 346
 ,, III—General, ... 347

LIST OF PLATES

I.	Breviary of John the Fearless, Duke of Burgundy. French, 1404–19. *Brit. Mus., Harl.* 2897 . *Frontispiece*	
		TO FACE PAGE
II.	Virgil. IVth cent. (?). *Rome, Vatican, Cod.* 3225. [From *Codices e Vaticanis selecti*, vol. i, 1899] . . .	6
III.	Gospels (Codex Rossanensis). VIth cent. *Rossano Cathedral.* [From Haseloff, *Codex purpureus Rossanensis*, 1898]	25
IV.	Gospels. Byzantine, XIth cent. *Brit. Mus., Burney* 19	37
V.	Simeon Metaphrastes. XI–XIIth cent. *Brit. Mus., Add.* 11870	52
VI.	Psalter of Melissenda, Queen of Jerusalem. Byzantine, 1131–44. *Brit. Mus., Egerton* 1139	60
VII.	Gospels (Book of Kells). Irish, VIII–IXth cent. *Dublin, Trin. Coll.* [From Abbott, *Celtic Ornaments from the Book of Kells*, 1895]	66
VIII.	Lindisfarne Gospels (Durham Book). *Circa* 700. *Brit. Mus., Nero D.* iv	74
IX.	Gospels ("Codex Aureus"). Carolingian, *circa* 800. *Brit. Mus., Harl.* 2788	90
X.	Gospel-book of S. Medard's Abbey, Soissons. Early IXth cent. *Paris, Bibl. Nat., lat.* 8850 . . .	94
XI.	Alcuin Bible. Carolingian, IXth cent. *Brit. Mus., Add.* 10546	96
XII.	Utrecht Psalter. IXth cent. *Utrecht University.* [From Pal. Soc. *Autotype Facsimile*, 1874]	110
XIII.	Liber Vitae of Newminster, Winchester. Early XIth cent. *Brit. Mus., Stowe* 944	118
XIV.	Psalter. English, XIth cent. *Brit. Mus., Tib. C.* vi .	120
XV.	Grimbald Gospels. Winchester, XIth cent. *Brit. Mus., Add.* 34890	132
XVI.	Bible. English, XIIth cent. *Winchester Chapter Library*	138
XVII.	Life of St. Guthlac. English, late XIIth cent. *Brit. Mus., Harley Roll Y.* 6	140

ILLUMINATED MANUSCRIPTS

		TO FACE PAGE
XVIII.	Codex Egberti. 977–93. *Trier, Stadtbibliothek.* [From Kraus, *Die Miniaturen des Cod. Egberti*, 1884]	148
XIX.	Psalter of Egbert, Archbishop of Trier, 977–93. *Cividale, Codex Gertrudianus.* [From Haseloff, *Der Psalter Erzbischof Egberts*, 1901]	152
XX.	Exultet Roll. Italian, XIIth cent. *Brit. Mus., Add.* 30337	166
XXI.	Psalter. English, early XIIIth cent. *Brit. Mus., Roy.* 1 D. x	176
XXII.	Psalter of Robert de Lindesey, Abbot of Peterborough, 1220–2. *Society of Antiquaries, MS.* 59	180
XXIII.	Bible. English, XIIIth cent. *Brit. Mus., Roy.* 1 D. i	184
XXIV.	Psalter of Prince Alphonso (Tenison Psalter). English, 1284. *Brit. Mus., Add.* 24686	190
XXV.	Psalter. French, XIIIth cent. *Brit. Mus., Add.* 17868	196
XXVI.	Gospel-Lectionary. Paris, late XIIIth cent. *Brit. Mus., Add.* 17341	198
XXVII.	Surgical treatise by Roger of Parma. French, XIIIth cent. *Brit. Mus., Sloane* 1977	200
XXVIII.	Somme le Roi. French, *circa* 1300. *Brit. Mus., Add.* 28162	202
XXIX.	Psalter. Flemish, XIIIth cent. *Brit. Mus. Roy.*, 2 B. iii	204
XXX.	Apocalypse. English, late XIIIth cent. *Oxford, Bodl. Douce* 180	216
XXXI.	Psalter. English, early XIVth cent. *Brit. Mus., Roy.* 2 B. vii	220
XXXII.	(Same)	222
XXXIII.	Psalter. East Anglian, early XIVth cent. *Brit. Mus., Arundel* 83	226
XXXIV.	Cuttings from a Missal. English, late XIVth cent. *Brit. Mus., Add.* 29704	232
XXXV.	Metz Pontifical. 1302–16. *Library of H. Y. Thompson, Esq.* (*formerly of Sir T. Brooke, Bart.*). [From Dewick, *Metz Pontifical*, 1902]	238
XXXVI.	Horae of Jeanne de Navarre. French, *circa* 1336–48. *Library of H. Y. Thompson, Esq.* [From H. Y. Thompson, *Hours of Joan II, Queen of Navarre*, 1899]	244
XXXVII.	S. Augustine, De Civitate Dei. French, late XIVth cent. *Brit. Mus., Add.* 15245	246
XXXVIII.	Horae. Flemish, *circa* 1300. *Brit. Mus., Stowe* 17	254

LIST OF PLATES

		TO FACE PAGE
XXXIX.	Niccolò di Ser Sozzo, 1334–6. *Siena, Archivio di Stato, Caleffo dell' Assunta*	258
XL.	"Très Riches Heures" of Jean, Duc de Berry, d. 1416. By Paul de Limbourg and his brothers. *Chantilly, Musée Condé*	272
XLI.	Bedford Hours. French, *circa* 1423. *Brit. Mus., Add.* 18850	274
XLII.	Horae of É. Chevalier, by Jean Fouquet, mid. XVth cent. *Chantilly, Musée Condé.* [From Gruyer, *Les Quarante Fouquet*, 1897]	280
XLIII.	Horae, School of J. Fouquet. French, *circa* 1470. *Brit. Mus., Egerton* 2045	282
XLIV.	Leaf from Choir-book. Sienese, early XVth cent. *Brit. Mus., Add.* 35254 C	288
XLV.	Scotus, Quaestiones in Sententias. Italian, 1458–94. *Brit. Mus., Add.* 15273	290
XLVI.	Liberale da Verona. *Circa* 1475. *Siena, Libreria Piccolomini. Gradual*	298
XLVII.	Sforza Book of Hours. Milanese, *circa* 1490. *Brit. Mus., Add.* 34294. [From Warner, *Sforza Book*, 1894]	300
XLVIII.	(Same)	302
XLIX.	Mandeville's Travels. Flemish, early XVth cent. *Brit. Mus., Add.* 24189	308
L.	Prayer-book. Flemish, *circa* 1492. *Brit. Mus., Add.* 25698	316
LI.	Horae ("Golf Book"). Flemish, early XVIth cent. *Brit. Mus., Add.* 24098	322

CORRIGENDA

Plate VII.   *For* VIIth cent. *read* VIII–IXth cent.
Plate XXXV.   *For* Sir T. Brooke, Bart., *read* H. Y. Thompson, Esq.
Plate L.   *For* Book of Hours *read* Prayer-book.

ILLUMINATED MANUSCRIPTS

CHAPTER I

THE ILLUMINATION OF CLASSICAL MANUSCRIPTS

THE opening chapter of a complete history of illuminated manuscripts, in the widest sense of the term, ought no doubt to be devoted to Egyptian papyri. Many of these were richly adorned with coloured illustrations; and specimens of this art survive dating back to the fifteenth century B.C., such as the famous Book of the Dead made for Ani, now in the British Museum. But the present work is less ambitious: only illuminations on vellum come within its scope, and only such of these, for the most part, as are of European origin. In one respect, however, we must extend the definition of illuminated manuscripts. Strictly speaking, the term is only applicable to manuscripts which are illustrated or ornamented in colours; some writers would even restrict it to those in which the precious metals too are used—which are "lit up" by gold or silver foil. But paintings and outline-drawings are so intimately connected (at all events, as applied to the embellishment of vellum manuscripts) that the latter can hardly be excluded from an attempt to describe the development of the illuminator's art.

Tradition assigns the invention of vellum to Eumenes II, king of Pergamum, B.C. 197–158, though the skins of animals, more or less specially prepared as writing material, had undoubtedly been used in Egypt long before his time. But the earliest definite reference

ILLUMINATED MANUSCRIPTS

to an illuminated manuscript on vellum occurs in Martial's Epigrams, written towards the end of the first century of the Christian era. Among other inscriptions for gifts of various kinds is one for a Virgil on vellum, having a portrait of the poet for a frontispiece (xiv. 186):—

Vergilius in membranis

Quam brevis inmensum cepit membrana Maronem!
Ipsius et vultus prima tabella gerit.

This gift-book has not survived to our days. It is interesting, however, to find that one of the few extant remains of classical book-illustration is a Virgil[1] containing the poet's portrait; not indeed on the first page, but on more than one of those which follow.

The distich just quoted proves that the art of miniature was practised in Martial's time. No specimens survive, however, which can be assigned to an earlier date than the fourth century; in fact, only three illuminated manuscripts of the classical period are now known to exist—the two Virgils in the Vatican and the Iliad at Milan. These are precious both for their rarity, and also as an indication of the style of much work which has now vanished; for the Iliad and the smaller Virgil show by the fully developed manner of their paintings that they are less the casual beginnings, than the last products, of an art. It seems unlikely, however, that this art had ever attained great proportions or enjoyed general popularity. No doubt there were many classical illuminated manuscripts (as there were many manuscripts of all kinds) which have perished, both separately and in the wholesale destruction of great libraries such as those of Alexandria, Constantinople, and Rome. But we may fairly assume that no greater proportion of these were destroyed than of other kinds. Indeed, books with paintings, being always more costly than plainly written copies, would be guarded more

[1] Cod. Vat. lat. 3867.

CLASSICAL MANUSCRIPTS

carefully, and we might therefore expect more of them to survive, relatively to the total number executed. The Ambrosian Iliad, for instance, was preserved purely for the sake of its pictures, all the plain leaves having long ago disappeared. But we find that whilst numerous codices of classical texts exist, in a more or less complete state, written in the fourth and fifth centuries, if not earlier, only the three above mentioned show any trace of illumination.

It may seem strange that the masterpieces of Greek and Roman literature, with their wealth of material, and with the numerous models afforded by paintings and sculptures of the best periods of Greek art, should not have produced a large and influential school of book-illustration. But illumination is an art which appeals chiefly to the class of mind that enjoys detailed beauty, small refinements, exquisite finish. The genius of Roman art was quite other than this. It was an art of display, which expressed itself chiefly in statuary, architecture, mural paintings; the ornamentation of great surfaces of the house and street. It raised triumphal arches and splendid tombs, but did not trouble itself much about the enrichment of books for private pleasure. The illuminated Homer or Virgil was always the fancy of an individual, never the necessity of the library.

One sort of book, however—the Calendar—seems to have been illustrated with paintings from a very early period, if we may accept the available evidence, which is rather of a second-hand kind, coming mainly, in fact, from a seventeenth century copy of a ninth century manuscript, which is supposed in its turn to have been copied from a fourth century original, now lost. This copy, now in the Barberini Library at Rome,[1] was made for that accurate and unprejudiced antiquary Peiresc, who showed a patience and common sense, in his deal-

[1] Published by J. Strzygowski, *Die Calenderbilder des Chronographen vom Jahre* 354, Berlin, 1888 (Jahrbuch des k. deutschen archäol. Instituts, Ergänzungsheft i.).

ILLUMINATED MANUSCRIPTS

ings with antiquity, far beyond the average of his own, or even of a later, day. It bears many evidences of authenticity, as well as some indication of the copyist's desire to "improve upon" his original. In a word, we have fairly good reason for believing the fourth century original to have been illustrated, and that in much the same way as the later copies, so far as the subjects are concerned; but it would be rash to draw any inference from the existing pictures as to the style of execution, or even the details of composition, of the lost archetype.[1]

The work in question is generally known as the Calendar of the Sons of Constantine, and its date is fixed, by the "Natales Caesarum" and other chronological notes, at the year 354 A.D. It purports to have been executed, probably at Rome, by Furius Dionysius Filocalus for a patron named Valentine. The drawings with which it is illustrated represent the cities of Rome, Alexandria, Constantinople, and Trier, personified in true classic fashion as female figures—Trier as an Amazon leading a captive barbarian; the planets, the sun and moon, the months, the signs of the zodiac. There are also portraits of Constantius II and Constantius Gallus Caesar. The figures of the months are specially interesting as the forerunners of the delightful Calendar-pictures prefixed to the Psalters and Books of Hours of the Middle Ages. They are generally nude or half-draped youths, and symbolize, more or less directly, the occupations proper to the various seasons. Thus March is a shepherd-boy, pointing upwards to a swallow; October, with a basket of fruit, is taking a hare from a trap. These

---

[1] The danger is well exemplified by a thirteenth century copy (Paris, Bibl. Nat., nouv. acq. lat. 1359) of an eleventh century chronicle of the abbey of S. Martin des Champs (Brit. Mus., Add. 11662). The miniatures in the copy correspond exactly with the drawings in the original as to subject and position in the text; but there the resemblance ceases. The later illustrator, with the sound artistic instinct which characterized his time, made no pretence of imitating the crude designs of his predecessor. See M. Prou in the *Revue de l'art chrétien*, 1890, pp. 122–8. On the other hand, some of the drawings in Harl. 603 (eleventh century), are almost exact reproductions of those in the ninth century Utrecht Psalter.

CLASSICAL MANUSCRIPTS

month-pictures exist, not only in the copies made for Peiresc, but also in a fifteenth century MS. at Vienna, from which Strzygowski has published five (January, April to July) to make good the deficiencies of the Barberini MS. The Vienna pictures are rectangular, without any ornamental framing; but those in Peiresc's copy are placed in decorated frames, with a pediment surmounted by a lunette addition, decorated with debased classical patterns, such as the Greek scroll, cable, egg-and-dog-tooth, very carelessly executed. Unless these are the tasteful addition of the ninth century copyist—a not improbable hypothesis—we have here the only evidence that classical illuminators ornamented, as well as illustrated, their books. The miniatures in the classical texts which we shall next consider are pictorial only; it is not until the sixth century that we meet with other instances of the use of decorative borders and conventional ornament.

Of the three classical manuscripts to which we have already referred, by far the best is the smaller of the two Virgils in the Vatican.[1] Its pictures are not all of equal merit, but the best are painted in so mature a manner, with so dexterous a technique, as to make one feel very sure that we have in them the only surviving work of a large and developed school of illumination. It has been very carefully studied by M. Pierre de Nolhac,[2] and published in photographic facsimile by the authorities of the Vatican Library.[3] In its present fragmentary state it consists of seventy-five leaves, containing parts of the Georgics and of the Aeneid; about one-fifth or one-sixth, perhaps, of the original manuscript. Nothing is known of its history until the fifteenth century, when it was at Naples, in the possession of Gioviano Pontano. In trac-

[1] Cod. Vat. lat. 3225, sometimes called "Schedae Vaticanae," but more generally known as "the Vatican Virgil"; the larger and artistically inferior Virgil, Cod. Vat. lat. 3867, being styled "Codex Romanus."

[2] In *Notices et Extraits*, xxxv., pt. ii., 1897, pp. 683-791.

[3] *Fragmenta et Picturae Vergiliana Codicis Vaticani* 3225, Rome, 1899 (vol. i. of *Codices e Vaticanis selecti phototypice expressi*).

5

ILLUMINATED MANUSCRIPTS

ing its subsequent adventures, M. de Nolhac has shown that it must have been seen by Raphael, who was inspired by more than one of its designs. The text is written throughout by one hand, in rustic capitals, a kind of script notoriously difficult to date with any confidence. The best judges concur, however, in assigning it on palaeographical grounds to the fourth century; and the fine execution of the earlier miniatures, the really classical pose and style of the figures, point to this rather than to a later date, when the artistic decadence consequent on the barbarian invasions was far advanced.

The book has now fifty miniatures, six occupying the full page, the remainder from half to two-thirds of a page. Each is enclosed in a rectangular frame of red, black, and white bands, the red decorated with gilt lozenges. There are nine illustrations of the Georgics, and forty-one of the Aeneid. In these paintings M. de Nolhac finds the work of three separate artists, of the same school and period, but of very different degrees of merit. To the best of the three (A) he assigns the Georgics series, pictures 1-9; to the worst (B), pictures 10-25; the remainder he gives to a third artist (C), inferior to A, but better than B. Sig. Venturi[1] agrees in attributing the first nine pictures to A, but would also credit him with thirteen of the C series (26-32, 40-4, 46); and he is disposed to assign seven of the B series (11, 15, 16, 18, 20, 22, 24) and three of the C series (35, 38, 45) to a fourth artist. It would be presumptuous to attempt to judge between these two distinguished critics. Provisionally, however, M. de Nolhac's hypothesis may be accepted as at least highly probable.

The illustrator of the Georgics[2] was evidently a painter of great skill and taste. His pastoral pictures show something of that sense of the idyllic in country life which is peculiar to the cultured dweller in cities. His figures, too, are well posed, graceful, in good proportion; the animals natural and full of movement. The freedom

---

[1] *Storia dell' Arte Italiana*, i., 1901, pp. 312-26.   [2] See plate ii.

PLATE II

VIRGIL. IVth CENT (?)
ROME, VATICAN, COD. 3225

CLASSICAL MANUSCRIPTS

and sense of space in these little pictures are truly artistic. They are painted with the direct touch of a person accustomed to work in a ductile medium. The colours are thick; many of the miniatures have suffered through this, the thickest layers having flaked off. There is no trace of preliminary outline-drawing. The soft handling of the draperies is very different from the crisp, hard manner of the Byzantine painters. The artist, too, is something of a naturalist. Not content with telling a story, he also composes a credible scene. His backgrounds have recess, his trees are not mere symbols; he even has some idea of perspective, both aerial and linear. As for his personages, slight and graceful in type, they seem to stand midway between the wall-paintings of Pompeii and those late-classical mosaics of Ravenna (Tomb of Galla Placidia and Baptistery of the Orthodox), which show a suppleness and sense of movement not yet crushed by the formalism and part-spiritual, part-decorative aims of Byzantine art.

Many of these excellences, however, belong to the individual artist, not to his school. The first sixteen of the Aeneid illustrations, be they by one hand or two, show a sad falling-off. Good modelling and composition vanish, so does delicacy in sense of colour. The artist (assuming him to be but one—in any case, the main characteristics are the same throughout) illustrates his subject, often with a certain vigour, but does not make a picture out of it. Often he loses all sense of proportion, tiny buildings being combined with figures twice their height. There is no hint of perspective; the painting in general is coarse and careless, and the attempts at facial expression merely grotesque. Perhaps the seven miniatures assigned by Sig. Venturi to a different hand are a trifle worse than some of the others; but all are bad, especially when compared with the charming pictures which precede them.

A marked improvement begins with Picture 26, and is sustained, more or less completely, to the end of the

ILLUMINATED MANUSCRIPTS

volume. The modelling and colouring become decidedly better; and in some of the pictures, such as the Death of Dido (27), there is a distinct effort to represent emotion. Individual figures and buildings are well done, but the artist lacks the power of successful combination. The miniature of Latinus receiving the Trojan envoys (41), however, is a really charming picture. The late-classical temple in the forest is painted with great delicacy, while the contrast between the cold, severe architecture and the deeps of the woods has not only been felt, but is communicated to the spectator.

The colour throughout the manuscript is deep, rich, and harmonious; and the first and third hands show considerable understanding of gradation, e.g. in the Boat-race scene (28), where the sea gradually changes from a dark tint in the foreground to pale green in the distance. The high lights of draperies and accessories are touched with gold. The flesh-tints are always brick-red, and recall (says M. de Nolhac) those of the Pompeian wall-paintings. Foliage is a dark green, in parts nearly black; but the second artist, in his careless hurry, sometimes uses blue. Otherwise, all three painters seem to have practically used the same paint-box, only distributing their tints with varying degrees of skill.

After the Vatican Virgil it seems natural to mention the fragments of the Iliad, now in the Ambrosian Library at Milan;[1] for the two manuscripts have much in common. The Iliad fragments consist of fifty-two separate leaves of vellum, containing fifty-eight miniatures, all the full width of the page, but of various heights. These are mostly on only one side of the leaf, the other side having portions of the text, in uncial writing of the fifth century; and it is evident that the book in its original state was a complete Iliad, profusely illustrated, com-

---

[1] *Homeri Iliadis pictae fragmenta Ambrosiana phototypice edita*, with preface by A. M. Ceriani, Milan, 1905. See too *Pal. Soc.*, i. 39, 40, 50, 51. The engravings published by Mai in 1819 and 1835 are not exact enough to be satisfactory for study, but his descriptions (which Ceriani reprints) are invaluable.

CLASSICAL MANUSCRIPTS

prising (according to Ceriani's estimate) 386 leaves with about 240 miniatures. What survives has evidently been preserved solely for its artistic interest: not only have the leaves been cut down as far as possible without encroaching on the pictures, but the text on the verso pages was covered, until Mai's time, with a paper backing, which was apparently put there as early as the thirteenth century.

Most of the miniatures are so stained and worn that it is difficult to judge of their original appearance. A largeness and freedom of manner, however, are evident, suggestive rather of mural painting than of illumination. Fine juxtaposition of mass is aimed at, rather than subtlety of line. It seems not improbable that the designs may have been copied from frescoes or other large paintings of the Augustan age, since lost. The style of the best is certainly Graeco-Roman, but the work is most unequal, some of the compositions being full of dignity, whilst others, weak, scattered, and lacking in proportion, seem to proceed from a different and very inferior school. Here, perhaps, antique models failed the artist. Many childish devices appear, such as making the slain in battle-pieces only half the size of the living, and the ridiculous—perhaps only symbolic—representation of Troy as a tiny walled space containing half a dozen soldiers. On the other hand, there are many charming single figures, especially Thetis, the winged Night, Apollo with his garland, sprig, and lyre, and the river-god Scamander; some of the battle-scenes, too, are full of life and vigour. There does not seem to be, even in the best pictures, anything like the fine artistic feeling and finished execution of the best miniatures in the Vatican Virgil; but the average merit of the book is perhaps higher. The pictures are enclosed in plain banded frames of red and blue. The favourite tints are white, blue, green, and purple, with a preponderance of red; no gold is used, its place being taken by a bright yellow. Some of the outlines are in pale

ILLUMINATED MANUSCRIPTS

ink; two of the pictures have landscape backgrounds, in the rest the backgrounds are plain. The coloured nimbi worn by the gods—Zeus purple, Aphrodite green, the others blue—are not without interest for the student of Christian iconography.

From these two books, which retain in an enfeebled form something of the grand and gracious manner of Graeco-Roman art, how great is the drop to our third and last classical manuscript! This is the larger illustrated Virgil[1] of the Vatican Library, numbered Cod. Vat. lat. 3867 and called the "Codex Romanus." Thanks to similarity of subject, age, and place, it has been persistently confused, even by those who should know better, with the probably older and certainly infinitely superior Cod. Vat. lat. 3225 described above—*the Vatican Virgil par excellence.* The Codex Romanus is a large, coarsely executed manuscript, whose exceeding ugliness has even caused some critics to suggest that it was decorated as a sort of artistic joke for the amusement of a Roman schoolboy! As the text, however, is as debased as the illustration, it would seem that its imperfections are the result of ignorance, not of a strained sense of humour. Expert opinion is divided as to its age: the form of writing—rustic capitals of an early type—has led the editors of the Palaeographical Society[2] to assign it provisionally to the first half of the fourth century, or possibly the closing years of the third; while other critics, judging by the corruptness of the text and the crudeness of the paintings, would relegate it to the sixth century or even later. The Vatican editors review the rival opinions carefully in their learned preface; their own judgment is that the manuscript is not later than the sixth century, nor earlier than the end of the fourth. The book certainly seems to belong to a period when the classical style had become

---

[1] *Picturae . . . Cod. Vat.* 3867, Rome, 1902 (vol. ii. of *Codices e Vaticanis selecti phototypice expressi*).

[2] Series i., pl. 113–14, and introd. p. vii.

CLASSICAL MANUSCRIPTS

a dead tradition, not a living force. This is strikingly apparent when one compares the feeble portraits of Virgil, which occur on three of the earlier pages, with their indubitable though distant prototype, the superb mosaic-portrait of Virgil sitting between Clio and Melpomene, recently found at Susa and published by the Fondation Eugène Piot.[1] But the shortcomings of the manuscript may perhaps be indications, not of late date, but of provincial origin. Inscriptions at the beginning and end show that in the thirteenth and fourteenth centuries it belonged to the abbey of S. Denis near Paris; and its editors suggest that it may possibly have been there from the eighth century onwards. In that case it might be presumed, without gross improbability, to represent a praiseworthy effort on the part of a Gaulish scribe and artist for the delectation of some wealthy patron; and to have visited Italy for the first time when it made its way, between 1455 and 1475, into the Papal Library.

Unlike its more comely neighbour and the Milan Iliad, the Codex Romanus is nearly complete; it consists of 309 leaves of very fine vellum, containing nearly the whole of the Eclogues, Georgics, and Aeneid. There are nineteen miniatures, many of them full-page, all of the full width of the text, mostly enclosed in rough banded borders of red and gold. The first seven (including the three portraits of the poet) illustrate the Eclogues, the next two the Georgics, and the last ten the Aeneid. The drawing is rough throughout, and the colouring harsh. The Virgil-portrait, which is twice repeated with practically no variation, and some of the scenes in the Aeneid were doubtless copied—as well as the painter could—from classical models. These were not necessarily miniatures; the patron's house may well have been adorned, like that at Susa, with a series of mosaics illustrating the Aeneid. In the rest, where the painter probably had nothing but his own imagination to guide him, the

[1] *Mon. et Mém.*, iv, 1897, pl. xx, pp. 233-44.

ILLUMINATED MANUSCRIPTS

designs are childish, grotesque, and monotonous, particularly in the pastoral pictures. It is perhaps worth noting that the nimbus here occurs, not only—as in the Ambrosian Iliad—as an attribute of the gods in council, but also on the heads of Aeneas and others when sitting in state, whether for consultation or feasting.

On the whole, the Codex Romanus is of little use for the study of classical illuminations; and its chance survival has done injustice to their memory. It is on the Ambrosian Iliad and the Vatican Virgil that our ideas of Roman miniature must be based; and perhaps also on a further series of books which, though not dating from such early times, seem to have preserved the ancient traditions with great fidelity. These are the illustrated copies of the Comedies of Terence, many of which have survived to us from the ninth and later centuries;[1] they seem to have enjoyed a great and unique popularity during the Dark Ages, and indeed right down to the twelfth century. Though differing considerably in age, they are much alike in style. A more or less fixed tradition for their illustration had evidently been early set up, probably in classical times; and since there are few more absolute despots than an established iconography, this tradition was never disobeyed.

By far the best of these manuscripts is No. 3868 in the Vatican Library. It is of the ninth century; and its finely painted miniatures have been said to make nearly all other illuminated copies of the Latin classics look squalid in comparison.[2] Of the remainder, perhaps the Paris MS. 7899, also ninth century, deserves the leading place. The Ambrosian MS. H. 75 inf., tenth century, is imperfect; it is copiously illustrated with rough but very expressive outline-drawings, tinted in blue and brown, of figures—the *dramatis personae* of the plays—

[1] *Terentius. Cod. Ambros. H. 75 inf. phototypice editus*, ed. Bethe, Leyden, 1903 (vol. viii of De Vries, *Codices Graeci et Latini*); with ninety-one reproductions from other Terence MSS. and printed books.

[2] *Ibid.*, col. 10.

CLASSICAL MANUSCRIPTS

sometimes with suggestions of a building, but with no attempt at background or illusion. Complete manuscripts usually have a portrait of Terence at the beginning, supported by two actors in comic masks. After this come the Comedies, with numerous sketches of the male and female performers gesticulating and pointing at one another in violent and apparently angry conversation. The men are nearly always masked; the ladies have streaming hair, and their attitudes and expressions are full of excitement. At the beginning of each play is a sketch of the faces of the characters, arranged in tiers, often looking out from the front of a theatre, but sometimes simply enclosed in a rectangular frame.

With the Terence codices our meagre supply of classical manuscripts comes to an end. There is an Iliad[1] in S. Mark's Library at Venice, of the tenth or eleventh century, but its few marginal drawings and full-page pictures are æsthetically negligible. The same may be said of the drawings of constellations which occur in manuscripts of Cicero's Aratea. An Aeneid was illuminated in 1198 by the monk Giovanni Alighieri, in gold and colours, and was preserved down to 1782 in the Carmelites' library at Ferrara;[2] but this was probably an isolated exception. The medieval Church, mother of the medieval arts, turned the art of the miniaturist to more pious uses than the illustration of pagan texts. Not until the fourteenth century was far advanced does the supply of illuminated classics recommence. Then, and still more in the following century, when the Renaissance had brought Greek and Latin literature into fashion again, we get a superb series of illustrated codices by Italian and French artists; but these, being classical only in subject, will be best treated along with other works of their school and date.

---

[1] *Homeri Ilias cum scholiis Cod. Ven. A, Marcianus* 454, ed. D. Comparetti, Leyden, 1901 (De Vries, *Codd. Gr. et Lat.*, vol. vi).

[2] See Brit. Mus., Add. MS. 22347, ff. 69, 73b; J. W. Bradley, *Dict. of Miniaturists*, i, 1887, p. 22.

CHAPTER II

EARLY CHRISTIAN ILLUMINATION TO THE END OF THE SIXTH CENTURY

WHEN in A.D. 330 the seat of Imperial government was removed from Rome to Byzantium, the centre of intellectual and artistic activity also moved eastwards. By this time the long-decadent Graeco-Roman art, the pagan world from which it had come, were almost dead. New influences were gradually making themselves felt: influences which finally developed, on their æsthetic side, into that which we call the Byzantine manner.

Battles have long raged about the question as to whence this new style drew its chief inspiration: whether from Syria or Alexandria, Byzantium or Rome. All, it would seem, contributed something towards it. This, however, is not the place for detailed discussion of questions which belong to the general history of art; the reader who wishes to grapple with the "Byzantine question" must study the writings of those who have devoted themselves to it.[1] Here, we are concerned with the evolution of style only in so far as it affects the art of illumination, which is seen, in the period which we are considering, "standing between two worlds": taking something from the past—as the early Christians took the symbols of the Catacombs—but re-making the ele-

---

[1] For a concise summary of most of the contesting theories see F. X. Kraus, *Geschichte der christlichen Kunst*, i (Freiburg i. B., 1896), pp. 538–50. But the literature has grown considerably in recent years; for fuller and more up-to-date treatment see M. Gabriel Millet's chapter on "L'art byzantin" in A. Michel's *Histoire de l'Art*, i, pt. i (Paris, 1905), pp. 127–301, with an extensive bibliography at the end.

ments derived from that past in the light of a new inspiration.

The new style, which resulted from the conflicting influences and eclectic culture of the early Byzantine Empire, is found fully developed in the mosaics of the sixth century. In illumination, if we judge—as we must—from surviving manuscripts, the process of assimilation was a slower one. Book-illustration lagged behind the other arts; and at the time when the great mosaics of Ravenna were being produced it showed, alongside the characteristics which link it with those works, strange barbarisms and survivals of dead tradition. The manuscripts which remain to us, however, are so few in number and so diverse in manner, and so little is known of their birthplace or their date, that the task of tracing their evolution is extremely difficult; the attempt to pronounce with any certainty upon the tendencies which they represent, practically a hopeless one.

It would be misleading to give the name Byzantine to these manuscripts of the transition period, for that peculiar and well-defined manner which is known as the Byzantine style is not yet developed in them. They show us an art which was in a fluid and transitional state, old memories and new ideas existing side by side. In some, the decay of the classical manner is still far more apparent than the new influence; in none has the new influence really "found itself" and attained the proportions of a style. Produced apparently in various parts of Europe and Western Asia, written mostly in Greek and under ecclesiastical influences, they are best described, perhaps, by the general name of *Early Christian;* since the new æsthetic ideals which they begin to exhibit, if not wholly to be attributed to the definite triumph of the Christian religion, at any rate developed side by side with it.

It is notorious that the early Church adapted, so far as she could, the elements of pagan symbolism to Christian use. The paintings of the Catacombs prove this sufficiently, and their testimony is confirmed by the manuscripts

ILLUMINATED MANUSCRIPTS

of the Early Christian period. This free adaptation of classical art is conspicuous in the first of the manuscripts which we have here to consider, so far as we can judge from its present much-damaged condition. This is the Quedlinburg Itala MS.,[1] which consists of five leaves from a copy of the "Itala," or Old Latin version of the Bible, written on vellum in fourth or early fifth century uncials.

In the seventeenth century the manuscript appears to have been at Quedlinburg, in Prussian Saxony, and to have fallen there into the hands of a bookbinder who thought it just good enough to use for lining-up the covers of his books. At all events, these five leaves were found there —two in 1865, two in 1869, one in 1887—in the bindings of seventeenth century municipal and ecclesiastical records. The last leaf contains text only; the other four, now in the Royal Library at Berlin, have one side filled with text (parts of the books of Samuel and Kings), and the other with illustrative miniatures, usually four to a page, in compartments formed by broad red bands. It has been suggested that one of the Saxon emperors may have brought the manuscript from Italy and given it to the monastery at Quedlinburg; but this is merely a conjecture. Certainly the pictures show close affinities with those in the Vatican Virgil, especially with those which M. de Nolhac assigns to the third hand; there is the same use of gold for heightening effects in dress and other accessories, the same antique conception of the human figure. The paintings are in thick body-colour, much of which has now disappeared, leaving the preliminary outlines bare (note the departure from the pure brush-work of the Virgil); but enough remains to give us some idea of the bright colouring and forcible modelling of these pictures in their original state. There are already traces of the method of treating the face with sharp high lights upon the forehead, which afterwards became a mark of the Byzantine school. The peeling of

[1] *Die Quedlinburger Itala-miniaturen der k. Bibl. in Berlin*, ed. Victor Schultze, Munich, 1898.

EARLY CHRISTIAN ILLUMINATION

the colours has revealed a curious feature in the shape of instructions to the artist, written in cursive script across the field of the pictures.

Classical methods still survive in the next great relic of Early Christian illumination, the Cotton Genesis. Presented to Henry VIII by two Greek bishops who, we are told, had brought it from Philippi, it was given by Queen Elizabeth to her Greek teacher, Sir John Fortescue, and by him again to Sir Robert Cotton. In 1618 Cotton lent it to Peiresc to collate its text; and that enthusiastic, if somewhat unscrupulous, antiquary made various pretexts for keeping it until he had had many of the pictures copied. He intended to have had them all engraved, but the project fell through, Cotton insisting at last on the return of the manuscript; and only two of the copies are extant.[1] This is much to be regretted; for the fire at Ashburnham House, in 1731, which wrought such havoc in the Cottonian Library, left only a mass of charred fragments to represent this once beautiful and precious volume. Some of these went astray, and are now in the Baptist College at Bristol; the rest, 150 pieces in all, have been inlaid in paper leaves, and are preserved in the British Museum.[2]

In its original state the manuscript contained the Septuagint version of Genesis, in uncial writing of the fifth or sixth century, illustrated with about 250 miniatures. None of these have survived completely; but the best-preserved fragments suggest strongly that the illumination of the book was a last bright flicker on the part of the expiring classical school. In many respects it reminds one of the best miniatures of the Vatican Virgil and of the Ambrosian Iliad. It shows traces of that suavity and grace which art, in her new and severely dogmatic mood, was soon to lose. On one or two of the

---

[1] Paris, Bibl. Nat., fr. 9350, ff. 31, 32, published with Peiresc's letters by H. Omont, *Facsimilés des Miniatures des MSS. grecs*, 1902. The second one may be compared with its now mutilated original, Otho B. vi, f. 18.

[2] Otho B. vi. See *Cat. Anc. MSS.*, i, p. 20, pl. 8.

pages finely designed figures, finished with deep rich colour and much use of fine gold lines, still remain to show us what these pictures must have been in their glory. That of Lot receiving the Angels (f. 26b), one of the best of these fragments, has still its delicate background of undulating country, the distant lake seen blue between the hills; all treated with a greater care and naturalism than we shall find in the manuscripts of the definitely formed Byzantine school. The angels, beautiful figures in rich draperies which combine the old fashions of Rome with the new ones of Byzantium in an interesting way, are painted with a high degree of finish. There is nothing barbarous here, though perhaps the thick dark outline, which surrounds the figures and indicates the details of the faces, is a decline from the softer modelling of the artist of the Georgics in Vat. 3225. Another charming fragment is f. 24, Hagar and the Angel. Not much more than suggestions of the angel's figure remain, but the left-hand portion of the picture is complete, showing Hagar seated on a boulder beside the well, with the wilderness stretching white beyond her to the horizon; modelling, drapery, and landscape are again excellent. The faces too are often treated with masterly skill, e.g. Eve on f. 3b, or Abraham's followers on f. 19, especially one seen three-quarter face, with exquisite features and eyes full of live expression. In some of the miniatures, as, for instance, Abraham and the Angels (f. 25), there is a trace of a more formal manner, stiff and hieratic, with severe modelling, which, coupled with the unclassical costumes, has been claimed as evidence of Byzantine origin. Other critics find traces of barbaric influence in the manuscript, e.g. Kraus,[1] who finds this in the "bearded heads," though as a matter of fact most of them are beardless! But any general imputation of barbarism is emphatically contradicted by the assured and graceful drawing still to be found in many of the

---

[1] *Op. cit.*, i, p. 459.

fragments, by the careful harmony of the colours, and by the indescribable but obviously classical trend of the whole work.

The miniatures which now remain are all enclosed in plain banded borders of red, black, and white or pale yellow; they are of the same width as the text, and are placed sometimes above it, sometimes below, occasionally two on a page, with or without a few lines of text between. Thus in general arrangement, as well as in the absence of conventional ornament, the manuscript agrees with the Vatican Virgil. The composition of the subjects—at least, of such as can still be traced—has been studied in detail by Dr. J. J. Tikkanen,[1] who points out that the designs recur in later representations of scenes from Genesis, notably in the series of mosaics which adorn the atrio of S. Mark's at Venice.

Court life at Byzantium, as we know, was characterized by pomp and ostentatious splendour of all kinds. Among other ways, the prevalent taste for luxury found expression in the production of sumptuous manuscripts, written in gold or silver uncials upon purple vellum, " burdens rather than books," as S. Jerome called them about the end of the fourth century, in a well-known passage of his Preface to Job. To this class, though to a somewhat later time, belong the next three manuscripts on our list: the Vienna Genesis, and the Rossano and Sinope Gospels. A still closer bond unites them, for their mutual resemblances are so striking as to leave little room for hesitation in referring all three to the same period and locality. The period is in all probability the first half of the sixth century. The locality is more doubtful—perhaps Byzantium itself, perhaps Syria, perhaps Asia Minor; Sig. Muñoz, their most recent critic of authority, decides for the last.[2]

---

[1] *Archivio Storico dell' Arte*, i, 1888–9, pp. 212, 257, 348; republished in German, in an expanded form and with many additional illustrations, in *Acta Societatis Scientiarum Fennicae*, xvii (Helsingfors, 1891), p. 205.

[2] A. Muñoz, *Il Codice Purpureo di Rossano e il Frammento Sinopense*, Rome, 1907, p. 27; but see A. Haseloff in *L'Arte*, 1907, p. 471.

ILLUMINATED MANUSCRIPTS

Nothing is known of the history of the Vienna Genesis[1] before its entry, between 1609 and 1670, into the Imperial Library at Vienna, where it is now preserved under the denomination Cod. Theol. graec. 31 ; nothing, that is, beyond an inference that it had previously been in Italy.[2] It consists of twenty-four leaves of vellum, stained in the dull and unpleasant purple so fashionable in the Dark Ages, and containing forty-eight miniatures, one on each page. The text, which fills the upper part of the page, is in silver uncials. It is not a complete copy of the Book of Genesis; apart from lacunae due to the loss of leaves, large portions are omitted—in fact, the scribe seems only to have aimed at supplying a continuous narrative to explain the illustrations. Evidently this was a sumptuous Bible picture-book, probably one of a large class which vanished either in consequence of the iconoclastic controversy, or during the innumerable "alarums and excursions" of the time. When we remember that, in Constantinople alone, the Senate House and the great church of S. Sophia, with all their treasures of sacred and profane art, had been twice burnt down before the end of the sixth century ; when we think of the wholesale destruction of sacred images and pictures —doubtless including pictured books—by the Iconoclasts, which began in 725 under Leo the Isaurian, and continued for over a century; the sacking of Constantinople in 1204, and its capture by the Turks in 1453, it is not difficult to understand why so few manuscripts dating from early Byzantine times remain to us. The rest have gone the way of other "missing links," to the confusion of the systematic historian.

The Vienna Genesis, therefore, may be taken as the

---

[1] *Die Wiener Genesis*, ed. Wilhelm Ritter von Hartel and Franz Wickhoff, 1895; forming a Beilage to vols. xv and xvi of the Vienna *Jahrbuch der kunsthist. Sammlungen*. See too Kondakoff, *Hist. de l'Art byzantin*, i, 1886, pp. 78–91.

[2] So Hartel, p. 99. Kraus says (i, 454) that it was acquired by "Angelo" Busbecke in Constantinople, about 1562, for the Imperial Library, evidently confusing it with the Dioscorides. See Busbecq's *Life and Letters*, 1881, i, 417.

EARLY CHRISTIAN ILLUMINATION

sole representative of a once numerous family of books. It is in fine preservation, and has long been one of the most celebrated of Early Christian manuscripts. Compared with the Cotton Genesis and the Quedlinburg Itala, redolent as they are of classical sentiment and tradition, its art seems crude and barbarous. But one cannot help being struck by one outstanding characteristic—the extraordinary vivacity which the artist has given to his scenes. In spite of drawing which is rough and faulty, often grotesque, and of colouring which is sometimes inharmonious enough to suggest complete carelessness of æsthetic possibilities, these little pictures live. They do not charm, but they arrest the attention. They display a positive genius for the direct telling of a story. Never was artist more "literary" than the illustrator of this book. The telling of Bible history, not the production of beauty, was his aim; but his stiff little figures, with their coarsely marked features and often absurd proportions, have the fascination which belongs to all fresh and active things.

Another characteristic of the Vienna Genesis is the persistent use of the "continuous" treatment, i.e. the representation in one picture, without any division, of successive scenes or moments in a narrative. This method, which became popular with all the arts in the Middle Ages, was already known in classical times; indeed, the reliefs of Trajan's column afford the most perfect example of its use. It occurs once in the Vatican Virgil, viz. in the Laocoon scene; but this is the first manuscript in which its capabilities are thoroughly exploited. In other respects the book is more conservative. We find in it many survivals from classical art, notably that old pagan device which took so strong a hold upon the Christian imagination—the personification of natural things. In the picture of Rebecca at the Well, the spring, besides being represented naturalistically, also appears as a half-draped nymph of distinctly classical type, pouring water from her urn; recalling the personification of Jordan in the famous fifth century mosaic of the Baptism of Christ, in the Baptistery at Ravenna.[1]

Many details of costume and ceremonial in these miniatures have been recognized as Byzantine; but the dignity of the fully developed Byzantine style is not even remotely suggested. The work is that of artists possessed of lively visual imagination but insufficient technical skill. The characters are personified successfully, and the types are well preserved, so that Joseph, Jacob, and other individuals are instantly recognizable in all the scenes where they appear. We see the stories briskly acted, as it were, by rather ridiculous marionettes. Backgrounds are introduced, for the most part, only to the extent required for the comprehension of the subject; but in the last twelve miniatures, and a few of the others, an attempt is made to heighten the pictorial effect by painting in a background, usually of greyish blue. The rest are painted direct on the purple vellum, sometimes within a plain red rectangular frame. Many are in two compartments, one above the other, but with no division except a strip of colour to represent the ground of the upper picture.

The Codex Rossanensis[2] is a book of very different character, though its superficial resemblances to the Vienna Genesis point to its being of much the same date and provenance. There is a change in the painter's standpoint, and tendencies begin to appear which afterwards became characteristic of Greek artists. It was unknown to the outer world until 1879, when a lucky chance revealed it to the eminent theologians Drs. Harnack and von Gebhardt. Rossano, in whose cathedral it is preserved, is an ancient city of Calabria, which

---

[1] Venturi, *Storia dell' Arte ital.*, i, pp. 127, 284; Diehl, *Ravenne*, 1903, pp. 5, 37, 40.

[2] O. von Gebhardt and A. Harnack, *Evangeliorum Codex graecus purpureus Rossanensis*, Leipzig, 1880. The miniatures were first published photographically by A. Haseloff, *Codex purpureus Rossanensis*, Berlin, 1898; afterwards, in colour, by A. Muñoz, *Il Codice Purpureo di Rossano e il Frammento Sinopense*, Rome, 1907.

EARLY CHRISTIAN ILLUMINATION

long maintained its Byzantine character. The Greek rite and language were used in its church down to the fifteenth century; and as late as the middle of the eighteenth the Gospel on Palm Sunday was read in Greek. Hence the survival of a Greek service-book is not very surprising. There is no tradition as to how the manuscript came there; perhaps, as has been suggested, it was the gift of an Emperor, or of a Patriarch of Constantinople. Its Eastern origin is clear, not only from the style and iconography of the pictures, but also from the remarkable agreement of its text with that of the fragment found a few years ago at Sinope,[1] and with that of the dismembered codex known to Biblical students as N, which was almost certainly written either at Constantinople or in Asia Minor.[2]

Nearly half the Codex Rossanensis is wanting, probably through fire, of which there are traces on some of the surviving pages; but luckily no damage has been done to the illuminated pages which remain. Of these there are fifteen, viz. twelve miniatures representing scenes from the life and parables of our Lord, a decorative frontispiece to the Tables of Canons, an ornamental border framing the first page of the Epistle from Eusebius to Carpianus, and a miniature of S. Mark. All but the last are at the beginning of the volume, which contains nearly the whole of the first two Gospels in Greek; the portrait of S. Mark is prefixed to his Gospel. When complete, the manuscript no doubt contained the four Gospels, with portraits of all the Evangelists, and with a longer series, probably, than now exists at the beginning. The Eusebian Canons must have followed the Epistle to Carpianus; and it is likely, as we shall see later, that they were enclosed in ornamental arcades. All the leaves are of purple vellum, and the text is in silver uncials, except the opening lines of each Gospel, which are in gold.

[1] See H. Omont in *Notices et Extraits*, xxxvi, pt. ii, 1901, p. 608.
[2] See H. S. Cronin, *Codex purpureus Petropolitanus* (*Texts and Studies*, vol. v, No. 4, Cambridge, 1899), pp. xv, xli, xliii.

ILLUMINATED MANUSCRIPTS

Of the twelve miniatures at the beginning, one is in two compartments, filling the whole page: in the upper, Christ before Pilate; in the lower, Judas returning the thirty pieces and hanging himself. The next page is entirely filled with the "Christ or Barabbas" scene. But in the other ten pages the miniature occupies the upper half only, the lower half being filled with a singular device, by which the eye is "brought to the picture," and which marks the introduction of that elaborate symbolism so congenial to the Byzantine temperament. This is the presence below each picture of four half-length figures of Old Testament prophets and types of Christ, who stand in tribunes inscribed with appropriate texts, and point upwards, each with his right hand, to the fulfilment of their prophecies. All have the nimbus. David appears most frequently, sometimes thrice on one page; he and Solomon are represented alike, with fair hair and short brown beards, and are distinguished by their crowns. The others are Moses, Isaiah, Sirach, and seven of the minor prophets; they are depicted indifferently, so far as individual discrimination goes, with one or other of three or four well-defined types of face. Hosea, for instance, has on one page a smooth, youthful face, which elsewhere does duty for Moses; on another, he is an old man with white hair and beard. But this apparent carelessness in no way diminishes the symbolic effect: they are important, not as persons, but as heralds of the Messiah, and their high office is to proclaim His presence, and to point out the mystical significance of His acts.

The choice of subjects too is in some respects unusual, and is instinct with the same theological spirit. Some of the compositions are, of course, those common to nearly all pictorial treatments of the life of Christ, e.g. the raising of Lazarus, the entry into Jerusalem, the Last Supper, Gethsemane, Christ before Pilate. Other subjects in the book, however, are less familiar. The fine dramatic episode of the choice between Christ and

PLATE III

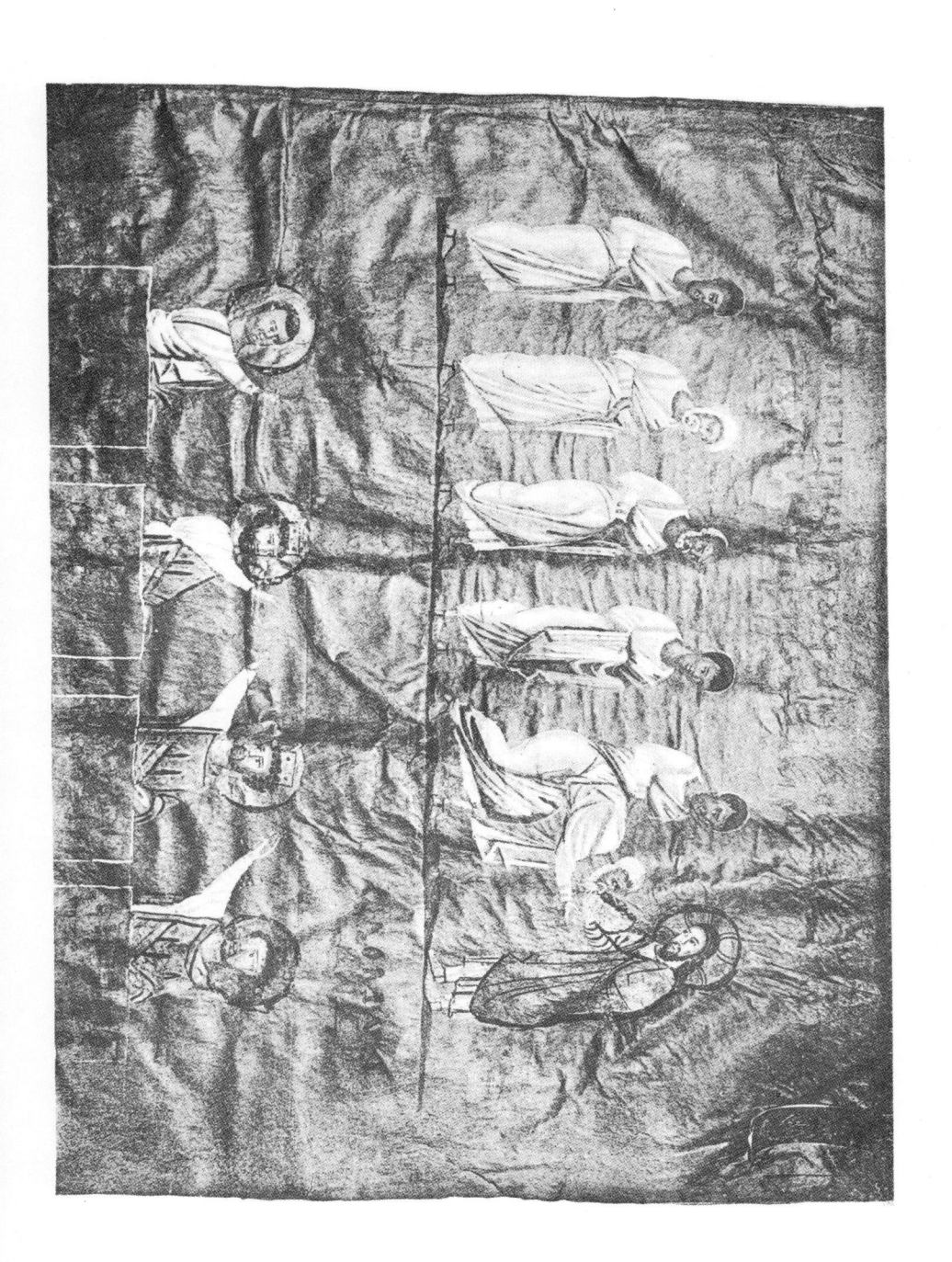

EARLY CHRISTIAN ILLUMINATION

Barabbas, here specially noticeable for the supernatural character given to Christ, soon dropped out of the traditional series. When in later times it became usual to represent the Crucifixion, no doubt the earlier scenes of the Passion were condensed. Two parables also are remarkable for their unusual treatment, viz. those of the wise and foolish virgins and of the good Samaritan. In the first, we see in the centre a closed door, barring the five foolish virgins out from Paradise, within which Christ stands, accompanied by the five wise virgins, who wear white cloaks and hold aloft their lamps, which have rather the appearance of flaming torches. The river of Eden, with its four heads, appears in the foreground, and in the background is a suggestion of a wooded park. In the second, the good Samaritan is represented by Christ Himself, three distinct phases in the story being in one undivided miniature—the only unequivocal instance of "continuous" treatment in the book. Christ, assisted by an angel, tends the wounded man, who lies prostrate on the ground; the second and third scenes are combined in true "continuous" method, our Lord being depicted as at the same time leading a mule on which the wounded man is seated, and giving money to the innkeeper.

But perhaps the most arresting pages in the whole book are the two which follow the miniature of the Last Supper and of Christ washing the disciples' feet. Under the form of the distribution of bread and wine to the apostles, they symbolize the mystical institution of the Mass.[1] The communicants approach in procession; the foremost, who is in the act of partaking, bows low and bends the knee, while the others stand or advance with devout expectancy expressed in every gesture. Christ, here the priest rather than the Redeemer, makes the initiate a participant in His own sacrifice. In this, as in the figures of the prophets, the theological spirit of Byzantine art clearly declares itself. In the distribution

[1] See plate iii.

of bread, Christ is at the extreme left-hand side of the picture, and the communicants approach from right to left; but this arrangement is reversed in the picture of Christ giving the cup. This circumstance has led Sig. Muñoz to argue, with much force, that the composition of the two miniatures must have been derived from a design which combined both scenes in a single picture. The Eastern Church possesses many such representations of the "Double Communion" in mosaic, though none of those now extant can be dated earlier than the eleventh century.[1] They have in the centre an altar, at each end of which is a figure of Christ as priest, sometimes accompanied by an angel as deacon, giving the sacred elements to the apostles, who advance in procession from right and left.

It is interesting, again, to find that at this early date the iconography of some of the principal scenes in the life of Christ had already become settled. Here we recognize the same arrangement of the personages, the same way of telling the story, that occurs again and again, almost without variation, in liturgical manuscripts of the Middle Ages. In the Raising of Lazarus, for instance, one of the spectators covers his nose with his cloak as the corpse issues from the grave—a touch of realism which wandered down the centuries, and appears, to give only a couple of instances, in Giotto's fresco in the Arena at Padua,[2] and in a fourteenth century East Anglian Psalter in the British Museum.[3] In the Entry to Jerusalem, again, the main outlines of composition are exactly the same as in almost any medieval miniature of the subject: the advance of Christ from left to right; the multitude carrying palm-branches, or spreading garments for the ass to tread upon; the spectators who climb trees to get a better view—all these are found in

---

[1] See P. Perdrizet and L. Chesnay in *Fond. E. Piot, Mon. et Mém.*, x, pp. 123–44, pl. xii.

[2] See No. 24 of the woodcuts published by the Arundel Society, 1855.

[3] Arund. 83, f. 124b.

EARLY CHRISTIAN ILLUMINATION

the Codex Rossanensis, and persisted unchanged down to the time of the Italian Renaissance.

The minuter details, however, of the miniatures in this manuscript have been shown conclusively by Dr. Haseloff and Sig. Muñoz to prove its affinity to the monuments of Eastern Christendom, as distinct from Western; e.g. Lazarus stands upright at the mouth of a cave, instead of rising from a recumbent posture in a coffin; and in the Entry into Jerusalem Christ sits sideways, facing the spectator, whereas in Western art He sits astride. Mention has already been made of the resemblance to the Vienna Genesis, which shows itself mainly in the facial types and in details of architecture and costume; also—it must be said—in the painter's lack of knowledge how to suggest a picture in three dimensions. There is little perspective, no atmosphere, no background, except in the Gethsemane scene, where the purple rocks of the foreground fade into inky darkness in the distance, with a blue and star-spangled sky above, and in some slight touches in the Parable of the Virgins. But the miniatures show a decided advance on the art of the Vienna Genesis. They are quiet in manner, with a sense of arrested movement very different from the brisk action of that work. A great dignity marks the conception of the characters, especially that of Christ, whose figure sometimes (as in the Trial before Pilate, and still more in the Choice between Christ and Barabbas) does actually suggest a spiritual presence. Here He is no more the beardless young god of the earliest Christian art, the so-called sarcophagus type; but a mature man with dark hair and beard, dressed in a deep blue robe and gold mantle, and wearing a gold nimbus on which the outlines of a cross patée are traced in double lines in a rather unusual way. Even in such animated scenes as the Entry into Jerusalem, the artist has succeeded in giving to His face and figure a grave, serene, and most impressive majesty. We are made conscious, through-

ILLUMINATED MANUSCRIPTS

out, that weighty things are happening in a solemn and inevitable way; and mere technical shortcomings are atoned for by sincerity and depth of feeling.

The two ornamental pages, though slight in themselves, deserve notice as early examples—perhaps the earliest extant—of purely decorative illumination. In the frontispiece to the canon-tables the title is enclosed within two concentric circles, the space between which is filled (except for medallion half-length portraits of the Evangelists, arranged symmetrically) with overlapping discs of various colours. Only the first page remains of the Epistle to Carpianus. The text is surrounded by a rectangular frame of gold, bounded by black lines and having pink rosettes, flowering plants in natural colours, black doves with white wings, and ducks of varied plumage painted upon it at regular intervals so as to form a symmetrical scheme. A similar interest attaches to the full-page miniature of S. Mark, who sits in a sort of basket-work arm-chair, his implements on a table beside him, and writes his Gospel on a roll spread over his knees, at the dictation of a nun-like woman who stands over him, and who has been interpreted as a personification of Divine Wisdom. She does not appear in later miniatures; in Western art her place is taken by the Evangelist's emblem. The architectural setting too is of an unusual type: a semicircular shell-pediment, coloured blue, pink, and gold in strips radiating fan-wise from the centre, and flanked by sharp-pointed gables terminating in gold discs, rests on an entablature supported by two pillars. In its composition generally, however, as well as in many of the actual details, this miniature may be regarded as the prototype of the long series of Byzantine, Celtic, and Carolingian Evangelist-portraits, which usually formed the chief adornment of manuscripts of the Gospels.

For twenty years the Codex Rossanensis was the only known representative of its class. But a second came to light in April, 1900, when the National Library in Paris acquired a precious fragment, which a French officer had

EARLY CHRISTIAN ILLUMINATION

discovered a few months before in the Greek colony of Sinope, on the northern coast of Asia Minor.[1] It is now numbered Suppl. gr. 1286, but is better known as the Codex Sinopensis. It consists of forty-three leaves of purple vellum, containing about a third of S. Matthew's Gospel in Greek, written throughout in gold uncials (unique in this respect among Greek Gospel-books), with five miniatures. The text, which M. Omont published in 1901,[2] is of the same recension as the Codex Rossanensis; the date is in all probability nearly the same; and the miniatures in the two manuscripts are closely allied.[3] Another leaf, which must have been in its proper place (between ff. 21 and 22) as recently as the end of the eighteenth century, is in the Gymnasium at Mariupol, near the Sea of Azov.

The miniatures in the Codex Sinopensis do not fill the whole page, but only the lower margin, coming below the text which they illustrate. Hence, they are on a smaller scale than those of the Rossano book; their execution is much cruder, less finished and dignified, suggesting an earlier phase in the development of the school. There are two prophets, instead of four, to each miniature; and instead of being ranged below the picture and pointing to it with uplifted arm and hand, in the emphatic manner of the Codex Rossanensis, they stand one on each side, their tribunes bounding the picture and somewhat dwarfing it, and themselves looking down on it and timidly extending two fingers; a much weaker conception. The subjects are the death of S. John the Baptist, the two miracles of feeding the multitude (the first badly mutilated), Christ healing the two blind men, and cursing the barren fig-tree. The figures are painted directly on the purple vellum, as in the Codex Rossa-

[1] First announced by M. H. Omont in the *Comptes rendues* of the Acad. des inscr. et belles-lettres, 1900, p. 215.
[2] *Not. et Extr.*, xxxvi, ii, pp. 599–675.
[3] The four complete ones of Cod. Sinop. have been reproduced in *Not. et Extr.* as above, and (in colours) in *Fond. E. Piot, Mon. et Mém.*, vii, 1901, pl. xvi–xix; all five in Omont, *Facsimilés*, pl. A, B, and in Muñoz, *op. cit.*, pl. A, B.

ILLUMINATED MANUSCRIPTS

nensis, but with still less attempt at background or perspective; not even the ground beneath their feet is indicated, except in the third picture, where the people sit in tiers on the grass. The anatomy and proportions are poor, the heads being usually too large for the stunted bodies and limbs. As in the Codex Rossanensis, Christ is represented with dark hair and beard, but the majestic calm and dignity so noticeable there are lacking; and the compositions are altogether more vivacious, less static. On the other hand, the artist has sometimes succeeded admirably with the faces, which are on the whole less ceremonial and more instinct with human life and individuality than those of the principal characters in the other manuscript, e.g. the expression of gentle benevolence with which Christ regards the two blind men, the fine thoughtful face of Moses in the third miniature, or the wild unkempt hermit who stands for Habakkuk in the fifth. The prophets here too are nimbed; David appears four times, always wearing a crown with a double row of pearls; Moses thrice, with a different face each time; Isaiah, Habakkuk, and Daniel once each, the last a beardless youth wearing a high cap adorned with pearls.

The ornamental pages of the Codex Rossanensis are paralleled by fragments of two other Greek Gospel-books of the sixth or early seventh century, one in the British Museum,[1] the other in the Imperial Library at Vienna.[2] The former consists of two imperfect leaves of vellum, gilded on both sides, and containing parts of the Epistle to Carpianus and of the Eusebian Canons. The Epistle is framed in a depressed arch, the Canon-tables in round-arched arcades; columns, pediment, and arches profusely decorated with geometrical patterns and other conven-

---

[1] Add. 5111, ff. 10, 11. See *Cat. Anc. MSS.*, i, p. 21, pl. 11. Two pages were reproduced by Haseloff, *Cod. purp. Ross.*, pp. 44, 45; and all four, in colour, by H. Shaw, *Illuminated Ornaments*, 1833.

[2] No. 847, ff. 1–6; described and reproduced, partly in colour, by F. Wickhoff in the Vienna *Jahrbuch*, xiv, 1893, pp. 196–213.

EARLY CHRISTIAN ILLUMINATION

tional ornament, especially floral scroll-work; with medallion-heads of saints, mostly of similar type to those in the Rossano title-page; and with birds, fishes, and flowers. The colours, among which blue and carmine predominate, are wonderfully fresh and well preserved, and stand out brightly against the gold ground which, though faded, still serves to suggest the pristine splendour of the manuscript. Especially noteworthy is the naturalism, both in colour and form, of a plant which springs from the capital of one of the columns on the first page: stalk, leaves, buds, and full-blown flower with deep crimson petals, all have the appearance of being faithfully copied from nature.

The Vienna fragment contains the Eusebian Canons, with frontispiece, and a title-page for the four Gospels. It is bound up at the beginning of a Latin manuscript (Rufinus) of about the same age, which has an almost identical frontispiece. The design in both is rigidly symmetrical; it consists of a cross enclosed by two concentric circles, and standing on a sort of Y-shaped device which spreads out at the foot, below the circles, into two wavy lines; each of these ends in a leaf, and has a flowering plant growing out of it. In the Greek page, the wavy lines also support two peacocks facing one another; the Latin has instead two birds of less determinate species (Prof. Wickhoff confidently calls them doves) just below the arms of the cross. This close agreement is of great interest, though not so helpful as it would be if the provenance of the two manuscripts were known. The Canon-tables are in arcades, usually round-arched, but with a gable top in one place; the arches and shafts of columns are covered with ornamental patterns, including cable, zigzag, and strapwork, and on one page are birds pecking at fruit. The title-page has a double banded frame covered similarly with decoration, but produces a less pleasing effect.

Our next manuscript is of Asiatic origin, but its connection with European art is too unmistakable and vital

ILLUMINATED MANUSCRIPTS

for us to ignore it. Among its many points of interest is a welcome feature—all too rare in these early manuscripts, and not so frequent as might be wished among those of later date—in the shape of an inscription telling us when, where, and by whom it was written. It is a copy of the four Gospels in Syriac, written in 586 by Rabula the Calligrapher in the monastery of S. John at Zagba, in Mesopotamia, and now preserved in the Laurentian Library at Florence.[1] Like the two Greek fragments which we have just noticed, and like almost all later Greek manuscripts of the Gospels, it contains the Eusebian Canons in decorated arcades. It has also seven full-page miniatures of surpassing interest for the history of Christian art, especially the four at the end of the book, which represent the Crucifixion, the Ascension, Pentecost, and Christ enthroned in a sanctuary. The Crucifixion appears here for the first time in illumination, and there are few extant examples of its treatment, in any form of art, which can be assigned with any confidence to an earlier date. As in many of the oldest representations of the subject, Christ wears a long sleeveless tunic (*colobium*), whilst the two thieves are draped in loincloths only. Above the arms of the cross are the sun and moon, emblems of mourning nature which recur again and again, e.g. in an English Psalter of the thirteenth century.[2] Longinus pierces the Saviour's right side with a lance, while a soldier stands on the other side holding up the sponge filled with vinegar. At the foot of the cross sit three soldiers dividing the raiment. The Virgin and S. John, and the three Maries, form the extreme left and right groups of the picture. Its special importance

---

[1] Fully described in the Catalogues of S. E. Assemani, 1742, p. 1, and A. M. Biscioni, 1752, i, p. 44. Both have woodcuts of the twenty-six illuminated pages, which are also engraved by R. Garrucci, *Storia della Arte Cristiana*, iii, 1876, tavv. 128–40. For photographic reproductions see Venturi, i, pp. 162, 163, and C. Diehl, *Justinien*, 1901, pl. iv, v, p. 500. Doubts have been raised as to the authenticity of the inscription, but may be disregarded in view of Ceriani's note in *Studia Biblica*, ii, 1890, p. 251.

[2] See pl. xxii.

EARLY CHRISTIAN ILLUMINATION

is iconographical rather than artistic, but from the latter point of view too it has just claims to consideration. There is a sketchiness and lack of finish about this miniature, as about all the illuminations in the volume; but the work is always wonderfully effective and expressive, and at times succeeds in conveying the idea of spiritual beauty and grandeur. In the Pentecost scene, for instance, there is great dignity in the figure of the Virgin, who stands in the central foreground with the apostles grouped about her, a composition which is repeated down to the end of the fifteenth century. The arcades are decorated with zigzag, check, meander, and other patterns, and peacocks and other birds appear on many of the pages, usually standing on the arches. On the margins outside the arcading is a series of small paintings of scenes from the Gospel-history. Among these is the Annunciation, in the divided form familiar to students of medieval Italian art: the angel in the left-hand margin, the Virgin in the right. Another very interesting scene recalls the "Double Communion" of the Codex Rossanensis, but the treatment is very different and far less solemn and impressive: Christ holds the cup in His left hand, while with the right He gives bread to one of the apostles, behind whom the other ten stand clustered. On the same page is the Entry into Jerusalem, much more compressed than in the Rossano book, but agreeing closely with it. A comparison of the two manuscripts has indeed led some critics to claim a Syrian origin for the Codex Rossanensis. But on the other hand it has been suggested that the Rabula Codex was copied from a Greek original—a suggestion to which the blundered inscription "Loginos" in Greek uncials, over the head of Longinus, seems to lend some support. Whatever may be the truth as to these theories, there can be no doubt that Byzantine and Western art owed much to Syrian influence.

This has been brought out clearly—if perhaps with something of the pardonable exaggeration of a pioneer—by Dr. Strzygowski, especially in his valuable monograph

ILLUMINATED MANUSCRIPTS

on the Etschmiadzin Gospel-book.[1] This is a tenth century copy of the Gospels in Armenian, bound up with two sets of illuminated pages in which he recognizes, largely from their resemblance to the Rabula-book, the work of Syrian painters of the sixth century. The same details of ornament—decorated arcades, peacocks, ducks, foliage, etc.—occur in both manuscripts, besides many of the same compositions. The most interesting feature, perhaps, is a sanctuary with a convex dome, not unlike a Chinese pagoda, surmounted by cross and orb and supported by Corinthian columns. This appears in a somewhat modified form in the Rabula-book,[2] and is repeated, with striking exactness, in the "Fountain of Life" pictures of the Carolingian Gospel-books of the ninth century;[3] a conclusive proof of the indebtedness of Carolingian to Eastern art.

The famous Vienna Dioscorides[4] is probably of earlier date than any but the first two of the manuscripts already mentioned in this chapter. Belonging as it does, however, to an entirely different class, it is best considered separately. The six full-page miniatures at the beginning form a link between the decaying Graeco-Roman art and the later Byzantine school; while the numerous and exquisite coloured drawings of plants and animals, with which the text is illustrated, make this manuscript the common ancestor of all the illuminated herbals and bestiaries of the Medieval and Renaissance periods. In this respect too it connects classical with medieval art; for Pliny[5] tells us that it was the custom for Greek medical writers to illustrate their works with paintings

---

[1] *Das Etschmiadzin-Evangeliar. Beiträge zur Geschichte der armenischen, ravennatischen und syro-ägyptischen Kunst*, Vienna, 1891 (*Byzant. Denkmäler*, i).

[2] Garrucci, tav. 129.

[3] See pl. x.

[4] Published in complete facsimile, with introduction by A. von Premerstein and others, as tom. x (pts. i and ii) of De Vries, *Codd. Gr. et Lat.*, 1906. Shorter notices abound; the most useful is that by E. Diez, "Die Miniaturen des Wiener Dioskurides," in *Byz. Denkm.*, iii, 1903, pp. 1–69.

[5] *Nat. Hist.*, xxv, 4.

EARLY CHRISTIAN ILLUSTRATION

of herbs. Since he goes on to complain of their general inadequacy, the Dioscorides probably represents the high-water mark of this branch of illumination, most of its successors falling far short of it in delicacy of execution. The six miniatures at the beginning are all badly rubbed, and the first (a peacock with outspread tail) is mutilated in addition. The second and third are of famous physicians in groups of seven, including Chiron the Centaur; the fourth illustrates the fable of the mandrake uprooted at the cost of a dog's life, and the fifth Dioscorides writing the description of the mandrake while an artist paints it, a lady personifying Discovery in both pictures. All these four are enclosed in banded frames, ornamented with wreaths, quatrefoils, lozenges, and scroll-work. The sixth is the dedication-page,[1] and shows the manuscript to have been executed for the Princess Juliana Anicia, probably in 512, on the occasion of her founding a church at Honoratae, a suburb of Constantinople; but at any rate before her death in 527–8.[2] It is a portrait of Juliana, enthroned between Prudence and Magnanimity in the central panel formed by two interlacing squares inscribed in a circle. The geometrical framework is adorned with cable-pattern, and in the interstices charming little putti play with emblems of the various arts patronized by the Princess. The composition of the group is exactly that of contemporary consular diptychs,[3] but the framing rather recalls mosaic ornament of an earlier period. Thus the transitional condition of art at the time is well exemplified by this manuscript, which forms as it were a symbolic link between the Classical and Byzantine styles.

[1] Often reproduced, e.g. in Kraus, i, p. 429; Venturi, i, p. 141. A splendid reproduction in colours accompanies Dr. A. von Premerstein's valuable article in the Vienna *Jahrbuch*, xxiv, pp. 105–24.

[2] *See* the facsimile ed., introd., cols. 7–9.

[3] Cf. Venturi, i, p. 367.

CHAPTER III

BYZANTINE ILLUMINATION

PRACTICALLY no Greek illuminated manuscripts of the seventh and eighth centuries have survived, and they do not begin to be plentiful until the closing years of the ninth: a lacuna largely due, no doubt, to the Iconoclastic controversy, which raged from 725 to 842, and which, though mainly concerned with paintings on a larger scale, must have been unfavourable to the preservation and production of works of art of all kinds. There is an evident continuity of tradition, however, between the Early Christian illuminations and those of the later, more definitely formed Byzantine school. Many of these later manuscripts were written and illuminated in Italy, especially in Southern Italy, where Greek influence persisted long after the decay of the Empire had become far advanced; many too were doubtless produced in the cities and monasteries of Western Asia, until the Turkish invasion swept away their civilization. But it is convenient and appropriate to group them all together under the name Byzantine, for a certain well-marked and easily recognizable manner is common to all; and this manner, whencesoever it primarily drew its chief inspiration, certainly flourished conspicuously in and about Byzantium itself, under the patronage of the Imperial court. The leading principles of Byzantine illumination became fixed, it would seem, about the end of the ninth century, in the time of Basil the Macedonian; it reached its highest perfection in the tenth and eleventh centuries, and then fell gradually into decadence until at last, lifeless in conception and coarse and weak in execution, it no longer deserved the name of art.

GOSPELS. BYZANTINE, XIth CENT.
BRIT. MUS. BURNEY 19

BYZANTINE ILLUMINATION

What, then, are the characteristics of this school, as we find them exhibited in the manuscripts of its great period? It has long been the custom to identify Byzantinism with formalism in art: with stately decoration rather than life, with the presentation of idea rather than of action. We know it as the conserving force which kept intact for centuries the traditional composition of sacred themes; we see its last descendants in the icons of the Greek Church, which still interpret the truths of eternity to the twentieth century in the artistic language of the tenth. This static, traditional, symbolic quality, however, only represents one of the main influences which went to the making of Byzantine art at its prime, though it happens to be the one which has survived to the present day, and which has become familiar to the casual tourist in the mosaics of Ravenna and other places. In the Greek illuminations of the ninth century we find not one but three styles or ideals, and endless combinations and permutations of these three, struggling for mastery.

The first of these, and perhaps the strongest, is the static or conservative ideal. This sets before it the representation of arrested action, not violent movement; aims at dignity, not energy. The Codex Rossanensis already hints at the beginning of this style, which at its best possessed a power of rendering spiritual values, of translating supernatural or natural majesty into terms of colour and line, which no other artistic system has ever approached. The main purpose of this art was theological, dogmatic, liturgical; profoundly anti-realistic, it preferred the solemn presentation of mysteries to the picturing of events. It achieved its purpose by a deliberate subordination of naturalism to idea. Its personages are symbols of something greater than themselves; their formal outlines, their carefully folded draperies, enhance like the vestments of priests the hieratic effect. In fact, there is a close parallel between Byzantine art of this kind and those formal liturgies and grave ceremonies

ILLUMINATED MANUSCRIPTS

which succeed by their very stateliness and remoteness from actuality in raising the mind to a plane of rapture and awe.

There can be little doubt that Byzantine illumination of this type was largely influenced by the contemporary art of mosaic. Many of its miniatures are but mosaics in little, and reproduce the usual accessories of such mosaics as are still to be seen in churches of the Byzantine style, just as Western illuminators of the thirteenth and fourteenth centuries copied the sculptured decorations of Gothic architecture. To the influence of mosaic may probably be traced the stiffness of the forms, the majestic pose of the figures, perhaps too the depth and richness of the colouring.

The second stream of influence, however, owes nothing to contemporary architecture or the style of decoration evolved in connection with it. Its origins are classical; and we find it in the ninth century existing side by side with the hieratic style, as in the early Italian Renaissance the pointed and classical styles dwelt together. It is evident that under Basil the Macedonian and his successors, after the long puritanic period of the Iconoclasts, beauty came into fashion again, and artists were called upon to satisfy the æsthetic cravings, as well as the religious instincts, of their clients. The masterpieces of classical art, of which many then existed that have since perished, were pressed into the service as models. Some miniatures, especially of the tenth century, are so imbued with the classical spirit that they have been held to be copies of lost originals dating back to the earliest periods of Christian art. But it is more probable that suggestions were adopted, or groups or single figures copied, from pagan paintings or sculptures of still greater antiquity. Whatever be the truth on this point, classical influence, at any rate, is evident and strongly marked; and that not only in such devices as the personification of qualities (e.g. Strength, Repentance, and so on), or of rivers, mountains, and towns, but also in the treatment of

BYZANTINE ILLUMINATION

individual figures and groups, and occasionally in the composition of a whole picture, as in the famous representation of David as Orpheus.

Finally, that lively and primitive manner, full of brisk movement and vividly depicted action, so noticeable in the Vienna Genesis, survived along with the Neo-Classical style and that remote and impassive dignity which descends from the Codex Rossanensis and the Ravenna mosaics. Many of the best manuscripts of the tenth and eleventh centuries show this manner in a high degree, sometimes actually in conjunction with the static style. In the representation of a martyrdom, for instance, the executioners are often animated figures, going about their horrid work with the utmost vigour, while the saint—a symbol of divine patience rather than the portrait of a living man—seems wrapped in another atmosphere than that of his persecutors.

The Vatican Library possesses a copy of Ptolemy's Tables,[1] written in 814, and adorned with representations of the sun, moon, months, hours, and signs of the zodiac, painted on blue or gold grounds; apparently carrying on the tradition of the Calendar of Filocalus, which has been noticed in chapter i. Astronomical and geographical personifications also appear in the Christian Topography of Cosmas Indicopleustes, composed about 547-9 on Mount Sinai, where its author, a native of Alexandria, had settled as a monk after a life of travel had earned him his surname. This work must have been illustrated from the first, as Dr. Strzygowski points out,[2] the text abounding in references to the diagrams and other illustrations. The best known, and probably the oldest, of

---

[1] Cod. Vat. gr. 1291. See P. de Nolhac in *Gazette Archéol.*, 1887, p. 233, and *La Bibliothèque de Fulvio Orsini*, 1887, p. 68; A. Riegl, Die mittelalt. Kalenderillustration, in *Mittheilungen d. Inst. f. oest. Geschichtsforschung*, x, 1889, p. 70.

[2] *Der Bilderkreis des gr. Physiologus, des Kosmas Indikopleustes und Oktateuch, nach Hss. der Bibl. zu Smyrna*, 1899 (Krumbacher's *Byzant Archiv*. Hef, t2), p. 54.

ILLUMINATED MANUSCRIPTS

the existing copies is the one preserved in the Vatican.[1] It has been assigned by some critics to the seventh, or even to the sixth, century; but we think it safer to accept the verdict of the editors of the New Palaeographical Society, who place it in the ninth century. Its miniatures, like those of most Byzantine manuscripts, are much disfigured through the colours flaking off; but it is evident, from what remains, that in finish and technique a great advance has been made on the Codex Rossanensis. Most of the subjects are Biblical, and the treatment is generally formal and anti-realistic, an effect which is heightened by the entire lack of background, giving the figures a disconnected appearance. The heads are in many cases too big for the bodies; and that excessive pleating of the draperies, which became a foible of Byzantine painters, is already noticeable. Isolated figures, however, are rich in solemn charm, such as the Madonna who stands with Christ, S. John the Baptist, Zacharias, and Elizabeth, in one of the full-page miniatures. In others, again, animation is portrayed with some success, as in the picture of the Babylonians amazed at the backward motion of the sun.

One of the best and most valuable documents for the study of Byzantine illumination of the ninth century is the Paris copy of the Sermons of S. Gregory Nazianzen,[2] a large volume with forty-six full-page miniatures, apparently executed for the Emperor Basil I (867-886), whose portrait, standing between the prophet Elijah and the archangel Gabriel, fills one of the pages, and whose patron S. Basil also figures prominently. Another page represents the Empress Eudocia with her two young sons Leo and Alexander; her eldest son, Constantine, who died in 880, is ignored, so the manuscript may be dated 880-6. Three distinct styles, all characteristic of

---

[1] *Le miniature della topografia cristiana di Cosma Indicopleuste, Cod. Vat. gr.* 699, ed. C. Stornajolo, 1908 (*Codd. e Vat. selecti*, vol. x). See too *L'Arte*, 1909, pp. 160-2; *New Pal. Soc.*, pl. 24; Venturi, i, pp. 153-7; Diehl, *Justinien*, pl. iii, pp. 265, 401, 411.

[2] Bibl. Nat., gr. 510. See Omont, *Facsimilés*, pp. 10-31, pl. xv-lx.

BYZANTINE ILLUMINATION

Byzantine illumination, are shown in the miniatures. First we have the archaic manner which recalls the Vienna Genesis: animated compositions in the "continuous" method, but quite lacking all sense of beauty; the figures are short, stiff, and awkward, with absurdly big heads and protruding eyes, and the attempts to render facial expression are generally grotesque. The miniatures painted in this manner are mostly on a comparatively small scale; several scenes on one page, either in separate panels or in a continuous series without division. The history of Jonah, for instance, is treated altogether in the continuous method, the whole story being crowded into one picture; that of Joseph combines both methods, the page being divided into five compartments, each of which contains several scenes; while a third page is in twelve compartments, each illustrating the martyrdom of an apostle. The other subjects are mostly Biblical; they include a picture of the Crucifixion with Christ in a long sleeveless tunic, and adhering in many other respects to the primitive type of the Rabula manuscript.

The second manner concerns itself solely with ornamental effect, and tends to stiff magnificence. In it we have the stately, bejewelled, highly decorative pages which recall the most gorgeous of the Byzantine mosaics. It is most noticeable in the portraits of Basil and Eudocia, already mentioned, and in the impressive figure of S. Helena, who stands, vested as empress, with three other saints in a splendid full-page miniature of an angel proclaiming the Redemption. This style was evidently considered the right thing for imperial portraits. We find it so used in many later manuscripts, e.g. for the portraits of Alexius Comnenus (Emperor 1081-1118) in a Vatican manuscript,[1] and for those of Nicephorus Botaniates (Emperor 1078-81) in the Paris manuscript of the Homilies of S. John Chrysostom;[2] in one of the

---

[1] No. 666, see Venturi, ii, pp. 462, 476.
[2] Bibl. Nat., Coislin 79; Omont, pl. lxi–lxiv.

ILLUMINATED MANUSCRIPTS

latter, representing Nicephorus with his chief officials, it is exaggerated into grotesquely wooden formalism. It is sometimes spoken of as "debased Byzantine"; but it certainly co-existed with the best manner of Byzantine painting, and was probably recognized as expressing—perhaps with a touch of satire—the quintessence of courtly ceremony. In the Gregory Nazianzen, for instance, it is found side by side with miniatures in which the prevailing influence is classical. Of these last, the most celebrated is the Vision of Ezekiel; they are not yet frankly Graeco-Roman, like many later miniatures (especially of the tenth and eleventh centuries), but combine the tightly clinging Byzantine draperies with the freer pose of classically conceived figures.

When we reach the tenth century, however, we find that the transitional phase represented by the Gregory Nazianzen has passed. The Paris Psalter,[1] with its allied manuscripts, and the Vatican Joshua Roll[2] are absolutely pagan in their art, if Christian in their subject. In fact, many of the compositions of the Joshua Roll are so full of the classical spirit that one is tempted to regard it as a production of the third or fourth century. But the Greek text which accompanies the drawings is written in minuscules of the tenth century;[3] and the drawings themselves are more nearly akin to miniatures of that period of classical renaissance than to any actually existing ones of earlier date, so we hesitate to accept the theory that a tenth century scribe, having found the pictured roll, proceeded to fill in the text. Another hypothesis, put forward by some critics of this much-disputed work, is that the pictures are a faithful copy from a much earlier original. It must be admitted that

[1] Bibl. Nat., gr. 139; Omont, pl. i–xiv.

[2] Cod. Vat. Pal. gr. 431; published photographically, partly in colour, by the Vatican authorities, *Il rotulo di Giosuè*, Hoepli, Milan, 1905. See too *Pal. Soc.*, i, 108.

[3] It is true that some of the figures have titles written against them in capitals; but this feature also occurs in such manuscripts as Paris 139 and Vat. Reg. gr. 1, both of the tenth century.

BYZANTINE ILLUMINATION

this view derives some support from the fact that gaps are left in the text, as though the scribe had sometimes been unable to read his original. This fact, however, only tends to prove that an earlier series of illustrations existed, having the same subjects as those in the Joshua Roll. It does not at all necessarily follow that the treatment was the same; and indeed it is difficult to believe that a mere servile copyist could have produced these spirited groups of soldiers, these charming and spontaneous personifications of cities, rivers, and mountains. On the other hand, it seems likely enough that the actual compositions, in their main outlines, were taken from earlier designs. It has been pointed out that many of the subjects are found in the fifth century mosaics of S. Maria Maggiore;[1] and we have seen in the Cotton Genesis an example of an illustrated Biblical codex dating back to the same period. The artist, then, may have had before his eyes an earlier set of illustrations, though it is highly improbable that he contented himself with copying them.

The history of the Joshua Roll is not known farther back than 1571, when it appears in a list of the manuscripts owned by Ulrich Fugger; but there are some accounts on the back, in Greek, written in the thirteenth century, showing that it was then in Greek hands. Its form is unusual, and it is not easy to see precisely for what purpose it was intended—perhaps as designs for a series of mural paintings. It is now in fifteen separate membranes, placed between the leaves of a large album; but until 1902 these membranes were glued together, end to end, and formed one long roll of vellum, thirty-two feet by about one foot—originally much longer, for it is clearly imperfect both at beginning and end. The back was left blank, and the front covered with drawings of the deeds of Joshua, forming a continuous series throughout the length of the roll, with abridged extracts from the Greek text of the book of Joshua, explaining

[1] See Venturi, i, 380.

ILLUMINATED MANUSCRIPTS

the several scenes, written in short columns below them. The outlines are drawn in brown ink, and some parts have been lightly tinted. Critics have doubted whether this incomplete colouring is not the work of a later hand; but if the drawings were meant to serve as models for mural paintings, the artist may well have thought it enough to indicate the respective colours of the various objects: armour blue, draperies brown, and so on. But whatever may be the true solution of the problems which confront the student of the Joshua Roll, no one could refuse to consider it a masterpiece. The drawings are broad in treatment, correct as to anatomy, and full of movement. In such scenes as the carrying of the Ark of the Covenant, or others in which crowds of soldiers are represented, depth as well as linear extension is suggested. The figures have unity with their surroundings, and the artist evidently aimed at producing an illusionist picture, not merely at representing an event. The influence of classical art is everywhere strikingly apparent; nowhere more so than in the personifications of cities, some of which are extremely beautiful, especially the graceful goddesses who represent Ai and Jericho. The whole composition has been compared, not unjustly, to the series of reliefs on Trajan's column.

The Paris Psalter, Bibl. Nat. gr. 139, is one of the most beautiful of Byzantine manuscripts. Acquired in Constantinople by a French ambassador in the sixteenth century, it had probably belonged to the Imperial Library. The text is in minuscules of the tenth century; and the fourteen full-page miniatures are doubtless of the same date, though M. Omont has shown that the fourteen leaves which contain them (each on a verso page, with the recto blank) are independent of the quires of text, and might possibly, therefore, have been inserted later.[1] The first of these is the famous picture of David with the harp, inspired by Melody; a design which seems to

[1] *Facsimilés*, p. 5

BYZANTINE ILLUMINATION

have become justly popular from the moment of its production. It appears again and again in later manuscripts, slavishly copied by hands of varied degrees of incompetence.[1] In all of them the main features of the composition are reproduced, and some repeat every detail: Melody sitting at David's right hand, with her hand on his shoulder; Echo, as a nymph peeping round a pillar in the corner; the reclining figure in the foreground who represents Bethlehem; even the individual animals which have been charmed to stillness by the music. But the Paris miniature is far superior to the others in freedom, grace, and proportion; and we can hardly be wrong in regarding it as their archetype. Its very excellence makes us doubtful about accepting the view that it is a copy of a lost antique representation of Orpheus. That the artist had much of the classical spirit is very plain; the central group, for instance, may be compared with a Pompeian painting of the death of Adonis.[2] But Byzantine miniatures of the tenth century abound in evidence of a classical renaissance; and the miniature in question, while doubtless owing its original idea to some Graeco-Roman picture of Orpheus taming the beasts, seems likely, from its free handling and easy grace, to have been the work of a brilliant artist who had absorbed the spirit of his model, rather than an exact copy made by a patient craftsman. Copies are nearly always tight and laboured—qualities not to be detected in this work.

Many of the other miniatures of the Paris Psalter, though perhaps not so beautiful as that of David and Melody, show the same classical influence, and rise to a high artistic level. Especially good are David slaying the Lion, with a beautiful Diana-like personification of Strength coming to his assistance; and Isaiah receiving inspiration, standing between the figures of Dawn and

---

[1] See Venturi, ii, fig. 306-11. To these may be added Brit. Mus., Add. 36928, f. 44b, late eleventh century.
[2] *Museo Borbonico*, ix, pl. 37.

Night. Dawn is a boy holding up a torch; the more poetically conceived Night is a regal-looking woman, her torch drooping and half-extinguished, and a scarf thrown like a cloud above her head. The effect is somewhat marred by the figure of Isaiah, whose draperies cling tightly in the manner already noted as characteristic of Byzantine painting. Two other fine pages are Nathan rebuking David, with Penitence standing near; and the Prayer of Hezekiah. A third page, David in imperial garb, standing between Wisdom and Prophecy, combines classic grace and dignity with the more rigid symmetry of a late-Roman consular diptych.

The remaining eight miniatures are probably the work of an inferior hand; they are akin to the Biblical scenes in the Gregory Nazianzen, and show little or no trace of classical influence, except in a few isolated figures, such as the personification of Meekness in the Anointing of David, or the charming nymph representing Boastfulness, who flees in dismay from the side of Goliath. We have in them crowded compositions, filled with vigorous but undignified and often ill-proportioned figures—the heads usually too big, and the legs too short. In the colouring too there is a noticeable falling off. Some of the scenes, however, are interesting on other than purely æsthetic grounds, e.g. the Crowning of David, who stands on a shield upheld by soldiers, illustrating the picturesque coronation ceremony of the Byzantine Emperors.[1]

The Paris Psalter is the best, as well as probably the earliest, extant example of what has been called the "aristocratic" group of Psalters, in contradistinction to the "monastic-theological" group, in which there are no full-page miniatures, but only marginal illustrations.[2] Other members of the group are No. 54 in the Ambrosiana, and two Mount Athos MSS., Vatopedi 609 and Pantocrator 49, of the tenth and eleventh centuries.[3] A small volume

---

[1] See Bury, *Later Roman Empire*, ii, 70.
[2] Tikkanen, *Die Psalterillustration im Mittelalter*, 1895, etc.
[3] Michel, i, i, 221–5.

BYZANTINE ILLUMINATION

recently acquired by the British Museum[1] belongs to the same class; it was executed about the end of the eleventh century, and contains eight full-page miniatures, mostly of subjects represented in the Paris manuscript. The colours have flaked off badly, so that some of the pictures are scarcely recognizable; but enough remains of the "David and Melody" composition and others to show that, although painted with much delicacy, they are lacking in ease and freedom. One feature worth noting is the magenta priming which appears where the gold background has peeled away; in most Byzantine manuscripts the gold leaf and pigments seem to have been laid directly on the vellum without any preliminary ground, though some twelfth century and later manuscripts show traces of red priming below the gold.[2] A much more stately volume is the Vatican Psalter, Cod. Vat. Pal. gr. 381, but of later date (twelfth to thirteenth century) and with only four miniatures,[3] each filling the whole page. Three of these are plainly derived from the Paris Psalter, with which they agree in practically every detail of composition, though far inferior in execution; these are David and Melody, David standing between Wisdom and Prophecy, and Moses receiving the law on Mount Sinai. The fourth miniature repeats this last subject, differently treated, and perhaps represents the renewal of the tables; it was no doubt copied from some illustrated Biblical manuscript, but the subject seems to have been comparatively rare.

With these Psalters must be classed a fine Bible in the Vatican, Cod. Vat. Reg. gr. 1. This, a votive offering in honour of the Virgin, was given by Leo the Patrician, a high official of the Imperial palace; and so is probably a fair sample of the best work of the court miniaturists of the time, i.e. the first half of the tenth century. Leo's gift comprised the whole Bible, in two volumes; but only

---

[1] Add. 36928.
[2] e.g. Brit. Mus., Add. 35030; also 19352, noticed below.
[3] *Collezione Paleografica Vaticana, I. Miniature della Bibbia Cod. Vat. Reg. gr. 1 e del Salterio Cod. Vat. Pal. gr. 381*, Milan, 1905.

vol. i remains, containing the text from Genesis to Psalms, with eighteen full-page miniatures, which have been published in the same volume with the four from the Psalter just mentioned. Two of these are identical in composition with miniatures in the Paris Psalter, viz. Moses on Mount Sinai and Samuel anointing David. A third, the Coronation of Solomon, differs only in names and minor details from the Coronation of David in the Paris manuscript. Other pages correspond equally closely with those of the Paris Gregory Nazianzen; while in style, as in probable date, the painting stands midway between that of the two Paris books—more finished than the Gregory, rougher than the Psalter.

The Neo-classical wave was spent by the end of the tenth century. Illuminations of later date show little trace of its influence, apart from direct imitations of older manuscripts, as in the Psalters already mentioned or in the Octateuch MSS. Of these there are five extant, of the eleventh and twelfth centuries: two in the Vatican,[1] one at Smyrna,[2] one on Mount Athos,[3] and one in the Seraglio at Constantinople.[4] They contain the first eight books of the Bible, in Greek, illustrated with a great abundance of small miniatures. Their artistic merit is not particularly great—in this respect one of the latest, the Vatican MS. 746, is decidedly the best; but they are of interest from their extraordinarily close agreement with one another, not only in the choice of subjects, but in the mode of treatment down to the minutest details of iconography. Moreover, it is obvious that the illustrations of the book of Joshua must have been derived from the Joshua Roll, or at least from a common ancestor.

[1] Gr. 746 and 747. Many of the miniatures are published in the introduction to *Il rotulo di Giosuè*, 1905.

[2] Strzygowski, *Bilderkreis*, pp. 113–26, pl. xxxi–xl.

[3] Vatopedi 515, described by H. Brockhaus, *Die Kunst in den Athos-Klöstern*, Leipzig, 1891, pp. 212–17.

[4] For reproductions, see Album to vol. xii of the *Bulletin de l'Institut Archéol. Russe à Constantinople*, 1907, which also contains many of the Smyrna and Vatopedi miniatures.

BYZANTINE ILLUMINATION

Just the same groups occur, in the same antique garb, though not handled in the same masterly way; the same personifications of cities, but with faint relics only of the delicate grace and charm of the original. One of these has by mistake been put in the picture following that to which it properly belonged; proving clearly that the archetype must have been a continuous series of paintings, whether the Vatican Joshua Roll or a lost one of similar design.[1]

Of the "monastic-theological" family of Psalters, i.e. those with only marginal illustrations, the earliest extant specimens date from the end of the ninth century.[2] The British Museum possesses a very fine example,[3] written in 1066 by the arch-priest Theodore of Caesarea for Michael, Abbot of the Studium monastery at Constantinople. Almost every one of its 208 leaves has the margins filled with paintings, for the most part executed with great delicacy. There are no backgrounds; the figures, with such few accessories as were indispensable for the representation of the scenes depicted, are painted direct on the plain vellum page, and so have at the first glance a quaint appearance of standing or walking upon nothing. The pigments have flaked away in many places; and an inspection of the places where this has happened discloses two interesting facts. In the first place, it is clear that the gold leaf was laid on a red priming, but where colours were used there is no trace of any preliminary preparation of the vellum surface. Secondly, outlines were drawn with the pen, very lightly, apparently in watered ink, before the colours were laid on; except where precise definition of form was not wanted, as in the case of watercourses, which are represented by broad wavy lines of blue. The figures, which are, of course, on

---

[1] Strzygowski, p. 120.

[2] Tikkanen, i, pp. 11 *seq.* For the one on Mount Athos, Pantocrator 61, see Brockhaus, pp. 177–83, pl. 17–20.

[3] Add. 19352. See *Pal. Soc.*, i, 53; F. G. Kenyon, *Facsimiles of Biblical MSS.*, 1900, pl. vii; G. F. Warner, *Reproductions from Illuminated MSS.*, ser. ii, 1907, pl. 2, 3.

a small scale, dainty rather than majestic, are on the whole admirably drawn, graceful, and well proportioned; and the varied scenes are vividly portrayed, despite the lack of background. The animated style predominates, but not to the exclusion of the statuesque, which is often used for single figures, e.g. for David standing, with hands uplifted in adoration, before an icon of the Saviour—a subject which recurs on page after page. The colouring is subdued for the most part, one of the prevailing tints being an almost leaden blue; but the pages are brightened up with touches of gold in the draperies, and with copious use of red, and the general effect is pleasing and harmonious.

The chief value of the Theodore Psalter, however, lies in the wealth and variety of its illustrations, rather than its purely artistic interest. The painter was not hampered in his choice of subjects by a sense of congruity. To illustrate the text was his purpose, whether by naïvely literal or elaborately symbolical methods. For instance, Ps. xi. 2 is represented by three wicked men shooting arrows with malicious vigour at the upright in heart (f. 10b); Ps. xii. 3, by an angel standing on the boaster's chest and snipping off " the tongue that speaketh proud things " (f. 11b); Ps. lxxviii. 25, by an angel giving a cake to an old man (f. 102); Ps. cxxvii. 1, by workmen with ladder, pulleys, etc., building a house (f. 170); and so on. Pictorial renderings of a less elementary kind are given to such passages as Ps. xxxix. 6, where we see porters and mule laden with money-bags, which the young heir is emptying at a girl's feet (f. 47). Ps. lxxviii, cv, and cvi are accompanied by pictures of the plagues of Egypt and the wanderings of the Israelites (ff. 99b–104b, 141b–44); and other scenes from the Old Testament appear, not only like these in direct illustration of the text, but allusively, as when the translation of Elijah is used to illustrate Ps. xlii. 6, or Job on the dunghill for Ps. cxiii. 7 (ff. 51b, 154). As in the Vatican Bible, Reg. gr. 1, and the Paris Psalter, gr. 139, we

BYZANTINE ILLUMINATION

have a coronation scene: opposite Ps. xxi. 3 stands Hezekiah, robed like a Byzantine Emperor, on a shield upborne by soldiers, while an angel reaching down from heaven sets "a crown of pure gold on his head" (f. 21). Pictures from the life of David are naturally to be found throughout the volume; including two charming pages at the end of the Psalms (ff. 189b, 190) which are filled with a consecutive series, Christ sending down an angel to David as he plays the flute among his flocks, David's colloquy with the angel, and finally his being anointed by Samuel.

The "monastic-theological" character of the book comes out in the scenes from the New Testament, the lives of saints and the history of the Eastern Church, which form a very large part of its illumination. The prophetic element in the Psalter is emphasized here, especially in pictures of the Gospel-story, where David often appears at one side pointing, as in the Codex Rossanensis, to the fulfilment of his prophecy. Many of the subjects are repeated in different parts of the book, with striking variations in the treatment—a fact which shows that the Byzantine rule of unchanging iconography had its exceptions. For instance, there are miniatures of the Crucifixion on ff. 87b, 96, 172b. In the second of these Christ wears a loin-cloth, in the two others the colobium; in the first and second Longinus with his spear is on the left, but the right-hand side has in the first the soldier with the hyssop, in the second the Virgin and S. John; in the third, the only figures besides Christ are the Virgin and S. John, standing on the right and left respectively, and bending over His feet. On f. 152 is a representation of the Double Communion, inferior in impressive solemnity and depth of feeling to the Codex Rossanensis, but interesting because of the figures of David and Melchizedek, who stand as witnesses on either side. The Iconoclastic Controversy is graphically depicted on f. 27b: the Patriarch Nicephorus and his friend Theodore, abbot of the Studium, are shown

ILLUMINATED MANUSCRIPTS

supporting an icon, and again protesting before the Emperor Leo, while his myrmidons are busy destroying the sacred images. The book shows no hint of the earlier classical revival, except in the somewhat grotesque personifications of rivers as men with urns, and of the winds as men blowing trumpets, and a representation of the Sun-god in his chariot on f. 61b, opposite Ps. l. 1.

Some of the illustrations of the Theodore Psalter were drawn from the lives of saints; for these the iconography had already become settled, probably soon after the completion of the great work of Simeon Metaphrastes, who flourished under Constantine Porphyrogenitus (912–58) and collected and amplified the lives of the early Christian saints. A Menology, abridged from his voluminous compilation, was made for Basil II (976-1025), and is now in the Vatican Library;[1] or rather, all that remains of it, viz. the portion for the half-year from September to February. It is a stately volume of 215 leaves, containing a miniature on each page, with the artist's name inscribed against it on the margin. Eight artists were employed, including two (Michael and Simeon) who are surnamed "of Blachernae"; so the manuscript was probably executed at Constantinople by the leading court miniaturists. It is certainly one of the finest surviving examples of its kind. There is not much width of range, the saints being usually depicted either in the *orans* attitude, standing rigidly with uplifted hands, or else while undergoing martyrdom; and despite the beauty of much of the painting, an effect of monotony is produced by the endless series of nuns and bishops standing before arcaded parapets or flanked by hills of impossible symmetry—even the livelier movements of the executioners tend to become stereotyped. All the

---

[1] Cod. Vat. gr. 1613. The text, with Latin translation and with engravings of the miniatures, was published by Card. A. Albani, *Menologium Graecorum*, Urbino, 1727; and the whole manuscript has since been reproduced, *Il Menologio di Basilio II*, Turin, 1907 (vol. viii of *Codd. e Vat. selecti*). See too Beissel, *Vat. Min.*, 1893, pl. xvi, *New Pal. Soc.*, pl. 4, and *Al Sommo Pont. Leone XIII omaggio giubilare della Bibl. Vat.*, 1888, pl. i (in colour).

PLATE V

SIMEON METAPHRASTES. XI-XIITH CENT.

BRIT. MUS. ADD. 11870

BYZANTINE ILLUMINATION

miniatures have gold backgrounds, and a strong family likeness altogether, so that it is difficult to recognize the individual characteristics of the several painters; Pantoleon, Michael the Little, and Simeon of Blachernae seem, however, to have been decidedly the best artists—the others were perhaps only painstaking and highly trained imitators. One of the most beautiful miniatures in the book is Simeon of Blachernae's painting of the Nativity.[1] The whole scene is in the open air, as it usually is in Byzantine art. In the centre lies the Babe in the manger, at the mouth of a cavern half-way up a hill. Mary sits on the rocks beside His head, Joseph below her to the left: and the centre of the foreground shows the Babe being washed in a bath which stands in a flowery meadow. At the top of the hill are two angels, and a third on the right-hand slope proclaims the glad tidings to an aged shepherd. The composition is symmetrical, but not to excess; and the whole picture is full of grace and charm. The Adoration of the Magi, which follows on the next page, is also by Simeon; it too has great merit, especially in the figures of Mary and the Child, and of the angel who leads the Magi into their presence; but it is marred by the grotesque costume of the foremost Mage, who crouches impossibly while still advancing with his gift. Another fine miniature,[2] by Pantoleon, represents the miracle of S. Michael and the hermit Archippus —a subject which we meet again in the Metaphrastes of the British Museum.

Landscape backgrounds figure largely in the Vatican Menology, treated according to the peculiar traditions of Byzantine painters and their successors the early Italian masters. The development of these traditions, from their first germs in Pompeian wall-paintings down to their last survival in the works of such painters as Benozzo Gozzoli and Filippo Lippi, has been traced by W. Kallab

---

[1] *Menologio*, p. 271; but Beissel's plate is more pleasing.
[2] *Menologio*, p. 17.

ILLUMINATED MANUSCRIPTS

in an interesting and copiously illustrated monograph;[1] and we need not do more than mention the subject very briefly here. The most striking feature in Byzantine landscape is the curiously conventional treatment of hills, which are represented as truncated cones with smooth, level table-tops, and with steep, symmetrical and absolutely smooth and arid slopes, often interrupted at regular intervals by ledges of the same evenness as the summits. Lower down are crags and boulders of similar form, like the stumps of neatly sawn-off tree-trunks. There is a far-away resemblance to some basaltic formations, such as Fingal's Cave or the Giant's Causeway, but the treatment is essentially non-naturalistic; it had become traditional before the end of the tenth century, and it persisted, in the Eastern Empire and Italy, till well on in the fifteenth.

Many of the compositions of the Vatican Menology are reproduced, on a smaller scale but with almost equal delicacy and finish, in a copy of the Lives of Saints for September, from Metaphrastes, executed about the end of the eleventh century or beginning of the twelfth.[2] At the head of each legend is a miniature, richly framed in ornament. One of these (f. 60) represents the Archangel Michael turning aside a torrent from the church and dwelling-place of the devout hermit Archippus.[3] This was plainly inspired by Pantoleon's painting in the Menology; the subject seems to have been a popular one —it occurs on f. 125 of the Theodore Psalter. Another subject, S. John in his old age dictating the Gospel to his youthful disciple S. Prochorus (f. 197b), occurs frequently in Greek Gospel-books, as we shall see presently. Six of the other headpieces contain scenes from the saints' lives and passions, in series of four or five small medallions. The remaining fourteen have single miniatures, like the two already mentioned. Seven of them represent martyr-

---

[1] "Die toscanische Landschaftsmalerei im xiv und xv Jahrhundert," in the Vienna *Jahrbuch*, xxi, 1900, pp. 1–90.

[2] Brit. Mus., Add. 11870.

[3] Pl. v.

doms; in the other seven the saints stand upright, sometimes in the regular *orans* pose, sometimes holding a small cross in the right hand.[1] The backgrounds are in reddish gold; the figures, painted in body-colour and highly finished, are long and slender, the faces dignified and pensive in expression, the draperies carefully shaded and arranged in fine folds. This is Byzantine work of a high order; rich and harmonious in colour, conceived in the solemn and ceremonial manner proper to the school. The saints, both male and female, are of ascetic type, with emaciated frames, contrasting strongly with the vigorous muscularity of their executioners. Apart from the figures, the treatment is conventional, as in the Vatican Menology. The artist places his martyrdoms among impossible hills, his saintly nuns and confessors before arcades and porticoes devoid of perspective, and prettily but improbably coloured in red, blue or green.

The Metaphrastes is the first of the manuscripts which we have been considering to show in a perfect form the characteristic conventional ornament of the Byzantine school. This ornament, in the best examples of great richness and beauty, irresistibly reminds every one who sees it for the first time of some Oriental pattern-work, and especially of Persian carpets or enamels. It is generally used at the beginning of a book or chapter, sometimes forming a framework or pendant to a miniature, as here,[2] but more often alone, the miniature (if any) being on a separate page within a plain banded frame, as in most of the Gospel-books. The form is square or oblong, sometimes with short depending borders. The decoration consists of a repeat-pattern of geometrical elements—circles, lozenges, and quatrefoils—together with strictly conventionalized flower and leaf ornaments. Sometimes the design is so close as to seem a mere floriated network; sometimes it has a rich border, and a more open pattern within. The ground is gold; the

[1] See Warner, *Reproductions*, i, 1, for one of the latter class.
[2] Pl. v.

ILLUMINATED MANUSCRIPTS

pattern is in the deep blue of Persian enamel, with myrtle-green and a little red. In later work pink, light blue, mauve, and other secondary shades are introduced; but as a general rule the better the example the nearer it keeps to the original blue-and-green effect. The whole is relieved with minute touches of white, which become coarse and heavy as the style deteriorates. A really good piece of this ornament is like nothing so much as a fine Persian praying-rug on a small scale; and it seems likely that the idea may have been borrowed from the Arabs, whose civilization was more or less in touch with that of Byzantium from the seventh century onwards. But it must be admitted that a scheme of decoration, out of which that now in question might conceivably have been evolved, appears at a still earlier date in Byzantine architecture, e.g. in the altar-screen and capitals at the church of San Vitale, Ravenna.[1] Obscure though the origin and early development of this headpiece may be, its successive stages of decadence may easily be seen from the long series of Gospel-books to be considered presently.

Byzantine miniature was at its prime in the tenth century—the age of the Joshua Roll and the Paris Psalter; but the next two centuries produced many manuscripts of great beauty and interest. Among these may be mentioned the Vatican Homilies of the monk Jacobus (Cod. Vat. gr. 1162, 11th cent.), a perfect example of the Byzantine conventual manner, and of additional interest because its exquisitely finished, if formal, groups of saints and angels can be compared with the laboriously careful, but greatly inferior, copies in a twelfth century manuscript at Paris (Bibl. Nat., gr. 1208).[2] Another fine manuscript of the eleventh century is the Scala Paradisi of John Climacus in the Vatican

---

[1] See Venturi, i, fig. 76-8, 82; C. Ricci, *Ravenna*, 1902, pp. 35-7, 40, 41. But a Moslem derivation is more probable. See the illustrations to F. Sarre's article on "Makam Ali am Euphrat" in the Berlin *Jahrbuch*, xxix, 1908, pp. 63-76.

[2] Beissel, *Vat. Min.*, pl. 15; Venturi, ii, pp 468-75, fig. 329-41.

BYZANTINE ILLUMINATION

(gr. 394),[1] setting forth the toilsome ascent of the spiritual ladder by means of allegorical miniatures and drawings, delicately executed in a manner somewhat resembling that of the Metaphrastes. Other copies of this treatise are extant, with independent but inferior illustrations.[2]

The so-called Melissenda Psalter in the British Museum[3] exemplifies the strange mingling of East and West brought about by the Crusades. Unlike the other manuscripts considered in this chapter, it is written in Latin, and its small, finely formed minuscules bespeak a Frankish scribe of no mean skill. The Calendar-ornaments too, consisting of the signs of the zodiac painted on gold grounds in small medallions, are Western in character; and so are the elaborate decorative initials at the beginning and principal divisions of the Psalter. But the miniatures, while purely Byzantine in iconography, are curiously un-Byzantine in colouring. The book is generally supposed to have been executed for Melissenda, eldest daughter of Baldwin II, king of Jerusalem, and of the Armenian princess Emorfia, his queen. Melissenda was married in 1129 to Fulk of Anjou, and was crowned with him on Baldwin's death in 1131. Throughout Fulk's reign she took an active part in the government, and for some years after his death in 1144 she held the regency for their young son, Baldwin III; she died at Jerusalem in 1161. Her name does not appear anywhere in the book, but the Calendar records the deaths of her parents (but not that of Fulk) and the capture of Jerusalem by the Crusaders (July 15, 1099), and the prayers contain many phrases which tend to show that the book was written in the Holy City. Moreover, its sumptuous appearance, in binding enriched with beautiful ivory carvings and studded with turquoises

---

[1] Beissel, pl. 14; Venturi ii, pp. 478-85, fig. 343-4; *Pal. Soc.*, i, 155.

[2] See Tikkanen in *Acta Societatis Scientiarum Fennicae*, xix, 1893, No. 2.

[3] Eg. 1139. See *New Pal. Soc.*, pl. 140; Warner, *Reproductions*, iii, 6. All the illuminations have been reproduced in colour, but not satisfactorily, by A. Du Sommerard, *Les Arts au Moyen Âge*, 1838-46, Album, ser. 8, pl. 12-16.

and rubies, makes it fully worthy of a royal patron. So we will not dispute its traditional association with Queen Melissenda's name; but it contains some phrases which suggest that it was intended, not for her own use, but for presentation to some lady in a religious house—perhaps her youngest sister Iveta, a nun at S. Anne's, afterwards Abbess of the nunnery of S. Lazarus at Bethany, which was founded and richly endowed by Melissenda herself.[1]

The book contains twenty-four full-page miniatures of the life of Christ at the beginning, and nine half-page miniatures of saints towards the end, all on gold grounds. The latter series is plainly the work of the Western (probably French) artist who painted the zodiac-medallions in the Calendar. He has faithfully copied the stiff and formal designs of a Byzantine menology of traditional type, but has completely altered the effect by the use of brighter, less sombre colours, by greater freedom and naturalism in flesh-tints and draperies, and above all by his delicate and skilful treatment of the faces, imparting to them an animation, in some cases even a touch of coquetry, quite alien to the spirit of Byzantine hagiographical art.

The scenes from the life of Christ are painted in a very different manner; they are by an artist whose signature, "Basilius me fecit," appears in uncial lettering on the last of the series. The name is Greek, and the compositions agree exactly with the established Byzantine traditions; but the attenuated, ill-modelled figures with impossibly long necks, the sullen, peevish faces, and especially the rich but unpleasantly vivid and unharmonized colouring, mark the presence of some other influence. If one compares these paintings with the corresponding scenes in a typical Byzantine manuscript of the same period, such as Harl. 1810, one is struck by the difference in treatment almost as much as by the similarity in design. The deep ultramarine of the Melissenda book looks rich and warm beside the leaden blue of

---

[1] See R. Röhricht, *Geschichte des Königreichs Jerusalem*, 1898, p. 228.

BYZANTINE ILLUMINATION

the Harleian MS., but its effect is constantly marred by the juxtaposition of ill-matched shades of crimson, green, and—most discordant note of all—a harsh magenta. The local colours are often quite arbitrary, e.g. in the picture of the Magi following their angel-guide the ground is magenta, and the hair and beard of one Mage are, like his horse, of a pale bluish green—a colour which also does duty for the ass ridden by Christ in the Entry into Jerusalem. The artist exaggerates the hard, dry manner which was one of the worst faults of the later Byzantine school; his scenes seem as if cut out against the gold background, without a hint of perspective. Little attempt is made to vary the types, or to depict facial expression; and the draperies are so treated as to give the effect of some hard substance, striped with fine lines, rather than of folded stuffs. The proportions are often absurd, as in the Raising of Lazarus, where the kneeling sisters and the men removing the sepulchre door, though all in the foreground, are mere pygmies; or in the Entry into Jerusalem, where the figure of Christ is dwarfed by the tall disciples—the ass too is of diminutive size, and is grotesquely represented as walking on air high above the ground.

Despite these shortcomings, however, the Melissenda book has much beauty, besides a well-nigh unique interest as a monument of one of the most picturesque episodes in the Middle Ages. Its pages glow as brightly now as when they were first painted, with none of the flaking-off that disfigures so many Byzantine miniatures. The pictures of the life of Christ form an unusually complete series, of great value for the study of iconographical details. Here, for instance, the Baptism-scene, unlike that in the contemporary Harl. 1810 (f. 95), still preserves the personification of Jordan, but shrunk to puny dimensions. The Harrowing of Hell[1] is represented in the symmetrical form long established in Byzantine tradition: Christ in the centre, beneath His feet the broken doors of

[1] Pl. vi.

ILLUMINATED MANUSCRIPTS

the tomb; in the left hand He holds a cross, with the right He raises Adam from the grave; Eve stands behind Adam, waiting her turn; on the right-hand side of the picture, balancing Adam and Eve, is a group of patriarchs headed by David and Solomon; two angels hover above Christ, to right and left, bearing standards inscribed "SSS" (Sanctus, Sanctus, Sanctus). This last detail seems to be rare; but the main outlines of composition stamp the miniature as one of a large family, other members of which are in Harl. 1810 (f. 206b)[1] and a Gospel-book dated 1128-9 in the Vatican.[2] The Ascension is represented by a still more symmetrical composition:[3] Christ enthroned, within a circular mandorla, is borne heavenwards by four angels; below, the central figure is the Virgin, and on each side of her stands an angel addressing a group of disciples. Again an almost exact counterpart, as regards design, is to be found in Harl. 1810 (f. 135b).[4]

As a rule, the decoration of Greek Gospel-books is restricted to portraits of the Evangelists and headpieces prefixed to the Gospels, sometimes with arcades for the Eusebian canons and ornamental initials. The two manuscripts, which we have mentioned in discussing the Melissenda book, are exceptional in containing some additional miniatures. Besides the four Evangelist-portraits and a painting[5] of Christ blessing the Emperors Alexius and John Comnenus, the Vatican MS., Urbino-Vat. gr. 2, which was executed in 1128-9, apparently for John Comnenus, has four full-page miniatures, one before each Gospel, viz. the Nativity, Baptism, Birth of S. John the Baptist,[6] and Harrowing of Hell. There is far greater wealth of illustration in the Harleian MS. 1810, also of the twelfth century. Inserted in the

---

[1] Reproduced, with other illustrations of the subject, by G. McN. Rushforth in *Papers of the British School at Rome*, i, 1902, pp. 114-19.
[2] Cod. Urbino-Vat. gr. 2, f. 260b, reproduced in *New Pal. Soc.*, pl. 106.
[3] Warner, *Reproductions*, iii, 6.
[4] *Ibid.*, i, 2.
[5] Venturi, ii, fig. 342.
[6] Beissel, *Vat. Min.*, pl. 14.

PLATE VI

PSALTER OF MELISSENDA, QUEEN OF JERUSALEM. BYZANTINE, 1131-44
BRIT. MUS. EGERTON 1139

BYZANTINE ILLUMINATION

text at varying intervals are sixteen miniatures of the life of Christ, each occupying about three-quarters of the page. All the subjects are represented in the Melissenda book, and for the most part by nearly identical designs. But the book now under consideration is thoroughly typical of Byzantine work of the time; and its miniatures, so far as their condition enables one to judge, are marked by the subdued colouring, dignified gestures, and gentle, pensive faces which characterize the school. One of the finest is the Annunciation (f. 142), large in manner and freely handled. Finer still is the Incredulity of Thomas (f. 261b), a very charming composition in blue and gold, and fraught with an intensity of spiritual emotion that recalls the Codex Rossanensis. Christ stands in the centre, between two groups of apostles. His face is beautiful, His figure majestic and well drawn, though emaciated; and the gestures and faces of the apostles express awe-struck, ecstatic wonder and reverence.

After the twelfth century the history of Byzantine miniature is one of rapid decadence. Having provided a starting-point for the Italian school, which continued its tradition with great success through the thirteenth and fourteenth centuries, it ceased to exist as an æsthetic power. That instinct for decorative fitness and for the solemn effects proper to religious art, which had been its distinguishing characteristic, died away; and nothing remained but those outward mannerisms which had always been the least satisfactory features of the style. Signs of decay had begun to show themselves, especially in the sense for harmonious colouring, before the end of the twelfth century; and the downward movement was no doubt accelerated by the disasters which befell the Eastern Empire about this time, culminating in the Latin conquest of Constantinople in 1204.

Before we pass on to the Western schools, a word must be said about the portraits of the Evangelists, which form the chief decoration of a very large number

ILLUMINATED MANUSCRIPTS

of copies of the Greek Gospels, ranging in date from the tenth century to the fourteenth. The series must have begun much earlier, as is evidenced by the portrait of S. Mark in the sixth century Codex Rossanensis, and by the four portraits in the Lindisfarne Gospels (*circ.* 700), which were plainly copied from Italo-Byzantine archetypes. But in this class, as in Byzantine illumination generally, the gap between the sixth century and the tenth has to be bridged over by inference and conjecture. One safe inference is that the symbolical figure of Divine Wisdom, which we saw in the Rossano book, was discarded during this dark period—it was felt, perhaps, to savour too much of pagan art. The absence of the four emblems constitutes a more complex problem. From a very early period the Christian Church had regarded the "four living creatures" of Ezekiel i. 5, the "four beasts" of the Apocalypse iv. 6, as symbols of the four Evangelists—certainly before the time of S. Jerome. When and where they were first introduced into Christian art is still undetermined; but in Western miniatures they appear almost invariably from the seventh century onwards, whereas in Byzantine they are practically unknown. Their first appearance among the Greek Gospel-books in the British Museum is in Add. 11838, written in 1326;[1] among those in the Vatican, we are told, they do not occur at all. It is difficult to account for their absence in the paintings of a school so devoted to symbolic imagery as that of Byzantium; and one is tempted to suggest that their use in art was a Latin invention, which did not become known to Greek-speaking Christendom until a comparatively late date. Certainly one of the oldest surviving instances of their occurrence is in the mosaics of the Baptistery of S. Giovanni in Fonte at Naples, *circ.* A.D. 400; and it is an interesting coincidence, to say the least, that the Durham Book (written at Lindisfarne *circ.* 700), which seems to have been copied from a Neapolitan archetype, contains pages

[1] *New Pal. Soc.*, pl. 130.

BYZANTINE ILLUMINATION

on which portraits of the Evangelists inscribed in Greek ("O agios Mattheus," etc.) are combined with the emblems, the latter inscribed in Latin ("imago hominis," etc.).[1]

After this digression, let us return to the Byzantine type, which is amply represented in Eastern monastic libraries, as well as in the Vatican,[2] the Imperial Library at Vienna,[3] the British Museum, and other great European collections of manuscripts. In point of artistic excellence the highest level, as with Byzantine miniatures in general, is reached in the tenth and eleventh centuries, and from the closing years of the twelfth century the deterioration becomes rapid and complete. As to the broad outlines of composition there is a conservatism verging on monotony, though the details vary in a way calculated at once to delight and perplex the archaeologist—and that not only from one manuscript to another, but from page to page within the same volume. The ground is almost invariably gold—but occasionally blue, as in a twelfth century MS. in the British Museum.[4] In some cases the backgrounds are more or less filled with buildings, in others they are quite plain. Landscape is restricted to one subject, S. John dictating to S. Prochorus, and is of the peculiar character already described. The Evangelists are always at work on their respective Gospels; the first three seated, and engaged in the actual writing, usually with an exemplar on a stand to copy from. For S. John two different compositions were recognized. In one, as we have seen in the Metaphrastes, he stands dictating to S. Prochorus, and at the same time looking heavenward for inspiration, which is symbolized by a hand issuing from part of a disc; this device also appears in the other type, where he sits alone writing. The cast of countenance is usually grave, thoughtful,

---

[1] For a fuller discussion of this question see *Burlington Mag.*, xiii, 162.
[2] Beissel, *Vat. Min.*, pp. 16–19, pl. ix–xi.
[3] *Jarhbuch*, xxi, pl. i–v.
[4] Add. 4949.

ILLUMINATED MANUSCRIPTS

ascetic, especially in the earlier manuscripts, with bulging, wrinkled forehead and prominent chin. A good example is the portrait of S. Mark[1] in Burney 19, a manuscript of the eleventh century, formerly in the Escurial Library. S. Matthew is always an old man, with white hair and beard. S. Mark is much younger, dark haired, sometimes of a strikingly Semitic type, e.g. in Add. 4949 and 22740, both of the twelfth century. S. Luke is a young man in his prime, fair, with good features of Greek type, and slight pointed beard; sometimes tonsured, as in Burney 19, Add. 4949, and Burney 20 (dated 1285). In Add. 22736, dated 1179, both he and S. John have almost girlish faces. But the latter is generally depicted as an old man, with long white beard and bald head, the forehead very large and dome-shaped. The accessories are, as we have said, of great interest for the student of archaeology, but too full of fanciful variations to afford him very secure data. For instance, the exemplar is of scroll or codex form according to the painter's fancy for the moment; and the form of the transcript varies equally but quite independently. In this connection we may note that in Burney 20 S. Matthew is copying or translating from a roll inscribed in Arabic—evidence of a current tradition, at all events, as to the original language of his Gospel. The table by the Evangelist's side is often covered with a complete outfit of writing implements: inkstand, knife, scissors, compasses, sponge, etc. The devices for adjusting the book-rest; the patterns of chair, table, and other pieces of furniture; the hanging lamp suspended over S. Luke's table in Add. 28815 (tenth century)—these are a few of the many points worth notice.

Enough has been said as to the headpiece decoration, which adorns the beginning of each Gospel in these manuscripts. But there is another feature which must not be ignored, viz. the initial-ornament, in which some of the earlier manuscripts are rich. One of the best in

[1] Pl. iv.

BYZANTINE ILLUMINATION

this respect is Arundel 547, an Evangelistarium or Gospel-lectionary, written in Slavonic uncials early in the tenth century. Its initials are of the type usually called Lombardic, and abound in variety and humour: fishes, birds, human limbs, human trunks without limbs, pitchers—these and many other objects are combined in all sorts of fantastic ways. It is worth remarking that similar initials occur in an Evangelistarium[1] written at Capua in 991 by a Sicilian monk, and in a copy of the Gospels[2] written in 1023, probably in Southern Italy; but they are also found in manuscripts of the tenth and eleventh centuries on Mount Sinai,[3] and are probably of Eastern origin.

To conclude this chapter, we cannot refrain (even at the risk of irrelevance) from mentioning a copy of the Greek Gospels[4] written at Rome in 1478 for Cardinal Francesco Gonzaga by a Cretan priest named John. The illuminations are unmistakably the work of an Italian artist; but while his miniatures of the Evangelists, and the charming headpieces which he has prefixed (following the Byzantine custom) to the Gospels, are thoroughly Italian in style, the single figures and small groups painted on some of the margins recall such manuscripts as the Theodore Psalter, and were plainly copied from Byzantine models.

[1] Cod. Vat. gr. 2138. See *Pal. Soc.*, ii, 87.
[2] Milan, Bibl. Ambros. B. 56 Sup. See *Pal. Soc.*, i, 130.
[3] Muñoz, *L'art byzantin à l'exposition de Grottaferrata*, 1906, fig. 56.
[4] Brit. Mus., Harl. 5790.

CHAPTER IV

CELTIC ILLUMINATION

HAVING sketched the development and subsequent decay of Byzantine illumination, we now turn from the extreme east to the extreme west of Europe, and follow, so far as existing materials will allow us, the history of a counter-movement which took its rise in the Irish monasteries at an early period—possibly even before the end of the fifth century; and which, spreading thence to Great Britain and the Continent, combined with Byzantine and other influences to form the decorative system which obtained in Europe from the ninth century to the twelfth.

The great characteristic of Celtic illumination is a complete disregard for realism and an impassioned understanding of conventional ornament. It is, indeed, by the use that it makes of decorative elements that the exact limitations of the school are fixed. The Classical style was entirely, the Byzantine mainly, pictorial; the Celtic is purely ornamental. In its disposition of lines and masses, its dexterous manipulation of a few forms and colours to form patterns of endless variety, it has never been surpassed. Another marked feature of the school is the adaptation of decorative motives which belong primarily and properly to work in three dimensions—to the allied, yet essentially distinct, arts of basketry, metalwork, and sculpture. Some purists object to this as a blemish; but we find it difficult to accept their strictures when feasting our eyes on the exquisite beauty of some of the pages in such books as those of Kells, Lindisfarne, or Lichfield.

The art of writing was probably introduced into Ireland, as a concomitant of Christianity, early in the fifth century;

PLATE VII

GOSPELS (BOOK OF KELLS). IRISH, VIIth CENT
DUBLIN, TRIN. COLL.

CELTIC ILLUMINATION

and the fervour with which the faith was embraced in the "Isle of Saints" led to the foundation of monasteries innumerable, in which the copying of the Gospels and of service-books was diligently practised, for use at home and on missionary enterprises. A distinctive Irish calligraphy was soon evolved, which preserved most of its characteristics almost unchanged down to the decay of writing as an art—a conservatism fruitful in perplexities for the palaeographer, and so adding to the difficulties of the would-be historian of Irish illumination. At first, probably, the scribes contented themselves with making unadorned copies of the texts. The archetypes brought over from the Continent by S. Patrick and his companions were very likely devoid of ornament; this would account for the absence of any trace of foreign influence in Irish book-decoration. No illuminated manuscripts of the Celtic school exist to which an earlier date than the seventh century can safely be assigned; but its first beginnings must be put a good deal earlier, for by this time we find already a fully developed and elaborate system of decoration, together with a very high degree of technical skill.

Before we come to notice individual manuscripts in detail, a few words must be said about the elements of ornamental design by which the school is characterized. These were formerly claimed as of Irish invention, but are now recognized as belonging (for the most part, at any rate) to the common stock of primitive art. They are roughly divisible into a few groups, and these again may be classified as arising from either geometrical or organic forms. The following list, though perhaps incomplete, contains the most frequent patterns:—

A. Geometrical

1. Ribbons: plaited, knotted, or used as frames to enclose ornament. These, with the spirals, really form the foundation of the Celtic decorative system.
2. Thread-like lines plaited or knotted; a more delicate and intricate variety of 1.

ILLUMINATED MANUSCRIPTS

3. Spirals, including the divergent spiral, or trumpet-pattern.
4. The triquetra, or three-spoked wheel pattern.
5. Dots, generally red, arranged in patterns, or outlining letters and frames.
6. Step-patterns of zigzag lines.
7. Tessellated patterns: tartans, lozenges, checks, key-patterns.
8. Network patterns of fine lines on a contrasting ground.

B. Organic Forms

1. The chief animal-designs are the so-called "lacertines," i.e. birds, dragons, serpents, hounds, etc., "stretched out lengthwise in a disagreeable manner," to quote Dr. Keller's graphic phrase.[1] These are plaited and twined together with a wonderful dexterity; their tongues and tails being prolonged into ribbons, and knotted or woven into a compact space-filling decoration. Like the spirals and ribbon-work, they are among the most distinctive features of Celtic illumination.
2. In the Book of Kells and other Irish manuscripts, use is made of the human figure for grotesques, corner-pieces, and terminals. It is always treated in a purely conventional manner, the hair and limbs often being prolonged into plaits, spirals, or ribbon-like edges for letters and frames.
3. Grotesque animals other than lacertines are sometimes, but sparingly, introduced.
4. Plant-forms occur, but rarely. The chief is the shamrock, much used in the Book of Kells and one or two other manuscripts. There are also a few examples of the vine; but on the whole, Celtic ornament cannot be said to have derived many of its patterns from vegetable life.

[1] See his article on Irish MSS. in Swiss libraries in *Mittheil. der Ant. Gesellsch. in Zürich*, vii, Heft 3, 1851, pp. 61–97; translated by W. Reeves in the *Ulster Journal of Archaeology*, viii, 1860, pp. 210–30, 291–308.

CELTIC ILLUMINATION

In the disposition of this mass of decoration, the Irish monks showed themselves to be great artists as well as expert craftsmen. They used their ornament in three ways. First, as rich frames enclosing full-page figure-subjects. Secondly, to enrich the opening pages of the Gospels, or other specially important parts of the text. Thirdly, for the complete pages of conventional decoration, often full of their peculiar symbolism, and usually having as foundation an elaborate cruciform design, which were generally prefixed to the Gospels and Psalms. In each case, the fundamental plan was much the same. Frames, capitals, or decorative pages were cut into variously shaped panels by flat ribbons, sometimes plaited at the corners, or bent to receive knotted and lacertine terminals. These panels were then filled with all-over patterns of one of the elements above described, so disposed as to give at once an impression of great variety and perfect harmony. In the best Irish manuscripts, such as the Book of Kells, every panel turns out on examination to be different, even plaits and knots being slightly varied. Nor did the artists rest content with the labour of producing their great cruciform and strap-work designs; they also made their pages of script splendid by the huge plaited initials, ending often in swans' heads, eagles, or human grotesques, and by the wealth of dotted work, spirals, and lacertines which filled the ground between and about the lines of text. The draughtsmanship is extraordinary, the most intricate enlacements and spirals, and the delicate openwork patterns which recall "drawn thread" work, being faultlessly executed in firm and accurate outline. The pattern thus made was then coloured, always in small detached patches, like champlevé enamel-work. There are no washes, broad masses, blendings of tone; everything is flat and definite. The range of colours was not large; often only red and yellow are used, in addition to the lustrous black ink. In manuscripts of greater importance green, violet, and brown are added; and finally, in a few books, blue, the rarest and most

ILLUMINATED MANUSCRIPTS

beautiful of the colours which the Irish painter had at his disposal.

It only remains to mention the figure-subjects, usually portraits of the Evangelists, occasionally a few scriptural scenes also, which the Celtic illuminators unfortunately felt it necessary to introduce into their works. Their genius, as has already been said, was for pattern-weaving, space-filling, symmetry; their world was a flat one, their art two-dimensional. The result of applying these peculiarities to the human figure may be imagined. Man, as seen by the Celtic artist, is a purely geometrical animal. His hair is a series of parallel lines or neatly fitted curves; his eyes, two discs set symmetrically in almond-shaped frames; his nose, an interesting polygonal device. His dress, cut up into arbitrary compartments, his straight toes and fingers, and his doll-like stare, complete an *ensemble* which may be successful as a decorative pattern, but has no relation to real life.

There is a good deal of uncertainty as to the dates of most of the extant examples of early Celtic illumination; fixed points are few, experts' judgments are many and various. So the order adopted in the following notes of individual manuscripts cannot claim finality as a precise chronological arrangement. A fixed point of great value is supplied by the Durham Book, which was written (according to a tradition recorded in the tenth century and accepted without dispute) at Lindisfarne, in Northumberland, between 687 and 721. The monastery at Lindisfarne had been founded by S. Aidan, from Iona, early in the seventh century; and the fully developed style and technical perfection of the purely Celtic work (i.e. all the decorative ornament) in this book compel us to assign the beginnings of Irish illumination to a much earlier period. But no actual specimens exist, probably, of greater antiquity than the seventh century.

One of the earliest, by common consent, is the Book of

CELTIC ILLUMINATION

Durrow,[1] a copy of the Latin Gospels now in the library of Trinity College, Dublin. It formerly belonged to Durrow monastery, in King's County, founded by S. Columba about A.D. 553, and was believed to have been the handiwork of the saint himself, on the strength of a colophon in which the scribe names himself Columba and claims to have written the whole book in twelve days. But the manifest impossibility of such a feat of rapid calligraphy has led to the conclusion that this colophon was copied from the archetype, doubtless a hastily written and unadorned codex. King Flann had a cumdach or shrine (now lost) made to enclose the volume, between the years 879 and 916, when it was already regarded as a precious relic; and we shall probably not be far wrong in assigning it to the seventh century. The ornament consists of five full pages of decorative design (one at the beginning, and one prefixed to each Gospel), another page with the four Evangelistic emblems, four more representing each of the Evangelists by his emblem, and elaborate initials at the beginning of each of the Gospels. The drawings of the emblems are crude, conventional, grotesque, especially on the page which contains all four.[2] In fact, the most noteworthy point about them is the winglessness of the man, lion, and calf—suggesting an early date. The decorative work, on the other hand, is well planned and firmly executed; it lacks the extreme delicacy and rich variety which we find in a few of the later manuscripts, but it is far from ineffective. The chief defects are a tendency to overcrowd the page by filling up all available spaces with close-set strap-work or tartan patterns of lozenges or squares, and a monotonous effect produced by

---

[1] J. O. Westwood, *Facsimiles of the Miniatures and Ornaments of Anglo-Saxon and Irish MSS.*, 1868, pp. 20–5, pl. 4–7; *National MSS. of Ireland*, ed. J. T. Gilbert, i, 1874, pp. viii–ix, pl. 5, 6; J. A. Bruun, *Celtic Illuminated MSS.*, 1897, pp. 45–7, pl. 1, 2; S. F. H. Robinson, *Celtic Illuminative Art*, 1908, pp. xix–xxi, pl. 1–4.

[2] Reproduced by Westwood, *Palaeographia Sacra Pictoria*, 1843–5, at end of Irish Biblical MSS. All the other illuminated pages are given in colours in his *Facsimiles*.

the exact symmetry of the design and by the too frequent repetition on one page of the same device without any variation. For instance, the page facing the beginning of S. Mark's Gospel is filled with fifteen circles in rows of three, connected by lozenges of trellis-work and filled with interlaced ribbons, all exactly alike except the central circle. Another page is given up almost entirely to spirals; another to rows of lacertines biting each other. Perhaps the finest page is that of which the centre is occupied by a sort of patriarchal cross surrounded with an elaborate pattern of interlaced ribbons; the borders filled with interlaced circles and strap-work. The ground of the decorative pages is usually black, that of the emblem pages the plain vellum. The colours used are few: red, yellow, and green predominate, brown also occurs, and rarely purple. Red dots are freely used, both for framing coloured ornament and for the groundwork of panels on which the letters are set.

There is not much to be said about the Book of Dimma,[1] another Gospel-book at Dublin (Trin. Coll.), written by one Dimma Mac Nathi, who is supposed to have lived in the first half of the seventh century. Besides the initial ornament, which is much slighter than in the Durrow Book, it contains four full-page miniatures, representing the first three Evangelists and the emblem of the fourth, drawn in outline on the vellum ground, and flatly coloured in segments, enclosed within frames filled with the usual plait and coil patterns with zigzags, lozenges, and simple tessellated work. The execution is poor, the general effect mean and barbaric—perhaps indicative of an early date.

Celtic illumination must have developed rapidly during the seventh century, for its close witnessed the production of one of the two most perfect existing specimens of the school; and that, too, not in Ireland itself, but in the

---

[1] *Nat. MSS. Irel.*, i, pp. xii–xiii, pl. 18, 19. Westwood, *Facsimiles*, p. 83, *Pal. Sac. Pict.*, Irish Bibl. MSS., pl. ii, 1; Bruun, pp. 60–1.

CELTIC ILLUMINATION

north of England. This is the famous Durham Book,[1] or Lindisfarne Gospels, a copy of the Gospels written by Eadfrith, Bishop of Lindisfarne (698–721), in honour of S. Cuthbert (d. 687); such at any rate is the tradition recorded by Aldred, who added an interlinear translation in the tenth century. Aldred goes on to credit Ethilwald with the binding and Billfrith with the ornamental metalwork of the outer cover, and finally names himself as translator, without saying a word as to the illuminations; so we may conclude that they were done by Eadfrith or under his supervision. Strictly speaking, therefore, the manuscript should be relegated to the Hiberno-Saxon class at the end of this chapter; but it seems better to discuss it here, in view of its great importance as a *point de repère* in the history of Celtic illumination. Its decoration consists of five cruciform pages, four portraits of the Evangelists, six pages of text, and sixteen pages of arcades enclosing the Eusebian Canons; besides a great wealth of initial ornament throughout the volume. Of the cruciform pages one is at the beginning of the volume, and one prefixed to each Gospel. The most perfect is that before S. Matthew; it consists of a cross of ornate and unusual design, enclosed in a rectangular frame and completely filled and surrounded with intricate interlacing and other decorative patterns. The general scheme in the others is the same, but only that which precedes S. John's Gospel approaches it in beauty; the other three are more rectilinear in design, and produce a much less pleasing and interesting effect. The first page of each of the Gospels and of S. Jerome's Epistle to Damasus is profusely decorated, and so is the page beginning with the words: "Christi autem generatio" (Matt. i. 18). Perhaps the finest of these text-pages is

---

[1] Brit. Mus., Nero D. iv. For descriptions and partial reproductions see Warner, *Illuminated MSS.*, pl. 1, 2, and *Reproductions*, iii, 1, 2; *Cat. Anc. MSS.*, ii, pp. 15–18, pl. 8–11; *Pal. Soc.*, i, 3–6, 22; Sir E. M. Thompson, *Eng. Ill. MSS.*, 1895, pp. 4–10, pl. 1; Westwood, *Facsimiles*, pp. 33–9, pl. 12, 13; Robinson, pp. xxii–xxiv, pl. 5–10; Bruun, pp. 48–60, pl. 3.

ILLUMINATED MANUSCRIPTS

that on which S. Luke's Gospel begins.[1] The general plan is the same in all: the text enclosed in a frame-border filled with interlaced work, spirals, long-necked birds, and other devices, and having the initial letter itself for the left-hand side; the initial, and usually the next few letters, of large size and ornamental design and filled with decoration like the border; the remainder of the text smaller and less elaborate, but adorned with touches of colour and surrounded with patterns of red dots. These eleven pages form the principal part of the purely Celtic illumination in the book. For varied intricacy of design they are surpassed only by the Book of Kells; and the softness and harmony of the colours, the skilful and delicate contrasts of blue, red, green, yellow, and purple, brought out the more effectively by touches of black in the spaces between the patterns, are unsurpassed by any other manuscript of the school. The text is a beautiful example of half-uncial writing, in ink whose lustrous blackness is perfectly preserved, and is enriched throughout with coloured initials of characteristically Celtic style: spirals, lacertines, interlacings, with plentiful use of red dots. The ornamentation of the Eusebian Canons is comparatively slight; but the delicately tinted arcades, with pillars and arches alternately filled with ornithines, or lacertines, and plaits, charm by their perfection of execution, if they do not astonish by their fertility of design.

All these are purely Celtic, though Celtic of a more advanced kind than we have yet seen. But when we come to the four full-page portraits of the Evangelists, the only examples of figure-drawing in the book, we break at once with the Irish tradition, though its flat and conventional technique is still apparent. These miniatures are thoroughly Byzantine in design: the seated scribes, drawn in profile, with cushion, desk, and footstool, one with the ceremonial curtain at his side, are obviously descended from the same stock as the portraits

[1] Pl. viii.

LINDISFARNE GOSPELS, CIRCA 700

BRIT. MUS. NERO D IV

CELTIC ILLUMINATION

in the Greek Gospel-books described in chapter iii. The relationship is proved, indeed, beyond a doubt by the inscriptions in a sort of Latinized Greek, "O agios Mattheus," "O agius Marcus," etc. But the addition of the evangelistic emblems, inscribed in Latin ("imago hominis," etc.), shows that the descent from a Greek archetype was not immediate;[1] and it is most probable that these portraits were inspired by Italo-Byzantine originals contained in the Neapolitan manuscript from which the text was presumably copied. The ground in these pages is a pale violet; there is no conventional ornament, except a little knot-work at the corners—a marked contrast to the luxuriant decoration by which the Celtic illumination is characterized. In each of them the Evangelist sits writing, with his emblem, winged, above his head; but S. Matthew's emblem also appears in the form of a man holding a book,[2] low down on the right-hand side of the miniature, almost hidden by a curtain.

The Gospels of S. Chad,[3] in the cathedral library at Lichfield, may probably be assigned to the beginning of the eighth century. This manuscript is to all appearance of purely Irish workmanship. The first owner of whom any record survives was one Cingal, who in the ninth century sold it in exchange for a horse; it was afterwards dedicated to S. Teilo, the patron saint of Llandaff, but found its way to S. Chad's Church at Lichfield, apparently before the end of the tenth century. Several leaves are missing, and those which remain have suffered badly through damp, especially as regards the colours. There is a full page of ornamental text at

---

[1] See above, p. 62.

[2] Westwood's interpretation of this figure as representing the Holy Ghost has been generally accepted hitherto; but his position in the picture, looking up with reverence to the saint, makes it improbable, and comparison with the corresponding miniature in the S. Gall MS. 1395 (Keller, pl. vii, *Ulster Journ. of Arch.*, viii, p. 302) leaves little room for doubt that the Northumbrian artist has duplicated the emblem. He has been followed by the illuminator of the Copenhagen Gospels (Westwood, *Facsimiles*, pl. 41).

[3] *Pal. Soc.*, i, 20, 21, 35; Westwood, *Facsimiles*, pp. 56-8, pl. 23.

ILLUMINATED MANUSCRIPTS

the beginning of each Gospel, and another at the words "Christi autem generatio"; also portraits of SS. Mark and Luke, and a leaf prefixed to S. Luke's Gospel, having the Evangelistic symbols in outline on one side, and a rich cruciform design of ribbons and lacertines on the other. This last page, by far the most beautiful in the book, has the same form of central cross as the first of the cruciform pages in the Durham Book; while the decorative scheme with which the panels are filled, though somewhat inferior in delicacy and variety, is not unlike that of the splendid S. Matthew page in the same volume. The finest of the text-pages is that with the words "Christi autem generatio," a superb example of Celtic illumination; the prevailing ornaments here are the triquetra, spirals, and interlaced long-necked birds. But when we look at the two portraits we are confronted with the limitations of the Celtic artist, and have to recognize how really barbaric his outlook was, when once he turned from traditional ornament to actual life. The drawing of the figure touches the limit of grotesque hideousness: the body, composed of a series of bulging curves; the hair, divided into neatly fitting segments and coloured red, yellow, and purple; the huge head, with its staring eyes and impossible nose —all combine to form a *reductio ad absurdum* of the Irish manner.

We come now to the Book of Kells,[1] justly celebrated as the supreme masterpiece of Celtic illumination. Formerly assigned to the seventh century or even earlier, it is now regarded by the best critics as a production of the eighth or early ninth century. This view is partly based on textual considerations, the volume containing the four Gospels in a mixture of the Hieronymian and Old-Latin versions resembling that found in the Gospels

---

[1] Westwood, *Facsimiles*, pp. 25-33, pl. 8-11; *Nat. MSS. Irel.*, i, pp. ix-xii, pl. 7-17; Robinson, pp. xxv-xxx, pl. 11-51; *Pal. Soc.*, i, 55-8, 88-9; T. K. Abbott, *Celtic Ornaments from the Book of Kells*, 1895, with fifty plates; Bruun, pp. 77-81, pl. 7-9; M. Stokes, *Early Christian Art in Ireland*, 1887, pp. 9-17.

CELTIC ILLUMINATION

of MacRegol (early ninth century); partly on artistic, for the profusion, variety, and perfection of its decoration undoubtedly point rather to the maturity than the primitive ages of Celtic art. It was probably executed in the Columban monastery of Kells, in Meath, where it remained, certainly from the beginning of the eleventh century, down to the dissolution of that abbey in 1541; it afterwards belonged to Archbishop Ussher, and is now prized as the greatest treasure in the library of Trinity College, Dublin, having come there with the rest of his books in 1661. Conjecture has identified it with a codex shown to Giraldus Cambrensis at Kildare, towards the end of the twelfth century, whose illuminations he describes in a remarkable passage[1] of enthusiastic appreciation; they were said, he tells us, to have been produced under the direction of an angel at the prayers of S. Bridget. But perhaps it is more natural to suppose that this was another example of a class now represented only by the Book of Kells.

More fully decorated than any other extant manuscript of its school, the Book of Kells forms a sort of compendium of Irish art: possessing—besides arcaded Canon-tables, portraits of Evangelists, numerous decorative pages and magnificent initials—full-page miniatures of the Temptation of Christ, His seizure by the Jews, and the Madonna and Child, which are unique in the history of Celtic painting. Historically interesting, however, these pages possess all the artistic vices of their school. The Madonna and Child, surrounded by four small angels with censers, and placed in an elaborately ornamented frame, seems like a caricature of some early Byzantine painting. It is solemn, but inept. Nothing could be less lifelike or more hideous than this Infant Christ, not even the large-headed, stony-eyed Madonna. But the beautifully jewelled wings of the angels, the soft bright colours, the woven patterns of the accessories, the clever space-filling, nearly succeed in turning what is

[1] Topographia Hibernica, ii, 38–9 (*Opera*, v, 123).

really an ugly picture into an interesting, even pleasing design. Better in every way is the miniature of the seizure of Christ. Here the artist, in spite of crude drawing and bad anatomy, has actually managed to convey the idea of unresistant suffering on the one hand, of malicious energy on the other.

But perhaps the best things in all three pictures are the figures of angels with wings outspread, which also appear with beautiful effect on many of the pages of lettering. Poor as to facial expression, they yet suggest something of mysterious dignity by the great sweep of those straight and jewelled pinions, which give majesty even to the slightly grotesque symbols of the Evangelists, thrice represented[1] between the arms of the mystical cross. These winged figures have a look which is magical, remote, profoundly un-European, reminiscent, indeed, of the deities of ancient Assyrian or Egyptian art. This feature of the Book of Kells and its congeners, together with the peculiar flamingo-like character of the lacertine birds, has led some writers to claim for Irish art an Egyptian inspiration.[2] In support of this claim it has been remarked that the earliest Irish monasteries were built on the same plan as those of the Egyptian hermits; and a piece of direct evidence is adduced from the Leabhar Breac, which mentions, among other foreign ecclesiastics buried in Ireland, "Septem monachos Aegyptios qui jacent in Disert-Ulidh." It has even been maintained that the conversion of Ireland was due to Coptic missionaries; but this cannot be regarded as anything more than conjecture. It is clear, however, that Irish ornament, whatever its origin, is not in its entirety a native product. Its plaits and knots are European in their distribution, and seem always to occur at a certain stage of primitive art. Its spirals are found on British shields of the second century (not to mention Cretan decoration of a much earlier period); its key and tessel-

---

[1] One of these representations is our pl. vii.
[2] See Keller, pp. 74, 79–81 (Reeves's translation, pp. 225, 229–30).

CELTIC ILLUMINATION

lated patterns seem relics of classic design. It is in execution and combination, not in invention, that the Irish illuminator excels.

In the ornament pages of the Book of Kells, and especially in the great designs of mingled lettering and decoration prefixed to each Gospel, his taste and dexterity are seen at their best. S. Matthew alone has six such pages, culminating in the superb illumination of the monogram " XPI," on which, as Miss Stokes has well said, " is lavished, with all the fervent devotion of the Irish scribe, every variety of design to be found in Celtic art, so that the name which is the epitome of his faith is also the epitome of his country's art."

But the Book of Kells is unique; not even the Durham Book can be compared with it for richness and variety, and no other extant manuscript of the school is worthy to be mentioned in the same breath. The style was here being used by a supreme artist; its usual interpreter was only a respectable craftsman at best. Of the remaining Irish manuscripts, perhaps the most important is the Gospels of Mac Regol,[1] in the Bodleian Library at Oxford, sometimes called the Rushworth Gospels from its donor, John Rushworth the historian. Its scribe, Mac Regol, has been identified with an Abbot of Birr, in Queen's County, who died in 820; and though this identification cannot be regarded as certain, it probably indicates the date of the manuscript correctly. The decoration is rich, but coarsely and unevenly executed; it consists of an elaborate page of lettering at the beginning of each Gospel, and portraits of SS. Mark, Luke, and John in highly decorated frames. The chief colours are brick-red and yellow, but green and dull purple are also used. There is no blue or pale violet. Most of the ornament is made up of plaits, spirals, lacertines, and open reticulated patterns. The strange women's faces seen on some pages of the Book of Kells

---

[1] Westwood, *Facsimiles*, pp. 53–6, pl. 16; *Nat. MSS. Irel.*, p. xiii, pl. 22–4; *Pal. Soc.*, i, 90, 91.

appear again, as well as the semi-human lacertines, their hair prolonged into plaits and spirals. The symbols of the Evangelists, which stand above their portraits, are covered with bright-coloured tartans, recalling the Book of Durrow. The Evangelists themselves are, as usual, quite conventional in drawing. Drapery is represented by a series of rather turbulent diagonal stripes, faces are flat and geometrical, perspective does not exist. Still, the book is of great value as representing, presumably, the average work of the period when Celtic art reached its culminating point in the Book of Kells. It is, at any rate, immeasurably superior, both in taste and execution, to most of its successors.

One of the best of these is the Gospel-book at Lambeth,[1] written for (or perhaps by) Maelbrigte Mac Durnan, who was Abbot of Armagh and Raphoe, and afterwards of Iona, and who died in 927. It is a small volume, written in minuscules, and adorned with four full-page portraits of the Evangelists and a cruciform page containing their emblems, as well as decorative text-pages at the beginning of each Gospel and at the words "Christi autem generatio." The colouring is on the whole delicate and pleasing, including bright red, a beautiful violet, two shades of green, and buff; and the ornamental work is rich and varied. But the figure-drawing is impossible, and the drapery still more so, appearing in a series of strange curvilinear folds. The four emblems are exceedingly weird, drawn in fantastic shapes, only just distinguishable by their heads, and coloured on the patchy, enamel-like system so often found in Celtic painting. An unpleasing peculiarity of the manuscript is the use of a heavy white body-colour for the faces, hands, and other parts of the figure, which are usually only drawn in outline on the vellum. The artist's passion for symbolism has led him to provide S. Luke

---

[1] S. W. Kershaw, *Art Treasures of the Lambeth Library*, 1873, pp. 27-9; Westwood, *Facsimiles*, pp. 68-72, pl. 22, and in *Archaeol. Journ.*, vii, 1850, pp. 17-25; *Nat. MSS. Irel.*, p. xvii, pl. 30, 31; Bruun, pp. 65-7, pl. 4-6.

CELTIC ILLUMINATION

with cloven hoofs; but it is hard to see why he should have treated S. Matthew[1] in the same way.

In the library of Trinity College, Dublin, are two manuscripts closely allied to the Gospels of Mac Durnan, although tradition assigns them to much earlier dates. These are the Book of Armagh,[2] written (there seems reason for supposing) in 807, and the Book of Mulling,[3] whose scribe has been identified with S. Mulling or Moling, Bishop of Ferns in Leinster, who died in 697. The former has only pen-and-ink work, but was evidently meant to be fully illuminated. The Evangelistic emblems, which appear all four on one page, between the arms of a cross, as well as singly, resemble those of the Lambeth book in having four wings each, but are much better drawn, less conventional, and more life-like, especially the prancing lion and the eagle with its talons embedded in a fish. The Book of Mulling has full-page miniatures of three of the Evangelists, standing upright with a book in the left hand; the pose of the figures, the absurd folds of drapery, the dead-white faces, the frame-borders filled with lacertines and other ornaments, all strongly resemble the portrait-pages in the Lambeth book. The colouring, however, is less delicate and more restricted in range—so restricted, indeed, that the artist has found it necessary to paint the hair blue, as well as the eyes!

Two more Irish manuscripts of the ninth or tenth century are just worth mentioning, as showing the depth of barbarism into which Irish illumination quickly relapsed. One of these is a Psalter in the British Museum;[4] damaged by fire, but not to such an extent as to mask the childish absurdity of its two drawings—David overthrowing Goliath, and David playing the harp—or the poverty of design in its interlaced borders and initials.

---

[1] This curious feature also occurs in the Book of Kells. See Abbott, pl. 33.
[2] Westwood, *Facsimiles*, pp. 80-2; *Nat. MSS. Irel.*, pp. xiv-xvii, pl. 25-9.
[3] Westwood, p. 93; *Nat. MSS. Irel.*, p. xiii, pl. 20, 21.
[4] Vitell. F. xi. See *Cat. Anc. MSS.*, ii, p. 13; Westwood, *Facsimiles*, p. 85, pl. 51, fig. 5, 6, and in *Archaeol. Journ.*, vii, pp. 23-5.

ILLUMINATED MANUSCRIPTS

The other manuscript, also a Psalter, is in the library of S. John's College, Cambridge.[1] It has three full-page miniatures, all extremely crude and barbaric: two are of the victories of David; the third is surely the most grotesque representation of the Crucifixion ever perpetrated in Christian art. Among other peculiarities are the intertwining folds of Christ's draperies (the figure is completely clothed, even to boots and stockings, the latter red), the armless angels with hands emerging directly from their bodies, and the ridiculous little figures of Longinus and the soldier.

Illumination continued to be practised in Ireland down to the thirteenth century, an ugly if pathetic memorial of its glorious past. There are drawings of the Evangelistic symbols in two twelfth century Gospel-books in the British Museum, viz. Harl. 1802 and 1023; those in the former, which was written by Maelbrigt hua Maeluanaigh at Armagh in 1138, being especially feeble and ugly.[2] But the decorations were for the most part restricted to interlaced and zoomorphic initials and borders; and these became stereotyped in design, coarse in execution, unpleasing in colour.[3]

But we must go beyond Ireland, beyond the British Isles, to give anything like a complete sketch, however brief, of Celtic illumination. As early as the sixth century a stream of Irish missionaries began to pour forth, who carried Christianity, and with it their own peculiar form of Christian art, into Great Britain and many parts of the Continent, notably Switzerland, South Germany, and Northern Italy; and the monasteries which they founded grew rich in manuscripts written and illuminated in the Irish manner. Not many of these have survived; and those that have are mostly—it must be

---

[1] MS. C. 9. See Westwood, *Facsimiles*, p. 84, pl. 30, and *Pal. Sac. Pict.*, No. 18; Burlington Fine Arts Club, *Exhibition of Illuminated MSS.*, 1908, No. 3, pl. 11.

[2] *Nat. MSS. Irel.*, pp. xx, xxii, pl. 40-2, 45; *Pal. Soc.*, i, 212.

[3] e.g. see Brit. Mus., Galba A. v and Add. 36929, two thirteenth century Psalters.

CELTIC ILLUMINATION

confessed— rather curious than beautiful. This is emphatically the case with the Book of Deer, a tenth century copy of the Gospels which belonged to the monastic settlement founded by S. Columba at Deer, in Aberdeenshire, and which is now in the Cambridge University Library.[1] The drawings of the Evangelists, which are repeated again and again on every available space throughout the volume, are merely childish; and their absurdity is not counterbalanced by any exceptional merit in the initial and border ornaments, which, though based on better models and more correctly drawn, do not rise above the simplest forms of plait, meander, and tessellated patterns. Celtic art in Wales reached a higher level, if we may judge by the Psalter executed by Ricemarch, Bishop of S. David's, in the latter part of the eleventh century. This manuscript, now in the library of Trinity College, Dublin,[2] has no miniatures, but its three ornamental text-pages, though not comparable to the best work of the school, still show some sense of decorative effect in their interlaced lacertine borders and zoomorphic initials.

Among the continental monasteries of Irish origin, two of the most famous are that founded by S. Columban at Bobbio, in Piedmont, and his disciple S. Gall's foundation in Switzerland. In these and the rest a great number of Celtic manuscripts accumulated: partly, no doubt, through donations from the parent church or from Irish pilgrims who visited these houses on their way to or from Rome; but mainly through the industry of the inmates, working under the direction of Irish calligraphers who had brought with them a knowledge, more or less perfect, of the principles of Celtic art. The Bobbio manuscripts have been dispersed; but the Irish influence in them would seem, judging by the few remnants now preserved in Turin, Milan, and Munich, to have yielded to that of

---

[1] Ii. vi. 32. The decorated pages are all reproduced in the Spalding Club edition, 1869. See too *Pal. Soc.*, i, 210, 211.

[2] Westwood, *Facsimiles*, p. 87; Bruun, p. 82, pl. 10.

ILLUMINATED MANUSCRIPTS

the local Lombardic and Italo-Byzantine schools, except for a few elements of ornament, especially plait and knot work and tessellated patterns.

The primitive traditions were maintained more closely at S. Gall,[2] contending influences being doubtless weaker there than in the Italian settlement. The famous Gospel-book (No. 51), which was probably written in the monastery about the end of the eighth or beginning of the ninth century, is actually nearer in style to the Books of Durrow, Lichfield, and Kells than many manuscripts of undoubtedly Irish execution. Its beautiful cruciform page contains panels filled with lacertines, and frame-compartments filled with plaits, spirals, and lozenges, all very perfectly drawn and delicately coloured. Blue, black, pale yellow, and red are the chief tints; no silver or gold. In the portraits of the Evangelists, each surmounted by his emblem as in the Durham Book, we find the rudimentary figure-drawing of the Mac Regol book and its successors; but these pages too are redeemed by the excellence of the frame-borders, filled with lacertines, interlacings, spirals, and other devices. The extraordinary miniature of the Crucifixion is decidedly more dignified, less grotesque, than that in the Cambridge Psalter: but there is an obvious kinship between them, and Westwood's remark on this picture and that of Christ in glory is not much too strong: "More barbarous designs could scarcely be conceived." This book is much the finest example of Celtic illumination preserved at S. Gall; but the others show the same faithful adherence to Irish traditions.

These traditions were firmly established in the north of England by the end of the seventh century, as is proved by the Lindisfarne Gospels. They appear very plainly

---

[1] See F. Carta, *Atlante paleografico-artistico*, 1899, pl. 10, 15; C. Cipolla, *Codici Bobbiesi*, 1907, pl. 39-41; *Pal. Soc.*, i, 121; L. von Kobell, *Kunstvolle Miniaturen*, p. 22, pl. 12, 13.

[2] See Keller's article, mentioned on p. 68 above; Westwood, *Facsimiles*, pp. 62-8, pl. 26-8. Copies of many of the miniatures and ornaments in these manuscripts were made for the Record Commissioners in 1833, and are now in the Public Record Office (Record Commission Transcripts, ser. iii, No. 156).

in two eighth century manuscripts, probably executed in the same district, and now in the Durham Cathedral Library. One of these[1] is an imperfect copy of the Gospels, having a splendid "In principio" page not unlike that of the Lindisfarne book, besides many fine initials; it also contains a full-page miniature of the Crucifixion, whose damaged condition is the less to be regretted since it is of the ungainly type represented in the Cambridge and S. Gall books—evidently the received Irish treatment of this subject. The other manuscript,[2] ascribed by tradition to the hand of Bede (but probably of somewhat later date), contains the commentary of Cassiodorus on the Psalms. It has two full-page miniatures, showing David as harpist and warrior respectively; the figures are rigid and rudely drawn, as usual, and the ornament of the enclosing borders, though richly varied (including lacertines, interlacings, and step-patterns), is less fine in execution than the decorative work in the Gospel-book. A still further decline is visible in the Prayer-book of Bishop Aethelwald of Lindisfarne, now in the Cambridge University Library,[3] with its quaint drawings of the Evangelists and their emblems.

But the Celtic spirit had by this time made its way southwards to Canterbury, where it was confronted with a rival influence introduced from Rome by Augustine and his missionaries. The result was a curious fusion of the two manners, a combination of classical composition with Celtic ornament, which is strikingly exemplified in the Psalter of S. Augustine's Abbey, Canterbury.[4] This manuscript, executed about the same time as the Lindisfarne Gospels, has initials which are already nearer to Franco-Saxon than to pure Celtic work. The body of

---

[1] A. ii. 17. See Westwood, p. 48; *New Pal. Soc.*, pl. 30.
[2] B. ii. 30. See Westwood, p. 77, pl. 17, 18; *Pal. Soc.*, i, 164.
[3] Ll. i. 10. Westwood, p. 43, pl. 24.
[4] Brit. Mus., Vesp. A. i. Westwood, pp. 10-14, pl. 3; *Pal. Soc.*, i, 18, 19; *Cat. Anc. MSS.*, ii, pp. 8-11, pl. 12-15; Thompson, *Eng. Illum. MSS.*, pp. 10-13, pl. 2; Warner, *Illum. MSS.*, pl. 3.

ILLUMINATED MANUSCRIPTS

these letters is black, with coloured terminals plaited together and surrounded by red dots. The plaits, however, are more open, less minute than in Irish illumination; the panels of lacertines have vanished, so has much of the spiral work. In their place we have a plentiful use of gold, a metal never found in Irish manuscripts, and very sparingly applied to the Lindisfarne Gospels. This, with the great black letters, produces an effect of sombre magnificence, very different from the gay yet austere delicacy of the best Irish initial-work, though distinctly traceable to its influence.

But when we come to the figure-composition, we see a style which has nothing at all to do with Celtic illumination, but is plainly the attempt of the native artist to copy a late-classical painting, which he may well have found in one of the books brought from Italy by Augustine.[1] Before Psalm xxvi, a full-page miniature shows David the Harpist enthroned, playing in concert with four other musicians, while two boys dance before him, a scribe standing on either side of the throne. Here all is painted in thick body-colour, faces and draperies are modelled and gradated, with green shadows on the flesh and white high-lights. The figures, though badly proportioned, are no mere geometrical shapes, but have life and movement; perspective is attempted, though in somewhat rudimentary fashion. The picture, in short, if not beautiful, aims at expressing actuality, and belongs to an altogether different order of things from the flat and conventional absurdities which passed as figure-compositions in purely Celtic manuscripts. Yet the arched frame enclosing it is richly ornamented with trumpet-pattern and interlacing, as well as with gilded rosettes and lozenges; so that the page presents an almost unique combination of Roman and Irish elements, welded together by an English painter.

[1] Sir G. Warner notes the interesting fact that a similar design occurs in a tenth century Bobbio MS.; the treatment is different, but again shows no hint of Celtic influence.

CELTIC ILLUMINATION

Something of this fusion is still to be seen in a late eighth century Gospel-book emanating from the same abbey,[1] but with a marked weakening of the Celtic influence. The tables of Eusebian Canons are enclosed in arcades, pillars and arches being profusely decorated with medallions and compartments filled with ornamental devices; but these include arabesque scrolls and many other non-Celtic patterns, and perhaps the most distinctive sign of Irish inspiration is to be seen in the plentiful use of red dots, which had by now become a recognized feature of English manuscripts, often forming the sole attempt at embellishment.

[1] Brit. Mus., Roy. 1 E. vi. Westwood, pp. 39-42, pl. 14, 15; *Pal. Soc.*, i, 7; *Cat. Anc. MSS.*, ii, pp. 20-2, pl. 17, 18; Warner, *Reproductions*, iii, 3.

CHAPTER V

THE CAROLINGIAN RENAISSANCE

WHEN Charlemagne became king of the Franks, in A.D. 771, he found himself at the head of a nation as inconspicuous artistically as it was militantly important. The existing remains of Merovingian, Lombardic, and Visigothic art, conveniently classed by some German critics under the general heading of "Wandering of the Nations style," can at best only be described as quaint, while at worst they are unspeakably hideous. They consist mainly, so far as the decoration of manuscripts is concerned, of strange initial letters and detached ornaments, based on fishes, birds, and dragons, with cable and plait patterns borrowed, in all probability, from Classical mosaics. These are generally drawn in coarse coloured outline and flatly tinted in crude colours, red, yellow, and green predominating. They are found in the seventh and eighth century MSS. of France, Spain, Germany, Lombardy,[1] the same patterns surviving in continental Romanesque stone-carving down to the twelfth century. Their strange, distorted shapes belong to a different world from the sophisticated ornament of Classical art; they are the ancestors of the long series of grotesques which became so constant and prominent a feature of Gothic design. There is a strong family likeness between these fantastic initials and those noted in chapter iii as occurring in Greek Gospel-books of the tenth and eleventh centuries—a likeness probably due to a common Oriental

[1] Many reproductions, especially from manuscripts now preserved in the Bibliothèque Nationale at Paris, are given in the Comte de Bastard's monumental *Peintures et ornements des manuscrits*, 1832–69. See too L. Delisle, *Mémoire sur d'anciens sacramentaires*, 1886 (*Mém. de l'Acad. des Inscr. et Belles-Lettres*, xxxii, i).

THE CAROLINGIAN RENAISSANCE

ancestry. In the horse-shoe arches, which occasionally appear on full pages of decoration, the influence of Moorish architecture is apparent. Here and there too are found pages filled with interlaced rings, lattice-work, and a few simple geometrical devices, faintly reminiscent of the least interesting pages in the Book of Durrow. This suggestion of kinship with Celtic art is borne out in the Gellone Sacramentary[1] by the symbolism which represents the first three Evangelists by their emblems, and S. John by a very Egyptian-looking eagle-headed man. This manuscript, however, is one of the latest productions of the Merovingian school (if school be an applicable word), and shows signs of its transitional character both in script and illuminations. In its sole miniature, for instance, of the Crucifixion (f. 143b), the figures of the hovering angels, and of Christ clothed in a loin-cloth reaching to the knee, suggest some early Italo-Byzantine archetype in fresco or mosaic, and have nothing in common with the barbarous design found in Celtic manuscripts. But whatever the precise source may have been of individual elements in pre-Carolingian illumination, its most salient characteristic is a bizarre, barbaric quality, symptomatic of a low state of culture.

With the third quarter of the eighth century, however, we enter on a new era. Charlemagne, when he was seized with the idea of reviving the Roman Empire, desired an imperialism which should be Latin in other things besides greatness of dominion. His scheme included an intellectual ascendency, and a transference of the faded glories of Classical art, the ripening ones of Byzantine, to his own capital and court. The name of Carolingian Renaissance is given to the resulting efflorescence of learning and the arts, which took place under his immediate influence. His school is unique in this, that it owed its inception to the personal encouragement of a prince, not to the genius of individual artists. We notice, in fact, in Carolingian

---

[1] Paris, Bibl. Nat., lat. 12048, ff. 42, 42b. For description of the MS. see Delisle, p. 80.

ILLUMINATED MANUSCRIPTS

manuscripts not so much greatness of technical achievement as a general magnificence of plan. Charlemagne "dreamed greatly"; his miniaturists, without a native tradition to help them, carried out his ambitions as best they might. Beginning at his capital of Aix-la-Chapelle, the artistic revival radiated throughout the Western Empire; influenced Southern England, already feeling the first stirrings of culture; and, under Charles's successors, determined the subsequent course of European pre-Gothic art.

In the decoration of books this artistic revival was essentially derivative and composite. Byzantine influence is at once discernible, not only in the purple pages and gold lettering of some of the most sumptuous manuscripts, but also in the composition of the portraits of Evangelists and other miniatures, and in the arcades enclosing the Eusebian Canons. To account for this influence, it is not necessary to lay much stress on the direct relations of Charles with the court of Constantinople—not even on the fact that a Greek tutor was sent thence to instruct his daughter, for some years betrothed to the Emperor Constantine VI. Still less need we suppose that the iconoclasm of Constantine's predecessors caused a great influx of Greek painters into Charles's dominions; the resemblance of Frankish to Byzantine miniature is in iconography rather than manner, the work of imitators rather than pupils. It is to Rome and Ravenna, doubtless, not to Byzantium itself, that we must look for the immediate source of this resemblance, as well as for that of the Late Classical and Early Christian elements which appear in Carolingian illumination. In 784 Charles despoiled Ravenna of marbles and mosaics for the enrichment of Aix-la-Chapelle; and it may be supposed that he did not return empty-handed from Rome, which he had already visited thrice (in 774, 781, and 787) before his coronation there as Emperor in 800. It is known, in fact, that he brought back Roman singers, in his zeal for bringing the Frankish liturgy into conformity with

GOSPELS ("CODEX AUREUS"). CAROLINGIAN, CIRCA 800

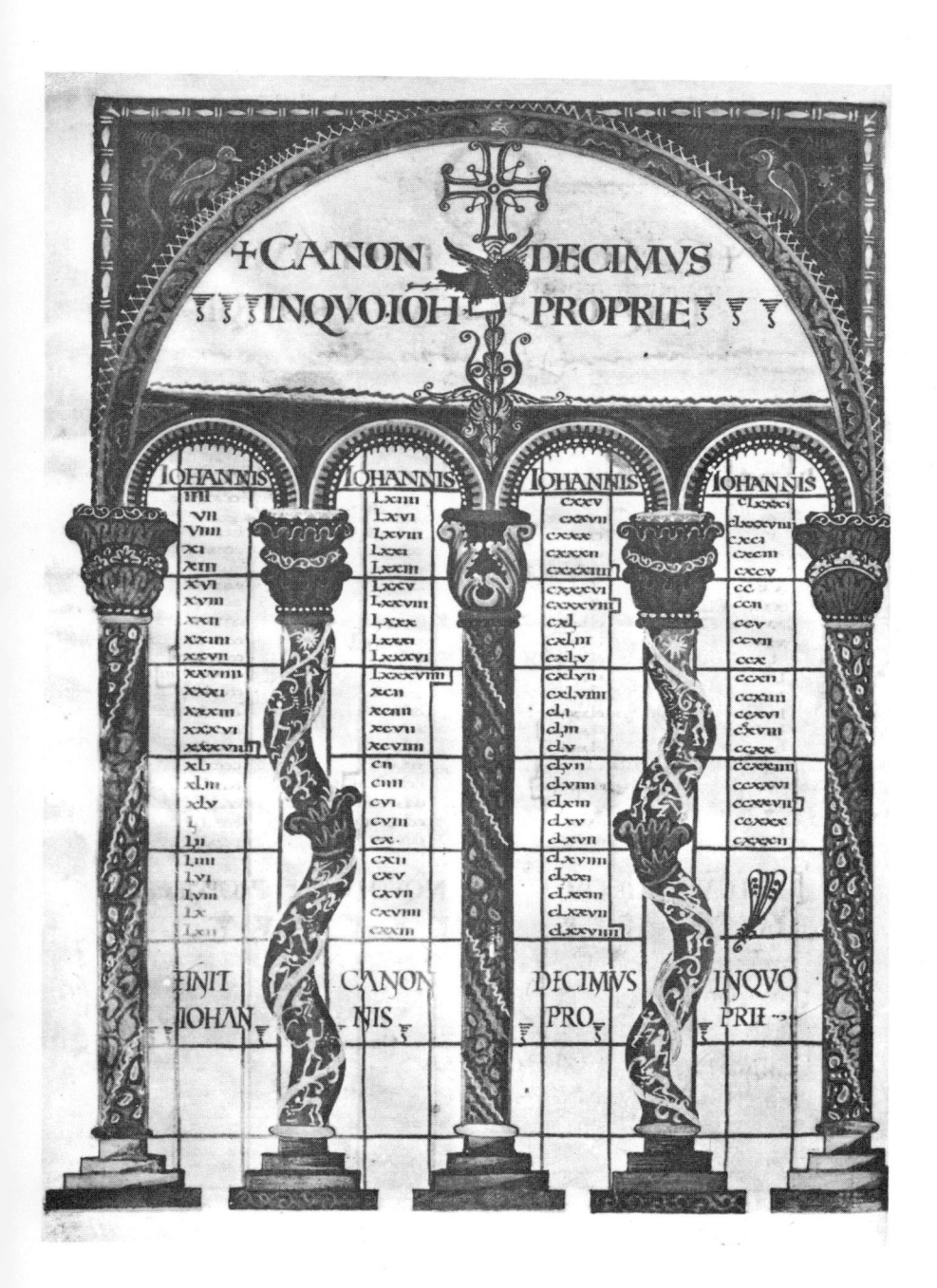

BRIT. MUS., HARL. 2788

THE CAROLINGIAN RENAISSANCE

that of Rome; and we can hardly doubt that he brought books too, and that some of these were illuminated.

The Syrian element in Carolingian illumination has already been noticed in chapter ii, in connection with the Rabula and Etschmiadzin Gospel-books.[1] There are hints of it in some of the decorations of Merovingian manuscripts, but it becomes more apparent in the succeeding period, especially in the pagoda-like dome which figures in representations of the Fountain of Life,[2] and in the frequent use of peacocks, pheasants, and other bird-forms as ornament—though the latter device might conceivably have been borrowed from Early Christian paintings.

Celtic influence too counted for much—as to decorative ornament, luckily, not figure-drawing. Frankish artists made no attempt to reproduce the minute and delicate intricacy of spiral, interlaced, and lacertine ornament which is the glory of Celtic illumination. But some of the simpler details were adopted, especially plait and knot-work, and the use of birds' or beasts' heads as terminals; and in Gospel-books the decoration of the initial-pages of script was closely copied. It is easy to understand the presence of Anglo-Irish ornament, when we consider the important part played by Alcuin in the Carolingian revival of learning. Not that he can be credited with a direct share in the artistic revival which accompanied it, or even with the introduction of the neat and well-defined script known as Caroline minuscule, which superseded the unshapely, illegible Merovingian hand; but when he left York for Charles's court, in 782, he must have taken with him, for use in the Palatine school, or requisitioned afterwards, when engaged on the revision of the Vulgate, manuscripts written and illuminated in Northumbria.

An elaborate and wellnigh exhaustive study of Carolingian illumination has been made by the late Dr.

---

[1] Above, p. 33.
[2] See pl. x.

ILLUMINATED MANUSCRIPTS

Janitschek,[1] who deduced from the extant manuscripts the existence of several local schools, having each their individual mannerisms. His classification is perhaps too rigid in some respects,[2] but his comprehensive survey of the materials makes his work an indispensable text-book of the subject; and the limits of the present book will not admit of more than a brief summary of his conclusions, with a few remarks on some of the most important manuscripts. According to Janitschek, then, at least six great schools of illumination flourished in the Frankish dominions early in the ninth century, viz. (1) the Palatine school, established in immediate connection with Charles's court, and usually working at Aix-la-Chapelle; (2) the school of Tours, founded by Alcuin, who retired from the court in 796 to become Abbot of S. Martin's; (3) Corbie, in Picardy, closely connected with the Tours school; (4) Metz; but Aix-la-Chapelle seems a more likely place of origin for the principal manuscripts assigned by Janitschek to this school; (5) Rheims, specially interesting as the probable birthplace of the Utrecht Psalter style, which counted for so much in English illumination; (6) the Franco-Saxon school, whose centre was perhaps the great Abbey of S. Denis; conspicuous for its use of Celtic ornament.

To the first of these schools, the Schola Palatina, Janitschek assigns three manuscripts only, viz. the Gospel-book in the Schatzkammer at Vienna, said to have been found on Charlemagne's knees when his tomb was opened in A.D. 1000; the Gospels of Aix-la-Chapelle Cathedral, and those of S. Victor-in-Santem, now in the Brussels Library (No. 18723). The style of these three books would scarcely be recognized by the casual critic as essentially Carolingian. The Evangelist-portraits with

---

[1] *Die Trierer Ada-Handschrift*, 1889 (Gesellschaft für rheinische Geschichtskunde, Publikationen, No. 6), pp. 63–111.

[2] Cf. the section on Carolingian miniature in A. Michel's *Histoire de l'Art*, i, i (1905), pp. 328–78. The writer, P. Leprieur, disputes many of Janitschek's views, especially as to the Metz school.

THE CAROLINGIAN RENAISSANCE

which they are illustrated are evidently derived from some excellent Classical, perhaps Roman, original; reproduced by artists who were thoroughly at home with their model and yet were no servile copyists, as is evident from the naturalistic manner and the grasp of values and the meaning of form which characterize their work. These paintings, in fact, show something of the true antique tradition in the pose of the figure, easy yet dignified; in its harmonious relation to its background; in the profoundly studied fall of the draperies. The same tradition is manifest, again, in the severe simplicity of the architectural decoration of the Canon-tables. It would seem, therefore, that the Carolingian Renaissance was based at the outset on all that was best in Classical art.[1]

As we move away from Aix-la-Chapelle to the provincial schools, we find ourselves travelling farther and farther away from this really beautiful restatement of the antique idea. It is supposed that the Palatine school produced its masterpieces during Charlemagne's reign, between 795 and 814; and that they became, together with the manuscripts imported by Charles and his counsellors, the point of departure for the national manner. This manner assumed its characteristic form in the monastic scriptoria which were founded, or at any rate encouraged, by the Emperor and his sons; but in most cases it came to its development, not in Charles's own day, but in the later times of Louis the Pious and Lothaire. Some writers have attributed this fact to the rather iconoclastic position which Charles took up during the great controversy; but a more probable explanation lies in the period of time which must necessarily elapse before a newly established school is fit to undertake the production of elaborately illuminated manuscripts.

It is, however, likely enough that Charles's views, liberal as they were, did tend to restrict the number of

[1] It must be noted, however, that Leprieur doubts whether these three manuscripts can be assigned to the Schola Palatina, or to so early a date as the lifetime of Charlemagne. See Michel, i, i, 335–6.

ILLUMINATED MANUSCRIPTS

subjects illustrated by the early Carolingian artists, and also helped that turn for symbolism which strikes such an unexpected note in the work of this otherwise prosaic school. After the Evangelist-portraits and Canon-tables (borrowed, as we have seen, from Greek Gospel-books), the most characteristic subjects in Carolingian illumination are the Hand of God giving the benediction; the Fountain of Life, an odd compound of East and West, with its Syrian pagoda-like temple, its peacocks and drinking stags; the Apocalyptic Adoration of the Lamb by the Elders; the Lamb with the chalice, symbolizing the Mass; and sometimes the Christ in Glory, of the beardless catacomb-type. These are the subjects proper to Gospel-books. The Alcuin-Bibles also illustrate Genesis, and occasionally Exodus; but never the life of Christ. This comes in later, the cycle of permissible subjects being gradually enlarged till, before the Ottonian period is reached, almost every event and parable in the Gospels has its authorized representation.

From the school attached to Charlemagne's court we naturally turn first to Tours, where his friend and adviser Alcuin spent the closing years of his life, from 796 to 804, as abbot of S. Martin's. There is a special fitness too in the fact that among the finest products of the Tours school are copies of Alcuin's revision of the Vulgate, though none of those extant, probably, were executed during his lifetime. We have no reason for supposing him to have concerned himself with pictorial illustration of the Bible; his great aim was to purge the text itself of errors which had crept in through the carelessness or ignorance of successive copyists. Indirectly, however, he must have influenced the formation of the distinctive Tours style, which is characterized in its conventional ornament by a blending of Celtic with Classical elements, through his importation of manuscripts from Northumbria (where Hiberno-Saxon illumination had already reached its prime) as well as from Italy. But it was under his successors that the school of Tours rose into

PLATE X

GOSPEL BOOK OF S. MEDARD'S ABBEY, SOISSONS. EARLY IXTH CENT.
PARIS, BIBL. NAT., LAT. 8850

THE CAROLINGIAN RENAISSANCE

artistic prominence, attaining its greatest perfection towards the middle of the ninth century.

The oldest surviving Alcuin-Bible—that in the Zurich Cantonal Library (Cod. 1)—is illuminated only with ornamental Canon-tables and initials. In these, weaving-patterns of Celtic type predominate, but are mingled with the palmette and acanthus, and Ravennate basket-capitals appear in the arcades. The Bamberg and London Bibles, however, show an increasing development in the direction of pure illustration, and a simultaneous abandonment of Celtic design. Subjects from the Old Testament are now represented, as well as Apocalyptic pictures such as the sacramental Lamb. In the Bamberg Bible (A. 1. 5) further Classical designs are found, in combination with the still prominent Celtic motives; and the miniatures of scenes from Genesis, in long narrow compartments, show the beginnings of a narrative art. This art is as yet very ugly and uncouth; but its compositions are obviously based on some Early Christian series, whose excellence of conception and sense of design are still visible, despite the barbarous ineptitude of the copyist. Midway between this rather primitive book and the finest work of the school, as exemplified in the Vivian Bible and the Lothaire Gospels, stands the Alcuin-Bible in the British Museum (Add. 10546).[1] This great book, probably executed about 840, is decorated with beautifully arcaded Canon-tables, in which the only relic of Celtic influence is the edging of red dots about the arches. It has also four full-page miniatures, prefixed to Genesis, Exodus, and the Gospels, and at the end of the volume. These are painted in a thick, gummy body-colour, with strong and unpleasant flesh-tints, and an entire want of harmony both in colour and composition. There is some attempt at naturalistic modelling, but this is almost nullified by the ill-proportioned, stunted figures and the harsh, ugly faces with staring eyes. The Genesis

---

[1] Fully described in *Cat. Anc. MSS.*, ii, pp. 1-4, with two plates (42, 43).

ILLUMINATED MANUSCRIPTS

pictures are evidently drawn from the same cycle as those in the Bamberg Bible, but they show a decided improvement in technique. Both these and the Exodus miniature (Moses receiving the law from God, and delivering it to the Israelites) are full of "vestigial relics" of Classical ancestry. The architecture of the Delivery of the Law is of the basilica style, with a coffered roof borne on Corinthian columns; the draperies, as in Late Classical illuminations, are much heightened with gold; and further evidence of Roman parentage is offered by the backgrounds, which are softly striped with blue, violet, and white—a fashion directly borrowed from Classical painting. Here, these backgrounds are used with excellent effect; but in the later work of the Carolingian illuminators the softness and airy gradations originally aimed at were lost, and the final result was a crude arrangement of hard contrasting bands of colour. In this disagreeable form, the striped background survived as a noticeable and persistent feature of the early German style. All the miniatures in the volume, except that prefixed to the Gospels (a full-page composition of Christ in glory, seated on a globe and surrounded by the Evangelistic emblems and the four Major Prophets), are divided into compartments by horizontal bands, as in the Bamberg Bible. The miniature at the end of the book, illustrating Apoc. iv and v, is in two compartments.[1] In the upper picture the sacramental Lamb and the Lion of the tribe of Judah are seen approaching, from left and right respectively, an altar on which the Book of Life is lying; at the corners are the Evangelistic emblems, holding each an open book. The lower represents God unveiling Himself, seated on a throne and surrounded by the four Apocalyptic beasts.

Closely related to the London Alcuin-Bible, though artistically superior to it, is the Bible[2] given to Charles

[1] Pl. xi.
[2] Paris, Bibl. Nat., lat. 1. See Bastard, *Peintures de la Bible de Charles le Chauve*, 1883.

PLATE XI

ALCUIN BIBLE. CAROLINGIAN, IXTH CENT
BRIT. MUS., ADD. 10546

THE CAROLINGIAN RENAISSANCE

the Bald by Count Vivian, as secular Abbot (845-50) of S. Martin's; which, with the Gospel-book [1] made for the Emperor Lothaire, probably about 840-3, represents the finest achievement of the Tours school. The miniatures in the Vivian Bible include all the subjects depicted in the London book, besides a series of scenes in S. Jerome's life, another of the conversion of S. Paul, and two full-page pictures: one representing David as harpist, with soldiers and musicians grouped around him; the other, Count Vivian and his monks offering the book to Charles the Bald. This last composition has its counterpart in the Lothaire Gospels, in a full-page portrait of the Emperor enthroned, with a soldier standing on each side. In these, as in the other miniatures of both manuscripts, there is abundant evidence of indebtedness to Late Classical art for composition and for individual motives; but the effect is marred by the stiff, awkwardly posed and often badly proportioned figures, with hard features and staring eyes; by the swirling draperies, foreshadowing the eccentricities of our own Winchester school; by the absence of perspective; and by the over-elaboration of ornament.

The best side of the style is certainly seen in the luxuriant decoration of the Canon-tables, which in the Vivian Bible and Lothaire Gospels is of singular beauty. The slender columns have foliated capitals of a Ravennate type; a Roman lamp hangs from the keystone of each arch; in the spandrels and lunettes are classical devices of drinking birds, centaurs, etc. Equally splendid are the initials, of strap or ribbon work, with Romanesque plant forms and monsters. In this decoration gold and silver are much used, and with excellent effect. Magnificence of ornament was the side of their art which the Tours illuminators really appreciated and understood. It was in this that they secured their greatest successes, not in their clumsy adaptation of Roman and Byzantine figure-subjects to the purposes of their own time.

[1] Bibl. Nat., lat. 266.

ILLUMINATED MANUSCRIPTS

The so-called Corbie school, closely allied to that of Tours and founded on it, came to its height about the third quarter of the ninth century, when Tours had already produced its best work. It is doubtful whether the manuscripts assigned to this school were actually executed at Corbie Abbey, near Amiens; but there seems good reason for localizing them at all events in the northeast of France. Three of the most famous were executed for Charles the Bald, viz. the Paris Psalter (Bibl. Nat., lat. 1152), written by Liuthard about 846-62; the Codex Aureus of S. Emmeran, a Gospel-book in the Munich Library (Cimel. 55), written in 870 by the same Liuthard and his brother Berengarius; and a small Prayer-book, in the Schatzkammer at Munich, specially interesting as the forerunner of the fourteenth and fifteenth century Horae, and as containing what is perhaps the earliest regular "pious founder" picture—a two-page miniature of Charles kneeling before the crucified Christ. To the same group too is assigned the great Bible of the monastery of S. Paul at Rome, which was probably executed for Charles the Fat (Emperor 881-8). The S. Emmeran book may be taken as the finest work of the school; indeed, so splendid is the effect of its illuminations that one is tempted to forgive the woodenness of the figure-drawing and the disproportionate elaboration of the frame-borders. Its most remarkable feature is the quantity and variety of the ornamental work. Every page is bordered, with Carolingian shell and wave patterns; plaits branching into foliated terminations; meander, key, and lozenge patterns; bands of imitation jewel-work on gold; and various designs of thick white dotted work upon a coloured ground. The draperies of the Evangelists are even more crumpled and turbulent than in the Lothaire Gospels; and their heavy faces are strongly marked with white lines, giving almost the appearance of mosaic.

The Bible of S. Paul's [1] is the most profusely illuminated, probably, of all Carolingian manuscripts.

[1] See Westwood, *The Bible of the Monastery of St. Paul near Rome*, 1876.

THE CAROLINGIAN RENAISSANCE

Besides a great wealth of miniatures illustrating Bible-history, and of frame-borders to the text-pages (similar to those in the S. Emmeran Gospels), it has huge ornamental initials to the several books. The miniatures are unequal in quality, and are clearly the work of more than one hand. The best of them show distinct traces of kinship with Byzantine miniatures of the ninth and tenth centuries, and were doubtless based on models imported from Italy. The resemblance is chiefly in the pose of the figures, and in some of the facial types, especially Moses in the Pentateuch scenes; in fineness of finish, modelling, and execution generally, the Western artist is immeasurably inferior. Many of the compositions were evidently copied from the Vivian Bible or its archetype, but the range of subjects illustrated is much wider. Interesting as the miniatures are, however, they are quite eclipsed in beauty by the decorative work, which is really admirable, particularly the delicate foliate terminations of the large initials.

Next in antiquity to the school of Tours, and surpassing it both in originality and productiveness, comes what Janitschek has designated the school of Metz, while admitting that the localization rests on inference and conjecture rather than certain knowledge. The manuscripts which he groups together under this head are beyond doubt closely related to one another, and it is natural to suppose that they emanated from the same school; but there is much force in Leprieur's contention [1] that this school was associated with the Imperial court—was the Schola Palatina, in short—and the title "School of Godescalc, or of the Ada Gospels," which he gives it, has at any rate the advantage of safety. Wherever its home may have been, this school produced, in the closing years of the eighth century and the first three decades of the ninth, a splendid series of manuscripts, including some of the finest examples of Carolingian art that have survived to our days. Pre-eminent among these are

[1] Michel, p. 336.

ILLUMINATED MANUSCRIPTS

some magnificent Gospel-books of large size, written in gold and profusely illuminated.

The earliest of these is the Godescalc book,[1] a Gospel-lectionary, written for Charlemagne about 781–3 by a monk named Godescalc. As might be expected from its early date, it is the artless performance of an inexpert painter who has an abundance of material to copy from, but cannot assimilate or reproduce it. Modelling and perspective are practically non-existent; the colouring is mostly pallid and weak; the drapery folds, indicated by heavy black lines, have little relation to actuality. These faults are especially prominent in the portraits of the Evangelists, which occupy the first four pages; a distinct improvement is visible in the " Majestas Domini" which fills the next page, representing the enthroned Christ as beardless, long-haired, almost feminine, wearing a nimbus with jewelled cross, giving the benediction with the right hand and holding a book in the left. The verso of this leaf is devoted to the subject usually called the Fountain of Life. The Syrian ancestry of this composition has already been mentioned, and is plainly shown here, as in the later and finer Soissons book,[2] by the strange portico under which the fountain is placed, and the long-tailed Oriental birds which hover about it, along with stags and more homely birds. The border-ornament is comparatively slight, consisting of banded frames filled with plait-work, step-pattern, and a few more of the designs usually found in early Carolingian books. The text-pages are stained purple—an effort at splendour which was fortunately not generally imitated by later artists of the school.

About the year 800 three manuscripts were produced so nearly related to one another that there is no room for hesitation in grouping them together as representing the school in its middle period. These are the Codex Aureus in the British Museum (Harl. 2788), the Gospels

---

[1] Paris, Bibl. Nat., Nouv. acq. lat. 1203 (anc. 1993).
[2] Pl. x.

THE CAROLINGIAN RENAISSANCE

in the Abbeville Library (No. 1), and the celebrated Ada MS. in the Trèves City Library (No. 22). The Harleian Gospel-book[1] is one of the most magnificent manuscripts remaining from the actual age of Charlemagne. Written throughout in gold, in double columns, every column is surrounded by a narrow illuminated border. In the first part of the book these are of gold also, patterned with plaited, tessellated, and key designs, grotesque birds, etc. But after the first few quires they begin to deteriorate; red, green, and dull purple, or bands of imitation marbling, take the place of the gold, and the fineness of execution is lost. In the Canon-tables too there is a change half-way through: the first six are very richly decorated, the golden arches with elaborate capitals and columns filled with plait and scroll work contrasting effectively with the paintings of birds and trees (often in monochrome, always in comparatively subdued colouring) which fill the spandrels. The absence of silver, and the habit of outlining the gold with a fine red line, give a particularly warm and glowing effect to these splendid arcades. In the last five tables much less gold is used, the pillars are of many-coloured marble, and there is not so much elaboration of ornament. By this change, however, monotony is avoided, and the gorgeous effect of the first part is enhanced; a curious variety is introduced, on one page, in the form of spirally twisted pillars covered with human figures in quaint attitudes.[2] Besides borders and Canon-tables, this Codex Aureus has a decorated title-page, full-page portraits of the Evangelists, and a magnificent text-page at the beginning of each Gospel. The portraits show a great advance on the primitive art of the Godescalc book, though the S. John has decided affinity with the Majestas Domini of the older manuscript. The

---

[1] Fully described in *Cat. Anc. MSS.*, ii, pp. 22-4, pl. 39-41. See too Warner, *Illum. MSS.*, pl. 4, 5, and *Reproductions*, iii, 4; Janitschek, *Ada-Hs.*, pp. 86-7, pl. 26-8; Kenyon, *Biblical MSS.*, No. 13.

[2] Pl. ix.

Evangelists are all of the young, beardless type which henceforth became traditional—a departure from the bearded faces of the Godescalc book; long-nosed, large-eyed, with high arched brows; solidly painted in body-colour, with green shadows on the flesh and heavy streaks of white for the high-lights. The anatomy is sometimes at fault, e.g. in the impossible wrench by which S. Mark is dipping his pen in the ink. But the faces have life and expression, especially Matthew and Mark; there are distinct signs of modelling and perspective; and the draperies, though much folded, are treated with a considerable measure of success. The compositions as a whole are evidently derived from late Roman, rather than Byzantine art. In the text-pages which face them, on the other hand, the main idea is Celtic; but this is profoundly modified by the free use of gold, by the purple grounds, by the abandonment of spirals, lacertines, and the most intricate plaited and knotted designs, and by the introduction of new devices: the initial "Q" of S. Luke's Gospel, for instance, encloses a picture of the Angel appearing to Zacharias—a form of illumination of which hints had already appeared in some of the initials in the Gellone Sacramentary, and which afterwards became an important feature in the decorative scheme of the Gothic schools.

The Abbeville and Trèves "Codices Aurei" resemble the Harleian so closely that only a few words need be added about them. The Evangelist types are practically identical in all three manuscripts, though not in all cases applied to the same Evangelist; and the general plan of decoration is alike in all three, but the sumptuous illumination of the Canon-tables in the Harleian MS. is not rivalled in the other two. The Abbeville MS., given by Charlemagne (according to tradition) to Angilbert, Abbot of S. Riquier from 790 to 814, has the imposing but unpleasing peculiarity of being written on purple. The Trèves MS. is supposed to have been given to S. Maximin's Monastery by Ada, a natural sister of Charlemagne, about the beginning of the ninth century;

though the simplest, it is perhaps, artistically, the finest of the three.

The full development of the school is exemplified in the Soissons Gospels,[1] a splendid Codex Aureus, one of the most perfect of all extant memorials of Carolingian illumination. Until 1790 it was preserved in S. Medard's Abbey, Soissons, the gift (according to a highly probable tradition) of Louis the Pious when he spent Easter there in 827. Besides portraits of the Evangelists, arcaded Canon-tables, and illuminated initial-pages to the Gospels, it has two full-page miniatures: the first, an allegorical picture of the Church in adoration, is not found in any other Carolingian manuscript; the second represents the Fountain of Life,[2] and agrees in conception with that in the Godescalc MS., but is obviously taken, not from that barbarous work, but from some well-composed and carefully drawn original. Common ancestry with the Godescalc MS. is suggested again by the bearded S. Matthew, but the other Evangelists correspond in type with those of the Harley, Abbeville, and Ada Gospels. The book has altogether a strong family likeness to these three, but shows a more advanced tradition as well as finer individual taste and skill. It resembles the first-named in having spiral shafts for some of the pillars supporting the Canon-arches; but its work is more delicate and finished throughout, its colouring is brighter and more pleasing, and its pages have less tendency to become overloaded with gilding and decoration. The figures too are much more vigorous and lifelike, especially in the Biblical scenes introduced into the spandrels and lunettes of the arches.

Since Janitschek has attributed these manuscripts to a school of illuminators working at Metz, he naturally groups with them the Sacramentary[3] of Drogo, Bishop of Metz 826-55; it has, however, little apparent con-

---

[1] Paris, Bibl. Nat., lat. 8850.
[2] Pl. x.
[3] Paris, Bibl. Nat., lat. 9428. See *New Pal. Soc.*, pl. 185-6.

nection with them. It contains no large miniatures; but their place is taken by an interesting series of large illuminated initials, quite different in style from anything to be seen in earlier Carolingian paintings. These initials are based on a combination of strap-work and scroll-like foliage, and many of them enclose delicately tinted drawings of scriptural incidents, executed in a manner plainly allied to that of the Rheims school, to be noticed presently. There are two Gospel-books at Paris,[1] whose decoration is of similar character; and these three are the only manuscripts to which the title "School of Metz" can safely be given. The Lothaire Psalter, recently bequeathed by Sir Thomas Brooke to the British Museum,[2] is perhaps rightly classed by Janitschek with the Soissons Gospels, as to place of origin; it is later, however (after 840), and altogether inferior in artistic merit and pretension, its chief point of interest being a full-page portrait of the Emperor Lothaire.

Two smaller offshoots from the main stem of Frankish illumination may be briefly mentioned. The school of Rheims, as seen in the Ebbo Gospels at Épernay (No. 1722) and the Blois Gospels at Paris (lat. 265), forms a connecting link between the early Carolingian art of what Janitschek calls the Palatine school and the pen-drawings of the celebrated Utrecht Psalter. From this point of view they will be discussed in the next chapter, where the Utrecht Psalter and its descendants are considered. The Épernay book, executed at Hautvillers, near Rheims, for Bishop Ebbo (816–35), is perhaps the most characteristic work of this school; but the Blois book is of special importance because, by its strong resemblance to the Gospels in the Vienna Schatzkammer, it suggests the archetype from which the Rheims artists procured their technique. This technique, in fact, with its attempt towards natural yet violent action, its ex-

[1] Bibl. Nat., lat. 9383, 9388.
[2] Add. 37768. See *Pal. Soc.*, i, 69, 70, 93–4 (then owned by Messrs. Ellis and White).

traordinarily agitated sketchy line, its crumpled clinging draperies, is what one might expect to result from the efforts of an inexperienced painter to imitate the delicately illusionist neo-classical art of the Palatine school. The Canon-tables, placed under classical pediments, are a departure from the Romanesque arcading usual in Carolingian manuscripts. On one of them sit two little carpenters, hammering nails into the cornice: a pleasant variation from the usual peacocks or ducks, and an early example of the illustration of contemporary crafts. Spiral columns occur here too, as in the Harley and Soissons Gospels.

The most salient characteristic of the Franco-Saxon school, which has been associated specially with the abbey of S. Denis, originally an Irish foundation, is the predominance of Celtic ornament, especially weaving and spiral patterns. These are sometimes, as in the little Gospel-book in the British Museum,[1] executed in true Celtic fashion in white line on a black ground. The curious looped corner-pieces, with swan-headed finials, are another mark of this school. Figure-painting, where it occurs, follows the usual Carolingian type, and shows some affinity with the style of the Tours school. Among the best examples of the school are the Gospel of François II and the Second Bible of Charles the Bald, at the Bibliothèque Nationale (lat. 257 and 2); and the Gospel-lectionary of S. Vaast, at Arras (No. 1045).

[1] Eg. 768. See Warner, *Illum. MSS.*, pl. 6, and *Reproductions*, i, 18.

CHAPTER VI

OUTLINE-DRAWINGS OF THE NINTH, TENTH, AND ELEVENTH CENTURIES, ESPECIALLY IN ENGLAND

WE have seen how the Celtic school, before it began to decay in its own home, sent offshoots eastward and southward, which deeply influenced the subsequent course of European illumination; and now we notice a return current from the Continent, bringing to England a new inspiration which—though not, strictly speaking, describable as illumination at all—became a determining factor in the development of early English miniature. This new inspiration was the art of freehand or outline illustration, which before its appearance in England in the tenth century had already enjoyed a century or more of life in Western Europe, and which arose—as so many of the best artistic inspirations have arisen—from the remains of Classical art. Though of continental origin, it was in England that this art developed its highest powers. It flourished here for more than two centuries, providing the Anglo-Saxon artist with a medium exactly suited to his temperament. Alternately the rival and assistant of the more orthodox illumination in gold and colours, it fused with it to form the beautiful eleventh century Winchester style, and bequeathed to the later English schools an understanding of pure line which profoundly affected their subsequent development.

The first sign of the new tendency, towards expression by line rather than mass, is seen in the celebrated and much-discussed manuscript called the Utrecht Psalter. This book first appears in history about the year 1625, being then in Sir Robert Cotton's library, where it bore the

OUTLINE-DRAWINGS

press-mark "Claudius C. vii"; but it had already disappeared from the Cottonian collection in 1674, and nothing more is known of its adventures until 1718, when it was presented to the University Library at Utrecht, of which it is now one of the chief treasures. It was seen there by Westwood, who first called public attention to it in 1859.[1] The antique appearance of its triple columns and its rustic-capital script misled him, on his first cursory inspection, into giving it a much earlier date than a later and more leisurely examination, by himself and other experts, was found to warrant; and for many years a great battle raged as to whether it was a relic of the fourth, ninth, or some intermediate century,[2] theologians who upheld the earlier date acclaiming it as evidence in support of the authenticity of the Athanasian Creed, which occurs in it (as in most medieval Psalters) among the Canticles and other pieces which follow the Psalms. In order to decide the controversy, the Utrecht authorities in 1873 allowed the manuscript to be deposited for a time in the British Museum, where it was examined by the leading authorities in this country; and all of them, with the single exception of Sir T. D. Hardy (who had already declared for the sixth century, and saw no reason to change his opinion), agreed in assigning it to the eighth or ninth century, with a preference for the ninth.[3] This judgment was afterwards confirmed by the best continental critics, and may now be accepted with confidence, later researches having furnished additional reasons in its support. One of its authors, Sir E. M. Thompson, has had the further satisfaction of seeing his *obiter dictum*, that "the MS. was probably written in the

---

[1] *Archaeological Journal*, xvi, 245–7.

[2] A full chronicle of the dispute may be seen in W. de G. Birch's *The Utrecht Psalter*, 1876.

[3] See *The Utrecht Psalter. Reports addressed to the Trustees of the British Museum on the Age of the MS.*, by E. A. Bond, E. M. Thompson, H. O. Coxe, and others (including Westwood), with preface by A. P. Stanley, D.D., 1874. During its stay in England the manuscript was photographed throughout for the Palaeographical Society, who published a complete *Autotype Facsimile* in 1874.

north-east of France," verified through the studies of Count Paul Durrieu,[1] who has shown conclusively that the illustrations must be classed with the productions of the Rheims school of Carolingian illuminators.

The Utrecht Psalter is a small folio of ninety-one leaves, and has 166 illustrative drawings. One of these occupies the whole of the first page; the others are of the full width of the page and about one-third of its height, and interrupt the three columns of text, sometimes coming at the top of the page, sometimes at the bottom, sometimes midway. They are freely drawn with the pen in dark brown ink, and left quite uncoloured. They are, in fact, outline and often impressionist sketches of crowded scenes containing an immense number of small restless figures, with tiny heads thrust forward eagerly, hunched-up shoulders, and long attenuated limbs; set in a landscape of crags, boulders, and rounded hillocks, with a few feathery trees. Apart from a little shading here and there, the work is done entirely by means of fine penstrokes, drawn apparently with extreme rapidity, and producing a remarkable effect of lively, agitated, even tempestuous movement; the draperies flutter wildly, and even the contours of the landscape have a wind-swept appearance. Despite its sketchy character, the drawing is firm and delicate, especially in the first part of the book—farther on the hand changes, and the work becomes altogether inferior. There are no frames or suggestions of pattern—no attempts at a decorative result. We have here the very opposite of Celtic ideals in art.

For many years after its discovery by Westwood, the Utrecht Psalter was generally regarded as an early specimen of the Anglo-Saxon school of outline-illustration which flourished in the tenth and eleventh centuries, but which has left no authentic remains of earlier date. M. Durrieu's careful researches, however, have proved beyond any reasonable doubt that the book must have emanated from the same school as the Ebbo Gospels at Épernay,

---

[1] *L'Origine du manuscrit célèbre dit le Psautier d'Utrecht*, 1895.

OUTLINE-DRAWINGS

which were executed, as we have seen,[1] at Hautvillers, near Rheims, between 816 and 835. The eye is caught at once, in the latter book, by the curious fluttering draperies, the nervous rapid strokes from right to left, which are such distinctive features of the Utrecht Psalter drawings, and descend through it to the artists of Winchester and Canterbury. Further, in several miniatures of the Ebbo Gospels figures and scenes occur which are identical with those of the Utrecht Psalter; and this at a date when nothing of the kind is known to have existed in England. Moreover, the knot-work initial B, in gold and colours, at the beginning of Psalm i in the Utrecht Psalter—its one piece of illumination strictly so called—is of a form which M. Durrieu finds peculiar to the Rheims school. It seems certain, therefore, that the art of outline-illustration was born on Frankish soil, and imported at a later date into the English schools.

The division of the page into three columns, and the use of an archaic form of writing, make it almost certain that the Utrecht Psalter is a copy of a much older codex; but there is far too much freedom about the drawings to let us regard them as mere copies, although the archetype may very probably have supplied the subjects. These, like many of the miniatures in contemporary Greek Psalters of the "monastic-theological" class,[2] are naïvely literal illustrations of single passages in the Psalms. On f. 8, for instance,[3] Psalm xiv (xv). 1 is illustrated by two continuous scenes: in the first, a man is being invited to enter the tabernacle, in the second he is resting on the holy hill. The drawings at the foot of the page refer to the next psalm, which follows overleaf—an arrangement which goes far towards proving that the artist took his subjects from the archetype, not from the text before him.

---

[1] Above, p. 104.
[2] See above, p. 49. The subjects of the Utrecht Psalter drawings have been described by A. Springer, "Die Psalterillustrationen im frühen Mittelalter," in *Abhandlungen der phil.-hist. Classe der k. sächs. Gesellschaft der Wissenschaften*, viii (Leipzig, 1883), pp. 228-94.
[3] Pl. xii.

ILLUMINATED MANUSCRIPTS

It is evident, at any rate, that he was to some extent inspired by designs in which Classical traditions still survived. Over and over again the true antique flavour is discernible: in the Three Maries at the Sepulchre on f. 8, in the warriors on f. 13b, in the Bacchante crowned with laurel on f. 82b. This method, moreover, of rough outline-illustration is paralleled by the Terence manuscripts described in chapter i, which have much in common with the Utrecht Psalter and its derivatives.

Either the Utrecht Psalter itself, or another Psalter of the same type and resembling it very closely, must soon have found its way to England: not only is its influence apparent in the English outline-drawings of the tenth and eleventh centuries, but three manuscripts are still extant which were obviously derived, if not directly copied, from it or one of its congeners. These are Harl. 603 (early eleventh century) in the British Museum, to be noticed farther on; the Eadwin Psalter (twelfth century, executed in the Canterbury Cathedral priory) at Trinity College, Cambridge;[1] and the Tripartite Psalter in the Bibl. Nat. at Paris (lat. 8846, formerly Suppl. lat. 1194, thirteenth century).[2]

In France too the style was practised contemporaneously, and on very similar lines to those taken by the English schools. The miniatures, drawings, and historiated initials of the Franco-Saxon Psalter at Boulogne,[3] for instance, are scarcely distinguishable from English work of the time, and show how small a claim our so-called native school has to originality. This book, executed between 989 and 1008 at the abbey of S. Bertin in S. Omer, is additionally interesting because it shows the progressive and informal art of outline-drawing at work upon compositions of the strictly conservative

---

[1] M. R. James, *Catalogue of Western MSS. in the Library of Trinity College, Cambridge*, ii, 1901, pp. 402–10.

[2] H. O[mont], *Psautier illustré* [1906].

[3] Bibl. Municip., No. 20. See *Pal. Soc.*, i, 97; Westwood, *Facsimiles*, pp. 104–7, pl. 37–9.

UTRECHT PSALTER. IXTH CENT.

OUTLINE-DRAWINGS

Byzantine type, and combined with decorative ornaments of Carolingian design. It is richly illustrated, and in more than one manner. There are drawings in outline, tinted work, and red outlines on a pale blue ground; all quite "Anglo-Saxon" in feeling, and excellent proof—if proof were needed—of the impossibility of dividing out the various artistic styles of the early Middle Ages into rigidly defined and mutually exclusive schools.

During the century following the appearance of the Utrecht Psalter, outline-illustration was greatly developed both here and on the Continent. Nor was its use restricted to liturgical books; it was applied, for instance, to that favourite moral discourse of the Middle Ages, the Psychomachia of Prudentius.[1] This work, an allegorical poem on the conflict between vices and virtues, was composed about the end of the fourth century, and its cycle of illustrations, like that of the plays of Terence, probably goes back to a very early period; at all events, it had assumed a fixed traditional form before the end of the ninth century, and is now extant in a numerous series of manuscripts, ranging in date from the ninth century to the twelfth, but scarcely varying in composition. Two excellent examples of these are now in the British Museum. The larger, and probably the earlier (Add. 24199), seems to have been executed in Bury S. Edmund's Abbey[2] about the end of the tenth century. Its best illustrations (for many of the later ones are by an inferior hand) are of the most charming type of line-drawing, here developed far beyond the lively impressionism of the Utrecht Psalter sketches. They are drawn in a thin brown outline occasionally touched with pale colour; each occupies about half a page, the figures being from two to three inches in height. These figures show con-

[1] See R. Stettiner, *Die illustrierten Prudentius-Hss.*, 1895, for descriptions of the manuscripts; for reproductions see his larger work with the same title, vol. i (200 plates), 1905.

[2] It belonged, at any rate, to the library there. See M. R. James, *On the Abbey of S. Edmund at Bury*, 1895, p. 71. Sir E. M. Thompson, however, considers it a continental production (*Eng. Illum. MSS.*, p. 19).

ILLUMINATED MANUSCRIPTS

siderable power of dramatic presentation; they are expressive and vivacious, their much-pleated draperies are elaborately finished. Here and there may be seen slight traces of the Classical art from which this style of drawing descends; but in the main the work has the characteristics of the now developing English school. The Cottonian Prudentius (Cleop. C. viii)[1] is a very charming little manuscript of the first half of the eleventh century; undoubtedly of English origin, the illustrations having descriptive titles in Anglo-Saxon as well as Latin. All the subjects illustrated in Add. 24199 reappear, executed with great firmness and delicacy in red and black, sometimes partly in green. There is practically no variation in the compositions, but the smaller scale of the figures and the greater severity of technique give this book a very different air. Occasionally the artist does add some new and charming touch; as where he makes Humility, her earthly task accomplished, spread great wings and fly up gracefully to heaven. This is far more poetical—besides being more faithful to the text—than the corresponding design in Add. 24199, where Humility stands, wingless, with hands uplifted; or in a third Museum MS. (Titus D. xvi), where she climbs a steep flight of stairs towards the sky. Such a picture as this, or the pretty scene of Love laying down his bow and arrows, or the series containing the gentle nun-like figure of Patience, incline one to forgive the occasional lapses in proportion, the exaggerated hands and feet, the fretful draperies, which here, as in all Anglo-Saxon drawings, tend to swamp the more classic attributes of dignity and repose. The other Cottonian Prudentius, Titus D. xvi, was executed at S. Alban's Abbey about 1100. It is still smaller than Cleop. C. viii, and contains fewer illustrations. Though inferior in quality to the best work in the two other copies, its drawings show the development that was taking place in English art. The draperies are not so over-pleated, nor do they flutter about so wantonly;

[1] *Pal. Soc.*, i, 190.

OUTLINE-DRAWINGS

the wrinkled hose and sleeves no longer appear. On the other hand, though the fighting scenes are full of vigour, there is none of the dainty charm which characterizes the earlier books. The faces are mostly repellent, with long hooked noses; in fact, the artist has only slightly caricatured his usual types in the two devils which he introduces (departing from tradition) into the picture of Luxury feasting.

Outline-drawings of the occupations proper to the several months are often found in the Calendars prefixed to Psalters and other liturgical books. These Calendar-pictures, to which we owe so much of our knowledge of the daily life of the Middle Ages, may be regarded as the far-off descendants of the somewhat dubious illustrations to the fourth century Calendar of Filocalus.[1] They first appear in a Vatican MS. (Reg. 438) containing the Martyrology of Wandalbert of Prüm, and probably written in France or Western Germany about the beginning of the tenth century.[2] In England, the earliest examples are of the eleventh century; and though their manner is distinctively Anglo-Saxon, many of their details suggest a Classical archetype.

The best-known instance of this is an eleventh century Hymnal in the British Museum (Jul. A. vi), which contains a complete set of these occupation-pictures, drawn with extraordinary delicacy and minuteness in brown outline on the lower margins of the Calendar-pages. The airy, dainty technique has something more of the Utrecht Psalter quality than is often seen in English work of this time; and the presence in the Calendar of such saints as Germain, Denis, Philibert, Bertin, Geneviève, and Lambert, along with Wilfrid and Cuthbert, and the absence of most of the distinctive South-English patrons, seem to suggest that it may have

---

[1] See above, p. 3.
[2] A. Riegl, "Die mittelalterliche Kalenderillustration," in *Mittheil. des Instituts für oesterr. Geschichtsforschung*, x, 1889, pp. 1–74. There is an interesting article by J. Fowler, in *Archaeologia*, xliv, 1873, pp. 137–224, on these occupation-pictures in various forms of art.

been copied *en bloc* from a French original—possibly in a Northumbrian monastery. The draughtsmanship has plenty of well-marked Anglo-Saxon peculiarities, in the slender long-legged bending figures, the wind-blown draperies, the lively action. But relics of a Classical tradition are still traceable, notably in the April scene of three patricians reclining on a lion-ended couch, whilst a servant offers them wine and a Roman legionary stands on guard. So too the May picture of shepherds with their flocks has something in common with the pastoral miniatures of the Vatican Virgil. January, with its ploughing scene, and October, with its hawking party, are more medieval, and foreshadow the more elaborate Calendar-paintings found in fifteenth century Horae and Breviaries.

Continental though its origin may have been, this cycle of Calendar-illustrations had evidently become naturalized in England by the eleventh century. The whole series appears again in a collection of astronomical and chronological treatises (Tib. B. v), contemporary with Jul. A. vi, though differing widely from it in style, this time drawn in thick outline and rather crudely painted in colours. The scale is larger, the dainty nervous manner is gone; but the compositions are identical in every detail, even to the lion-ended couch in the April scene, the attitude of the hay-makers in June. As given in these two manuscripts, the series is as follows :—

January.	Ploughing with four oxen ; sowing.
February.	Pruning trees.
March.	Breaking up the soil ; sowing.
April.	Feasting in state.
May.	Shepherds with their flocks.
June.[1]	Felling trees.
July.[1]	Hay harvest.
August.[1]	Corn harvest.

[1] So Jul. A. vi; Tib. B. v. has the same compositions, but in different (and obviously wrong) order, viz. June, Corn harvest ; July, Felling trees ; August, Hay harvest.

OUTLINE-DRAWINGS

September.   Boar hunt.
October.   Hawking.
November.   Halloween fire.
December.   Threshing and winnowing.

There is no *a priori* improbability in the supposition that these designs are of continental origin. The copying of fine manuscripts—illuminations as well as text—was a regular and important part of the work of a medieval scriptorium; and the havoc wrought by the Danes all over England in the ninth century must have left but few examples of native art to serve as models. Hence recourse would naturally be had to manuscripts imported from the Continent; we have, in fact, direct evidence of this in the Prudentius MSS., and in the imitations of the Utrecht Psalter. Of the three existing specimens of the latter class, the oldest is Harl. 603 in the British Museum, written in Southern England—perhaps at S. Augustine's, Canterbury—about the beginning of the eleventh century.[1] As far as the compositions are concerned, it is (except for a few pages near the end) a copy of the Utrecht Psalter; but its variations in detail suggest a long series of successive copies intervening between it and its archetype. By this time, as we might expect, the Classical flavour of the original has evaporated; and the Anglo-Saxon love of coloured line has substituted blue, green, red, and sepia for the uniform brown ink of the original. The distribution of colour is quite arbitrary, e.g. hair and foliage are sometimes coloured blue. The nervous technique of the Utrecht Psalter has now vanished, and is replaced by the firm outline of an artist who is at home with his medium. Once, at the end of Psalm xxx (xxxi), where the Utrecht Psalter has left a blank space, the illustrator leaves his rôle of copyist, and produces a really beautiful drawing (partly sketched in pencil only), in the pure

---

[1] Thompson, *Engl. Illum. MSS.*, pp. 16–18, pl. 3; M. R. James, *The Ancient Libraries of Canterbury and Dover*, 1903, pp. lxxi, 532.

ILLUMINATED MANUSCRIPTS

Anglo-Saxon manner of his own time, of a great angel helping the Psalmist to climb a steep and rocky ascent, while the devil tries to hold him back with a trident. If, as seems probable, this scene is by the same artist as the rest of the book, we must suppose him to have adopted a deliberate archaism when working from the traditional Psalter designs.

It was in the closing years of the tenth century that Anglo-Saxon outline-drawing attained its greatest perfection; above all, at Winchester, which maintained an artistic primacy down to the end of the twelfth century. One of the most beautiful examples of the style is a full-page miniature of the Crucifixion, prefixed to a late tenth century Psalter[1] which was probably written at Winchester. It is drawn in reddish brown and pale blue outline; and though it shows the characteristic faults of the school in the bowed shoulders of the Virgin, in the unduly large hands and feet of S. John, and in the agitated draperies, yet for tenderness of feeling and purity of line it has seldom been surpassed in any period. That the tenth century draughtsman did not always reach such a level is shown by the Leofric Missal,[2] now in the Bodleian Library (No. 579). This very interesting little book was given to Exeter Cathedral by Leofric, its first bishop, about the middle of the eleventh century. It is in two distinct parts: the first part, a Sacramentary, is early tenth century Franco-Saxon work; the second, a Calendar with paschal tables, etc., was written in England about 970, and includes three full-page miniatures in red, green, blue, and purple outline. These represent a king, emblematic of Life, holding a lettered scroll; a particularly hideous figure of Death; and two almost charming, curly-headed, eagerly gesticulating figures. The flimsy agitated draperies and long toes and

---

[1] Brit. Mus., Harl. 2904. Thompson, p. 23, pl. 6; Warner, *Illum. MSS.*, pl. 7, and *Reproductions*, ii, 4.

[2] Westwood, *Facsimiles*, p. 99, pl. 33; *The Leofric Missal*, ed. F. E. Warren, 1883.

OUTLINE-DRAWINGS

fingers are thoroughly characteristic; and these bright, light pages, though not more than second-class of their kind, are curiously attractive when contrasted with the heavier and more ornate manner of the late-Carolingian illumination in the same volume.

Passing on to the eleventh century, we find the Winchester school well to the fore with two manuscripts executed at the royal foundation of Newminster, afterwards Hyde Abbey, and now in the British Museum. One of these (Tit. D. xxvii[1]) is a very small volume, written about 1012-20, partly by the monk Aelfwin, who was afterwards abbot; it contains the Offices of the Holy Cross and Trinity, with two full-page drawings in tinted outline. The first, a Crucifixion, is interesting for the personifications of sun and moon. The second, a symbolic representation of the Trinity, is in the best and least exaggerated manner of eleventh century Anglo-Saxon drawing: the faces are gentle and winning, the arrangement of the figures is unusually skilful. The Father and Son sit side by side, really dignified and beautiful personifications; beside them stands the Virgin, the Dove settling on her crown, in her arms the Child, symbolizing the human as distinct from the divine character. All these are enclosed in a jewelled circle, beneath which Satan, Judas, and Arius crouch in fetters above the open jaws of hell.

Still finer is the Newminster Liber Vitae, or register and martyrology (Stowe 944),[2] drawn up about 1016-20, and prefaced by three pages of admirable drawings, lightly and delicately sketched in brown ink, and touched here and there with yellow, red, green, and blue. On the first page are portraits of King Canute and his queen Aelfgyfu, offering a large gold cross on the altar. They are watched from below by the monks in their stalls;

---

[1] *Pal. Soc.*, i, 60; W. de G. Birch, *On Two Anglo-Saxon MSS.*, 1876 (Roy. Soc. of Literature, *Transactions*, new series, xi, pt. iii).

[2] Birch, *Liber Vitae*, Hampshire Record Soc., 1892; *Pal. Soc.*, ii, 16, 17; Warner, *Reproductions*, ii, 6.

ILLUMINATED MANUSCRIPTS

and two attendant angels hover above them, pointing upwards to Christ, who appears within a mandorla, between Our Lady and S. Peter, the patrons of the abbey. All this is disposed with great skill on the narrow upright page. Having done justice to the munificence of the reigning monarch, the artist now turns to matters of wider import, and depicts on the next two pages[1] the final rewards of good and evil. The first and second compartments of this design represent S. Peter receiving the blessed at the gate of heaven, and rescuing a soul by main force from the clutches of the devil; the third shows an angel locking up the damned in hell. All the naïve beauties of the developed English style are foreshadowed in this drawing: in the courteous *empressement* with which S. Peter welcomes the elect; in the gentle, piteous appeal with which the poor little soul in jeopardy looks up to him; in the simple and joyous expressions of the tonsured saints.

A third example of Winchester work is the so-called Caedmon MS. in the Bodleian,[2] which was perhaps executed for Abbot Aelfwin at Newminster about 1035. It contains a series of Anglo-Saxon poems, treating of the fall of Satan, the Creation, and various incidents of early Bible history, and thus resembling Caedmon's work in subject at any rate. These are copiously illustrated with outline-drawings, mostly in brown ink, the rest in red, green, or black. The illustrations to the first part are full of action, but show little sense of proportion or design. Some of the large draped figures are finely conceived; some, as the delicious angel who stands on tiptoe at the gate of Eden, have the ingenuous fascination of Winchester art at its best. All attempts to represent

---

[1] Plate xiii shows the right-hand page, which contains the principal part of the design. On the left-hand page are only, in the first compartment, two groups of saints and martyrs led by angels towards the gate of heaven; in the second, two nimbed spectators of the contest.

[2] Junius 11, described, with facsimiles of the drawings, in *Archaeologia*, vol. xxiv, 1832, pp. 329–40. See too Westwood, *Facsimiles*, p. 111; *Pal. Soc.*, ii, 14, 15.

PLATE XIII

LIBER VITAE OF NEWMINSTER, WINCHESTER. EARLY XITH CENT.
BRIT. MUS. STOWE 944

OUTLINE-DRAWINGS

the nude are of course disastrous: Adam and Eve only become endurable when the Fall has driven them to adopt the wrinkled draperies which leave room for all the cunning convolutions of the Anglo-Saxon line. After the Flood the style of illustration changes. The figures are more slender, but of better proportions; the draperies flutter more violently, having at times an almost ragged effect.

Early English outline-drawing is seen at its best in these three delightful books; soon after their production the delicacy of the style began to decline. About the middle of the eleventh century the custom of strengthening and enhancing the ink outlines with a narrow band of colour had crept in, to destroy the purity of line and crispness of effect once characteristic of the Anglo-Saxon technique; and we find the art of outline-illustration becoming confused with the essentially distinct one of illumination in gold and colours. A good example of the work of this period is to be seen in a glossed Psalter at the British Museum (Tib. C. vi), which has at the beginning a series of scriptural scenes,[1] each occupying the full page, drawn with a fine hard black line and re-outlined in bright colours. The firmness and delicacy of line are still excellent, though somewhat obscured by the tinting. But the faces are monotonous, flat, expressionless, with small staring eyes, the attitudes often ungainly, the anatomy impossible; and the proportions vary absurdly, single figures (e.g. the Christ in the Harrowing of Hell, or the angel in the Maries at the Tomb) by their vast size and free technique suggesting mural rather than book decoration. Farther on in the volume are a few miniatures elaborately painted in body-colour, besides pages framed in coloured rod-and-leaf borders of the style usually associated with Winchester, and fully illuminated initials.

A still better instance of the mingling of linear and

[1] See pl. xiv for the last of the series, Michael contending with the dragon. Another (Christ before Pilate) is in *Pal. Soc.*, i, 98.

ILLUMINATED MANUSCRIPTS

surface art is the Cottonian MS.[1] of Aelfric's paraphrase of the Pentateuch and Joshua, written in the eleventh century, and profusely illustrated with coloured drawings which, never attempting either beauty or naturalism, often show a considerable, if grotesque, dramatic force. All have the plain vellum page for background—no suggestion of landscape or atmosphere. About half have been left in various stages of incompleteness: in some cases the blank spaces have not even been touched; in others the draperies have been roughly blocked in with a first coat of thick colour, and the figures sketched in outline, often without features. Of the remainder, which were evidently regarded as finished, the majority are painted in body-colour, the folds of the draperies shaded and heightened with white, the faces covered with a shiny pigment; but some have been treated according to the draughtsman's ideals, carefully outlined in various light colours, without modelling or chiaroscuro. The types of figures and the methods of composition hardly vary throughout the book, so this divergence in technique cannot well be set down to difference of date or place.

Winchester doubtless held the leading position during this period, in outline-drawing as in painting; but both arts were also practised successfully, though with less originality, at Canterbury. In Harl. 603 we have seen what is perhaps (though by no means certainly) an example of the work of S. Augustine's abbey; there is better evidence for assigning to the cathedral priory a set of Easter tables[2] written about 1058, and adorned with one long narrow illustration, running like a frieze across the tops of two opposite pages. This is drawn in black outline, and touched with green and red; it represents Christ in glory giving a roll of instructions for finding Easter to an angel, who delivers it to Abbot Pachomius and his monks. With its short sketchy strokes, nervous

---

[1] Claud. B. iv. See *Pal. Soc.*, i, 71, 72; Thompson, pp. 25–6, pl. 8; Kenyon, *Biblical MSS.*, No. 21.

[2] Brit. Mus., Calig. A. xv, ff. 120–43. See *Pal. Soc.*, i, 145.

PLATE XIV

PSALTER. ENGLISH, XIth CENT.
BRIT. MUS. TIB. C VI.

OUTLINE-DRAWINGS

impressionist manner, and vivid sense of life, it shows very strongly the influence of the Utrecht Psalter style, no longer dominant at Winchester. This is only to be expected, when we remember that about a hundred years later that famous manuscript was copied in the same monastery, where it was probably deposited on its arrival in this country. The antique flavour, however, has vanished. Pachomius and his monks, who hurry *ventre à terre* to meet the angel, have already the placidly benevolent, almost babyish expressions so often seen in English monastic types.

With the Norman Conquest a new influence came into English art; it ended the Anglo-Saxon school, but far from killing the art of outline-drawing, it transformed and beautified it. The exquisite illustrations of the Guthlac Roll in the twelfth century, the Matthew Paris drawings in the thirteenth, and the delicate tinted drawings of Queen Mary's Psalter at the beginning of the fourteenth century will serve to show how great a contribution this method of freehand illustration, imported (it would seem) towards the end of the ninth century, preserved and perfected during the tenth and eleventh centuries, made to the final development of book decoration in England.

CHAPTER VII

ENGLISH ILLUMINATION TO A.D. 1200

AT the beginning of the eighth century English illumination was dominated, as we saw in chapter iv, by the influence of two schools, divergent, even antagonistic, in their aims: the Celtic, coming from Ireland by way of Iona and Lindisfarne, and the Late Roman or debased Classical, imported into Southern England through the mission of S. Augustine. In the Canterbury Psalter (Vesp. A. i) these two influences appear in juxtaposition rather than fusion; and the ravages of the Danes have left us no means of judging whether such a fusion actually took place, or what the resultant style was like. Most probably the art of illumination perished altogether in those troublous times, except for the somewhat perfunctory decoration of initial letters. We know that King Alfred did much for the revival of learning; and the New Minster which he founded in his capital of Winchester became at a later date—with the neighbouring Old Minster, S. Swithin's cathedral priory—the home of English illumination. But the lost art required time to reassert itself; and there is no evidence that anything was effected in this direction during Alfred's own reign. Lack of tradition and of good models must have made the initial stages slow and difficult; and it is not surprising that no specimens of the new school of Anglo-Saxon miniature exist which can be assigned to an earlier date than the reign of Alfred's grandson, Athelstan (925-40).

The manuscript commonly known as King Athelstan's Psalter[1] is a composite little volume: the nucleus was

[1] Brit. Mus., Galba A. xviii. See Westwood's *Facsimiles*, pp. 96-8, pl. 32; *Cat. Anc. MSS.*, ii, p. 12, pl. 28.

written on the Continent in the ninth century, but many additions were made in England towards the middle of the tenth century, including a Calendar decorated with roughly coloured drawings of the zodiacal signs and of saints, enclosed in circular or rectangular frames, and also three full-page miniatures drawn in heavy black outline and painted in rather pale colours. The first two represent Christ in glory, surrounded by choirs of angels, prophets, and saints; unusual and interesting compositions, doubtless copied from some foreign original, probably on a much larger scale. The third represents the Ascension; and the manuscript once contained a fourth, of the Nativity,[1] now bound up in the Bodleian MS., Rawlinson B. 484. The ground of the second miniature is black, and there is more finish altogether about it than in the other two, which are painted on the plain vellum; but in all three, as in the Calendar decorations, there is a rude, inchoate appearance, as of an untrained copyist striving laboriously to reproduce the model set before him; there is no gradation or perspective, the faces are expressionless, the heads and hands much too big, the drapery lines too heavy and uniform, both in the black pen-strokes and in the curves of white paint. In short, this book represents the beginning of a movement to replace the lost art of Hiberno-Saxon illumination by a new style, founded on continental models, and shows the defects natural to work of this character. No evidence is forthcoming to support the tradition which makes Athelstan the patron for whom these paintings were done, but it is highly probable that the book in its original state was given to him, considering his connection with Charles the Simple, Otto the Great, and other continental potentates through the marriages of his sisters; and the decorations subsequently added, crude and tentative as they are, may be taken as representing the best work of which English artists were at that time capable.

[1] Reproduced by Westwood, who was the first to recognize its connection with Galba A. xviii.

ILLUMINATED MANUSCRIPTS

Progress from this point was rapid, and the latter half of the tenth century finds the Winchester school at its zenith. The general decline of the monasteries which, joined with the Danish wars, had put an end to artistic production for the time being, was abruptly checked by the reforms introduced under S. Dunstan. His exile in 956-7 had given him an opportunity of studying the Benedictine rule at Ghent, and its subsequent introduction into most of the English monasteries was undoubtedly due to his influence, though he did not take an active part himself in the movement, which was carried on chiefly by S. Oswald, Bishop of Worcester, and S. Aethelwold, Bishop of Winchester. The appointment of the latter indeed, in 963, marks an epoch alike in the monastic and artistic history of England. He had already, as Abbot of Abingdon, sent to Fleury for instruction in the rule of S. Benedict, and begun to enforce its observance in his abbey; and he signalized his promotion to Winchester by expelling the secular clerks from both Old and New Minsters, and bringing monks from Abingdon to fill their places. The reform thus instituted spread by degrees to all parts of the country. Its introduction synchronized with a great advance in the art of illumination, an advance in which Winchester led the way; and the two movements are assuredly related more closely than by a mere coincidence in time. Foreign influence is plainly discernible in the new style of book decoration, both in the composition of miniatures and in the elements of ornament; and Sir G. Warner's suggestion[1] that Fleury supplied this influence, as well as a stricter ideal of monastic life, seems highly probable.

The accession of King Edgar in 959, followed as it was by his selection of Dunstan for chief adviser and for Archbishop of Canterbury, was no doubt an important contributory cause of the development of the new style, which first appears in his foundation charter granted to

---

[1] *Illum. MSS.*, p. iv.

New Minster in 966.[1] This document, written throughout in gold, is in book form, and has for frontispiece, on a pale purple ground, a votive picture of the king, between the Virgin and S. Peter, offering his charter to Christ, who appears above in a mandorla supported by four graceful angels. These are disposed with a regard for space-composition not always seen in the work of the Winchester school. King Edgar's angular attitude, his wrinkled sleeves and hose, the Virgin's folded head-dress, the pleated draperies, all exactly reproduce the technique of Anglo-Saxon outline-drawing. But the heavy painting and lavish use of gold take away the sense of airy impressionism which constitutes the special charm of that style. The drapery folds are now indicated by alternate lines of white and of dark local colour. Limbs and features are still defined by heavy lines, but there is a good attempt at modelling, and the faces are by no means void of life and expression; in fact, the advance on the crude paintings of King Athelstan's Psalter is enormous. The surrounding frame, of two gold rods entwined with blue, green, buff, and dull red foliage, may be pointed out as an excellent example of the characteristic Winchester ornament in its first stage. It is probably based on the border decoration found in later Carolingian manuscripts such as the Bible of S. Paul's, and is indirectly derived from Classical leaf-mouldings. Its pedigree appears more clearly in some of the later manuscripts, where the border consists of a repeat-pattern of small crisp leaves strictly confined in panels or between straps and rods, except at the corners, where the foliage breaks out from these bounds, twining itself about the confining rods and corner-pieces, and sprouting freely in all directions. In the page now under consideration there are no corner-pieces, and the foliage projects beyond the framing rods the whole way round.

The next example of Winchester work is beyond all

[1] Brit. Mus., Vesp. A. viii. See Westwood, *Facsimiles*, pp. 130-2, pl. 47; *Pal. Soc.*, i, 46-7; Warner, *Reproductions*, i, 4.

question the masterpiece of the school. This is the magnificent Benedictional of S. Aethelwold in the Duke of Devonshire's library,[1] written by Godeman, a monk at Winchester, for Aethelwold, about 975-80, and enriched with thirty full-page miniatures and thirteen pages of text enclosed in arches or rectangular borders, besides some other illuminated pages now lost. That the artist understood the use of pen or pencil far better than that of paintbrush is strikingly apparent. The colouring of the miniatures is for the most part inharmonious and unpleasing: a harsh vivid green, ill matched with dull shades of purple, mauve, and other secondary tints—all painted in thick body-colour, and broken and modelled with white. The general effect, however, is brightened by a plentiful use of gold. The treatment of the faces shows little advance on the Athelstan Psalter: they are mostly painted a sort of pinkish brick-red, heavily overlaid with streaks of white. In the borders a richer effect is aimed at, gold and bright colours predominating; and the result is generally successful. The draughtsmanship is excellent throughout, firm and clear, and already giving promise of the delicacy which, as we saw in the last chapter, characterized English, and particularly Winchester, drawing in the eleventh century; this is shown very plainly in the last miniature in the book, which has only been coloured in part, the rest being drawn in red outline. Many of the compositions are evidently derived, directly or indirectly, from Italo-Byzantine archetypes: in the miniature of the Baptism, for instance, the river-god of Jordan appears with his urn, as in the mosaics of the Ravenna Baptistery—an unexpected bit of paganism to light upon in an English book of King Edward the Martyr's time. Some of the miniatures are set in arches or under pediments, flanked with Oriental-looking buildings; but the majority are

---

[1] *The Benedictional of St. Aethelwold*, ed. G. F. Warner and H. A. Wilson, Roxburghe Club, 1910. See too *Archaeologia*, xxiv, pp. 1-117; Westwood, pp. 132-5, pl. 45; *Pal. Soc.*, i, 142-4; Burlington F.A. Club, No. 11, pl. 17.

ENGLISH ILLUMINATION TO 1200

enclosed in rectangular borders of typical Winchester style: frames of gold panelled or entwined with acanthus leaves, with sprays of foliage at the corners and centres of the sides.

Contemporary with this Benedictional is the Harleian Psalter (2904), whose beautiful drawing of the Crucifixion was mentioned in the last chapter. It also contains large initials for Psalms i (Beatus vir), ci (Domine exaudi), and cix (Dixit Dominus), finely illuminated in gold and colours. In all three the plan is the same: a gold frame divided into panels filled with leaf-moulding, dogs' heads with open jaws, plait-work terminals to the upright part of the frame, the body of the letter filled with intertwining scrolls of foliage. The "B" is specially interesting as representing the model on which the initial letter of English Psalters was based for the next three centuries.

In the companion volume to S. Aethelwold's book, the so-called Benedictional of Archbishop Robert,[1] now in the Public Library at Rouen, the peculiarities of the Winchester style are still further developed. This manuscript, which was probably given to his cathedral by Robert of Normandy, Archbishop of Rouen 990–1037, seems to have been written at Newminster for the use of Aethelgar, sometime Abbot, who became Bishop of Selsey in 980, Archbishop of Canterbury (in succession to Dunstan) in 988, and died in 990. Its decoration is comparatively meagre, consisting only (in its present state) of three full-page miniatures and five pages of text surrounded with borders in gold and colours. The compositions are practically identical with those of the corresponding pictures in the Benedictional of Aethelwold, but there are signs of advance in the pose and proportions of the figures and in the treatment of the faces;

---

[1] Ed. H. A. Wilson, Henry Bradshaw Soc., 1903. See too *Archaeologia*, xxiv, pp. 118–36; Westwood, p. 139. Besides episcopal benedictions at Mass, it contains a collection of pontifical offices, including the rite of consecration of the Anglo-Saxon kings; so it should strictly be called a Pontifical.

ILLUMINATED MANUSCRIPTS

the border ornament is of the same type as in the earlier book.

The Rouen Library possesses another volume of the same class in the Missal of Robert of Jumièges.[1] This manuscript, executed at Winchester, probably at Newminster, about the beginning of the eleventh century, was given by Robert of Jumièges, when Bishop of London (1044-51), to the abbey at Jumièges, of which he had formerly been abbot. It contains thirteen full-page miniatures, enclosed in arches or rectangular frames of the regular Winchester type, besides three elaborately bordered pages at the beginning of the Canon of the Mass. The art, however, is decidedly inferior to that of the two Benedictionals. Many of the figures are so thin as to be almost grotesque; and the ornamental frames and arches tend to overload the page and to detract from, instead of enhancing, the effectiveness of the picture enclosed. In the Crucifixion page, particularly, the comparatively small and insignificant figure-composition is completely overweighted by the magnificent but inappropriate luxuriance of the surrounding border. It would seem, in fact, as though this initial phase of the Winchester school had already reached its prime before the end of the tenth century, and had at once (as so often happens) begun to decay.

The excellence and shortcomings of Newminster work at this period are well shown, again, in the Gospels of Trinity College, Cambridge,[2] written apparently by the same scribe as the Missal just mentioned, and decorated with great magnificence. The pages devoted to the Eusebian Canons are specially splendid, with their gilded columns and round, triangular or trefoil arches, having angels, saints, peacocks, dragons, etc., in the tympana and spandrels, as in Carolingian manuscripts of the ninth century. Each Gospel has a full-page miniature of the Evangelist and an elaborate initial page of text, and there

---

[1] Ed. H. A. Wilson, Henry Bradshaw Soc., 1896; Westwood, pp. 136-8, pl. 40.
[2] B. 10. 4. See Westwood, p. 140, pl. 42; *New Pal. Soc.*, pl. 11, 12.

is also a miniature of Christ in glory; all these enclosed in rectangular borders, profusely foliated, and mostly decorated with medallion busts of saints and with ornamental corner-pieces. Gold is lavishly used, and the range of colours is wide, especially in the decorative frames, which are almost exaggeratedly luxuriant, giving the book a rich, even gorgeous effect. But a less attractive side is shown in the crumpled, fluttering draperies, so unsuited to the thick opaque medium used by the Winchester painters, in the large ill-drawn hands and feet, in the inept attempt at full-face portraiture.

By the end of the tenth century the art of illumination had begun to revive in other places besides Winchester, though the Wessex capital continued to hold the leading place. As examples of work done elsewhere, we may mention three manuscripts, now in the British Museum, which there is good reason for associating with Christ Church, Canterbury. The first of these is the recently acquired Bosworth Psalter,[1] written late in the tenth century, perhaps during the archiepiscopate of Dunstan (959–88), who is said to have been a skilled painter himself,[2] and who doubtless encouraged the decoration, as well as the transcription and study, of books. There are no miniatures in the Bosworth Psalter, but the large initials of Psalms i, li, and ci, filled with interlaced foliage and adorned with dragons, lions' heads, etc., are very spirited and successful, and are interesting as being among the earliest examples of English initial-ornament of this type. The second manuscript, Arundel 155,[3] is also a Psalter, and appears to have been written at Christ Church between 1012 and 1023. Like the tenth century Harleian Psalter, No. 2904, it combines outline with fully illuminated work. The tables which follow the Calendar

---

[1] Add. 37517. See *New Pal. Soc.*, pl. 163-4; Warner, *Reproductions*, iii, 5; F. A. Gasquet and E. Bishop, *The Bosworth Psalter*, 1908.

[2] Two miniatures purporting to be by him are extant, viz. Bodl. 578, f. 1, at Oxford, and Claud. A. iii, f. 8, in the British Museum. See Westwood, pp. 125, 126, pl. 50.

[3] Warner, *Illum. MSS.*, pl. 10.

are set in arcades outlined in red, the tympana of the last two (ff. 9b, 10) containing partially tinted outline scenes of Pachomius and his monks, closely allied to those described at the end of chapter vi as occurring in Calig. A. xv, a manuscript probably emanating from the neighbouring abbey of S. Augustine. On f. 133, again, is a representation of S. Benedict giving his rule to monks, partly coloured and partly left in outline. The principal feature of the book, however, is the illuminated initial and border decoration of Psalms i, li, and ci, especially the first, which has a frame of gold bands enclosing and surrounded by foliage, with gold quatrefoils at the corners, and an initial "B" obviously modelled, like the border, on Winchester work of the tenth century. The "D" of Psalm ci is interesting as an early example, in English art, of the historiated initial; enclosing a crude representation of David beheading Goliath.

The third manuscript,[1] a copy of the Latin Gospels, early eleventh century, is also decorated in the Winchester style; but it contains an inserted copy of King Canute's charter to Christ Church, Canterbury, so the natural presumption is that it was executed in the latter place. Its illuminated pages (the first of each Gospel) have, indeed, a heavy, almost sombre, magnificence very different from the brightness and freedom of the best productions of the Newminster artists. The gold bands are very broad, the foliage is close-set and monotonous, and the general effect of the colouring is dull, a brownish tone prevailing. Here again is a historiated initial, the "Q" of S. Luke's Gospel being filled with a miniature of Christ in glory.

Another Gospel-book of about the same date, also in the British Museum (Harl. 76), deserves mention for the excellence and variety of the arcades which enclose the Eusebian Canons. These pages, richly gilt and brightly coloured, are very effective, with angels, saints, lions, dragons, etc., filling the spandrels and tympana.

[1] Roy. 1 D. ix. See Warner, *Reproductions*, i, 6.

The manuscript belonged to Bury S. Edmund's, and was perhaps painted there; it has obvious kinship with the Missal of Robert of Jumièges, but it may be that this only illustrates the widespread influence of the Winchester school.

At the beginning of the eleventh century that school, as exemplified by the Missal of Robert of Jumièges, was already showing signs of deterioration. The downward tendency, however, was speedily checked: in the Grimbald Gospels,[1] written at Newminster early in the century, we have a charming example of the next phase in the development of the style. The portraits of seated Evangelists, looking up to their emblems for inspiration, preserve in their composition some faint suggestion of Byzantine or Carolingian archetypes; but the slender boyish figures and crumpled robes have not much in common with the Greek austerity or Teutonic solidity of these remote ancestors. The streaky backgrounds of earlier Winchester miniatures are abandoned in favour of the plain vellum, and the features are drawn in outline only. But the elaborate frames do all that is necessary towards richness of decoration; especially those which surround the portrait of S. John[2] and the first words of his Gospel, which are an interesting departure from the usual type of Winchester ornament. These frames are built up of silver panels, with gold circles at the corners and centres. The three topmost circles on the miniature page contain each a representation of Christ in glory, and are supported by exquisitely drawn angels, whose outlines are quaintly contrived to suggest the foliate ornament of the conventional border. Four of the other circles contain groups of adoring saints; in that beneath the Evangelist's feet two angels offer up the souls of the departed in a cloth. The panels are filled with half-length figures of adoring kings. The frame of the text-page is similarly constructed, but has

[1] Brit. Mus., Add. 34890. See Warner, *Illum. MSS.*, pl. 9, and *Reprod.*, i, 5.
[2] Pl. xv.

ILLUMINATED MANUSCRIPTS

the Madonna and Child in the central medallion at the top, the others containing angels and saints. The delicacy of the drawing, particularly of the angels, which are really charming, and the pleasing colour-scheme, which is founded on blue and its derivatives and uses silver (now tarnished, alas!) as well as gold for the heightening of effect, mark out the Grimbald Gospels as one of the finest examples of eleventh century English work.

As the century advanced the Winchester illuminators turned their attention to the decorative rather than the illustrative side of their art—to the development of initial and border ornament rather than to improvement in figure composition; that is, if we may judge by a Psalter in the British Museum,[1] written at Newminster about 1060. Like so many manuscripts of the time, it combines outline-drawings with paintings in body-colour; the former style being represented by the signs of the zodiac, excellently drawn in red outline to illustrate the Calendar, and by a full-page Crucifixion in black outline, tinted blue, green, and red. It is interesting to find that the composition of the latter is practically identical with that of the much smaller and rather earlier drawing in the Newminster Office of the Holy Cross,[2] having Sol and Luna above the arms of the cross, and also a rarer feature, the Dextera Domini issuing from a cloud above the head of Christ. The body-colour illuminations consist of initials and borders to Psalms i, li, and ci, and a full-page miniature of the Crucifixion opposite Psalm li. This last, painted on the plain vellum ground, within an illuminated frame-border, is of a most unusual type: the emaciated, ill-drawn figure of Christ is flanked by two stiff, mushroom-like trees, which stand in the positions usually assigned to the Virgin and S. John, below the arms of the cross. The four borders show considerable variety in the details of design. That of Psalm ci

---

[1] Arundel 60. See Westwood, p. 121, pl. 49; Thompson, p. 24, pl. 7; Warner, *Illum. MSS.*, pl. 11, and *Reprod.*, ii, 7, 8.

[2] Tit. D. xxvii, noticed above, p. 117.

GRIMBALD GOSPELS. WINCHESTER, XIth CENT.
BRIT. MUS. ADD. 34890

adheres most closely to the traditional type, but is distinguished by a not unpleasing restraint, the tendency to raggedness and over-luxuriance, noticeable in most of its predecessors, being severely pruned away: the framing bands are now reduced, on this as on the three other pages, to narrow wands; and the leaf-ornament, now purely conventional, is entirely confined between them except at the corners and centres. On the other pages the foliage is rather of the scroll-like order, interrupted at the corners, in the border surrounding the Crucifixion, by medallions containing the emblems of the Evangelists; and a new feature appears in the borders to Psalms i and li, the framing wands being bent and intertwined. It is in initial ornament, however, that the most significant progress has been made. The ideas suggested by the tenth century illuminators are developed to the utmost, and enriched by the introduction of new elements: elaborately intertwined spiral scrolls of foliage (almost recalling the intricacies of Celtic decoration) fill the body of the letter, and human figures, dragons, and other animal forms begin to appear. The "B" of Psalm i combines this decorative wealth with a miniature of David playing the harp. In short, the transition to the regular Gothic system of initial ornament is already far advanced. The manuscript has no silver or gold; its colour-scheme is on the whole soft and pleasing, the predominant tint a subdued blue.

Before leaving the eleventh century, we must mention a little book more interesting, perhaps, for its history and associations than for its intrinsic merit as a work of art, viz. the Gospel-book of S. Margaret of Scotland, now in the Bodleian Library.[1] Mr. Falconer Madan[2] has set forth its romantic story in full: how it was turned out as lumber from the shelves of a small parish library in Suffolk, advertised for sale as a fourteenth century

[1] Lat. Liturg. f. 5. See *Pal. Soc.*, ii, 131, and the facsimile reproduction, ed. W. Forbes-Leith, s.J., 1896.
[2] *Books in Manuscript*, 1893, p. 107.

copy of the Gospels, and acquired for a trifling sum by the Bodleian authorities, who at once recognized it as English work of the eleventh century; and how it was subsequently identified through the discovery of some Latin verses on a fly-leaf, narrating its miraculous recovery in an uninjured state, after being dropped into a stream by the priest who was carrying it to a tryst for the taking of an oath—an incident recorded in the life of S. Margaret, sister of Edgar Atheling and wife of Malcolm Canmore, King of Scotland. The piety of this saintly queen, the civilizing power of her gentle life, and the devotion which she inspired in her warlike, illiterate husband, provide one of the most beautiful episodes in early Scottish history; and the book thus happily recovered a second time has no merely casual association with her, for her biographer tells us that " she had always felt a particular attachment for it, more so than for any of the others which she usually read." She had doubtless brought it from England in 1067, when she fled for refuge to Malcolm's court.

The portraits of the Evangelists, with which this book of Gospel-lessons is decorated, are characteristic of their period and country. Specially noticeable are the inflated and swirling draperies, the predominance of pale secondary colours, and the plain vellum backgrounds. The emblems do not appear; the designs are of the simplest character, and are framed in plain rectangular bands of gold and pink, sometimes enclosing an arch with buildings in the spandrels. The bearded type of S. John is unusual; and so, fortunately, is the extraordinary figure of S. Luke sitting cross-legged on his stool. The faces are rather expressionless, and on the whole the art cannot be called better than second-class.

With the twelfth century English art enters upon a period of experiment and transition.[1] Many things combined to encourage the influx of new ideas and con-

---

[1] There is an interesting and well-illustrated article on English twelfth century illumination, by A. Haseloff, in Michel, ii, i, 309-20.

sequent readjustment of old traditions and standards. The first shock of the Norman Conquest was well over, and the Normanizing of English civilization, which had begun in Edward the Confessor's time, was fairly complete. The Crusades were beginning to bring westward a fuller knowledge of Byzantine and Syrian art. In architecture, the Romanesque was at its last and most magnificent period, the Gothic was about to be born; and we find, as might be expected, some reflection of this transitional phase in the minor art of illumination. The parallel, indeed, is not complete; but both arts alike evolved in the course of the century the beginning of the pure Gothic style.

Nearly all the best examples of English illumination that have come down to us from the tenth and eleventh centuries were produced at Winchester. But this exclusive predominance now comes to an end, and in the twelfth century we find well-established schools flourishing at Durham, Westminster, Bury S. Edmund's, and in many other places. At the very beginning of the century, in fact, the last-named school is represented by a series of thirty-two full-page miniatures of the life, passion, and miracles of S. Edmund, prefixed to a copy, apparently of slightly later date (*circ.* 1125-50), of the text which they illustrate.[1] These pictures have plenty of graphic force, but are destitute of charm. Particularly repellent is the prevailing type of face, with long nose, receding chin, and prominent eyes. There is no attempt at realistic figure-drawing; impossibly thin, flat-chested bodies, supported by immensely long, attenuated legs, suggest the human frame well enough for the artist's purpose, which is to tell his story with unmistakable clearness, and which (to do him justice) he never fails to achieve. Gold is used, but sparingly, and is not raised or burnished; the colouring generally is somewhat harsh,

[1] This very interesting manuscript is in Sir G. L. Holford's library. For description and reproductions see *New Pal. Soc.*, pl. 113-15; also Burl. F.A. Club, No. 18, pl. 23.

ILLUMINATED MANUSCRIPTS

and the choice of tints quite arbitrary—red, green or violet horses being among the vagaries met with. In the text are some excellent examples of the initial ornament, the development of which formed one of the salient characteristics of twelfth century illumination in England, as well as in France, Germany, and the Low Countries. The chief elements of this ornament are scrolls of foliage, diversified with human, animal, and monstrous forms; later in the century the larger initials are often historiated, but the purely decorative designs are also used right on through the thirteenth century.

Closely related to the miniatures just mentioned are twelve pages of Gospel pictures in compartments, prefixed to a New Testament which formerly belonged to Bury S. Edmund's and was doubtless written there, and which is now in Pembroke College, Cambridge.[1] These are outline-drawings, partly tinted, and are mostly on a much smaller scale than the paintings in Sir G. L. Holford's book; but the resemblance, especially in the facial types, is so striking as almost to suggest identity of hand. It is evident, however, that these mannerisms were distinctive of English painting generally at this period. They are to be seen in a most sumptuously illuminated Psalter, executed at S. Alban's during the time of Abbot Geoffrey (1119-46), and now at S. Godehard's Church in Hildesheim.[2] This splendid book has no less than forty-two full-page miniatures, besides a great wealth of initial ornament. The miniatures, which represent the Fall of Man, David as musician, scenes from the life of Christ, and SS. Martin and Alban, are framed in rectangular borders of meander, leaf-moulding, and other patterns. The initials are filled with figures, which are sometimes merely fanciful, boys riding on monsters, etc., but more often illustrate passages in the psalms to which they are prefixed. There is great freedom and variety in the

---

[1] No. 120. See M. R. James, *Cat. of the MSS. at Pembroke Coll.*, 1905, pp. 117-25 (two plates); Burl. F.A. Club, No. 23, pl. 28.

[2] See Adolph Goldschmidt, *Der Albani-Psalter in Hildesheim*, 1895.

designs, and the proportions and modelling of the figure are better than in the Life of S. Edmund, though still too thin and long-limbed. The faces too have much more individuality, but the unlovely types of the Holford and Pembroke books have a tendency to predominate here too.

Henry of Blois, brother of King Stephen, and Bishop of Winchester from 1129 to 1171, was a learned and munificent prelate, a liberal patron of the arts; and it is to his encouragement, doubtless, that two fine examples of Winchester illumination owe their existence. Both were executed, apparently, at his cathedral priory during his episcopate, and one of them still belongs to the Dean and Chapter of Winchester, but the other passed soon after its completion into the possession of the nuns at Shaftesbury, and is now in the Cottonian collection at the British Museum.[1] The latter, which is perhaps the earlier of the two (probably written before 1161), contains the Psalter in Latin and French, preceded by thirty-eight full-page miniatures, painted on backgrounds of deep blue, most of which has, however, been scraped or washed off, presumably by some unscrupulous artist who had run short of that pigment. The first twenty-seven and the last nine represent scenes from the Bible; between them are two paintings, of the Assumption and Enthronement of the Virgin, which, though apparently part of the original volume, are in marked contrast with the rest, being very beautiful examples of the early Italo-Byzantine manner, both in design and colouring. Sir G. Warner suggests that they were copied from Italian pictures brought over by Bishop Henry, who is said to have bought works of art during his visit to Rome in 1151-2; if so, the copyist has caught the spirit of his original with extraordinary success—and one feels almost inclined to suggest instead that the bishop must have imported Italian artists too. The remaining miniatures in Nero C. iv are characteristically English, and are curious and

[1] Nero C. iv. See *Pal. Soc.*, i, 124; Thompson, pp. 29-33, pl. 9; Warner, *Illum. MSS.*, pl. 12, and *Reprod.*, iii, 7-9.

interesting rather than beautiful. The fluttering draperies of the earlier Winchester style are now replaced by garments which cling closely to the form. The proportions of the body are rather bad; but the hair and faces, shaded with pale sepia, are very carefully treated. Among the most effective miniatures are the Jesse-tree, with its white curling tendrils; the two angels with spreading wings, setting up the cross on an altar; and the last of the series, an angel locking the door of the Jaws of Death upon the damned, who are tortured in various ways by sprightly, gargoyle-like fiends.

Much more stately is the second of these two Winchester books: a magnificent Bible,[1] in three great volumes, decorated throughout with splendid historiated initials in gold and colours, and with two full pages of outline-drawings. Monumental Bibles were evidently the fashion in the latter half of the twelfth century: of those now extant, this is perhaps the finest; another (to be noticed presently) is now in the Bibliothèque de Ste. Geneviève at Paris; a third is Bishop Hugh Pudsey's (1153-94), at Durham. The Winchester Bible is believed to be the one which King Henry II borrowed from S. Swithin's priory and then presented to his Carthusian foundation at Witham, in 1173, but which was soon afterwards restored by S. Hugh, then Prior of Witham, to its rightful owners. Its miniatures have much in common with those of Nero C. iv: the same clinging draperies, the same grave, solemn faces. The art, however, is of a much higher quality: the figures are well modelled and of good proportions, the grouping often shows a fine instinct for composition, and there is altogether a much more perfect finish. These differences unquestionably bespeak a superior artist; they also denote, probably, a slightly later date, a more settled, less tentative phase in the development of the school. The colouring is extraordinarily rich and beautiful, dark tones predominating, especially a deep blue. The framework of the

---

[1] See *Pal. Soc.*, ii, 166-7; Burl. F.A. Club, No. 106, pl. 78.

PLATE XVI

BIBLE. ENGLISH, XIIth CENT.
WINCHESTER CHAPTER LIBRARY

ENGLISH ILLUMINATION TO 1200

initials themselves is usually filled with leaf-moulding or foliated scroll-work: plaits, dogs' heads, grotesques, and other forms of ornament also occur. Good examples of these initials are to be seen on the first page of the Psalms,[1] which are given in both "Gallican" and "Hebrew" versions in parallel columns, so that the miniaturist had to supply a "B" for each column; and in doing this he has blended uniformity with variety most happily. Each pair of scenes represents two victories of Good over Evil: in the two loops of the right-hand "B," Christ casts out a devil and makes His triumphant descent into Hades; on the left, these events are typified by David's conflicts with bear and lion.

The Bible at S. Geneviève's[2] was written late in the twelfth century by a scribe of English parentage, one Manerius, who describes himself as "scriptor Cantuariensis"; so there is some presumption that it was executed at Canterbury, but no certainty, for he does not say where he wrote it, and the earliest fact known of its history is that in the eighteenth century it belonged to a church near Troyes. It may possibly, therefore, have been written and illuminated in France—at no time is the difficulty of discriminating French from English illumination greater than in the twelfth and thirteenth centuries. Like the Winchester Bible, it is in three large volumes; the foliate decoration of its initials is freer and more naturalistic, but the miniatures which many of them enclose, while spirited and interesting, are inferior as regards the treatment of the face, and the proportions and modelling of the figure. The "I" of Genesis occupies a whole column, and is filled with scenes of the Creation and Fall—a feature of Bible-illustration which became traditional.

Besides the Life of S. Edmund, two other pictorial biographies of English saints deserve notice, both

[1] Pl. xvi.
[2] *New Pal. Soc.*, pl. 116–18.

ILLUMINATED MANUSCRIPTS

executed towards the end of the twelfth century. One is a little Life of S. Cuthbert, written at Durham and illustrated with forty-five full-page miniatures[1] in gold and colours. These are enclosed in plain banded frames, without conventional ornament; the backgrounds are mostly gold, sometimes red or blue, in one case diapered (an early instance of what afterwards became the normal pattern of background). The pictures are on a modest scale, but very charming: the treatment of the face is very careful, and usually judicious, though sometimes marred by excessive use of white paint; the proportions are good, except for the extended fingers, which are still too long occasionally; and the colours are pleasing, especially the red and blue. The other manuscript is the famous Guthlac Roll in the British Museum,[2] a long strip of vellum covered with eighteen beautiful outline-drawings[3] of events in the life of S. Guthlac, probably executed in his abbey at Croyland. Here we find the English tradition of linear design, freed from Anglo-Saxon extravagances, steadied and matured by contact with other arts. The line has now become firm and clean; there is still a tendency to elongate the bodies and enlarge the extremities unduly, but the lively quaintness of the characterization, whether of angels, demons, or human beings,[4] gives these drawings an almost unique charm.

From the middle of the twelfth century till well on in the fourteenth the book most frequently used for the exercise of the illuminator's art was the Psalter. Those of S. Alban's (at Hildesheim) and Winchester (Nero C. iv) have already been noticed. Another fine one is the

---

[1] Reproduced in *The Life of Saint Cuthbert*, ed. W. Forbes-Leith, s.j., 1888. See too Burl. F.A. Club, No. 17, pl. 22. The manuscript is now in Mr. Yates Thompson's library.

[2] Harley Roll Y. 6.

[3] Reproduced by W. de Gray Birch, *Memorials of St. Guthlac*, 1881. See too Warner, *Reprod.*, i, 8. Dr. Birch suggests that they are the working drawings for a series of stained-glass medallions.

[4] Pl. xvii shows the saint expelling a demon, and receiving the tonsure.

PLATE XVII

LIFE OF St GUTHLAC. ENGLISH, LATE XIIth CENT.
BRIT. MUS. HARLEY ROLL Y 6

ENGLISH ILLUMINATION TO 1200

Huntingfield book in Mr. Pierpont Morgan's library,[1] having at the beginning forty pages of Biblical pictures and portraits of saints, besides a splendid "B" (to Psalm i) enclosing a Jesse-tree, and many decorative or historiated initials. The Psalter known as that of S. Louis, in the Leyden University Library,[2] executed in England about the end of the twelfth century, also contains a long series of Old and New Testament miniatures. The forms are severe and emaciated, with prominent eyes and grave expressions; the modelling is only moderately good, the bodies being short, with large extremities; the composition is crowded, sometimes "continuous." Two Psalters at the British Museum, written about the end of the twelfth century, though much less profusely illuminated than those just mentioned, deserve some notice. Harl. 5102 has some fine initials, especially the "D" of Psalm cix, which contains a representation of the Trinity, on a background of stippled gold; but its chief interest lies in the five full-page miniatures which seem to have been inserted, but which are plainly contemporary: one of these depicts the martyrdom of S. Thomas of Canterbury (1170), and is perhaps the earliest extant painting of that event, being only some twenty or thirty years later. A much more beautiful book is Royal 2 A. xxii, the Westminster Abbey Psalter.[3] It has five full-page miniatures at the beginning, painted in thick body-colour on burnished gold grounds, and representing the Annunciation, Visitation, Madonna and Child, Christ in glory, and David as harpist. Ultramarine, red, and green are the principal colours—the first-named especially deep and rich. The rounded, gentle face of the Virgin, and the stronger, more severe male types, show considerable power of modelling and expression; especially fine is

---

[1] M. R. James, *Cat. of MSS. of J. Pierpont Morgan*, 1906 (five plates); Burl. F.A. Club, No. 36, pl. 35.

[2] Lat. 76 A. See *Miniatures du Psautier de S. Louis*, ed. H. Omont, 1902 (*Codd. Gr. et Lat.*, Suppl. ii).

[3] See Thompson, pp. 33–5, pl. 10; Warner, *Illum. MSS.*, pl. 14, and *Reprod.*, i, 9, 10.

the picture of David, a truly regal, dignified figure. The "B" of Psalm i is elaborate, as usual, and is a good example of its kind, consisting of convolutions of foliage-scrolls, with animals' figures, and with three small medallion-scenes of the life of David; but it is from the beauty of the miniatures, above all, that the Westminster Psalter derives its value.

CHAPTER VIII

GERMAN, FRENCH, AND FLEMISH ILLUMINATION, A.D. 900-1200

THE outburst of magnificent, if ungainly, art which had characterized the Carolingian period declined towards the end of the ninth century. The chief centres of this art, as we saw in chapter v, were in Northern France and the Franco-German borderland: at Aix-la-Chapelle, Tours, Rheims. But the troubled times which saw the decay of the Carolingian line in France were unfavourable to artistic activity, and Germany begins now to take the leading place, especially during the brilliant period of the Ottonian dynasty, from the accession of Otto the Great in 936 to the death of Henry II, the Saint, in 1024. The not inaptly so-called Ottonian Renaissance doubtless owed much to the marriage of Otto II, in 972, to the Byzantine princess Theophano, whether she actually brought Greek artists in her train or only paintings and other objects of art from the Eastern imperial court; but the movement had probably begun before this date. Reichenau, at any rate, on Lake Constance, had long been famous as a school of painters; and many of the finest Ottonian illuminations, especially the earlier ones, emanate from this centre. Towards the end of the tenth century the artistic revival began to spread northwards: S. Bernward, Bishop of Hildesheim near Hanover (993-1022), instituted a school of illumination and metal-work in his cathedral city, and the Reichenau influence was brought to Trèves by Archbishop Egbert (977-93). The Bavarian schools too, especially that of Ratisbon, began to flourish about the same time; throughout Germany, in fact, this was a time of great energy in artistic production, though the resulting achievements were for the most part (so far at least as miniature is concerned) interesting rather than beautiful. By the twelfth century, a definite style with well-developed decorative features was thoroughly established in Western and Central Europe; and such books as the great Bibles of Worms, Floreffe, and Arnstein, and that lost treasure-house of medieval allegory, the Hortus Deliciarum, were preparing the way for the exquisite thirteenth century Gothic art of France and the Low Countries.

Few German illuminated manuscripts remain to us from the first half of the tenth century; and these few represent the decay of the Carolingian rather than the rise of any new progressive style. One of these books, however, must be mentioned, though its claim to notice arises less from its intrinsic merit than from its historical associations. This is the Gospel-book of King Athelstan,[1] given him (as the inscription "Odda rex, Mihthild mater regis" seems to indicate) by Matilda, widow of Henry the Fowler, and her son Otto the Great (who had married Athelstan's sister Edith in 929), between Henry's death in 936 and Otto's coronation as Emperor in 962; and afterwards given by Athelstan to Christ Church, Canterbury, where tradition says that it was kept for use as the oath-book at the coronation of the English kings. It is decorated with portraits of the Evangelists, arcades for the Eusebian Canons, and large ornamental initials. Gold and silver, the former edged with red, are profusely used in the arcades and initials, whose style is best described as debased Carolingian; and this abundance of the precious metals, together with the illustrious names of donors and recipient, justifies the assumption that the book, ugly as it is, may be taken as representative of the best work produced in the "dark age" which gave it birth. The Evangelists Mark, Luke, and John—rather small huddled figures painted on dull green backgrounds

[1] Brit. Mus., Tib. A. ii, described in *Cat. Anc. MSS.*, ii, pp. 35-7.

GERMAN ILLUMINATION, 900-1200

—show traces of the influence of the ninth century Rheims school, but without its artistic merit. Their strong flesh-tints contrast disagreeably with the cold tones of their draperies; their huge hands, their heads twisted round in the effort to gaze upwards, suggest the incompetent copyist of a good model. The Matthew miniature is quite different in style; with its thick soft technique and pale colouring, it represents a type which afterwards became characteristic of one branch of Ottonian art.

The Gregorian Sacramentary in the Heidelberg University Library (Sal. ix[b]) is assigned by Dr. A. von Oechelhäuser[1] to the first half of the tenth century; but its affinity with the Gospel-book at Darmstadt (Cod. 1948)[2], executed for Gero, Archbishop of Cologne 969-76, is so close that we can hardly suppose the two books to be at all widely separated in point of age, if indeed they are not actually by the same hand, as Janitschek held them to be. In any case, the Heidelberg book is one of the earliest extant productions of the great Benedictine Abbey at Reichenau, which, as we have said, occupies the foremost place in the history of German tenth century schools of painting. The style of the Reichenau artists, judged by existing miniatures and by the wall-paintings discovered there in 1880,[3] seems to have been founded (as to iconography and types of figure-drawing) on Early Christian models of the Roman type; indirectly, perhaps —for Dr. Haseloff[4] sees in the miniatures only a continuation of the tradition of the "Ada-Gospels" group of Carolingian illuminators. But a new feature appears

---

[1] *Die Miniaturen der Universitäts-Bibliothek zu Heidelberg*, pt. i, 1887, pp. 4-55, pl. 1-8.

[2] *Ibid.*, pp. 14-16, 32-3, pl. 9. Haseloff, *Der Psalter Erzbischof Egberts von Trier, Codex Gertrudianus*, 1901, p. 119, pl. 61 (2), 62.

[3] See Kraus, *Geschichte d. chr. Kunst*, ii, i, fig. 28-35.

[4] For the subject of the present chapter, see his articles in Michel, *Hist. de l'Art*, i, ii, 714-37, 744-55, ii, i, 297-309, 320-9; and, for a more detailed study of Ottonian illumination, his masterly introduction to the *Codex Gertrudianus*.

ILLUMINATED MANUSCRIPTS

in the patterned backgrounds introduced into some of the pages of Reichenau manuscripts and their derivatives; the patterns used are either geometrical designs or else forms of birds or monsters, and were probably suggested by tile-work or textile fabrics—in neither case do they improve the pictorial effect in figure-scenes, but when confined to the purely decorative pages they are less inappropriate.

In the Heidelberg Sacramentary these tendencies are already prominent. Its two full-page miniatures, of Christ and the Virgin, each enthroned within a circular border filled with the common Carolingian device of semicircles arranged mosaic-wise, have the hard, clumsy figures of mediocre Carolingian painting; but the beardless, long-haired, almost feminine-looking Christ is of the type characteristic alike of Early Christian (fourth to fifth centuries) fresco and of Ottonian illumination. The "Vere dignum" page, within a frame of Carolingian meander, has its background diapered with a repeat-pattern of crosses and rosettes, in true Reichenau style; a much less pleasing background, of horizontal bands of green and blue, disfigures the "Te igitur" page, and occasionally reappears in other Ottonian manuscripts; on these two pages and elsewhere throughout the book are initials of intertwined branch-and-leaf work, which tends to curl about itself in the characteristic German manner. We have here, in fact, an almost complete epitome of the Ottonian style, already distinct from the great mass of Franco-German work of the ninth century.

Closely allied to the Heidelberg manuscript are the Gero Gospels at Darmstadt, mentioned above, and the Reichenau Sacramentary at Florence.[1] The former repeats the miniature of Christ in a circular glory with hardly a variation, except for a slightly improved technique. The latter has no miniatures, but its decorative pages are covered with geometrical repeat-patterns, or with the beasts and long-tailed birds which the

---

[1] Haseloff, *Cod. Gertr.*, pp. 115–17, pl. 59, 60.

GERMAN ILLUMINATION, 900-1200

Reichenau painters borrowed, probably, from Oriental silks. Precisely similar backgrounds appear on almost all the illuminated pages[1] of the Psalter at Cividale, which was executed for Egbert, the great Archbishop of Trèves (977-93), but which is usually known as the Codex Gertrudianus from the insertions made in the eleventh century by a Russian lady named Gertrude. At the beginning of this book are four pages depicting its presentation by Ruodpreht (presumably the scribe or illuminator) to Archbishop Egbert, and its dedication by him to S. Peter. The remaining miniatures represent fourteen of Egbert's predecessors, each standing in the *orans* attitude, and are interspersed throughout the Psalter, opposite fully illuminated initial pages which match them as to border and background. The initials are more pronouncedly Ottonian than in the Heidelberg Sacramentary, the leaf-terminals being now replaced by little round knobs.[2]

The Reichenau school reached its culminating point in another of Archbishop Egbert's books, the Codex Egberti *par excellence:* a Gospel-lectionary, now in the public library at Trèves,[3] which was executed for him by the monks Keraldus and Heribertus. A purple dedication page at the beginning shows these two, shrunk in modesty to diminutive proportions, offering the book to the majestic prelate, who sits towering above them in dignity. The portraits of the Evangelists follow, painted on backgrounds filled with geometrical patterns like those in the Psalter, and with their emblems above their heads; but otherwise adhering closely to Byzantine models, both in the simplicity of the compositions and in the grave, thoughtful, ascetic type of face. But it is the fifty-one miniatures illustrating the Gospel-lessons which give the book its exceptional interest and value.

---

[1] These are all reproduced in the elaborate and profusely illustrated monograph by Sauerland and Haseloff, referred to above, p. 145.

[2] See pl. xix.

[3] Kraus, *Die Miniaturen des Codex Egberti in der Stadtbibl. zu Trier*, 1884.

ILLUMINATED MANUSCRIPTS

These are framed in rectangular bands with no ornament beyond a simple lozenge-pattern, and mostly occupy half-page spaces in the text; where they fill the whole page, they often contain two scenes with differently coloured backgrounds, but without formal partition.[1] In such details as these, and still more in the whole spirit and manner of the paintings themselves, they recall vividly the Vatican Virgil and the Quedlinburg Itala, and show quite unmistakably the influence of Early Christian art of the fourth or fifth century: the spaciousness of the compositions; the lightness and freedom of the style; the slender, expressive figures, distinctly reminiscent of antique grace; the softly shaded backgrounds. The range of subjects includes many that are new to Frankish painting; though we know from the sixth century mosaics of S. Apollinare Nuovo at Ravenna that they had long been used by artists of the Italo-Byzantine school. It is curious that in these same mosaics we recognize the youthful long-haired Christ of the Codex Egberti and other Ottonian illuminations.

The pre-eminence of the Reichenau scriptorium at this time may be gauged by the fact that Pope Gregory V (996-9) granted special privileges to the abbey in exchange for liturgical manuscripts to be supplied to Rome. Its artists were commissioned by Egbert, as we have seen, to enrich his library at Trèves; and their influence was undoubtedly felt in the monastic schools of illumination which were now springing up in all parts of Germany. Whether executed in Reichenau or elsewhere, the Gospels of the Emperor Otto (apparently Otto III, crowned by Gregory V 996, died 1002) in the cathedral at Aix-la-Chapelle[2] have many features in common with the books which we have been discussing. The Evangelist types are very like those of the Codex Egberti; the beardless, long-haired Christ is quite of the Reichenau type; and there is a certain flavour of Early Christian

---

[1] See pl. xviii.
[2] Beissel, *Die Bilder der Hs. des Kaisers Otto im Münster zu Aachen*, 1886.

PLATE XVIII

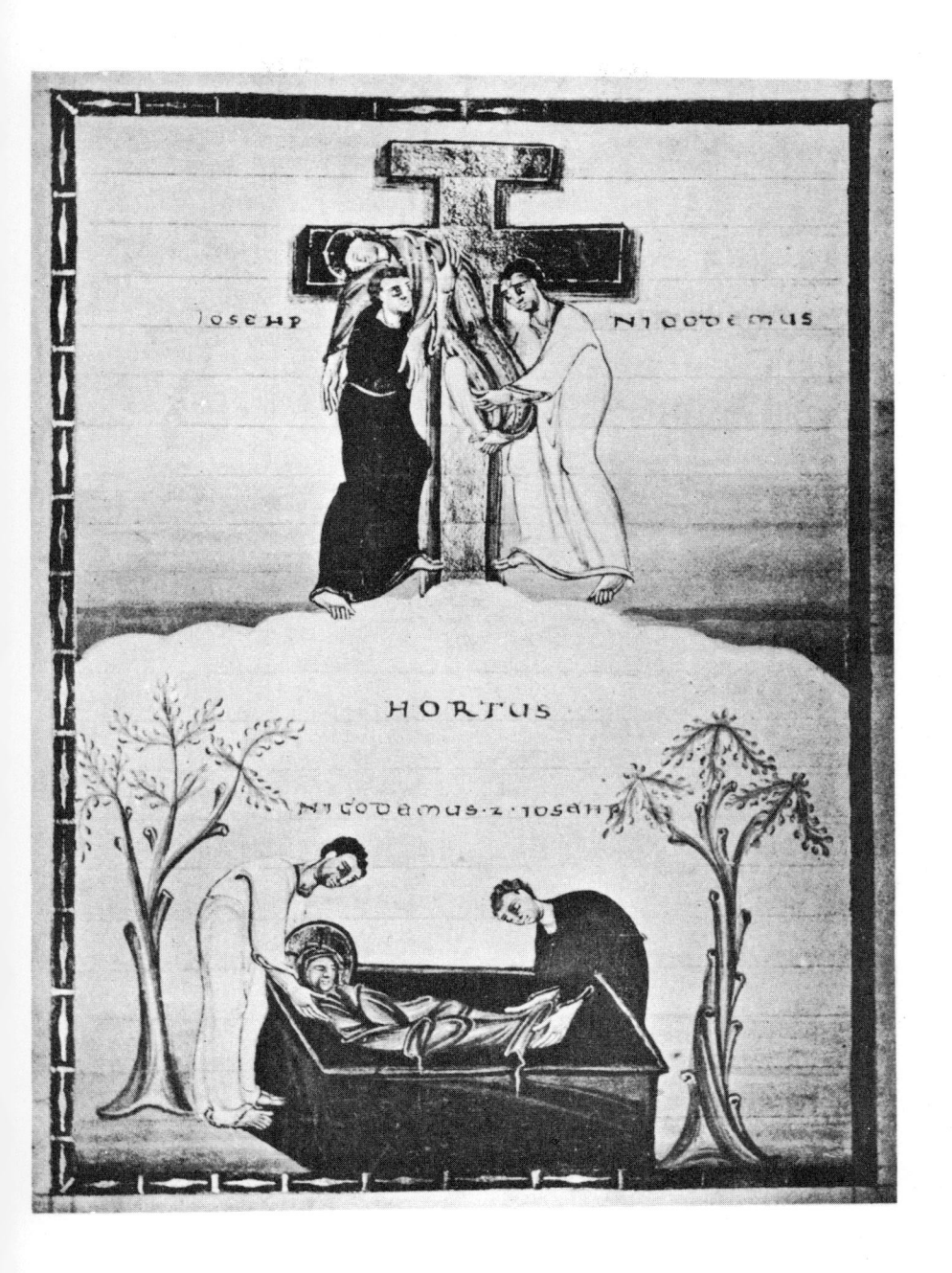

CODEX EGBERTI. 977-993
TRIER, STADTBIBLIOTHEK

GERMAN ILLUMINATION, 900-1200

tradition about many of the Gospel illustrations. But along with these resemblances are many points of difference. The backgrounds have neither the delicate gradations of the Codex Egberti, nor the tapestry-like patterns which form such a feature in the manuscripts of undoubted Reichenau origin; but are blue or purple for the dedication pictures, and gold for the illustrations to the text. The crowded compositions, clumsy figures, and absurd proportions suggest the crudity of primitive Byzantine miniatures such as those of the sixth century Codex Sinopensis, rather than the Classic grace and spaciousness of the earlier paintings whose manner survives in the finest Reichenau work. Moreover, the Carolingian tradition appears plainly in the arches, sometimes surmounted by pediments, often decorated with birds and plants in the spandrels, which enclose the miniatures; also in the apotheosis of Otto, who sits, enthroned within a mandorla, with the four Evangelistic emblems holding a veil before him—a composition which recalls the Apocalyptic picture at the end of the Alcuin Bible.[1]

The Aix-la-Chapelle book is related to two other Ottonian manuscripts—the Echternach Gospels at Gotha and the Bamberg Gospels at Munich. The former,[2] which belonged to Echternach Abbey, near Trèves, is in its original binding, with the portraits of "Empress" Theophano and "King" Otto on one of the covers, fixing the date of execution between the years 983 and 991, when Theophano was regent for her young son, Otto III. The binding is considered to be Trèves work, and it seems probable that the manuscript was written and illuminated in or near that city. It is chiefly remarkable for its great wealth in illustrations of the Parables. The Munich MS. (Cim. 58),[3] which formerly

[1] Pl. xi.
[2] Described by Beissel, *op. cit.*, pp. 18-28, and Janitschek, *Geschichte der deutschen Malerei*, 1890, pp. 66-70 (plate).
[3] Described very fully by W. Vöge, *Eine deutsche Malerschule um die Wende des ersten Jahrtausends*, 1891, pp. 7-98, fig. 2-15. See too L. v. Kobell, *Kunstvolle Miniaturen*, pp. 20-1, pl. 8-10; *Cod. Gertr.*, pl. 57; Janitschek, pp. 72-3 (plate).

ILLUMINATED MANUSCRIPTS

belonged to Bamberg Cathedral, contains a dedication picture, filling two pages, of Rome, Gaul, Germany, and "Sclavinia" offering tribute to the young Emperor, Otto III, who sits in state, with prelates and warriors standing round his throne. This miniature, almost a replica of one of Otto II painted for Archbishop Egbert's Registrum Gregorii,[1] dates the manuscript 996–1002. But the special interest of the volume lies in the scenes from the Gospels, many of which are identical, as to the main outlines of composition, with the corresponding pictures in the Codex Egberti and the Aix Gospels. The treatment generally resembles the latter rather than the former, and is more Germanic and "modern" than either; but in a few cases—notably the Crucifixion, Descent from the Cross, and Entombment—every detail of the Codex Egberti groups is copied, and the posing of the slim lithe figures is reproduced with amazing fidelity.

The Bamberg Lectionary at Munich (Cim. 57)[2] is of slightly later date, having been written for Henry II, apparently between his accession in 1002 and his coronation as emperor in 1014, and given by him to the great church which he founded at Bamberg. Its dedication page has in its upper compartment Henry and his wife S. Cunigunde, two timid little figures, presented by SS. Peter and Paul to Christ, who crowns them. Below are personifications of countries and provinces, holding up the orb of sovereignty, chaplet, and tributary offerings. The illustrations of the life of Christ agree in composition, for the most part, with those in the manuscripts which we have just been discussing—particularly the Descent from the Cross and the Entombment; but in execution there are distinct signs of decadence, e.g. in the treatment of draperies, which are over-accentuated either by making them cling too closely to the limbs, or by

---

[1] Now at Chantilly. Reproduced in Michel, i, ii, pl. 9, *Cod. Gertr.*, pl. 49.

[2] Vöge, pp. 112–29, fig. 16[1], 19, 22–9, 43; Kobell, p. 24, pl. 13–15; *Cod. Gertr.*, pl. 58.

GERMAN ILLUMINATION, 900-1200

giving them a tendency to flutter in a way suggestive of the contemporary Winchester mannerism. Both faults appear in the miniature of the Angel and the Shepherds, together with ungainly posing, absurd proportions (especially the ridiculous little *horses*—instead of the usual sheep—grazing in the foreground). An unusual feature is the landscape of boulders, which is probably derived, along with the tightly clinging draperies and some details of composition, from Byzantine paintings of the tenth century.

One of the most important artistic centres in Germany at the beginning of the eleventh century was Hildesheim, where a great revival of ecclesiastical art—especially in metal-work, enamels, and illumination—took place under the auspices of S. Bernward,[1] who reigned there as bishop from 993 to 1022. A friend of the Empress Theophano, and tutor to her young son Otto III, he had enjoyed special opportunities for studying all that was best in European art of the time ; and the school which he established in his cathedral city shows something of the eclecticism which might naturally be expected. The tradition that he was himself a miniaturist seems to have no foundation ; but many of the books that were executed for him are still preserved in Hildesheim Cathedral. The most noteworthy of these are a Gospel-book[2] and a Sacramentary, the former probably and the latter certainly the work of Guntbald the Deacon, who wrote another Gospel-book, less richly ornamented, in 1011 ; also a Bible, written about 1015, with an elaborate and interesting frontispiece. In these manuscripts the Reichenau fashion of filling the backgrounds with a repeat-pattern is adopted, but with a difference : the patterns seem founded less on textile designs than on those found in champlevé enamel, though there is no evidence that Bernward's craftsmen actually practised the

---

[1] See Beissel, *Der hl. Bernward von Hildesheim als Künstler und Förderer der deutschen Kunst,* 1895.

[2] Beissel, *Des hl. Bernward Evangelienbuch im Dome zu Hildesheim,* 1891.

latter art. The whole technique of his books suggests indeed, by its severity and disposition of line, its lack of perspective and modelling, its rigid, non-realistic rendering of the human form, an acquaintance with the arts of metal-work and enamelling rather than the more plastic ideals proper to the miniaturist. This predilection for conventional forms is joined, however, to an elaborate and sometimes impressive symbolism, e.g. in the Crucifixion miniature of the great Gospel-book, where Christ's feet rest on the emblem of S. Luke (the Evangelist whose narrative is being illustrated, and who appears himself, writing his Gospel, in the lower compartment of the same page), and where Terra and Oceanus, as well as the more usual Sol and Luna, look on in astonishment. This antique idea of the amazed Earth and Ocean before the divine power is used again with fine effect in the miniature of the Incarnation, prefixed to S. John's Gospel. Above, in the firmament of heaven, God sits enthroned on the globe, holding the Agnus Dei and the Book of Life, a six-winged seraph on either side; below His feet the Child in a manger-cot hangs suspended from a star, while Terra and Oceanus, classical half-draped figures, raise themselves to gaze up in wonder.

S. Bernward's Gospel-book was probably written between 1011 and 1014; his Sacramentary is slightly later, and shows distinct signs of development in its one miniature, a Crucifixion prefixed to the Canon of the Mass, with the opening words "Te igitur" embodied in the design, the "T" forming the cross, with elaborately plaited terminals. The figure-drawing is much less flat and rigid, though the aim is still symbolical and decorative rather than realistic. The effect is unfortunately marred by the striped background—an ugly device which also disfigures many pages in the Gospel-book.

A much higher degree of technical perfection was reached by the contemporary artists of the Bavarian schools; especially at Ratisbon, as the famous Utacodex witnesses. This manuscript, now in the Munich

PSALTER OF EGBERT, ARCHBISHOP OF TRIER, 977-993

CIVIDALE, CODEX GERTRUDIANUS

GERMAN ILLUMINATION, 900-1200

Library (Cim. 54),[1] is a Gospel-lectionary, and was executed for Uta, Abbess of Niedermünster at Ratisbon (1002-25), who appears in a dedication picture at the beginning of the book, offering it up to the Madonna and Child. Its splendid pages blend in a remarkable manner the Carolingian tradition of ornate magnificence with Byzantine wealth of symbolic imagery, and already foreshadow, in the slender figures and in the medallion-scenes set in the frames, the fully developed Gothic miniature of the thirteenth century. The mystical tendency is shown very strikingly in the miniature of the Crucifixion, where the crucified Christ appears as priest and king, wearing a crown and vested with stole and tunic, attended by allegorical figures of Life and Death, Grace and the Old Law.

But the Uta-codex is exceptional, wellnigh unique, among the great mass of eleventh century German illuminations that have survived. For the most part these are characterized by poverty of invention, heaviness and hardness in drawing, and harshness and want of harmony in colouring. The same compositions are copied again and again with wearisome iteration of design, and with steady deterioration in treatment. In initial-ornament, the interlaced branch-work of the Heidelberg Sacramentary is repeated with scarcely any variation, until with the twelfth century the historiated initial begins to make its appearance, and with it the initial decorated with forms of animals and monsters; a revival rather than a new movement, for both motives were used by Carolingian painters, as we have seen, e.g. in the Sacramentary of Drogo. A good example of the transition is Egerton 809 in the British Museum, a Gospel-lectionary written about the year 1100, apparently for S. Maximin's monastery at Trèves. Its four full-page miniatures (Nativity, Maries at the Tomb, Ascension, Pentecost) are hard, flat, and uninteresting, while its

[1] G. Swarzenski, *Die Regensburger Buchmalerei des X. und XI. Jahrhunderts*, 1901, pp. 88-122, pl. 12-18.

ILLUMINATED MANUSCRIPTS

initials are mostly of the stereotyped pattern, gold branch-work, red-edged, with knobby terminals, tastelessly disposed on green and bright blue grounds; but the monotony is occasionally broken by the introduction of small miniatures and serpentine forms—crude and insignificant in themselves, but welcome signs of incipient progress.

The twelfth century was pre-eminently a time for the production of huge Bibles, on the Continent as in England. Two splendid examples of German work are the Worms and Arnstein Bibles in the British Museum, both of them produced in the Rhineland. The earlier of the two is the Worms Bible (Harl. 2803-4),[1] apparently written in 1148. It has the usual German defect of an excessively hard and dry technique, and in its figure-painting shows little advance beyond the average work of the preceding century. The illumination consists of a large decorated initial at the beginning of each book—in some cases historiated, but generally filled only with scroll-work and leaf-ornament; two miniatures of S. Jerome writing; one of David as harpist, prefixed to the Psalms; arcaded Canon-tables; and portraits of the Evangelists. The miniatures are crude, flat, and coarsely executed; it is in the initial-ornament that the illuminators of this and similar books show to most advantage. The gold and silver branching has now vanished; in its stead we have white or coloured foliage-scrolls with gold bands, painted on coloured grounds and often combined with plait-work and human or serpentine figures. Sometimes the colouring is subdued and pleasing, more frequently it is harsh and gaudy, bright greens and blues, ill-matched, predominating to an unpleasant extent.

The Arnstein Bible (Harl. 2798-9)[2] is far superior to the Worms MS., and shows the best side of German twelfth century illumination. It was written towards

[1] Warner, *Illum. MSS.*, pl. 16.
[2] Warner, pl. 18.

GERMAN ILLUMINATION, 900-1200

the end of the century for the Premonstratensian abbey of Arnstein, near Coblentz, and, with two other twelfth century books from the same foundation—a Passionale (Harl. 2800-2) and a copy of Rabanus De Laudibus S. Crucis (Harl. 3045)—,forms a valuable monument of this great period of Rhenish art. The Bible and the Passionale have a long series of very fine initials of white foliated branch-work, outlined in red upon soft blue and green fields. Dragons and birds are often added to the intertwining stems and leaves, and form effective head and tail-pieces to the letters. Human figures too are sometimes introduced as part of the decorative scheme. The second volume of the Bible is more richly illuminated than the first, having great initials in gold, silver, and colours prefixed to Proverbs and to each of the Gospels; these initials are similar to the rest in general plan, but contain in addition large figures of Solomon and the Evangelists writing, with smaller half-length allegorical figures in medallions. The colouring is much more harmonious in tone than that of the Worms Bible, and the technique far less harsh. The De Laudibus S. Crucis, besides richly illuminated initials in silver, gold, and colours, has several pages filled with curious mystical diagrams, which have no interest from the purely artistic point of view, but are enclosed in border-frames decorated with various repeat-patterns in red outline on blue and green grounds; the great feature of the book is the depth and warmth of the colouring in the initials.

The curious symbolism of this last-named book links it with a far more beautiful and celebrated manuscript, now unhappily destroyed: the Hortus Deliciarum, composed, written, and illuminated by Herrad von Landsperg, Abbess of Hohenburg in Alsace, 1167-95, for the edification and delectation of her nuns. This great and unique work, with all its wealth of miniatures, was burnt at Strassburg during the siege of 1870. Fortunately, copies had previously been made of several of the miniatures,

ILLUMINATED MANUSCRIPTS

and these have been published by the Society for the Preservation of the Historical Monuments of Alsace.[1] The book was a sort of encyclopaedia of religious and philosophical knowledge, illustrated by paintings of scriptural, symbolical, and other subjects. These show a largeness and originality of conception which the *naïveté* of the drawing could not conceal.

In Germany, as elsewhere, the monastic scriptoria were not given up exclusively to the transcription and embellishment of religious books. A vernacular literature was growing, which demanded its copyists and illustrators. Shortly before the year 1200 there was made, in a Bavarian monastery, a copy of Heinrich von Veldegke's Eneidt, a free German paraphrase of Virgil's epic. This manuscript, now in the Berlin Library,[2] is illustrated with seventy-one fine drawings in red and black outline, on panelled grounds of crimson, blue, green or buff. The scenes, in spite of faulty technique, are full of action: feasts and battles, ships, castles, armed knights, fill the pages with a riot of chivalry delightful in itself, though having little relation to the dignities of the antique world.

Not much need be said about French or Flemish illumination during the period dealt with in this chapter. The art was almost paralysed by the constant strife and disorder which accompanied the decline and extinction of the Carolingian dynasty, and which by no means ceased with the conversion of the Counts of Paris into nominal Kings of France; and its recovery was doubtless retarded, and its progress checked, by the puritanical tendencies of the Cistercian Order, which, founded at the end of the eleventh century, spread with such amazing rapidity in the next century under S. Bernard, especially in France, the land of its birth. The S. Omer Psalter at Boulogne, written 989–1008, has already been men-

---

[1] *Herrade de Landsberg, Hortus Deliciarum*, ed. G. Keller, 1901. See too, for reproductions in colour, *Hortus Deliciarum de Herrade de Landsperg*, Paris, 1877.

[2] MS. germ. fol. 282. See F. Kugler, *Die Bilderhs. der Eneidt* [1834]; Janitschek, pp. 113–15.

FLEMISH ILLUMINATION, 900-1200

tioned in chapter vi, as showing the close connection between English and North French work at that time; and the same interdependence appears half a century later in a Gallican Missal, written probably for some church in the north of France, and now in Mr. Yates Thompson's library.[1] The miniatures in this manuscript, though less thickly painted and more subdued in colouring, show a strong resemblance to those in contemporary manuscripts produced in Southern England; especially in the draperies, the elongated fingers, and in the border decoration of frames filled with leaf-moulding and set with rosettes and medallions.

An important school of writing and illumination existed from early times in the Benedictine abbey of Stavelot or Stablo in Belgium, many of whose manuscripts have found their way to the British Museum. Among these is a tenth century Missal (Add. 16605), whose decoration shows the continuance, rather than development, of the Franco-Saxon style. It has no figure-compositions, only a few initials in gold and colours, and four pages of the Canon (Preface, Te igitur, and Paternoster) written in silver uncials on a purple ground, with large interlaced initials in gold, green, and white; the first two enclosed in frames whose panel and corner ornaments, like the whole of the decorative scheme, are quite in the manner of the S. Denis school. A Psalter from the same abbey, also of the tenth century (Add. 18043), shows no trace of this influence, and is more nearly allied to the Boulogne Psalter, so far as one may judge by the brightly yet softly coloured pages, with gold and red plait-work initials enclosing quaint little figures, prefixed to Psalms li and ci; the initial-page of Psalm i—doubtless the most elaborate of the three—has unluckily been cut out.

Better known, and more significant for the student of illumination, is the great Stavelot Bible (Add. 28106-7),

[1] No. 69. See *Illustrations of 100 MSS. in the Library of H. Y. Thompson*, i, 1907, pl. 1-3.

ILLUMINATED MANUSCRIPTS

in two huge volumes, written by the monks Goderannus and Ernestus in 1093–7; the precursor of the series which includes the Winchester, Worms, and Arnstein Bibles. Its illumination consists of large historiated or decorated initials to the several books; an "In principio" series of medallion-scenes from Genesis and the life of Christ, enclosed in an ornamental frame and filling the first column of the book of Genesis; Canon-arcades of no particular merit or interest; and one full-page miniature. This last, representing Christ in glory, surrounded by the emblems of the Evangelists in medallions, and enclosed in a frame filled with a meander pattern, is thoroughly Carolingian in spirit, and is chiefly remarkable for the immense size of the central figure. The initials vary considerably: most of those which are merely decorated with branching scroll-work (sometimes with animal forms entangled in the foliage), as well as some of those enclosing miniatures, are comparatively coarse. But many of those in the first volume contain illustrations in which the figures are drawn in outline and left wholly or partially uncoloured; and these are for the most part drawn with much delicacy, expressiveness, and even charm. Especially good are the miniatures prefixed to Exodus, Judges, and the first and second books of Kings; David beheading Goliath, in the last of these, is the very embodiment of youthful grace and energy.

Another Belgian monastery which has contributed largely to the British Museum Library is the Premonstratensian abbey of S. Mary De Parco, near Louvain. Its Bible, written in 1148 in three large volumes (Add. 14788–90), has only one full-page illumination, a very elaborate design prefixed to Genesis and containing the words of the first verse: Christ in glory in the centre, scenes from Genesis in medallions round the frame; the interspaces filled with foliate scroll-work, birds, archers, etc. Gold and silver are freely used, and the colouring is warm and rich, so that the total decorative effect is splendid, despite a certain coarseness in the figure-drawing.

FLEMISH ILLUMINATION, 900-1200

The initials sometimes contain figures, but are for the most part merely handsome examples of the current decorative style, being made of plaited gold ribbons placed on a coloured field and entwined with white vine-stems, or else of coloured foliations on a gold ground. Dragons are used for the tails of letters, and the white vine-branches are finely patterned with red and green pen-work.

The initials of the great two-volume Bible from Floreffe Abbey,[1] near Namur, written about 1160, are of a simpler character. They are of the usual scroll and dragon type, very finely drawn in red and black outline, with great elaboration of detail, but without any illumination properly so called. The miniatures, which occur in the second volume only, are brilliant in colour but rather hard in technique. The subjects are mystical and allegorical: the sacrifices of the Old and New Dispensations, the theological and cardinal virtues, etc. Despite its faults of hardness and flatness, this book with its neat execution and its slender, almost Gothic figures, shows that Flemish painting had by this time reached at least as high a level as that of the contemporary German schools.

[1] Brit. Mus., Add. 17737-8. See Warner, *Illum. MSS.*, pl. 15, and *Reprod.*, iii, 10; *Pal. Soc.*, i, 213.

CHAPTER IX

ITALIAN ILLUMINATION BEFORE 1300

THE materials for an orderly and consecutive history of early Italian illumination can hardly be said to exist; here, at any rate, only the slightest sketch can be attempted. That Byzantine influence predominated until well on in the Middle Ages need scarcely be stated; it has already been pointed out, in chapter iii, that many Greek manuscripts were written in Italy, and illuminated in a manner not to be distinguished from that of Byzantine painters. There can be little doubt, however, that illuminators working in Rome, Naples, and other Italian cities were also influenced by what they saw of wall-paintings, mosaics, and other monuments of Late Classical and Early Christian art. The seventh century Latin Gospels at Cambridge,[1] for instance, afford some evidence of this. This book belonged to S. Augustine's, Canterbury, at least as early as the ninth century, and it is highly probable that it came originally from Italy, perhaps from Rome itself. Its two remaining pages of illumination show little trace of Byzantine influence, except indirectly in the composition of S. Luke seated within an alcove; the additional figure of his emblem in the tympanum is most likely an Italian invention,[2] and the little scenes from the life of Christ are essentially Western in iconography and debased Roman in manner. Corroborative evidence may be deduced from the painting of David and his musicians in the Canterbury Psalter,[3]

---

[1] Corpus Christi College, No. 286. See *Pal. Soc.*, i, 33, 34, 44, and for coloured reproductions J. Goodwin, *Evangelia Augustini Gregoriana*, 1847 (Cambridge Ant. Soc., No. 13), pl. 6, 7.

[2] See above, p. 62.

[3] Brit. Mus., **Vesp. A.** i, noticed above, p. 86.

ITALIAN ILLUMINATION BEFORE 1300

which combines Celtic ornament with Classical composition, the latter almost certainly based on an Italian original of the seventh century or earlier.

In Northern Italy, overrun as it constantly was by invading hordes, Byzantine and Roman influence declined in art as in politics; and the few extant examples of the book-decoration practised in those troublous ages have a barbaric stamp plainly marked upon them. The outline-sketches which adorn (?) the fifth-seventh century Psalter at Verona[1] are too rude to deserve the name of art. More ambitious are the paintings of the famous Ashburnham Pentateuch,[2] now in the Bibliothèque Nationale at Paris (nouv. acq. lat. 2334), which were probably executed in North Italy towards the end of the seventh century. The title-page, with its peacocks, looped-back curtains, and rosetted arch, is of the ordinary Byzantine type; but formal regularity and adherence to convention appear only in this design. The illustrative miniatures, on the contrary, are graphic and forcible, but crude almost to barbarism. Crowded scenes jostle one another, often without partition, filling up the page regardless of composition or artistic effect. The figures are vigorous and expressive, but have no suggestion of grace or dignity, and the heads are much too big. In fact, if these pictures are indebted to Byzantine art at all, it is to Byzantine art of the untutored kind represented by the Vienna Genesis. The painter is at his best in pastoral scenes, e.g. Adam and Cain ploughing; his drawing of plants and animals is far in advance of his mastery of the art of picture-making. On the whole, this manuscript, interesting and valuable in itself, occupies an almost isolated position in the history of art, and has little relation to the subsequent development of Italian illumination.

---

[1] A. Goldschmidt, "Die ältesten Psalterillustrationen," in *Repert. f. Kunstwissenschaft*, xxiii, pp. 265-73.

[2] O. von Gebhardt, *The Miniatures of the Ashburnham Pentateuch*, 1883; *Pal. Soc.*, i, 234-5.

ILLUMINATED MANUSCRIPTS

In such places as the famous Chapter Library at Verona, examples may be seen of Italian illumination between the eighth and eleventh centuries; but these (setting aside the direct copies of Byzantine manuscripts, to which allusion was made just now) have few of the characteristics which one would expect to find in the native country of antique Roman art. They appear crude and barbarous when compared with the best work of contemporary Carolingian, Ottonian, and Early English illuminators; and a national Italian style can hardly be said to have evolved itself before the twelfth century. In monasteries like Bobbio, founded by Irish missionaries, Celtic influence appears, not only in illuminations directly copied from, or at least founded on, Irish models, but also in the blending of Celtic ornament with Byzantine figure-composition and dress;[1] and this influence is plainly discernible in the South Italian scheme of decoration from the tenth century onwards, where Celtic plait-work and convolutions of interlaced ribbons or foliage-stems are combined with monsters whose weird forms bespeak a Lombardic origin, and sometimes with intertwined branch-and-leaf work in gold on coloured grounds, a motive evidently borrowed from Ottonian illumination. An excellent example of the mingled styles found in early Italian manuscripts is the Sacramentary written for S. Warmund, Bishop of Ivrea in Piedmont, about the year 1000, and still preserved in the Chapter Library there.[2] The opening page of the Canon has the words "Te igitur" in gold interlaced lettering similar to that found in German manuscripts of the same period, together with a very Byzantine-looking figure of S. Warmund in the *orans* attitude as though saying Mass, and wearing the rectangular nimbus appropriated to living persons in early Italian art. On the other hand, the really fine

---

[1] See, for instance, the tenth–eleventh century Bobbio Psalter at Munich (Cod. lat. 343), in Kobell, p. 22, pl. 12, 13.

[2] F. Carta, C. Cipolla, and C. Frati, *Atlante paleografico-artistico*, 1899, pp. 21–2, pl. 23–4.

ITALIAN ILLUMINATION BEFORE 1300

miniature of the Maries at the Tomb is thoroughly instinct with Classical tradition : in the slender dignified forms of the women, in the great angel with his flowing draperies, in the sleeping soldiers.

It is to the Benedictine monasteries of Southern Italy, and particularly to the great parent house of Monte Cassino, founded by S. Benedict in the sixth century, that we must look for the beginnings of Italian illumination as a continuous and progressive art.[1] Lombard and Saracen invasions, and a subsequent fire at Teano, where the monks had taken refuge about the beginning of the tenth century, have left us no relics of the book-painting practised at Monte Cassino during the first three centuries of its history. But there is little sign of artistic tradition in the earliest extant work of the school, a copy of Paul the Deacon's Commentary on the Rule of S. Benedict, written at Capua between 915 and 934, and preserved in the library at Monte Cassino (No. 175). Besides its frontispiece (Christ in glory, with the emblems of the Evangelists and two adoring angels), it has a miniature of Abbot John giving the book to S. Benedict, who sits in a jewelled chair with an angel standing behind him. The ornamental framing of the frontispiece recalls the Book of Durrow and other early Irish manuscripts : a broad band entwined upon itself so as to form one large central circle and four small ones, and divided into panels filled with interlaced ribbons. The figure-drawing, however, on both pages is rudimentary, not in the grotesquely conventional Irish manner, but rather as though ineptly copied from models which had some relation to actual life ; the chief fault is in the proportions, especially those of the two adoring angels, whose crouching bodies and limbs are shrunk almost to nothing, while their heads, hands, and feet are enormous.

With the eleventh century, the number of extant

[1] See É. Bertaux, *L'art dans l'Italie méridionale*, i, 1904, pp. 155–67, 193–212, etc. ; Oderisio Piscicelli Taeggi, *Le Miniature nei codici Cassinesi* (Litografia di Montecassino, 1887, etc.), and *Paleografia artistica di Montecassino*, 1876.

ILLUMINATED MANUSCRIPTS

illuminated manuscripts from Monte Cassino becomes far greater. The art had not made much progress by the time of Abbot Theobald (1022-35), if we may judge by the miniatures in a copy of S. Gregory's Moralia written for him (Monte Cassino, No. 73), with their wooden faces, stiff, unlifelike figures, and poverty of design. But the abbacy of Desiderius, who was elected in 1058 and became Pope Victor III in 1086, marks an epoch in the history of Benedictine art in Southern Italy; and that in miniature as well as architecture, mosaic, and wall-painting. He imported Greek artists from Constantinople to decorate the abbey church with mosaics; and the figure-compositions in the manuscripts illuminated for him, whether painted by Greek masters or Italian pupils, are purely Byzantine in conception and manner. The decorative ornament of the initials, on the other hand, is quite independent of Byzantine influence; in it, the Celtic and Lombardic elements have now combined to form the characteristic South Italian style of the eleventh and twelfth centuries: interlaced straps, ribbons, and tendrils, with greyhounds, birds, human figures, and grotesques.[1] Both styles appear to great advantage in the beautiful Life of S. Benedict made for Abbot Desiderius about 1070, now in the Vatican Library (Vat. lat. 1202): another of his books, a volume of Homilies, still at Monte Cassino (No. 99), is decorated with exquisite drawings by a monk named Leo, executed in 1072.

Under Desiderius, Monte Cassino became one of the chief centres for the production of a class of manuscripts peculiarly South Italian, and specially interesting to students both of liturgiology and of Romanesque art. These are the illustrated Exultet Rolls,[2] which were

[1] The British Museum, which is not strong in early Italian illuminations, has a twelfth century Psalter (Add. 18859) with good initials in this, the typical Cassinese style. Mr. Yates Thompson's fine Martyrology, also of the twelfth century, is profusely decorated in the same manner. See Burl. F.A. Club, No. 5, pl. 13.

[2] These are discussed very fully, with illustrations, by Bertaux, pp. 213-40. See too the splendid series of coloured reproductions published at Monte Cassino, *Le Miniature nei Rotoli dell' Exultet*, ed. A. M. Latil, 1899, etc.; Venturi, *Storia dell' arte italiana*, iii, pp. 726-54.

ITALIAN ILLUMINATION BEFORE 1300

used in the ceremony of consecrating the great paschal candle on Easter Eve. One of the most impressive services in the liturgy of the Roman Church at the present day, this dedication of the holy candle—symbolizing at once Christ Himself and the Pillar of Fire which led the Children of Israel in the wilderness—was in the Middle Ages a ceremony of almost sacramental solemnity: a fact attested not only by the Exultet Rolls of which we are now speaking, but also by the magnificent sculptured candlesticks of the Romanesque period, specially intended for the paschal candle and placed near the ambo from which the Exultet was declaimed, which are still to be seen in many of the churches in Southern Italy. The Exultet itself, the text inscribed on these rolls, is the strange, mystical, almost rhapsodical chant sung by the deacon during the consecration and lighting of the candle: named from its opening phrase, "Exultet jam angelica turba caelorum, exultent divina mysteria!" Included in the Missal as early as the seventh century, it is here written separately on a long strip of vellum, and illustrated with pictures drawn in the reverse direction, so as to be visible right way up to the congregation as the deacon went on with the chant, letting the unrolled portion fall over the front of the ambo before him.

These illuminated Exultet Rolls seem only to have been used in Southern Italy, and there only for a comparatively short time, the surviving examples (which are all written in the well-marked script known to palaeographers as Lombardic minuscule) ranging in date from the beginning of the eleventh century to the end of the thirteenth. As to subjects and compositions they resemble one another very closely, though some are much more copiously illustrated than others. The most complete ones begin with a miniature of Christ in glory, or else (in two of the later ones) of a prelate enthroned between two priests. Then comes an immense and elaborately decorated initial "E" to the word "Exultet," with the "angelica turba" rejoicing, some rolls adding the

ILLUMINATED MANUSCRIPTS

Agnus Dei with six-winged seraphs and the Evangelistic symbols. The next picture in order, illustrating the words "Gaudeat et tellus," etc., is curiously Classical in conception. In the Bari Roll, written before 1028, Earth is represented as a dignified matron, fully draped, standing between two trees with animals grouped about her feet; but in most of the later rolls, including that in the British Museum,[1] she appears sitting on the ground or else emerging from it, half-draped or nude, with ox and serpent or two other creatures feeding at her breasts—a personification of the Universal Mother obviously inspired by pagan art. Interspersed among such pictures as these are others, showing the successive stages of the ritual performed during the chant: the censing, blessing, and lighting of the candle, the insertion of the five grains of incense, etc. Interesting as these are to the student of Christian archaeology, they are necessarily monotonous in subject, compared with the rich variety of the allegorical or literal illustrations of the text. The latter include, besides those mentioned, the Crucifixion, the Passage of the Red Sea, the Harrowing of Hell, and the Fall of Man; also Mother Church, a queenly figure extending protective arms over clergy and laity; and a very curious and distinctive scene, warranted by the text and yet suggestive of the Georgics rather than of Christian imagery: the bees, symbolical of the Virgin Birth, gathering honey and producing the wax of which the paschal candle is made ("Alitur enim liquantibus ceris, quas in substantiam pretiosae hujus lampadis apis mater eduxit.") In some rolls the symbolism is enforced by a miniature of the Nativity, with bees hovering around the crib; more commonly by a separate picture of the Annunciation, or of the Madonna and Child with adoring angels.

Until the end of the eleventh century, most of these rolls have little artistic merit; some indeed—notably the

---

[1] Add. 30337, assigned by the editors of the *Palaeographical Society* (i, 146) to the twelfth century, but Bertaux, who says (p. 226) that it came from Monte Cassino, calls it late eleventh century.

EXULTET ROLL, ITALIAN, XIITH CENT.

BRIT. MUS., ADD. 30337

ITALIAN ILLUMINATION BEFORE 1300

three in Gaeta Cathedral—are of almost repulsive ugliness, and their misshapen figures seem like childish caricatures of some worthier model, whose composition alone the copyist was able to preserve. The improved technique which afterwards begins to appear is generally accompanied by a closer adherence to Byzantine iconography, as well as a closer resemblance to Byzantine style; and M. Bertaux is doubtless right in giving a large share in the credit for this change to the school of Monte Cassino, and to Abbot Desiderius in particular. It was here, apparently, and probably not long after the time of Desiderius, that the Exultet of the British Museum (Add. 30337) was executed. Though damaged by the flaking away of the colours, it remains one of the finest surviving examples of its class; and its best miniatures already foreshadow that lovely early Italian style which, seen at its best in the Sienese and Umbrian schools, added dramatic expression and a light and brilliant colouring to the grand and spiritual Byzantine types on which it was founded. Its prevailing tints are blue and red; and these, with a plenteous use of gold, give its paintings a rich, bright, and yet charmingly soft and harmonious effect. The workmanship is uneven; but in the best pictures, such as the Harrowing of Hell,[1] with its splendid rushing figure of Christ, one sees more the large free manner of the fresco painter than the comparatively cramped technique of the miniaturist.

From this and other manuscripts it is evident that by the beginning of the twelfth century the Benedictine schools of Southern Italy had already advanced far in the evolution of a distinctive style of illumination; founded, so far as initial-ornament is concerned, on a mixture of Celtic, Lombardic, and Teutonic (Ottonian) elements; and deriving the composition of its miniatures mainly from Byzantine sources, but improving on its models by adding a largeness of manner and a warmth and richness of colouring which were afterwards among the most

[1] Pl. xx.

ILLUMINATED MANUSCRIPTS

striking characteristics of Italian painting. This instinct for colour, indeed, was already a national trait; it shows itself not only in the South Italian schools, but quite as strongly in the twelfth and thirteenth century illuminations of Northern Italy, which would often be difficult otherwise to distinguish from contemporary productions of Germany and Flanders. This applies specially to initial-ornament, where the Italian artist seems often to have been content to copy the designs of Northern illuminators, only replacing their light blue and pale green fields by brilliant ultramarine or crimson backgrounds, on which orange-yellow or gold letters, panelled with geometrical patterns in red, white, and blue, and filled with intertwining white vine-tendrils, stand in sharp relief. The British Museum possesses two excellent examples of this style in Harl. 7183 and Add. 9350. The former,[1] a very large volume containing Homilies for Sundays and Festivals from Advent to Easter Eve, was written early in the twelfth century. Most of its initials are of the type described, but often with figures of birds and animals introduced as additional ornaments. Some are historiated with half-length portraits of the saints to whose Homilies they are prefixed; these are flat, wooden, monotonous, altogether on a lower level than the purely decorative work, which is executed with great finish, shows much inventive faculty in the variety of its designs, and is altogether beautiful of its kind. In some cases the initial consists of a bird or monster, usually in white on a blue or crimson background; a favourite device of this kind is an " S " formed by a long-necked bird standing on its own tail and biting its back. Add. 9350 is a much smaller book, a glossed Psalter written about the end of the twelfth century; and its initials are on a less ambitious scale, with less intricate decoration; the colour effect too lacks something of the brilliancy and warmth of Harl. 7183, the blue being somewhat paler. Its miniature of David with his four musicians,

[1] See *Pal. Soc.*, ii, 55.

ITALIAN ILLUMINATION BEFORE 1300

all red-haired, red-nosed, and ill-proportioned, shows again how much better decorative ornament was understood at this time than figure-painting. In the fifteenth century it was bequeathed to the famous Dominican priory of S. Mark at Florence; but nothing is known as to its place of origin. These two manuscripts are good examples of the models chosen by "humanistic" Italian scribes and illuminators in the Renaissance period, and imitated with such bewildering accuracy.

How strong a hold Germanic influence had obtained in Northern Italy may be seen in such manuscripts as the Gospel-book[1] in Padua Cathedral, written in that city in the year 1170. This book has many full-page miniatures, painted in body-colour on dull gold grounds. White, emerald-green, violet, light blue, and crimson predominate. The colouring is often quite arbitrary—blue hair, green nimbi, etc.; the handling particularly harsh. The stiff and numerous folds of the draperies are outlined with hard bands or hems of colour, the large oval eyes and clumsy features are indicated by coarse lines. In fact, these miniatures with their pale hard colouring, angular figures, dry technique, and elaborate post-Carolingian architecture of striped and patterned pillars upholding round arches and many-coloured battlements, might pass as the production of some highly conservative Flemish or German scriptorium. Quite admirable, on the other hand, are the grotesque forms of birds, fishes, dragons, and demons, of which the chief initials are built up, and which are paralleled by the quaint and vigorous carvings that abound in North Italian churches of the Romanesque time.

It was in the thirteenth century that the Byzantine influence which had so long affected the course of South Italian sculpture, architecture, and painting, flowed over the whole of the peninsula, producing a sudden outburst of pictorial art, often of peculiar loveliness, in which the stateliness of Byzantium, her Oriental faculty for pre-

[1] See Venturi, iii, pp. 450–2, 454.

senting spiritual mysteries under the guise of earthly magnificence, was softened, humanized, by the gentler temper of the Italian religious mind. Italy in the thirteenth century was profoundly moved by the Franciscan spirit, which, though at first inimical to the production of works of art, was finally responsible for that sweetness and simplicity of outlook which charms us in the fresco-painting of the early Italian school, and gives its peculiar quality of grace to Italo-Byzantine art. This art was applied with special success to the illumination of liturgical books. Here its admirable convention, richness of colour, and extraordinary power of rendering spiritual themes produced a sudden revival of the miniaturist's art, in which Italy as a whole had so long been content to lag behind her northerly neighbours. Whilst England and France were in the heyday of their Early Gothic period, the illuminators of Padua, Parma, and Bologna looked eastwards for inspiration; and Italian miniature began to be henceforth sharply differentiated from that of the rest of the world.

How complete was the transition from the vague eclecticism, which makes North Italian illuminations of the twelfth century so perplexing to the student, to the formal but finished style of the thirteenth century, is well shown by a comparison of the Paduan Gospel-book of 1170, just described, with an Epistolar[1] made for the same cathedral eighty-nine years later. The art of the Gospel-book cannot be called either beautiful or religious. That of the Epistolar, on the contrary, despite the faulty proportions and overcrowded compositions, is essentially mature, noble, profoundly spiritual. The pictures express both dignity and emotion: things so opposed in their tendencies, that they are only found together in art of a high order. The Byzantine parentage of the Epistolar is obvious, but its defects, no less than its special merits, mark it off as a native product; and as a matter of

[1] Venturi, iii, pp. 486-9.

ITALIAN ILLUMINATION BEFORE 1300

fact it was written at Padua by a priest named Giovanni di Gaibana, who finished it in 1259, and whose portrait is appended, sitting at a desk and writing the words " Ego presbyter Johannes scripsi feliciter." Turning to the miniatures, we find a long series of full-page pictures of the lives of Christ and the saints, painted on highly burnished gold backgrounds in just such deep rich colours as are to be seen in the altar-pieces of Duccio and other Italian painters who employed the *maniera bizantina*: deep blue predominates, relieved by scarlet, pinkish purple, and a little green. Instead of hard contours and flatly laid tints, we have admirably modelled figures (though imperfect as to proportions, the heads being too big), whose dark complexions, with greenish shadows and sharp high-lights on forehead, cheek, and nose, sufficiently betray their Byzantine ancestry; as do also the static character of the whole work, the sudden failure of the artist when, as in the Death of S. John Baptist, he tries to represent violent action, and the poetic majesty of his design when, as in the Death of the Madonna, he is content to give new life to the old, formal compositions. The vivacity of expression which, without impairing the impressive character of his scenes, gives them a dramatic force often lacking in the mystical and ceremonial art of the Greek painters, owes something, perhaps, to Northern influence; or more probably to the Benedictine art of South Italy, for the same quality is noticeable, as we saw, in the twelfth century Exultet Roll in the British Museum.

By the end of the thirteenth century a well-marked type of conventional border-ornament had been evolved, which persisted, of course with many slight variations, throughout the fourteenth century in Italian illumination, and which assuredly owes nothing to Eastern influences; it is, in fact, closely allied with, and most probably derived from, the pendent "bar-border" initial-ornament which is one of the features of thirteenth century English and French book-decoration. Its main elements are: (1) The thin wand or rod, normally straight and rigid, but capable

ILLUMINATED MANUSCRIPTS

of being tied in knots, twisted or plaited; (2) The long lobed and pointed leaf, the lobes generally on one side only: this may spring from the wands or from the initial letters, or may be an independent growth twined round them; (3) Cup-shaped beads threaded on the wands and stems: though this style of ornament is more specially typical of fourteenth century Italian manuscripts, it had already come into use before the end of the period now under discussion, particularly at Bologna, where a school of miniature was growing[1] which was afterwards to attain a position of considerable importance. Another device found in Italian borders towards the end of the thirteenth century was doubtless borrowed from Northern Europe, where it was much more frequently practised and with much freer play of fancy and humour, especially in England, North France, and the Low Countries. This is the frankly comical use of human, animal, and grotesque figures: a hare hunting a man, two men fighting a gigantic snail, and such-like extravagances. They are not very common in Italian art,[2] but are noteworthy as an instance of the constant interchange of artistic ideas between different, even distant countries.

We cannot leave the thirteenth century without some mention of a manuscript interesting for the delightfulness, no less than for the uncommon character, of the drawings that it contains. This is a copy of the Emperor Frederic II's treatise *De arte venandi cum avibus*, written about 1260, presumably in Sicily or Southern Italy, and now in the Vatican Library (Cod. pal. lat. 1071).[3] It introduces us to a class of art curiously unlike most of what Italy was producing at the time. The accuracy and beauty of its marginal paintings of birds and falconers indicate rather a close study of nature than the slavish copying of traditional models. We have here

[1] See Venturi, iii, p. 457 *sq*.
[2] For examples see Venturi, iii, pp. 458–61, and a small Bible in the British Museum, Add. 37487.
[3] Venturi, iii, pp. 756–68; Beissel, *Vat. Min.*, pl. 20.

ITALIAN ILLUMINATION BEFORE 1300

indeed a technical accomplishment and beauty of line, quite Greek in their perfection, employed upon pictures of contemporary life; and these bright and lifelike scenes, with their intensely open-air atmosphere, are a refreshing contrast to the solemn, monastic spirit which pervades so much of Italian illumination in the thirteenth century.

CHAPTER X

ENGLISH ILLUMINATION IN THE THIRTEENTH CENTURY

THE twelfth century, as we saw in chapter vii, was a transitional period in English book-decoration; and its close witnessed the birth of a new style, which may well be called Gothic from its intimate connection with the architectural style that supplanted the Romanesque about the same time. In the main, Gothic illumination is minute, refined, delicate, contrasting sharply with the broad manner of the preceding age. At its best it is, indeed, the most perfect realization of the aims and ideals proper to the miniaturist's art, as distinct from skilful adaptations of the designs and methods of other arts, mosaic, wall-painting, weaving, or metal-work. Not that miniature was specially isolated and self-contained during the Gothic period—on the contrary, at no time is its kinship with the sister arts more apparent; but that somehow the decorative and illustrative ideas characteristic of this remarkable age happened to be specially suited to the limitations under which the miniaturist worked. This applies to France equally with England, at all events during the earlier part of this period. For the first two-thirds of the thirteenth century, indeed, French and English illumination resemble one another so closely as to be practically indistinguishable—be the initial credit due to this country or to that. Later on, as we shall see, the two followed somewhat divergent paths; and the development of the art, which in England was abruptly checked about the middle of the fourteenth century, proceeded continuously in France right on to its

ENGLISH ILLUMINATION, 13TH CENT.

decay in the tasteless magnificence of the Renaissance period.

The miniaturist was encouraged to cultivate a more minute style by the reduction of scale in book-production generally, which began to come in about the year 1200. Huge tomes like the Winchester and Durham Bibles were no longer in vogue; a demand arose for books of a handier size, in particular for single volumes of portable dimensions containing the whole of the Latin Bible. These were a special feature of the thirteenth century, and immense numbers of them still exist; their multiplicity was due in part, no doubt, to the efforts of Paris University to purify the Vulgate text, but they also testify to the zealous activity of the itinerant friars. With this reduction in *format* came also a diminution in the size of the lettering, a small, exquisitely neat and clear minuscule script replacing the large, bold characters of the twelfth century book-hands; so that the artist was impelled by his sense of due proportion, as well as by his now restricted allowance of space, to alter his methods. Initial-ornament, already a prominent feature of twelfth century book-decoration, began to engross his attention more and more at the expense of the full-page miniature; the historiated initial so affecting his style in figure-composition that when whole pages were still given up to miniatures it became usual to divide them into compartments, each containing a picture not much more spacious than those enclosed in the larger initials. A very interesting and distinctive feature of the initial-ornament of this period is the pendent tail, out of which were gradually evolved the luxuriant borders which so light up the pages of French fifteenth century Books of Hours. At first this tail merely wanders a little way down the margin, to end in a leaf or knob; gradually it lengthens until it reaches the foot of the column of text, when it proceeds next to turn the corner, becoming eventually a complete border which surrounds the text on all four sides. The main part is at first quite straight and rigid; hence the

ILLUMINATED MANUSCRIPTS

term "bar-border" is sometimes given to this type of decoration in the comparatively simple and undeveloped form which it kept throughout the thirteenth century. But the straight edge soon began to be replaced by a series of cusped lines, or other curves; and small figures, human, animal, or grotesque, further relieve the rigidity, perching on the bars or forming terminal ornaments. Finally, the bars themselves turn into foliage-stems, putting forth leafy branches of ever-increasing lightness, intricacy, and variety, bearing flowers and fruit as well as leaves without regard for species. This last development hardly appears before 1300, and does not reach its full luxuriance until the beginning of the fifteenth century; but a tendency had already begun, as early as the middle of the thirteenth century, to transform part of the bar into a thin cylindrical rod, adorned at intervals with rings and other ornaments—a device which became, as we saw in chapter ix, the foundation of the typical fourteenth century border in Italy.

The great majority of the most finely illuminated English manuscripts of the thirteenth century are Psalters. At the beginning of the century these usually open with a series of pages filled with miniatures of the life of Christ, two on a page, enclosed within narrow banded frames. The British Museum possesses two typical examples of the class in Roy. 1 D. x[1] and Arundel 157,[2] practically identical in amount and subjects of illumination, but differing widely in artistic merit. As neither of them mentions the translation of S. Thomas of Canterbury in the Calendar, it is fairly safe to conclude that they were written before 1220. The Calendar of the former points somewhat dubiously to Winchester as the place of origin, that of the latter more decisively to Oxford; but both are plainly derived from a common archetype, and belong, so far as the miniatures are concerned, to the same transitional class as the Westminster Psalter (Roy. 2 A. xxii), noted at the end of chapter vii, though to a

[1] Warner, *Reprod.*, iii, 14.   [2] *Ibid.*, iii, 16.

PSALTER. ENGLISH, EARLY XIIITH CENT.
BRIT. MUS. ROYAL 1 D X

ENGLISH ILLUMINATION, 13TH CENT.

slightly more advanced stage; having the same depth and splendour of colour, the same free use of burnished gold, the same simplicity of design. The Royal MS. is much the finer of the two. Its miniatures have plain backgrounds, alternately of highly burnished gold, and of deep blue or lake powdered with red rings and a small pattern of white dots. The deep, rich blue, so popular in the thirteenth century, is the dominant note of the colour-scheme; it is balanced by red, light green and lake, and the harmony is completed by passages of warm and cold grey, and of white draperies lightly shaded with buff, grey, and pink. The blue is of a warmer tint than in the Westminster Psalter, and the colour-effect as a whole is brighter; the faces, which are of longer, more emaciated types, are equally expressive but less livid in hue, having now a hectic spot of red on the cheek, besides sharply defined white high-lights on forehead, nose, and chin. In the best pictures, where few figures occur, such as the Annunciation, Visitation, and the Magi scenes,[1] there is a largeness of manner suggestive of fresco-painting rather than miniature, and not often found after this date in English illumination.

The Calendar-illustrations are thoroughly typical of the period, each month having (besides an elaborate decorative initial in gold and colours) representations of the zodiacal sign and an appropriate occupation, each enclosed in a small medallion. The occupation-scenes are no longer complete pictures, as in the eleventh century Calendars described in chapter vi, but are so compressed as to be little more than symbols, having mostly only a single figure. The subjects differ little from those of the older cycle except in distribution among the several months; but we notice with regret that the November Halloween Fire is now replaced by the less picturesque, more prosaic and utilitarian, fattening or killing of pigs.

After the preliminary Gospel-pictures and Calendar, thirteenth century Psalters have as a rule few illuminations

[1] Pl. xxi.

ILLUMINATED MANUSCRIPTS

beyond a highly decorative *Beatus vir* on the opening page and a more or less elaborate initial to each psalm, those at the principal divisions being specially large and usually enclosing miniatures. Roy. 1 D. x has a splendid *Beatus vir*: the " B," whose loops are formed of an intricate interweaving of spirals made of slender leafy stems terminating in monsters' heads and joined to the upright shaft by elaborate lattice-work, is placed on a finely chequered ground; minute animals are caught in the spirals, and the surrounding frame has four scenes from the life of David in gold medallions. Nine of the psalms (Pss. xxvi, xxxviii, li, lii, lxviii, lxxx, xcvii, ci, cix) have initials historiated with scriptural subjects: in these the miniature is painted on a background of burnished gold stippled with a dot-pattern, and the whole letter is set in a rectangle of diapered blue or lake. The initials to the other psalms are smaller, but not less finely finished and delightful to behold; a few contain figures, but the majority are filled with purely decorative designs of foliage and grotesques. It is noteworthy that some of them already show the beginnings of the pendent ornament which afterwards grew into the complete bar-border. Another feature of this and other English thirteenth century Psalters is the practice of filling up the spaces left at the ends of verses with pen-work designs in blue or red; these are sometimes mere flourishes or geometrical patterns, but often they are spirited and humorous drawings of fishes, birds, dogs, dragons, etc. Later on it became customary to illuminate these line-endings fully with diaper patterns or heraldic devices; but the effect of outline-drawings, such as those in this manuscript, is infinitely more telling.

As to the general character of its decoration, Roy. 1 D. x may be taken as representative of its class; but in artistic excellence it is far above the average. Admirable as its large miniatures are, with their beautiful colouring, simple, dignified compositions, and careful treatment of the face, they are fully matched by the exquisite delicacy

ENGLISH ILLUMINATION, 13TH CENT.

and rich variety of the decorative designs and the fine execution of the smaller miniatures. Arundel 157 may almost be called a coarser, more commonplace replica. Its initials and Calendar-medallions are only slightly inferior; its *Beatus vir* is actually finer, being on a larger scale and more elaborately intricate in design, while no less splendid in colouring—indeed, few more perfect pages exist, if any, of this particular kind. But the Gospel-miniatures at the beginning are distinctly on a lower level than those in the Royal MS. Practically identical in subject, main outlines of composition, and general scheme of arrangement, they fail altogether to produce the same pleasing effect. The figures are smaller, less dignified, with something of the gaunt ungainliness which characterized English figure-drawing nearly a century earlier, as in the Holford MS. of the Passion of S. Edmund;[1] the faces have the same touches of red and white, but are not treated with the same masterly delicacy. Finally, the colouring, though bright and varied, has not the same rich, soft charm, chiefly through the painter's lack of sure instinct for harmony in colour. In short, the manuscript is not the production of a great artist, but represents excellently the average work of an exceptionally interesting period in the history of English illumination. Among other characteristics of Gothic art, it illustrates the whimsical habit of collocating the sublime with the ridiculous: the solemn prayers which follow the Litany having initials historiated with such incongruous subjects as a monkey riding on a lion's back.

Another Psalter of the same period, but decorated in a very different manner, is Lansdowne 420 in the British Museum, emanating perhaps from Chester, since S. Werburga and her mother S. Eormenilda receive special honour in the Calendar. Like the two books just dealt with, it has excellent line-endings in blue and red outlines (fishes, human heads and limbs, etc.); but here the resemblance ends. The ten pages of Gospel-miniatures at the begin-

[1] Above, p. 135.

ning are evidently inspired by a series of medallions in stained glass. The pictures, two on a page, are painted on gold, red or blue grounds in roundels, which are placed on square fields of a contrasting colour; the gold burnished and stamped with a star-pattern, the coloured grounds patterned with white dots and rings. The stiff, elongated, angular figures have all the severity proper to the glass-painter's technique, their heavy black outlines reproduce the leads exactly, and the drapery folds are indicated in the same style by thick lines; the colouring shows a strong preponderance of deep blue and red. The *Beatus vir* page is of an unusual and amusing type. The " B," made of narrow entwined ribbons on a gold field, forms a small and rather insignificant foundation; but round about it, on a blue ground patterned with white branch-work, are eight gold medallions containing delightful figures of animal musicians—donkey and harp, cat and fiddle, etc. Outside all this is a frame holding more medallions of a less frivolous character.

The Psalter of Robert de Lindeseye, Abbot of Peterborough, in the library of the Society of Antiquaries,[1] cannot be many years later than the manuscripts which we have been considering, its date being fixed between the Translation of S. Thomas of Canterbury in 1220 and the death of Abbot Robert in 1222; but its beautiful miniatures already show the thirteenth century style in full maturity. The most striking of these is a Crucifixion,[2] drawn and painted with exquisite delicacy on a rich background of burnished and patterned gold. The anatomy is by no means faultless, the limbs of Christ being attenuated beyond all possibility; but this, like the touch of sentimentality in S. John's expression and pose, is a trifling blemish resulting very naturally from the extreme refinement and genuine feeling with which the whole picture is instinct. Especially charming is the graceful figure of the Virgin, balancing that of S. John; again

---

[1] No. 59. See Burl. F.A. Club, No. 37, pl. 36.
[2] Pl. xxii.

PLATE XXII

PSALTER OF ROBERT DE LINDESEY, ABBOT OF PETERBOROUGH, 1220-22.
SOCIETY OF ANTIQUARIES, MS. 59.

ENGLISH ILLUMINATION, 13TH CENT.

a thought too graceful, perhaps, for absolute dramatic fitness. The shaft and arms of the cross are covered with a symmetrical leafy stem—a very unusual feature; less rare, especially about this time, are the half-length figures of the Old and New Dispensations, and of Moses balanced by S. Peter, in medallions at the corners. The only other full-page illuminations, Christ in glory and *Beatus vir*, are equally fine in execution, though less original in design;[1] and five of the psalms have initials enclosing spirited and delicate miniatures. In all these the colour-scheme, dominated by the highly burnished and elaborately patterned gold, and by a lovely deep soft blue, is at once splendid and harmonious.

Much more abundant, but incomparably rougher, is the decoration of the Carrow Psalter in Mr. Yates Thompson's library.[2] Executed towards the middle of the thirteenth century (certainly after 1233), probably in the neighbourhood of Bury S. Edmund's, it belonged in the fifteenth century to the nuns of Carrow by Norwich. Despite their lack of finish, its numerous miniatures are interesting as the precursors (though the parental relation is not obvious) of the exquisite paintings of the early fourteenth century East Anglian school. Many of the subjects too are unusual: the initial "B," for instance, contains six scenes from the legend of S. Olaf, and the full-page miniatures include a graphic representation of the murder of S. Thomas of Canterbury, and a curious picture of an angel giving Adam a spade and Eve a distaff. Moreover, this manuscript is one of the earliest to use the trefoil-arched canopy, so characteristic a device in early Gothic architecture.

Leaving the Psalters for a while, we come to another class of manuscript even more distinctive of the thirteenth century, viz. copies of the Latin Bible. Of the vast

---

[1] It may be noted that both subjects reappear, treated in a strikingly similar manner, on a leaf inserted at the beginning of the much earlier Canterbury Psalter, Vesp. A. i. See Warner, *Reprod.*, iii, 15.

[2] No. 52. See H. Y. Thompson, *Descriptive Catalogue*, 1902, pp. 2–11, and *Lecture on some Eng. Illum. MSS.*, 1902, p. 13, pl. 2–4.

numbers of these volumes which have survived to the present day, the great majority are veritable pocket-books, and have more interest palaeographically than artistically, being remarkable rather for the minute neatness and regularity of their script than for the wealth of their decoration; the latter being generally confined to a foliated or historiated initial at the beginning of each book, sometimes with the addition of a series of Creation-scenes and a Jesse-tree at the beginnings of Genesis and Matthew respectively. From either point of view their direct utility for study is diminished by the fact that so few contain precise indications of date or provenance; even the country of origin can rarely be determined with certainty, French and English work, both in writing and illumination, being at this period so remarkably alike. In Burney 3,[1] luckily, the British Museum possesses an excellent example of the class, which is provided with these essential data: the Bible of Robert de Bello, Abbot of S. Augustine's, Canterbury, 1224–53, for whom it was presumably written and illuminated in his own abbey. Intended, no doubt, for library and not for pocket use, it is on a somewhat larger scale than the diminutive volumes just mentioned, though a mere pygmy compared with the huge Bibles of the preceding century; it may very well be taken, however, as a representative of the former class in everything but actual size. The chief decoration is at the beginning of Genesis: the "I" of *In principio* forming a broad band which fills the left-hand column and all the lower margin of the page, and contains a series of medallion-scenes from Genesis on burnished gold grounds. The initial "I" of S. John's Gospel is treated in a similar way, filling the whole space between the two columns of text, as well as part of the upper and lower margins, and containing, in a series of long narrow panels, representations of the Evangelist with an eagle's head and of incidents from his Gospel. At the beginning of S. Matthew is a Jesse-tree, as usual.

---

[1] Warner, *Reprod.*, i, 11; *Pal. Soc.*, i, 73–4.

ENGLISH ILLUMINATION, 13TH CENT.

In these, as in the smaller historiated initials of the other books, the style of the painting is rather flat, though the figures are well and accurately drawn; the colour-effect generally is pallid, a very curious whitish blue predominating. The chapter-initials, coloured blue or red, are decorated with pen flourishes in the same colours, often elaborate and very delicately executed. This kind of ornament became a great feature of thirteenth and fourteenth century illumination; it reached its greatest perfection in England about the beginning of the fourteenth century; in Italy, where its development was carried further, about half a century later.

A more beautiful manuscript, indeed the very flower of its class, is Royal 1 D. i,[1] a Bible written about the middle of the thirteenth century by one William of Devon; few English manuscripts of its time can approach it in perfection of taste and technique. Its historiated initials, with their exquisite little figures on burnished gold or diapered backgrounds, are finished with microscopic exactitude; they are prolonged into bar-borders which often surround the text on three sides, supporting delicious little grotesques and sometimes ending in slender foliage-stems. Only two pages have miniatures unconnected with initials. The first of these,[2] after the concluding lines of S. Jerome's Prologue to the Pentateuch, is filled with canopied panels of red, lake, or deep blue, either diapered or else powdered with tiny patterns of white dots and rings. In the topmost compartment is the Coronation of Christ by the Father; below this, the Crucifixion between two seraphs. The lowest division has in the centre the Virgin and Child, with a small miniature below of S. Martin and the beggar; on the sides, SS. Peter and Paul. At the foot of the page is a kneeling monk, perhaps William of Devon, perhaps the person for whom the

[1] Thompson, pp. 36-8, pl. 11; Warner, *Illum. MSS.*, pl. 20, and *Reprod.*, ii, 10; Kenyon, *Biblical MSS.*, pl. xix.
[2] Pl. xxiii.

183

ILLUMINATED MANUSCRIPTS

book was written. The second miniature-page, prefixed to the Psalms, is also divided into compartments; the backgrounds are blue or lake, powdered with gold discs and a white dot-pattern; the subjects depicted are the Crucifixion, the martyrdom of S. Thomas of Canterbury, the story of the Virgin helping him to mend his shirt, and an apparition of Christ to him or some other archbishop. The prominence given to S. Thomas has led to the suggestion that the manuscript was written at Canterbury, where S. Martin too had long been held in special reverence, as well as the Apostles Peter and Paul, the original patrons of S. Augustine's Abbey. This, however, is mere conjecture; nothing is definitely known of the history of the book, beyond the name of its scribe, which may be taken as guaranteeing its English origin. Of the other pages, the most richly illuminated are the first page in the volume, having a miniature of S. Jerome writing enclosed within the initial, and borders decorated with exquisite little figures of archers, rabbits, birds, and grotesques, and monks drawn in outline and delicately tinted; the *In principio* of Genesis, with a series of tiny panels under cusped arches, containing miniatures of the Creation, Fall, and Atonement; and the Prologue to S. Matthew, with a Jesse-tree in the initial. In these miniatures, as in the historiated initials of the several books, the figures are of the slender, dignified type characteristic of the best Gothic art. The chapter-initials throughout the volume are enriched with red and blue pen-work decoration of the utmost delicacy.

Firm and delicate draughtsmanship formed the groundwork of all the best English illumination of this period, as of those which preceded and followed it; and the practice of illustrating books in outline, either lightly tinted or left quite uncoloured, did not fall into complete desuetude, though the prevailing taste at this time was for books resplendent with burnished gold and rich warm colouring. The scriptorium of S. Alban's Abbey, in particular, has left us several fine manuscripts of the former

PLATE XXIII

BIBLE. ENGLISH, XIIIth CENT.

BRIT. MUS. ROYAL 1 D I

ENGLISH ILLUMINATION, 13TH CENT.

class, containing the historical writings of Matthew Paris. A monk at S. Alban's from 1217, he made himself proficient in writing, drawing, painting, and metal-work, and from 1236 till his death in 1259 he was head of the scriptorium, as well as historiographer of the abbey. Many of these manuscripts[1] are undoubtedly written by him, and illustrated either by him or under his direction. One of the most interesting is Royal 14 C. vii, containing his Historia Anglorum and the concluding portion of his Chronica Majora. Where the latter work ends, at the year 1259, there is a drawing of Matthew Paris on his deathbed, doubtless inserted by the monk who continued the chronicle. We also see him kneeling before the Virgin and Child in a full-page drawing, perhaps by his own hand, at the beginning of the volume. This picture, on a plain vellum background, framed in bands of pale green and red, is the most charming thing in the book. The Madonna is of the perfect Gothic type, with long curling hair; her face is shaded very slightly with bistre, but the draperies are tinted green, grey, purple, blue, and buff, and the folds indicated by black pen-strokes. This page is followed by lightly tinted outline-drawings of the kings of England from William I to Henry III, four on a page, on coloured backgrounds under horseshoe arches; they are represented as sitting stiffly and symmetrically, without much attempt at portraiture. In Claudius D. vi, an abridged chronicle of England, we have several pages of similar drawings of kings, from the legendary Brutus down to Henry III, firmly outlined in brown ink, very faintly tinted in water-colour, and placed against strong backgrounds of lake or chalky blue; there are occasional touches of graphic symbolism, as in Canute holding a battle-axe, or John with his crown nearly tilted off. More strictly outline-work is the illustration of the Lives of the Two Offas in Nero D. i:[2] a long series of excellently

---

[1] For an account of them see Madden's and Luard's introductions to his *Historia Anglorum* and *Chronica Majora* in the Rolls series.

[2] Thompson, pp. 41–2, pl. 13.

ILLUMINATED MANUSCRIPTS

dramatic drawings, very large and open in manner, filling the upper half of each page. Especially fine are the first six pages, dealing with the early life of the first Offa, the grievously afflicted and miraculously cured son of King Waermund: the pathetic figure of the young prince, the distress of his father and the faithful nobles, the malevolence of the traitor Rigan's evil counsellor ("malorum persuasor"), are all portrayed with real power and skill. The remaining scenes are not only in a much more sketchy, less finished state, but seem to be the work of an inferior artist; they too, however, though lacking in delicacy, are full of freshness, vigour, and dramatic force. Towards the end of the volume, which is filled with historical documents and notes, chiefly relating to S. Alban's Abbey, is a full-page drawing of the elephant which Louis IX sent to England in 1255 as a present to Henry III. This drawing is usually attributed to Matthew Paris, and it certainly does him no discredit.

It naturally suggests a large class of manuscripts which must be mentioned, though they do not lend themselves readily to precise chronological or topographical arrangement. These are the illustrated Bestiaries, the medieval handbooks of natural history. Based on the Etymologiae of Isidore, and more remotely on Pliny and "Physiologus," they were often illustrated profusely, especially during the twelfth and thirteenth centuries, with coloured drawings of beasts birds, and fishes actual or fabulous; more rarely with fully illuminated miniatures in gold and colours. They are often found in conjunction with illustrated Herbals, which trace their descent, almost in an unbroken line, from the famous Dioscorides MS. of the sixth century described at the end of chapter ii;[1] having the same carefully outlined and delicately tinted drawings of plants, the monotony of their solid instructiveness always broken by a picture of the ill-fated dog chained to the mandrake's monstrous roots. A good example of this combination is Harl. 4986

[1] Above, p. 34.

ENGLISH ILLUMINATION, 13TH CENT.

(twelfth century), though here the Bestiary illustrations are decidedly inferior to those of the Herbal. One of the finest extant Bestiaries, now in Mr. Pierpont Morgan's library,[1] was executed in England shortly before 1187, when a Canon of Lincoln gave it to Worksop Priory; another excellent specimen, perhaps slightly later, is Harl. 4751.[2] The most interesting of the pictures are, of course, those which illustrate the supposed habits of the creatures described: the pelican feeding her young with her blood; the unicorn crouching entranced at a maiden's feet; the watersnake spitefully entering the jaws of a sleeping crocodile in order to devour his entrails; the whale plunging into the depths, to the consternation of the sailors who have lighted a fire on its back; the wondrous white bird *caladrius*, which perches on a king's sickbed and either looks him in the face and cures him, or else turns its back on him, forecasting his speedy death.

In the second half of the thirteenth century English illumination was approaching its climax, which it reached soon after the year 1300. The ascetic, emaciated types of face and figure began to assume softer, more rounded and gracious contours; and in like manner the severe restraint of the bar-border was relaxed, branches shooting freely in all directions, bearing leaves in ever-increasing luxuriance, and giving shelter to all manner of dainty, whimsical, fantastic creatures, as well as to birds and animals often painted with amazing fidelity to nature. Nor is this advance in freedom and luxuriance accompanied by any decline in delicacy of drawing or refinement of taste; on the contrary, technique improved steadily in every way, and at the same time the artistic instinct became more sure. Of the many fine books of this period, which have survived to the present day, only a very small selection can be mentioned here; most of these are Psalters, but a

---

[1] No. 107. See M. R. James, *Catalogue* (2 plates); Burl. F.A. Club, No. 80, pl. 69.

[2] Warner, *Reprod.*, iii, 13.

ILLUMINATED MANUSCRIPTS

rival was already beginning to appear in the Book of Hours, afterwards by far the most popular of illuminated manuscripts. The British Museum possesses two good examples of the latter class in Eg. 1151[1] and Harl. 928, both very small books, and both profusely decorated with dogs, rabbits, birds, and grotesques, either placed on bar-borders or filling the margins. Eg. 1151 has no large miniatures, but instead there are exquisite little historiated initials at the beginnings of the several offices, hardly to be surpassed for minuteness of detail and delicacy of execution. The figures, set against finely diapered backgrounds, are drawn in very fine black outline, the faces and some of the draperies left white. Tradition not having yet fixed the range of subjects for illustrating the Horae, the artist has sometimes given us delightful scenes of contemporary life, e.g. on f. 47 we have a charming little picture of musicians playing while a youth and two ladies dance. Harl. 928 begins, like the Psalters, with a series of full-page miniatures of the life of Christ; these, like the historiated initials in the text, are less delicate and finished, more archaic in style, than the paintings in Eg. 1151; but the grotesques which are scattered over the margins are full of variety and humour.

Interesting though these little volumes are, however, they are completely eclipsed by the splendid Psalters executed about the same time. Foremost among these is a magnificent book in the Duke of Rutland's library,[2] written about the middle of the century and decorated as far as Psalm cx with extraordinary wealth and profusion. One of its special features is that six of the psalms have full-page or nearly full-page miniatures prefixed; all finely painted and elaborately finished, though varying considerably in style and merit. The most beautiful by far is the picture of Saul aiming a javelin at David: the faces are delicately drawn and full of expression, especially that of a slender graceful woman who stands beside

---

[1] Warner, *Reprod.*, i, 12.
[2] *New Pal. Soc.*, pl. 64–6; Burl. F.A. Club, No. 43, pl. 41.

ENGLISH ILLUMINATION, 13TH CENT.

the infuriated king, her hand uplifted in gentle protest. Expressive faces and gracefully modelled figures are noticeable again in the miniature of Balaam and the angel, where the ass (apart from its blue colour) is depicted with a spirited naturalism not often found at so early a date. The Jacob's Ladder miniature has something of the charm of these two; and that of David playing on an organ is remarkable both for the rare interest of the subject to historians of music, and also for the vigorous, well-modelled figure of the youth who works the bellows. These six psalms and three others have large illuminated initials, the first eight enclosing miniatures, the last (Ps. cx) filled with conventional foliage ornament. The Calendar has the usual two roundels for each month, containing the zodiacal signs and occupation-pictures on burnished gold backgrounds. Psalm i has a splendid initial-page: the framework of the "B" formed by two long-necked dragons with tails ending in convolutions of foliage, and by two lions back to back, with men astride both lions and dragons, fighting the latter or seizing one another by the hair; the loops historiated with David as Harpist and the Judgment of Solomon; between the "B" and the rectangular frame, and at the four corners of the latter, are seven roundels of the Creation and Fall. The other psalms have finely illuminated initials, sometimes enclosing figures, but more often filled with decorative designs of foliage. The borders are not of the typical bar-border kind, but consist of a broad vertical band of gold, or of blue and red covered with white tracery, running down the left-hand side of the page and having the gold verse-initials set within it, with dragons, birds, or other designs at the terminations; helping to enhance the rich, ornate appearance of the book. A far more striking feature, however, of the Rutland Psalter is the abundance, variety, and excellence of its marginal decoration: coloured drawings of single figures or small groups, sometimes exquisitely graceful, always instinct with life and humour, fill the lower margins of many pages; besides the usual gro-

ILLUMINATED MANUSCRIPTS

tesques, animals, and fanciful creatures such as mermaids and centaurs, there are illustrations of the games, pastimes, and ordinary pursuits of everyday contemporary life—chess-playing, wrestling, tumbling, etc.—as precious to the antiquary as they are delightful to the ordinary beholder.

The leading characteristics of English illumination at the close of the thirteenth century are well seen in two manuscripts now in the British Museum, which were both not improbably executed in a Dominican house, perhaps the Blackfriars in London, viz. the famous Tenison Psalter[1] and the Ashridge Petrus Comestor;[2] although neither of them contains any large miniatures. The Tenison Psalter, so called because it once belonged to Archbishop Tenison, was originally intended, as the arms on the first page show, for presentation to Alphonso, son of King Edward I, on his marriage with the Count of Holland's daughter Margaret; but the abrupt change after the first quire to a more commonplace style of decoration has led to the inference that the illumination of the book was interrupted by the young prince's death in 1284, a few days after the sealing of the marriage contract, and that its completion was afterwards entrusted to inferior artists. In its present state the volume begins with three pages of finely executed figures of saints; but these, like the small miniatures of the life of Christ which fill the next three pages, are later insertions, and we are here concerned only with the opening quire of the Psalter text itself. The first page is framed in a gold-edged band of tiny lozenges, alternately blue and crimson; on this border, and in the margins outside, are exquisitely painted birds —gull, bullfinch, etc., drawn and coloured with scientific accuracy, and standing in the most lifelike attitudes—also other figures, lion, leopard, an ape shooting a crane, and at the foot of the page a dainty little David slinging a stone at Goliath; David also appears as harpist in the

[1] Add. 24686. See *Pal. Soc.*, i, 196; Thompson, p. 39, pl. 12; Warner, *Illum. MSS.*, pl. 22, and *Reprod.*, iii, 17.
[2] Roy. 3 D. vi. See *New Pal. Soc.*, pl. 13.

PSALTER OF PRINCE ALPHONSO. ENGLISH, 1284

BRIT. MUS. ADD. 24686

ENGLISH ILLUMINATION, 13TH CENT.

initial "B," a gracefully posed, well-proportioned figure set on a background of patterned gold. The succeeding pages, though less elaborate, are decorated in the same delicate and perfectly finished manner;[1] they have only partial bar-borders, ending in curved and leafy stems, and supporting a great variety of charming and amusing groups or single figures: a monkey riding on a grotesque bird's back, a merwoman suckling her young, a lady stag-hunting, etc.

The Petrus Comestor (Roy. 3 D. vi) was given to Ashridge College by its founder, Edmund, Earl of Cornwall (d. 1300), and must have been executed for him in or soon after 1283. It is therefore contemporary with the Tenison Psalter, to which it bears a striking resemblance, though a much larger volume; having the same cusped and foliated bar-borders, the same admirably drawn and painted birds, animals, and grotesques. In one respect it is even richer in decoration, for each book has a large initial enclosing a finely executed miniature.

Some of the most beautiful examples of thirteenth century English illumination are copies of the Apocalypse; no mention has been made of them in this brief sketch, as they will be discussed later on in the chapter devoted to the Apocalypse manuscripts of various countries and periods, which form a distinct class.

[1] See pl. xxiv.

CHAPTER XI

FRENCH, FLEMISH, AND GERMAN ILLUMINATION IN THE THIRTEENTH CENTURY

THERE are few facts more striking in the history of illumination than the sudden emergence of France, about the beginning of the thirteenth century, from the comparative obscurity in which she had lain ever since the decay of Carolingian art, and her rapid advance to the leading position which she occupied from the time of S. Louis (1226-70) until the middle of the fifteenth century. Many causes must have combined to bring about this remarkable result, and it would be impossible to analyse them fully in a brief sketch like the present; two things, however, may be suggested as probable factors. In the first place, the advent of a strong ruler in Philip Augustus (1180-1223) removed an obstacle to the progress of peaceful arts by reducing the country to a more settled and orderly condition; and secondly, the growing importance of Paris as the French capital, and of its University as one of the chief European centres of learning, drew artists and students thither from all parts, and created a great demand for book-production there. For the decoration of books, English artists were perhaps employed at first to some extent; at all events, there is a very close resemblance between French and English work during the greater part of the thirteenth century, in the early stages of Gothic illumination, before the French schools had evolved that distinct national style which continued to develop for nearly a couple of centuries, producing in its various phases a succession of manuscripts of surpassing loveliness.

The best representative of the early period is the

FRENCH ILLUMINATION, 13TH CENT.

Ingeburge Psalter[1] at Chantilly, executed in or shortly before 1213 for Ingeburge, the ill-used wife of Philip Augustus, perhaps as a memorial of her reconciliation with her husband after twenty years of estrangement. The style of the miniatures shows a strong English influence; austere and simple types, rich colour, a general impression of splendour and severity. The twenty-seven pages of preliminary paintings, mostly two on a page, on burnished gold backgrounds, illustrate scenes from the Old Testament, the Life of Christ, Pentecost, the Last Judgment, the Burial and Coronation of the Virgin, and the legend of her deliverance of Theophilus from the toils of the devil. Their subjects point to a connection with the so-called S. Louis Psalter at Leyden, mentioned in chapter vii;[2] but the style is more advanced, with less stiffness and a greater attempt at grace and gentleness of expression, and is altogether much nearer to that of another English manuscript, the early thirteenth century Psalter Roy. 1 D. x.[3] As in that book, and in most Psalters of the thirteenth century, whether French or English, the Calendar is decorated with medallions of the zodiacal signs and figures symbolical of the occupations proper to each month, the text of the Psalms with a full-page *Beatus vir* and initials enclosing small miniatures of the life of David. There is no direct evidence as to where the Ingeburge Psalter was executed, but the saints' names in Calendar and Litany indicate the north of France, possibly Paris itself.

Closely related to the Ingeburge Psalter, and, like it, showing strong affinity to English art in general and to the Leyden S. Louis Psalter in particular, is the Arsenal MS. 1186;[4] a Psalter formerly preserved in the Sainte

---

[1] Described by the Duc d'Aumale, *Musée Condé, Chantilly. Cabinet des Livres. MSS.*, vol. i, 1900, pp. 9-12. See too L. Delisle, *Notice de douze livres royaux*, 1902, pp. 1-17, pl. 1-3.

[2] Above, p. 141.   [3] Noticed above, p. 176.

[4] All its miniatures have been reproduced by H. Martin, *Psautier de St. Louis et de Blanche de Castille* (*Joyaux de l'Arsenal, I* [1909]). See too Delisle, *12 livres roy.*, pp. 27-35, pl. 8.

ILLUMINATED MANUSCRIPTS

Chapelle, and executed (according to an ancient and credible tradition) for Blanche of Castile, the pious and devoted mother of S. Louis, probably between the date of her marriage in 1200 and her husband's accession as Louis VIII in 1223. In the arrangement of its preliminary miniatures this manuscript follows the method used in the contemporary English Psalter, Lansdowne 420, described in chapter x,[1] most of them being enclosed in medallions, two of which, slightly interlaced, fill the page. The subjects are nearly identical with those of the Ingeburge Psalter; but artistically the work hardly reaches quite so high a level, its manner being less large and spacious, more minute. The page devoted to the Crucifixion and Descent from the Cross is specially interesting as containing one of the earliest appearances of the symbolical representation of the Old and New Dispensations, which became so popular in Gothic art: the former, a tottering woman, holds a broken lance in one hand, while the Tables of the Law fall from the other; the latter is a woman standing erect, holding cross and chalice. The initials to the Psalms are mostly historiated with the usual subjects; but the "D" of Psalm ci has a lady kneeling before an altar—probably a portrait of Blanche herself.

These two manuscripts show the high-water mark of French illumination at this period. The average work was of course greatly inferior, as may be seen, for instance, in a Missal[2] written in 1218 by an Amiens clerk named Geroldus, in an unidentified abbey dedicated to SS. Stephen and Martin, and probably situated in the north-east of France. Little or no advance is apparent here on the art of the twelfth century, especially in the one large miniature, a full-page Crucifixion, prefixed as usual to the Canon, and characterized chiefly by coarse heavy drawing and hard dull colouring. Less unpleasing, but equally primitive, are the few historiated initials; and the

---

[1] Above, p. 179.
[2] Brit. Mus., Add. 17742. See *Pal. Soc.*, ii, 194.

FRENCH ILLUMINATION, 13th CENT.

decorative initials, filled with intertwined foliage-stems, lions, greyhounds, etc., have little to distinguish them from those found in late twelfth century books such as the great Bibles described in chapter viii.

Pre-Gothic crudity still lingers in the miniatures of the Vie de S. Denis,[1] executed in 1250 at the great abbey founded in his honour; graphic, clear, and forcible though they be, viewed merely as illustrations of the narrative. They naturally challenge comparison with the late twelfth century English pictures of the life of S. Cuthbert;[2] but in point of artistic finish they fall far short of the earlier work. The fact is that about this time illumination was ceasing to be the monopoly of the religious orders, and was beginning to grow into a recognized and organized craft. Names of illuminators begin to appear in records; and though it happens but rarely that the work of an individual can be identified, there can be no doubt that most of the finely illuminated manuscripts which France, and more particularly Paris, soon began to produce in such abundance, were executed by these professional painters, and not by monks or clerics.

At the same time secular subjects naturally began to claim a larger share of the miniaturist's attention. Reference has been made in chapter x to the vogue which illustrated Herbals and Bestiaries enjoyed in the twelfth and thirteenth centuries; and another class of scientific picture-book, more strictly scientific and therefore far less popular and numerous, is of too great interest to be passed over in silence. The great majority of medieval text-books of medicine and surgery have no illustrations at all, but some contain diagrams carefully drawn in outline, and a few have fully illuminated pages in gold and colours. The British Museum possesses an admirable specimen of this last class in Sloane 1977, a French translation of Roger of Parma's Treatise on Surgery,

---

[1] Bibl. Nat., nouv. acq. fr. 1098. Reproduced in 1906, *Vie et Hist. de St. Denys*, with preface by H. Omont.
[2] Above, p. 140.

ILLUMINATED MANUSCRIPTS

written about the middle of the thirteenth century. At the beginning are sixteen full-page miniatures, each divided into nine compartments,[1] and planned so as to combine professional instruction with a reminder of the homage due to religion: the three topmost compartments containing scenes from the life of Christ, etc., painted on gold or diapered grounds under trefoil-arched canopies, and forming a complete series from the Annunciation to the Last Judgment; while the remaining compartments are filled with illustrations of surgical treatment, on plain blue or lake grounds. Farther on in the volume are four pages, each in twelve compartments, entirely devoted to surgery, preceded by a full-page representation of the master and his pupil in the dispensary. The delicate and expressive draughtsmanship of these little pictures is a delight to the layman, while members of the faculty find an added joy, not unmixed with surprise, in recognizing their scientific soundness and accuracy.

Still, despite the occasional production of such works as this and other secular writings (histories, romances, *chansons de geste* and other poems) in a decorated form, theology and liturgy continued to supply the principal field for the exercise of the illuminator's craft. In France, as in England, copies of the Latin Bible were produced in great numbers; but these volumes are for the most part interesting as curiosities, from the exquisite minuteness of script and figure-initials, rather than strictly beautiful or important in relation to the development of art. There is no need, therefore, to add to what has been said on this subject in chapter x, beyond mentioning one single example of a French Bible. Add. 35085 in the British Museum, written in a Dominican house in France (perhaps at Clermont in Auvergne, where it was in the sixteenth century) about the year 1250, is an excellent specimen of the most compressed type, its pages measuring but five inches by three; its Jesse-tree

---

[1] See pl. xxvii; Warner, *Reprod.*, i, 21.

PLATE XXV

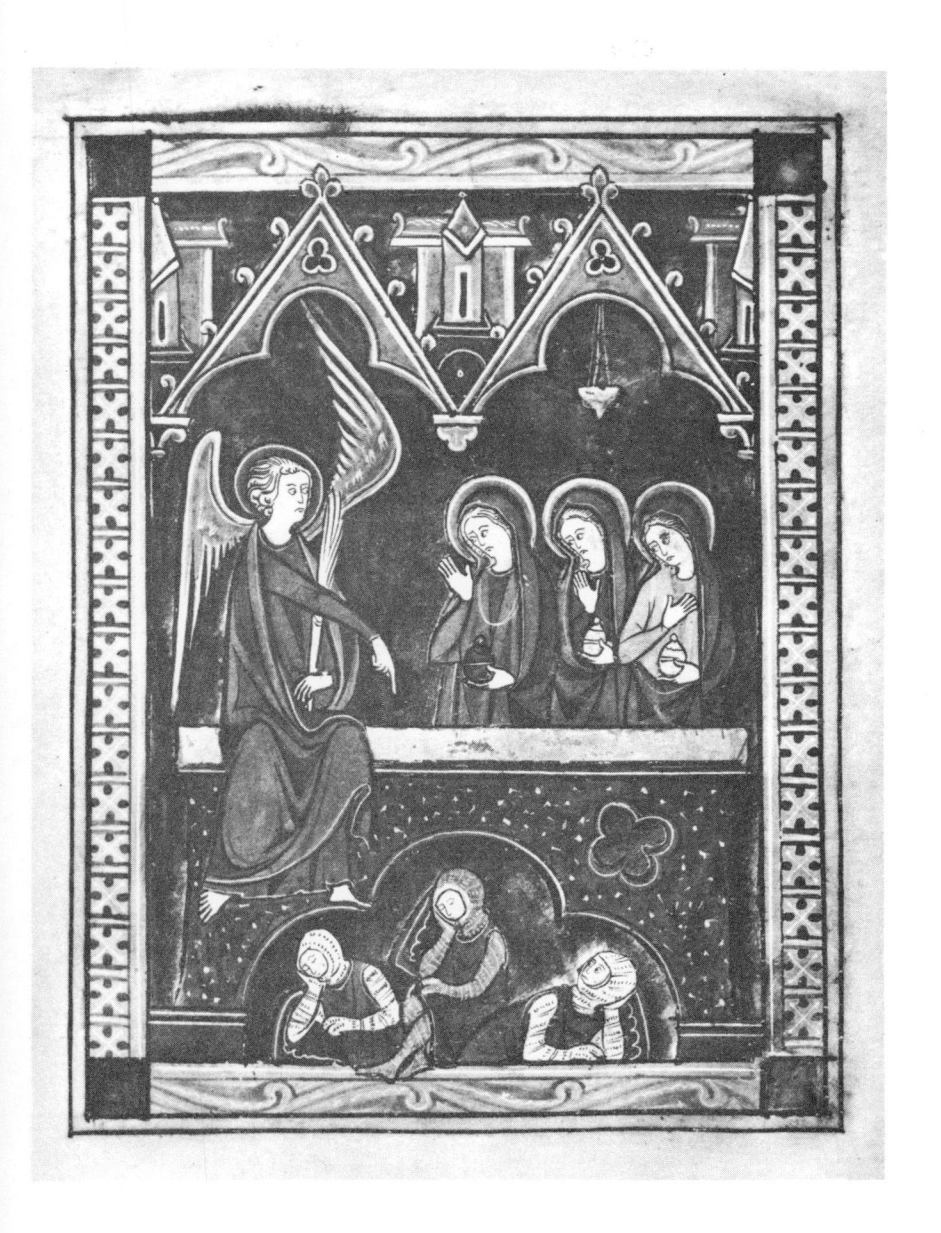

PSALTER. FRENCH, XIIITH CENT.
BRIT. MUS., ADD. 17868

FRENCH ILLUMINATION, 13TH CENT.

and its tiny miniature-initials, with architectural backgrounds and partial bar-borders usually ending in a single leaf, are marvellous in their combination of accuracy and softness.

Far more important artistically are the Psalters, among which are nearly all the finest manuscripts of this period. Royal 2 B. ii,[1] written for an inmate of an abbey of nuns, perhaps near Nantes, is a good example of the work of the middle of the century. It has no full-page miniatures; but the Calendar squares and medallions are finely painted, and eight of the psalms have large initials enclosed in diapered rectangles, and containing exquisite miniatures on backgrounds of burnished gold. These are thoroughly characteristic, and show at a glance with what speed and sureness French illumination had already developed: in the minuteness of the execution, the slender delicacy of the figures, the rich harmony of the colouring. The modelling of the draperies is partly obtained by slight deepening of the local colour, partly by fine black pen-lines, which are also used for the details of the pale and often really beautiful faces.

Slightly later in date, and more advanced in technique, is Add. 17868,[2] a Psalter executed certainly in Northern France, perhaps at Rheims.[3] In its preliminary series of eighteen full-page miniatures of the life of Christ, on grounds of raised and brilliantly burnished gold, we have a collection of true Gothic types: slender, pale-faced, sweet though formal personages, now far removed from the crudely outlined figures of the earlier time. The architectural ornament too is typical of Gothic art, and particularly of that branch of it which flourished in France at this period: trefoil-arched gables supported by very slender columns. Besides the usual historiated initials, the text of the Psalter is decorated with bar-

---

[1] Warner, *Illum. MSS.*, pl. 24, and *Reprod.*, ii, 19.
[2] Pl. xxv. See too Warner, *Illum. MSS.*, pl. 25, and *Reprod.*, i, 20.
[3] See Vitzthum, *Die Pariser Miniaturmalerei von der Zeit des hl. Ludwig bis zu Philipp von Valois*, 1907, p. 56.

borders, supporting delicious little manikins, rabbits, and other figures, on almost every page. In short, without being absolutely first-rate of its kind, this book represents admirably the average of its class—and that an exceptionally charming one.

For the very best work of the time we must turn to the productions of the Paris school, and particularly to two exquisite little Psalters which are closely associated with S. Louis himself.[1] The more complete of these, now in the Bibliothèque Nationale (lat. 10525),[2] was made for him in Paris between the years 1253 and 1270; the other, an almost exact replica, whose mutilated remains are preserved in Mr. Yates Thompson's collection, was made, evidently in the same place and about the same time, for a lady whom Mr. S. C. Cockerell[3] has identified with Isabelle, sister of S. Louis and foundress of Longchamp Abbey, where she lived from 1260 until her death ten years later. The Paris book has no fewer than seventy-eight full-page miniatures of Old Testament subjects at the beginning; only six of the corresponding series remain in the Yates Thompson MS. Both books are remarkable, among other things, for their exquisite architectural backgrounds, consisting in every instance of two or four bays of a Gothic interior, with gables, wheel or quatrefoil windows, and fretted arcadings and pinnacles above; forming as it were a scenic setting before which the personages of Bible-history play their parts like actors in the miracle-plays, which were actually performed in churches. These personages indeed, full of that gentle and ingenuous gaiety of which Gothic painters held the secret, seem less historical characters than the delighted actors of a pious play. One thinks of a Morality, or of the "Gestes" of Moses, Abraham, or Solomon—not of the solemn periods of the

---

[1] See Haseloff, *Les Psautiers de St. Louis*, 1900 (*Mém. de la Soc. Nat. des Antiquaires de France*, lix, pp. 18–42); Delisle, *12 livres roy.*, pp. 37–51, pl. 9–12.

[2] Omont, *Psautier de St. Louis. Reproduction des 86 miniatures* [1902].

[3] *Psalter and Hours of Isabelle of France*, 1905.

vores. Cum producunt
iam ex se fructum: sci
tis qm prope est estas.
Ita et uos cum uideritis
hec fieri: scitote quoni
am prope est regnum
dei. Amen dico uobis:
quia non preteribit ge
neratio hec. donec oi
a fiant. Celum z terra
transibit:
uba autem
mea: non
transient.
fiz. iiij. S.
Mathm.
N illo tx:
Dixit
ihs turbis
et discipu
lus suis. A
men dico
uobis: n
surrexit i
ter natos

mulierum maior iohe
baptista. Qui aut mi
nor est in regno celo
rum: maior est illo. A
diebz autem iohannis
baptiste usqz nunc reg
num celoz uim pati
tur. et uiolenti rapi
unt illud. Omnes e
nim pphe z lex: usqz
ad iohem pphauerunt.
Et si uultis recipere io
hannes ipse est heli
as qui uenturus est.
Qui ht aures audi
endi audiat. fiz. vij.
Initiu sci euuangly. S.
Marci.
Rincipium euuan
gely
ihu xpisti fi
ly dei. sicut
scriptum est

GOSPEL LECTIONARY. PARIS, LATE XIIIth CENT.

BRIT. MUS. ADD. 17341

FRENCH ILLUMINATION, 13TH CENT.

Vulgate text. The grave, ascetic faces met with in paintings of the time of Philip Augustus are replaced by gentler, more rounded and cheerful types; showing how the simple and joyous spirit of S. Francis, "the little troubadour of God," had penetrated to the arts, and banished the awe and terror with which the older miniaturists approached the sacred mysteries.

The Little Psalter of S. Louis and its companion represent the highest achievement of thirteenth century illumination in France. In the treatment of the face and figure they are indeed in advance of their time, and most of their contemporaries still retain something of primitive austerity. This is noticeable in a fine Gospel-lectionary in the British Museum (Add. 17341),[1] of the latter part of the thirteenth century. It follows the use of Paris, where it was evidently written, being a copy of a slightly earlier book which was given by S. Louis to the Sainte Chapelle, and is now in the Bibliothèque Nationale (lat. 17326). Its decoration is restricted to miniature-initials with partial borders attached; the initial " I," which occurs most frequently (in the prefatory phrase " In illo tempore"), being an oblong frame, sometimes of the full height of the column of script, enclosing one or more miniatures illustrating the text, with lacertines, foliage-scrolls, and other conventional ornament filling the rest of the frame. Though exaggeratedly long and attenuated, the figures are not ungraceful, and the draperies are now softly and realistically modelled by means of gradations of colour. A marked advance is perceptible in the bar-borders, which end in light and delicate leafy sprays, and on which are placed exquisite little figures of rabbits, birds, and grotesques. The foliate scroll-work inside the initial-frames is finely finished, and already foreshadows the rich designs which fill the margins of fifteenth century Horae.

Much more primitive is the art of the Moralized Bible,

---

[1] Pl. xxvi. See too Warner, *Illum. MSS.*, pl. 26, and *Reprod.*, ii, 20; Vitzthum, pl. 5, 6.

ILLUMINATED MANUSCRIPTS

a vast compilation in four volumes, two in the British Museum (Harl. 1526-7),[1] one at Paris (Bibl. Nat., lat. 1150), and one at Oxford (Bodl. 270b); forming one member of a large family of picture-books for religious instruction.[2] Every page has two narrow columns of text and two wide ones of miniatures: the text-column consisting of two short passages from the Bible, each followed by a moralization or allegorical interpretation; the picture-column, of four illustrative paintings on gold grounds in medallions placed one below the other, the spaces between them and their oblong frame being covered with a diaper pattern. These pictures are well adapted for their purpose, the scenes being depicted with unmistakable clearness and force; but as works of art they compare ill with the beautiful books we have been considering, the figures being stumpy and badly proportioned, the drawing heavy, with hard black outlines, the colouring harsh and inharmonious, and the technique absolutely flat. The British Museum possesses an uncoloured copy of the same work,[3] perhaps a little later in date, and of much greater artistic merit. Here the illustrations, again eight on a page, are square instead of round, and are freely and crisply drawn in brown ink without any use of colour. Simple, expressive, dramatic, they tell their stories apparently without effort, yet always with effect. Charming female types, with draped heads; a majestic lady with a chalice, typifying the Church; plump monks and bishops; bearded persons in conical hats—these and other delightful figures beflower the pages and give a mixed but altogether pleasing impression of brisk narrative, popular theology, and sure and easy draughtsmanship.

Of the many fine liturgical manuscripts produced in the closing years of the century, one of the most interesting is a Book of Hours at Nuremberg (Stadtbibl., Solger in 4°, No. 4).[4] Its contents seem to indicate that it was

---

[1] Warner, *Illum. MSS.*, pl. 27, and *Reprod.*, i, 22.
[2] See Delisle, "Livres d'images," in *Hist. Litt. de la France*, xxxi, 213-85.
[3] Add. 18719.   [4] Vitzthum, pp. 47-54, pl. 9.

PLATE XXVII

SURGICAL TREATISE BY ROGER OF PARMA. FRENCH, XIIIth CENT.
BRIT. MUS. SLOANE 1977

written in England, or at all events for an English lady; the decoration, however, is essentially French in manner, and is evidently the work of an artist trained in France, if not actually a Frenchman. An inserted inscription at the end shows that about the year 1400 the book was given by King Charles [VI] of France to the Queen of England (probably Isabella, wife of Richard II, or Catherine, wife of Henry V, both being his sisters). Nothing is known of its earlier history, but its original owner was evidently a lady possessed of wealth as well as of excellent taste. Apart from the great beauty of its workmanship, the Nuremberg Horae is interesting by reason of the unusual composition of the full-page miniatures prefixed to the several Hours of the Virgin. These are divided into compartments, in which the Joyful and Dolorous Mysteries of Our Lady are represented side by side. Thus the Nativity and the Adoration of the Shepherds are balanced by the Arrest of Christ and His appearance before Pilate; the Annunciation and Visitation, by Christ bearing the Cross and being stripped by the soldiers; the Crucifixion, by the Ascension. The figures are painted on backgrounds of stippled gold; the faces are left white, and finished with a fine pen-line; the draperies are modelled by gradations of the local colours, in which vermilion, blue, and pink predominate. Before the Hours, there is a series of charming single figures of saints standing under canopies; these are more conventionalized than the scenes which follow, and are almost architectural in their studied Gothic pose.

Still greater perfection is shown in a beautiful collection of religious treatises, written and illuminated in France about the year 1300. At some unknown stage in its history this book was divided into two volumes, which parted company and found their way eventually, one into the British Museum, the other into Mr. Yates Thompson's library. The former, numbered Add. 28162,[1] contains the

---

[1] *Pal. Soc.*, i, 245, 246; Warner, *Illum. MSS.*, pl. 33, 34, and *Reprod.*, iii, 19.

ILLUMINATED MANUSCRIPTS

Somme le Roi, a very popular compendium of Catholic doctrine, which was composed in French prose for Philip III by his confessor, Frère Laurent, in 1279. The text, which is adorned with well-executed initials enclosing foliage-scrolls or figures, and prolonged into bar-borders with cusped or leafy terminations, is preceded by a series of full-page miniatures illustrating the Decalogue, the Creed, the cardinal virtues, and the seven deadly sins with their corresponding virtues. These last are allegorically presented, and sometimes followed by their Biblical types: Humility and Pride, for instance, by the Publican and Pharisee; Love and Hatred, by David and Jonathan, and by Saul casting a javelin at David; Mercy and Avarice,[1] by Abraham welcoming the three angels, and by the widow distributing her oil freely. These scenes are painted on backgrounds of burnished and patterned gold, and placed within Gothic arcades. The dominant colour is scarlet, which, combined with the gold ground, produces a very brilliant effect. The figures, though rather large for the size of the pictures, are charming, especially the Lady Amitié in her garden, the widow pouring out her oil, and the three adorable angels who come to Abraham disguised as pilgrims with staff and wallet, but wearing the nimbus and rainbow-coloured wings without any attempt at concealment.

Mr. Yates Thompson's volume[2] has only four full-page miniatures; but the first three of these are superior to anything in the Somme le Roi, having a beauty of conception, a delicacy and refinement of colouring, and a perfection of technique, which mark them out as among the most exquisite productions of the illuminator's art. Two of them illustrate the Sainte Abbaye, the allegorical tract with which the volume opens. The first depicts the ideal state of the mystical Abbey of the Holy Ghost: Madame Charité the abbess and Sainte Sapience the

[1] Plate xxviii.
[2] See M. R. James, *Descriptive Catalogue*, 1898, No. 40, pp. 225-32; H. Y. Thompson, *Illustrations*, vol. i, 1907, pl. 6-9.

PLATE XXVIII

SOMME LE ROI. FRENCH, CIRCA 1300
BRIT. MUS. ADD. 28162

FLEMISH ILLUMINATION, 13TH CENT.

prioress kneel in prayer, and Honesté with her birch rod admonishes the novices who stand before her with their lesson-book; above the abbey is a representation of the Trinity and the heavenly host. The next picture is in two compartments: in the upper, a priest celebrates Mass in the abbey church before the assembled sisterhood, the nun-sacristan pulling vigorously at the bell-ropes; the lower compartment represents a priest and clerks, fully vested, walking in procession, followed by the abbess and her nuns. The third page illustrates another tract in the volume, the "Livres de lestat de lame," and shows the three states of good souls—penitence, devotion, and contemplation—in the person of a nun who confesses, prays, and kneels in ecstasy before a vision of the Trinity. There is a wonderful dreamy charm about these exquisite miniatures of conventual life, with their subtle harmonies of colour, the subdued tints of the nuns' habits contrasting effectively with the splendour of the heavenly personages and the delicately coloured architectural backgrounds. We have here, in fact, the work of a great artist in full sympathy with his subject; while the remaining miniature in this book, like all those in the Somme le Roi, more brilliant yet somehow lacking in poetic flavour, is only an admirable example of one of the most perfect schools known in the history of illumination.

Flemish illumination in the thirteenth century developed on similar lines to that of England and France, though at first with lagging footsteps. Such books as the Missal of S. Bavon's, Ghent (Brit. Mus., Add. 16949), written about the year 1200, show little promise of the glory which awaited Flemish painting. Its decorated initials, of white foliage-scrolls on pale blue fields powdered with white spots, are still of the regular twelfth century type; and its one full-page miniature,[1] a Crucifixion prefixed to the Canon of the Mass, is archaic, stiff, and lifeless, void alike of realism, grace, and impressiveness. This manuscript can only be regarded as typical

[1] Warner, *Reprod.*, ii, 34.

ILLUMINATED MANUSCRIPTS

of Flemish art at the very beginning of the century; but until well on in the second half the figure-drawing was uncouth and the technique altogether far behind that of the French and English schools. The British Museum possesses a good many Psalters of this period of gradual transition from comparative barbarism to real artistic excellence; but none of them can be compared with the splendid productions of contemporary French or English miniaturists. One of the most important of these is Royal 2 B. iii, executed apparently towards the middle of the century, certainly after 1228, as S. Francis occurs in the Calendar. Its full-page miniatures[1] of the life of Christ, some of which are interspersed among the Psalms, instead of being prefixed in the usual manner, have something of the largeness and simplicity found in English work a few decades earlier; but the dignity and feeling, which in the latter go so far to make up for faulty drawing, are altogether lacking here. The figures, heavily outlined in black, are stiff, ill-proportioned, and badly drawn; the pallid faces are mostly of unlovely, almost grotesque type; the grouping shows no attempt at effective composition. As to colouring, the backgrounds of raised and highly burnished gold brighten up the pages, but the general effect is sombre, hard, and streaky. A very dark blue, characteristic of thirteenth century Flemish painting, predominates; and on this and the other colours, which are for the most part pale and dingy, white paint has been applied lavishly for highlights.

The Flemish cycle of Calendar-pictures, as shown in Roy. 2 B. iii and other Psalters of this period, has one or two peculiar features. The signs of the zodiac are not represented as a rule; and the occupation-pictures, though containing single figures only, are comparatively large in scale, and are painted on blue or pink grounds framed in gold. The subjects too are peculiar in some respects, notably those for February (a woman holding a great

[1] See pl. xxix.

PLATE XXIX

PSALTER. FLEMISH, XIIITH CENT.
BRIT. MUS. ROY. 2 B III.

FLEMISH ILLUMINATION, 13TH CENT.

Candlemas taper), June (a man carrying a load of wood), and October (grape-picking). This distinctively Flemish series appears, for instance, in Add. MSS. 19899 and 24683, two Psalters of about the same date as Roy. 2 B. iii, but of even ruder, more archaic technique; also in Roy. 2 A. iii, a very small book, executed apparently in or near Maestricht. In this last-named manuscript, however, the tiny figures are on gold grounds in medallions, and the treatment shows something already of the refinement and delicacy typical of the best thirteenth century art. Harl. 2930, another Maestricht Psalter, probably of slightly later date, has no Calendar-decoration, but its miniatures and historiated initials and bar-borders, with birds and grotesques, form an interesting link between the crudity of the earlier period and the finished excellence of the school now beginning to approach maturity. Its colouring is rich and brilliant, but the effect is spoilt by the predominance of a vivid and unpleasant crimson.

The Maestricht artists seem to have worked by preference on a small scale; the masterpiece of the school, a Book of Hours of the very end of the century,[1] is even more diminutive than these two Psalters, its leaves measuring only $3\frac{3}{4}$ by $2\frac{3}{4}$ inches. This is indeed a wonderful little book. Its miniatures of the Childhood and Passion are charming, with exquisitely drawn figures, well posed and carefully draped, the faces finely outlined with the pen. It is in the marginal ornament,[2] however, that its special interest lies. Bible-history, legends of the saints, folk-lore, scenes in daily life, are illustrated with an exuberance of fancy and a delightful inconsequence thoroughly typical of this fascinating phase in the history of art, when austerity and genial humour strove for the mastery. To enumerate even the principal subjects would be impossible here: we have the monkeys' castle besieged by foxes with catapults and other engines; the fox shamming death; the three living and three dead

---

[1] Stowe 17. See Warner, *Reprod.*, ii, 35.
[2] See pl. xxxviii.

kings; an abbess spinning, whilst her white cat brings her a new spindle in its mouth; wrestlers, tilting knights, tumblers, musicians. The patroness of the book, a lady in an ermine cloak, appears frequently—once in a full-page miniature, kneeling before a crucifix.

Another remarkable monument of Franco-Flemish art of this time is a little book which once formed part of the Sneyd Collection, and passed, on its dispersal, into the possession of Mr. Bernard Quaritch, for whom it was described by Dr. M. R. James.[1] Its contents are of a very miscellaneous character, consisting of legends, hortatory and other tracts, passages from the Bible and the Fathers, etc., put together somewhat after the fashion of the Hortus Deliciarum, and very richly illustrated. Its art has certain affinities with that of Stowe 17, but is more French in style. It opens with a series of full-page tinted drawings of scenes from the lives of the Hermits, including one very naïve and charming picture of an angel cooking a hermit's supper over an open fire. After this we have many illuminated illustrations of Christian dogma, the arts and sciences, and allegories of monastic discipline; and two long series of designs, the one intended as mystical representations of the attributes of the Trinity, the other as expositions of the symbolic meaning of the Song of Solomon. Many of the subjects are extremely rare, if not unique, in the history of illumination; so that even apart from the richness and ingenuity of the borders and grotesques with which the latter part of this delightful little volume is filled, its importance as a treasure-house of medieval symbolism can scarcely be over-rated. The colouring, with its almost exclusive use of white, gold, rose, deep blue, and scarlet, and the elaborately diapered and stippled backgrounds, do not differ markedly from those found in contemporary French work. In fact, Flemish illumination, so backward at the beginning of the century, had by its close thoroughly

[1] *Description of an Illuminated MS. of the Thirteenth Century*, 1904.

GERMAN ILLUMINATION, 13TH CENT.

absorbed the spirit of the French Gothic, and become less a distinct and native style than a branch of that great school of art.

In striking contrast to these minute volumes, so far as scale is concerned, is a great Antiphoner in three stately volumes, dated 1290, and emanating, as the researches of its present owner, Mr. Yates Thompson,[1] have proved, from the Cistercian nunnery of Beaupré near Grammont. Despite their large size, its historiated initials are not lacking in delicacy, and with its cusped and leafy borders and marginal figures show how thoroughly the new spirit had by now been assimilated. Especially charming in their demure grace are the kneeling patronesses, " Domicella de Viana " and " Domicella Clementia."

The Gothic movement, which produced such a remarkable development of the art of illumination in England, France, and Flanders during the thirteenth century, left Germany almost untouched. German miniaturists were content, for the most part, with the artistic formulae, compounded of Byzantine and Romanesque traditions, which had been elaborated during the twelfth century. They placidly repeated the old harsh, lifeless types, the hard flat technique, the crude and discordant scheme of colour, of the style which the Rhenish schools had brought to such perfection as it was capable of by the end of the twelfth century. In fact, Germany ceased to take a leading place in the history of book-decoration, and the subsequent course of German illumination becomes a matter of interest for the specialist rather than for the student of the art in general, and of its most beautiful forms in particular. Some mention should indeed be made of such fine manuscripts as the Weingarten Missals in Lord Leicester's library at Holkham,[2] and of the numerous and exceedingly interesting group

---

[1] See his *Descriptive Catalogue*, iii, 1907, pp. 55–74 (No. 83); Burl. F.A. Club, Nos. 61–2, pl. 54.

[2] Nos. 36, 37. See L. Dorez, *Les MSS. à peintures de la bibl. de Lord Leicester*, 1908, pl. 5–8, 12–21.

ILLUMINATED MANUSCRIPTS

of early thirteenth century Psalters which Dr. Haseloff[1] has subjected to so searching a study, and which is represented in the British Museum by Add. 17687[2] and 18144. This must suffice, however, in a brief sketch like the present.[3]

[1] *Eine thüringisch-sächsische Malerschule des 13. Jahrhunderts*, 1897.
[2] Warner, *Illum. MSS.*, pl. 19, and *Reprod.*, i, 41.
[3] For fuller treatment of German thirteenth century miniature see Haseloff in Michel's *Hist. de l'Art*, ii, i, 359–71, and the bibliography on pp. 419–20.

CHAPTER XII

ILLUSTRATIONS OF THE APOCALYPSE

EXCEPT the Psalms and Gospels, no part of the Bible was more popular than the Apocalypse in the Middle Ages as a subject for pictorial illustration. Painters of the Carolingian period had already begun to find themes in it for some of their most interesting miniatures,[1] as we saw in chapter v; and a long series of compositions, illustrating the whole book, seems to have been devised about the same time. This series is found in manuscripts from the ninth century onwards, especially in the thirteenth and fourteenth centuries; usually in company with the complete Latin or vernacular text, often with a commentary in addition, but sometimes with nothing beyond descriptive legends written across the field of the pictures. So numerous, important, and distinctive a family do these manuscripts form that it seems most convenient to consider them as a separate class, irrespective of date or nationality.

The first appearance of a regular series of Apocalypse-pictures is in the illuminated copies of a Commentary on the Apocalypse, composed by the Spanish monk Beatus towards the end of the eighth century. These range in date from the ninth century to the thirteenth, and are all, or very nearly all, of Spanish origin.[2] In the history of illumination generally Spain occupies quite a secondary position; one might even say a negligible position, apart from these illustrations of the Apocalypse and the initial-

---

[1] See pl. xi.
[2] For a descriptive list see Delisle, *Mélanges de Paléographie et de Bibliographie*, 1880, pp. 117-47, supplemented by Konrad Miller, *Die ältesten Weltkarten*, Heft i, 1895, pp. 10-22, and by Dr. James and Dom Ramsay in the account of Mr. Yates Thompson's MS., cited below.

ILLUMINATED MANUSCRIPTS

ornaments (of a bizarre type, partly Merovingian and partly Celtic in style) found in the Mozarabic liturgical books and other manuscripts of the tenth to twelfth centuries.[1] In later times Spanish illumination was essentially derivative and imitative, French, Italian, and Flemish influence appearing in turn, or sometimes simultaneously, producing an oddly mixed and unsatisfactory result. It was not until illumination had ceased to exist as a living art that the great school of Spanish painters came into being.

Of the Beatus manuscripts, the oldest now extant is that in Mr. Yates Thompson's collection,[2] written A.D. 894 in a hitherto unidentified monastery dedicated to S. Michael; clearly in Spain, as is proved by the form of script (Visigothic minuscules), by certain peculiarities in spelling, and by the presence of marginal notes in Spanish. The cycle of pictures, however, most probably goes back a good deal earlier, for the contrast between the excellence of the compositions and the ineptitude of the technique suggests that the illustrator of this manuscript was a copyist rather than an original artist. Moreover, in all the manuscripts the illustrations of Beatus, and of S. Jerome's commentary on Daniel which usually follows it, are practically the same as to number and subject, showing plainly that all are derived from one common archetype, dating perhaps from the lifetime of Beatus himself. The British Museum possesses one of these Beatus-codices,[3] written in Silos Abbey between 1073 and 1091, and illuminated by Pedro the Prior, who finished his work in 1109; and its agreement with the Yates Thompson MS. is almost exact, despite the interval of more than two centuries which separates them. In style

---

[1] The British Museum has some characteristic examples in Add. 30844-6, 30850, and 30853, from Silos Abbey in the diocese of Burgos, and Add. 25600 (see *Pal. Soc.*, i, 95) from S. Pedro de Cardeña in the same diocese.

[2] No. 97, described very fully by Dr. James in the *Catalogue*, ii, pp. 304-30, with additional notes by Dom H. L. Ramsay on pp. 373-6.

[3] Add. 11695. See *Pal. Soc.*, i, 48-9; Férotin, *Hist. de l'abbaye de Silos*, 1897, pp. 264-9.

ILLUSTRATIONS OF THE APOCALYPSE

too, as well as subject, there is a great resemblance; the Silos manuscript is slightly less rude and primitive than its predecessor, but the general character is much the same in both, and either of them may be taken as typical of the whole group.[1]

So strange and barbarous is the art of these manuscripts, that one is reminded of the worst productions of the Celtic school. But while Celtic miniatures are generally cheerful in their grotesqueness, here we find an air of settled melancholy; dark and heavy colour accentuating the effect of coarse outlines and dull, gloomy faces. The figures are stiff and wooden, more like rudely made dolls than human beings; the faces are monotonous and ill-drawn, with low foreheads and large staring eyes; there is no attempt at modelling or perspective. The compositions, on the other hand, large and elaborate (many of them occupying the full page, and some extending over two pages), are often well planned and impressive. Moorish influence is seen in the uniform employment of the horseshoe arch in buildings, frames, and arcades; also, perhaps, in the horizontally striped backgrounds of red, yellow, dark blue, dark green, and other colours, a prominent feature in these paintings. The conventional ornament is far better than the figure-compositions, as so often happens in primitive art. Patterned frames, decorated with cable, plait, and knot, surround the most important miniatures; in the later manuscripts of the group great cruciform pages appear, and symbolic representations of the glorified Christ, obviously modelled on the emblematic designs of the Celtic and Carolingian Gospel-books, though never approaching their delicate exactitude. The initials and tail-pieces too deserve mention. Those in the Silos manuscript are often spirited and amusing: fishes, birds, beasts, and human forms, brightly coloured and sometimes very quaintly combined, form the initials;

---

[1] Another good example, one of the latest of the group, is MS. Lat. 8 in the John Rylands Library at Manchester. See *New Pal. Soc.*, pl. 167.

ILLUMINATED MANUSCRIPTS

among the tail-pieces are various exploits of Reynard the fox, besides figures of musicians, soldiers, etc.

With the thirteenth century begins that remarkable series of Gothic illustrations of the Apocalypse, of which MM. Delisle and Meyer have made so comprehensive and minute a survey.[1] Though the subjects are the same, the treatment in these later and more northerly manuscripts (mostly produced in England, France, or Flanders) is, as might be expected, very different from that of their semi-barbarous Spanish ancestors. In the best we find some of the most perfect examples of early Gothic painting, with a poetic fancy exercising itself on material of the most suggestive kind; in the worst, an abundance of that medieval humour which found such congenial expression in the gargoyles and grotesques of ecclesiastical sculpture.

These manuscripts must have been extremely numerous. M. Delisle mentions no less than fifty-nine, ranging in date from the beginning of the thirteenth to the end of the fifteenth century; and he describes many of them in full detail, especially the first sixteen, for which he gives a tabular list of all the miniatures. He divides them into two families, according to the subjects illustrated; but this classification cannot be rigidly applied, for many of the manuscripts which he assigns to the second family contain one or more of the scenes which he regards as distinguishing marks of the first. One might, no doubt, choose other principles of grouping, e.g. separating the illustrations in tinted outline from those painted in body-colour, or those which are accompanied by the text from those which merely bear scrolls with descriptive legends. Any such system, however, would be open to objection: the full truth as to the interdependence of these manuscripts which remain, and of the many more which must have perished, to say nothing of

---

[1] *L'Apocalypse en français*, 1901, forming an introduction to the facsimiles of the miniatures in Bibl. Nat. MS. fr. 403, published by the Société des anciens textes français.

ILLUSTRATIONS OF THE APOCALYPSE

their connection with Apocalypse-illustrations in other forms of art,[1] is too obscure and complicated a matter to be ascertained readily or stated tersely. No attempt can be made here, at any rate, to do more than call attention to one or two of the most important of these interesting specimens of the illustrative art of the Middle Ages.

Two excellent and closely related examples of the tinted outline class are the Bodleian MS. Auct. D. 4. 17[2] and the Paris MS. Bibl. Nat. fr. 403,[3] both produced in England about the beginning of the thirteenth century. They belong to what M. Delisle calls the first family, and begin and end with scenes from the life of S. John. The former contains no text beyond explanatory inscriptions in red and blue letters on the backgrounds of the miniatures, which fill the page, being usually divided into two compartments. No such inscriptions appear in the Paris MS., though blank tablets and scrolls evidently intended for their reception are in most of the miniatures; but the full text of the Apocalypse, with a commentary, both in French, occupies the lower half of each of the pictured pages. Leaning towards the grotesque rather than the poetical, these drawings are truly illustrative, unconstrained, and full of life. The type of figure is much the same in both manuscripts: large, rather elongated personages, angels and saints having sleek rounded faces, while devils, false witnesses, and executioners have rugged features, with extraordinary hooked noses. The compositions in the Oxford MS. have a tendency to be overcrowded, the artist's desire to illustrate every detail of his subject being stronger, apparently, than his instinct for spaciousness of design. The Paris MS. errs less in this respect. Amongst much that is grotesque, it has several impressive, some almost beautiful miniatures; especially the Marriage of

---

[1] See, for instance, Delisle's interesting chapter on the tapestries in Angers Cathedral, pp. clxxvi–cxci.

[2] Reproduced by the Roxburghe Club, *The Apocalypse of S. John the Divine*, ed. H. O. Coxe, 1876.

[3] Published in facsimile by the Soc. des. anc. textes fr., as noted above, p. 212.

the Lamb, which already shows signs of the delicate charm distinctive of the best Gothic art.

Akin to these two books is the British Museum MS. Add. 35166,[1] executed in England late in the thirteenth century. Though placed by Delisle in the second family, it includes the two series of scenes from the life of S. John (the second series unusually long), so it forms a link between the two families; it also contains a somewhat rare subject, "the woman drunken with the blood of the saints" (Apoc. xvii. 6), very graphically treated. The miniatures, which are drawn in outline and tinted in pale colours, fill only the upper half of each page, the lower half containing the full Latin text with a Latin commentary; there are no descriptive legends inside the frames of the pictures. The paintings are softer, more delicate and less crisp than those of the Oxford and Paris MSS.; the faces, mostly gentle to the point of weakness, are rendered expressive by skilful and delicate pen-work; the figures are long and slender, but not ungraceful; the draperies are well handled, with gradation of local colour as well as pen-strokes. Burnished gold is used for nimbi and other accessories, and parts of the backgrounds are painted red, blue or green in body-colour. There is less vivacity but more dignity, on the whole, than in the two earlier books.

Much more beautiful than any of these three, indeed one of the finest of all extant copies of the Apocalypse, is MS. R. 16. 2 in Trinity College, Cambridge.[2] Written in England, not improbably at S. Alban's, about the year 1230, this splendid manuscript is hardly surpassed by any of its contemporaries. Its ninety-one miniatures, while lacking the minute delicacy of the smaller designs which adorn the best French and English Psalters of the time, atone for this deficiency by the richness of their colouring and the dramatic force and vigour of their compositions.

[1] Warner, *Reprod.*, ii, 12.

[2] *New Pal. Soc.*, pl. 38–9. Reproduced for the Roxburghe Club, ed. M. R. James, 1910.

ILLUSTRATIONS OF THE APOCALYPSE

It is in the battle scenes, naturally, that the latter quality is displayed most effectively; the artists (for more hands than one are discernible) are less successful in their treatment of subjects of a more reposeful character. In fact, if we divide the Apocalypse MSS. into two classes accordingly as the grotesque or poetical imagination predominates, the Trinity MS. must be assigned to the former rather than the latter, though by no means void of single figures rich in delicate charm, such as the winged woman flying into the wilderness (xii. 14).

The poetical and devotional element is uppermost in Mr. Yates Thompson's beautiful manuscript,[1] written towards the end of the thirteenth century, and very profusely illuminated in England or the north of France. Like the Lambeth MS. 209, with which it is closely related, it contains the Latin text with the commentary of Berengaudus;[2] but it stands alone in the wealth of its decoration, having no fewer than 152 miniatures, which illustrate not only the usual cycle of subjects from the Vision itself, but also their scriptural and historical antitypes as set forth in the commentary. Interesting by reason of its symbolism, the book is also delightful from an artistic point of view, for its graceful figures, with naïve appealing expressions, and for the beauty and variety of its colouring, burnished gold and deep blue being freely used, as well as the more delicate harmonies of grey, green, and white.

The Lambeth Apocalypse[3] belongs to the same period, perhaps a trifle later, and was probably written and illuminated at S. Augustine's Abbey, Canterbury. It has seventy-eight half-page miniatures in plain banded frames,

---

[1] No. 55. See *Catalogue*, ii, pp. 20–39; H. Y. Thompson, *Lecture on some Eng. Illum. MSS.*, 1902, pp. 16–20, pl. 7–13; Delisle and Meyer, pp. xc–cvi, and Appendix, pl. 7–12.

[2] For other illustrated copies containing this commentary, though not artistically related to the above, see Burl. F.A. Club, Nos. 88, 89, pl. 74.

[3] No. 209 in the Archiepiscopal Library. See S. W. Kershaw, *Art Treasures of the Lambeth Library*, 1873, pp. 47–54 (2 plates); *Pal. Soc.*, ii, 195; Burl. F.A. Club, No. 87, pl. 73.

and at the end a series of tinted drawings of scenes in the life of Christ, miracles of the Virgin, and figures of saints. In the miniatures, pale and delicately drawn figures are contrasted against brilliant backgrounds of blue, purple, or stippled and burnished gold, usually consisting of a central panel framed in a broad border, the blue and purple sometimes diapered. The figures are slender and elegant, the angels being particularly graceful. The outlining and modelling of the flesh are in sepia, giving a much softer effect than the usual black ink; the drapery folds are indicated with light colours, chiefly grey, brown, and green. Specially pleasing is the figure of S. John, a tall slim person with curly hair and short beard, who appears, as usual, in every picture as spectator or interlocutor.

Less powerful and original than the Yates Thompson MS., but more delicately lovely, is Douce 180 in the Bodleian.[1] This exquisite book shows English painting of the late thirteenth century at its best; it has advanced beyond the formalism and severity of Early Gothic, and has not yet begun to grapple with the problems and subtleties of modern art. The white vellum backgrounds, soft pale colours, and careful space-filling, together with the sweet and gracious forms of the personages represented, give these miniatures a dainty, poetical, and altogether irresistible charm. Some of them are merely drawn in outline, in others the colouring and gilding have been left at various stages of unfinishedness. The angels are of monastic type, massive and dignified, with tonsured heads, grave and gentle expressions. One of the most delightful miniatures in the book is that of the vineyard,[2] where the successive incidents of Apoc. xiv. 17-20 are naïvely depicted in one composition, without a hint of division and yet with no overcrowding of the canvas: the angel with the sickle coming out of the temple, taking

---

[1] *Pal. Soc.*, ii, 77. The editors judged it of French origin, but linguistic considerations point to England. See Delisle and Meyer, p. cxxi.

[2] Pl. xxx.

t alius angelus exiuit de templo quod est in celo habens
et ipse falcem acutam. Et alius
angelus exiuit de altari qui habet
potestatem supra ignem et clamauit uoce magna ad eum qui habebat falcem acutam dicens. Mitte falcem acutam et uindemia uos
uinee terre. quoniam mature sunt
uue eius. Et misit angelus falcem
suam in terram et uindemiauit ui-
neam terre. Et misit in lacum ue-
dei magnum. et calcatus est lacus
extra ciuitatem: et exiuit sanguis
de lacu usq; ad frenos equorum p

stadia mille sexcenta. et cetera.

Et alter angelus exiuit de templo et clamauit uoce magna ad eum qui sedebat super nubem dicens.
mitte falcem tuam et mete. electos qui intrat terra laborant designat. per templum autem uni-
uersitas ipsius est: ecclesia designatur. Clamauit
ergo ad eum qui sedebat super nubem ut mit-
teret falcem suam in terram et meteret. quia sanc-
ti uiri uidentes mundum in maligno positum
cuiusq; miserias hominum deprecantur. ducit ut
regnum ter ueniat. in quo ab hominib; angustiis
liberata corpora pariter rapiente in eternum cum domino exultabunt. Similiter et alius angelus
qui exiuit de altari qui habebat potestatem. super igne
eandem significacionem habet quam et secundus
qui de templo exisse dictus est. Significat namq; e-
lectos electos in ierra uiuum laborantes. altare aute
etiam significat. sicut templum. per ignem uero
caritatem possumus intelligere. quam in cordib;
sanctorum spiritualib; fomentis spiritus sanctus
exurit. Super hunc ignem sanctam potestatem ha-
bere dicuntur. quia ipsi caritatem possident et pos-
sideantur ab ea. Iste ergo angelus clamauit ad ter-
cium angelum secundam falcem gerentem. que
xpm significasse diximus ut uindemiare bonos
uinee pro quod impii designantur. quia uisi
sunt uidentes condere genus humanum a demonib;
decipi. innocentes simpios seducere mundumq; seca...

ILLUSTRATIONS OF THE APOCALYPSE

his instructions from the angel at the altar, and cutting the clusters of grapes, while two small horses gaze somewhat apprehensively at the red stream which flows towards them. The serene, graceful, leisured dignity of the picture contrasts whimsically with the majestic terror of the text.

The best thirteenth century Apocalypse manuscripts are, as we have seen, of English origin; and fine examples continued to be produced in this country during the early years of the succeeding century, though none have survived which approach the perfection of their predecessors. Only three need be mentioned here, all in the British Museum. Roy. 19 B. xv[1] has seventy-two miniatures of varying size and of widely varying degrees of excellence; the best, by an artist whose hand is also recognizable in the famous Psalter of Queen Mary (Roy. 2 B. vii, to be noticed in chapter xiii), are quite charming. They are effective through simplicity rather than strength of colour, relying for effect on the contrast between backgrounds of soft red and blue, and white or faintly tinted figures delicately sketched in pen outline. The faces are rounded in contour and suave in expression, the figures graceful, though tending to an artificial statuesqueness of pose. Simplicity of composition as well as colour marks the happiest efforts of this artist, as in the exquisite design of the angel casting a millstone into the sea (xviii. 21). Roy. 15 D. ii,[2] unlike most of these manuscripts, is a volume of huge size, containing besides the Apocalypse a copy of the Anglo-Norman poem Lumière as Lais; a combination also found in the contemporary MS. B. 282 of the Royal Library at Brussels. It probably belonged to Greenfield nunnery in Lincolnshire, and its decoration, which consists mainly of initials containing miniatures or ornamental foliage, with cusped bar and line-and-leaf borders attached, is typical of the East Anglian school

---

[1] *Pal. Soc.*, i, 223; Thompson, *Eng. Illum. MSS.*, pp. 53–5, pl. 16; Warner, *Illum. MSS.*, pl. 30, and *Reprod.*, i, 13.

[2] Warner, *Reprod.*, ii, 13.

ILLUMINATED MANUSCRIPTS

which flourished in the first half of the fourteenth century. The figures in the miniatures have a certain family likeness to those of Roy. 19 B. xv, though decidedly inferior to the best work in that book; the backgrounds are mostly covered with a large diaper-pattern. The colour-scheme is harmonious and pleasant, but the technique is absolutely flat, without gradation or perspective; the drapery folds are indicated by heavy black lines. A great feature of East Anglian illumination is the use of foliage, treated with some attempt at naturalism, for initial and border ornament; and that occurs on almost every page of this manuscript. Add. 18633 is perhaps a little later than the two Royal MSS., but can hardly be assigned to a later date than the middle of the fourteenth century. It contains a paraphrase of the Apocalypse, in Anglo-Norman verse, which is found in some half-dozen illuminated copies ranging from the beginning to the middle of the century.[1] All the manuscripts of this group seem to be artistically as well as textually allied, and their archetype is clearly related to Bibl. Nat. fr. 403 with its hook-nosed devils. The art of Add. 18633 is not of a high order, but it is quite expressive as illustration. The backgrounds are mostly blue or pink, diapered, but are sometimes of stippled gold. On the whole the drawing is hard, the technique flat, the composition stiff; the architecture, however, is good and interesting. Silver is used for armour and other accessories.

Franco-Flemish Apocalypses are represented in the British Museum by two early fourteenth century manuscripts, Add. 22493 and 17333. The former, a fragment of four leaves, the upper half of each page filled by a miniature, is a fair sample of the average work of its school, with its neatly diapered backgrounds, its hard but clean and decided drawing, and its depth of colour, especially its dark blue. Much finer is the art of Add. 17333,[2] a really beautiful manuscript, which formerly

---
[1] See Delisle and Meyer, p. cxxiii; *Romania*, xxv, 178.
[2] Warner, *Illum. MSS.*, pl. 35, and *Reprod.*, i, 23.

ILLUSTRATIONS OF THE APOCALYPSE

belonged to the Carthusian monastery of Val-Dieu, near Mortagne. It has eighty-three half-page miniatures, drawn and painted with great delicacy and finish, on backgrounds of plain dark colour, or more often diapered with a great variety of tessellated patterns. Buildings are drawn with no less minute accuracy than in Add. 18633; and the slender graceful figures, the exquisite expressive faces, the finely painted birds and monsters which enliven the borders, combine with the harmonies of colour and composition to put this in the front rank of Apocalypse manuscripts.

About the middle of the fourteenth century the demand for these illustrations seems to have ceased among connoisseurs of art; for a marked and rapid decline is apparent in the quality of those produced after that time, and their chief interest, as regards the history of design, lies in the fact that they form a link in the chain which connects the Spanish paintings of the ninth century with Dutch or German woodcuts of the fifteenth.

CHAPTER XIII

ENGLISH ILLUMINATION IN THE FOURTEENTH AND FIFTEENTH CENTURIES

THE first quarter of the fourteenth century was the real flowering-time of English illumination. Other periods have bequeathed to us an abundance of good work, each with its special points of excellence, but also with its special foibles. In this, however, a peculiarly satisfying balance was struck between the various conflicting elements of book-decoration : realism, imagination, and tradition, illustration and ornament, were blended with unerring nicety of adjustment, by artists possessed of a greater technical dexterity and a more thorough naturalism than their early Gothic predecessors; and a harmonious perfection resulted, which has hardly been surpassed in all the history of the art.

This perfection was already foreshadowed in the closing years of the thirteenth century, to which Mr. Pierpont Morgan's "Windmill" Psalter[1] perhaps belongs, though its rich, fully developed style suggests rather the opening years of the fourteenth. It is indeed not easy to find a parallel to the two magnificent pages with which Psalm i begins. The first is filled with the initial " B," on a diapered ground, enclosed in a rectangular frame set with medallions of the Creation, etc., on gold grounds, and itself enclosing a Jesse-tree. The letter " E," continuing the word *Beatus*, takes up half the next page ; it is surrounded with a wonderfully delicate and intricate lacework design of leaves and flourishes drawn in red and

---

[1] M. R. James, *Cat. of MSS. in the Library of J. Pierpont Morgan*, pp. 41–3 (four plates); Burl. F.A. Club, No. 47, pl. 44.

PLATE XXXI

oment le diable vint en forme de femme a la femme Noe e demanda v son mari. Ço rt
E ele visoit qe ele ne sout ou il est ale pur toi trair e tute le mund prehne ces greines
e fere vn aboyson e le touer a boyre e il te dirra tut. E issint fist ele.

a comence Noe a charpenter e le primer coup qil ferut tute le mound te espir
E lors vint vn aungel a li e il cria merci. Le angel li dit tu as malfet mes pris
ne ces verges e les closes e chune ta neef le menz qe tu purras. Car le flod est
envenaunt

PSALTER. ENGLISH, EARLY XIVTH CENT.
BRIT. MUS. ROY. 2 B VII.

ENGLISH ILLUMINATION AFTER 1300

blue outlines and faintly washed with pale green, and it encloses paintings of an angel and of the Judgment of Solomon—over Solomon's head, the windmill to which the book owes its name. The remaining decoration of this interesting book consists of finely historiated initials at the usual divisions of the Psalter, and of humorous and spirited line-endings (grotesques, rabbits, monsters, etc.) in outline or body-colour.

If the Windmill Psalter represents the opening bud, it is assuredly the fine flower of early fourteenth century illumination, in its fullest perfection, that we see in the beautiful manuscript known as Queen Mary's Psalter. Kept in its native country through the vigilance of a London customs-officer, who seized it in 1553, just as it was on the point of being sent abroad, and presented it to the Queen, whose name it now bears, it has been ever since one of the chief treasures of the old royal collection, in which it is numbered 2 B. vii.[1] For a Psalter it is an unusually thick volume, its exceptional wealth of miniatures and marginal drawings leaving but little space for text on most of the pages. Prefixed to the Calendar is a long series of scenes from Old Testament history, over two hundred in all, mostly two on a page, framed in plain vermilion bands with three leaves growing out of each corner. These drawings, firmly but delicately executed in the finest possible outline, far freer and more truly spontaneous in manner than any previous works of the kind, are lightly tinted in violet, green, and reddish brown. The compositions are spacious and simple; the figures graceful, with just a hint of dainty self-consciousness in their pose; the facial types often of great beauty. As is usual in such series, a comparatively small number of models is made to serve for many personages. The subjects are described in French legends, quaint in phrasing and often of considerable length; they are not

---

[1] See *Pal. Soc.*, i, 147; Thompson, *Eng. Illum. MSS.*, pp. 43–5, pl. 14, 15; Warner, *Illum. MSS.*, pl. 28–9, and *Reprod.*, iii, 20–2; N. H. J. Westlake and W. Purdue, *Illustrations of O.T. Hist. in Qu. Mary's Psalter*, 1865.

ILLUMINATED MANUSCRIPTS

restricted to the scriptural narrative, but include many stories of apocryphal origin, e.g. that of the devil instilling jealous suspicions into Noah's wife, in order to hinder the building of the ark.[1]

These drawings are followed by a nearly full-page Jesse-tree and some pages filled with figures of Christ and His kindred, etc., all painted in body-colour on grounds of burnished gold or diapered colours, but obviously by the same artist as the tinted drawings. Then comes the Calendar, remarkable for the elaboration and originality with which the zodiacal signs and monthly occupations are treated in a series of frieze-like designs running across the full width of the pages.

After the Calendar, the text of the Psalms is introduced by a frontispiece of the Annunciation and Visitation. The lower margin of every page is now filled with an admirable tinted drawing, in the same style as the scenes from the Old Testament, but on a smaller scale, and with much greater freedom of range as to subject. Beginning with a long series of illustrations of medieval animal-lore—the phoenix, the panther whose fragrance attracts other animals, the tiger brought to a standstill by a mirror which the hunted man has dropped, the water-snake eating his way through a crocodile, sirens capturing mariners, etc.—the artist goes on to illustrate all manner of contemporary games, sports, and pastimes, often with grotesque monsters for performers. Then come the miracles of the Virgin, followed by the lives and martyrdoms of the saints. The book is further enriched, not only with historiated initials at the usual divisions, but also with a great number of large miniatures of the life of Christ, delicately drawn and brilliantly painted on stippled gold or diapered backgrounds.[2]

[1] Pl. xxxi.

[2] See pl. xxxii, representing the Cana marriage-feast just after the miracle, a servant offering a cup of the new wine to the ruler of the feast. This treatment of the subject is rare; in the contemporary Taymouth Horae it follows a picture of the more familiar scene, servants filling the jars with water. See H. Y. Thompson, *Catalogue*, ii, p. 63.

PLATE XXXII

PSALTER. ENGLISH, EARLY XIVth CENT.

BRIT. MUS., ROY. 2 B VII.

ENGLISH ILLUMINATION AFTER 1300

Queen Mary's Psalter stands alone in its dainty and exquisite beauty; in point of variety and brilliance of decoration, however, it is rivalled, if not surpassed, by its contemporaries of the East Anglian school. An Apocalypse[1] belonging to this remarkable group was mentioned in the last chapter; but its finest representatives are a set of Psalters, which take a very prominent place in the history of English illumination. All are executed with the highest degree of finish, and all are characterized to a great extent by the same mannerisms.[2] These are easier to recognize with the eye than to describe in words; they may be briefly summed up, however, as consisting of (1) a rich and harmonious colour-scheme, with plentiful use of burnished and patterned gold; (2) luxuriance of ornament, especially in the designing of frame-borders and initial-decoration, where plant forms, animals, and human figures are entwined together in an effective and distinctive manner, red and green ivy, vine, and oak-leaves, the last combined with acorns, being specially prominent; (3) a passion for the droll and grotesque, not peculiar indeed to this school, but very noticeable and pronounced in it. This last trait suggests a connection with late thirteenth century Flemish art, as exemplified in Stowe 17;[3] and very likely East Anglian art did owe something to Flemish or North-French influence. In the main, however, it was undoubtedly a native growth, and its half-century of duration (1300-50) was the brightest period in English illumination.

Mr. Sydney Cockerell claims the Rutland and Tenison Psalters[4] as ancestors of the East Anglian school; but no evidence has been adduced to connect them with it locally, and they have but little resemblance to it in point of style, apart from the use of grotesques, which is too common in

---

[1] Roy. 15 D. ii. See above, p. 217.
[2] These are well brought out in Mr. S. C. Cockerell's valuable and sumptuously illustrated monograph on *The Gorleston Psalter*, 1907.
[3] Above, p. 205.   [4] Noticed above, pp. 188, 190.

ILLUMINATED MANUSCRIPTS

late thirteenth century work to be considered a distinctive attribute of one particular school. It is quite otherwise with the Peterborough Psalter in the Royal Library at Brussels.[1] The contents of this splendid book prove beyond question that it was done for (and in all probability at) Peterborough; its date has been variously put by good judges as *circa* 1250 and *circa* 1300, so we may safely assign it to the latter half of the thirteenth century. There is still a good deal of archaic angularity about its miniatures; but the borders contain all the elements of ornament noted above as characteristic of the early fourteenth century East Anglian school, though they lack the rich exuberance of fancy and the fineness of finish which make the best productions of the school so delightful to behold.

Of these, one of the earliest and most interesting is Arundel 83 in the British Museum;[2] a volume containing two incomplete manuscripts, of similar contents, age, and style, bound up together. The first is a Psalter, preceded by a Calendar and several pages of allegorical designs, and followed by Canticles, Litanies, Office of the Dead, and Hours of the Passion, the last imperfect. The second is a mere fragment textually, though artistically the richer and more beautiful of the two; it consists of Calendar and allegorical designs, followed by a series of miniatures of the life of Christ, in compartments, and by some remarkable full-page miniatures. In the second Calendar, under November 25, Robert de Lyle has recorded his gift of the book to his daughters Audrey and "Alborou" in succession, with remainder to the nuns of Chicksand in Bedfordshire. His note is dated 1339, and the manuscript is probably some twenty or thirty years earlier; his family association with Mundford in Norfolk supports the evidence of style in favour of an East Anglian provenance. The arms on the first page of the other MS. seem to indi-

---

[1] Nos. 9961–2. For full description and reproductions, partly in colours, see *Le Psautier de Peterborough*, ed. J. van den Gheyn [1907], forming fasc. 2–3 of *Le Musée des Enluminures*.

[2] *Pal. Soc.*, i, 99, 100; Thompson, pp. 55–8, pl. 17; Warner, *Illum. MSS.*, pl. 31, and *Reprod.*, iii, 23–5; Cockerell, *Gorleston Psalter*, pl. 20, 21.

cate that it was made either for Sir William Howard, who died in 1308 and was buried at East Winch near Lynn, or for Alice Fitton his wife. The opening page of the Psalter is, as usual, the most elaborate: the " B " encloses a Jesse-tree, and the two columns of text are framed in a border resplendent with gold and colours, filled with intertwining foliage-stems whose curves form panels for figures of Patriarchs and Prophets on both sides, a Crucifixion at the top, and the Evangelistic emblems at the corners. At the foot of the page, between text and frame, is a lively picture of a woodland scene, with stag and hind, rabbit, and a fowler crouching under a bush and luring birds with an owl; all carefully and admirably painted, and full of an animation the more vivid from its contrast with the conventionalism of the more strictly appropriate scriptural figures. The other divisions of the Psalter have miniature-initials on grounds of burnished and stippled gold, and borders of cusped bars and foliage-stems, supporting grotesques and decorated with ivy, oak and vine leaves; daisy-buds, afterwards a favourite device in English borders, also occur.

The emblematic diagrams, which figure in both manuscripts, are exceedingly curious: they include a seraph whose wings are inscribed with moral qualities, illustrations of the Creed, tables of virtues and vices, and a representation of the Cross as the Tree of Life. In the second manuscript the series is fuller, and contains a painting of the stages of human life in ten medallions, the first an infant on its mother's lap, the last a tomb; also the Three Living and Three Dead Kings—a subject found in East Anglian wall-paintings of this period,[1] and very popular at a later date in Flemish Books of Hours.

Of greater artistic merit, indeed of singular beauty, are the additional pages in Robert de Lyle's book. The life of Christ miniatures are in two series, by two different

[1] e.g. at Gorleston, possibly the birthplace of this very book, and at Wickhampton and Belton. See Cockerell, p. 7, and G. E. Fox in the *Victoria History of Norfolk*, vol. ii, 1906, p. 547.

ILLUMINATED MANUSCRIPTS

hands: the first eighteen, arranged in compartments, six to a page, within cusped quatrefoils, are exquisitely painted in subdued tints, a soft greyish blue predominating, and are set on grounds of stippled gold and diapered colours alternately. The faces are too long for correct proportions, anatomy is often at fault, and the compositions are lacking in vigour and movement; but with all this there is an indescribable charm about the pictures, the gentle, reposeful faces and quiet, solemn gestures expressing well the reverential awe with which the artist approached his subject. The remaining eight, separated from these by some pages, are in the same style, but of somewhat inferior workmanship. Two of the intervening pages are filled with large miniatures which show East Anglian painting at its best. One of these[1] represents the Madonna and Child under a canopy, against a background of gold highly burnished and covered with a finely stippled pattern of foliage scroll-work; the Child is playing with a goldfinch, and the Virgin's feet rest on a dragon and a lion; in the spandrels are angels with censers, and on either side are saints in niches. The other is a Crucifixion, painted on a background of lozenges filled with fleurs-de-lis and heraldic lions; at the foot of the cross Adam sits up in his tomb and holds up a chalice to catch the Redeemer's blood; at the top are two angels with discs to represent the sun and moon, between them a pelican feeding her young, an emblem of the Redemption.

We come next to two Psalters definitely associated with Gorleston in Suffolk, two miles south of Yarmouth; both of the very highest excellence, and closely allied to the Arundel MS. These are MS. 171 in the Public Library at Douai,[2] and the book which was long famous as Lord Braybrooke's Psalter, but is now one of the gems in the collection of Mr. C. W. Dyson Perrins, who prefers to call it the Gorleston Psalter.[3] The Douai Psalter was

---

[1] Pl. xxxiii.   [2] *New Pal. Soc.*, pl. 14–16; Cockerell, pl. 16–18.

[3] It forms the main subject of Mr. Cockerell's often-cited monograph, in which pl. 1–14 show eight full pages and a great number of marginal subjects.

PLATE XXXIII

PSALTER. EAST ANGLIAN, EARLY XIVTH CENT.

BRIT. MUS., ARUNDEL 83

ENGLISH ILLUMINATION AFTER 1300

given, as an inscription on the fly-leaf shows, by Thomas, vicar of Gorleston, to a certain Abbot John; and it contains two series of chronological notes, referring specially to the diocese of Norwich, and fixing the date of the book between the years 1322 and 1325. These same notes occur, be it observed, in a Breviary of the Norwich diocesan use (Brit. Mus., Stowe 12),[1] which in its present condition has no large miniatures, but whose border and initial ornaments make it an interesting, if not quite first-rate, example of East Anglian illumination. The Perrins Psalter has the Dedication of Gorleston Church marked in the Calendar (Mar. 8) as a "majus duplex" festival, and special prominence is given in the illuminations to S. Andrew, to whom the parish church at Gorleston was dedicated. Moreover, it has so marked a resemblance to the Douai Psalter in point of style, that they may both be referred without hesitation not only to the same locality but also to the same period and the same scriptorium, if not indeed to the same individual artists. Each of them has a magnificent *Beatus vir* page, much richer than that in the Arundel MS.: an elaborate Jesse-tree in the "B," the frame-border filled with figures of kings and scenes from the life of Christ, finely painted on patterned gold grounds in panels formed by intersecting oak or vine stems. The Perrins MS. has a hunting scene at the foot, corresponding to the woodland scene in Arundel 83; in the Douai MS. there is instead a picture of David bringing the ark to Jerusalem, with all the stately pomp of a medieval church procession. This page is preceded in the Douai book by two splendid full-page miniatures, of the Virgin and Child and the Crucifixion; both subjects were probably in the Perrins book too originally, but only the latter remains. The Douai miniatures, like the Arundel Madonna, are on backgrounds of gold punctured with a scroll-work pattern of foliage; a further point of resemblance is the goldfinch with which the Child is playing. The Perrins and Douai Crucifixions are so

---

[1] *Pal. Soc.*, ii, 197; Warner, *Illum. MSS.*, pl. 32, and *Reprod.*, ii, 14.

much alike that Dr. James assigned them both to the same hand; Mr. Cockerell, however, who had the advantage of seeing them together, thought them more probably the work of "two artists who worked side by side." It is quite clear that many hands contributed to the embellishment of these and other allied manuscripts—that there was, in fact, an active, flourishing, and highly accomplished school of illuminators established at this time somewhere in the neighbourhood of Norwich, perhaps at Gorleston. The Franciscans and the Austin Friars had houses at the latter place, but we have no grounds for attributing these books to either of those orders, or even to clerics at all, religious or secular; at this period it seems more likely, as Mr. Cockerell says, that "the best of the artists were laymen, who contracted for given pieces of work, and moved from place to place, at the beck and call of various patrons."

We must not leave the Perrins Psalter without a word as to the small marginal figures and the still smaller ones in the line-endings, which for variety, humour, and vivacity are unrivalled among the productions of this the best period of the school. Practically the whole range of human activities, as known to the artists, is represented: ecclesiastics, warriors, hunters, musicians, blacksmiths, etc., practising their respective callings. But it is in whimsical caricature above all that the illustrators delighted, giving free play to an absolutely riotous fancy: foxes masquerading as bishops, rabbits conducting a solemn procession, apes hunting on horseback or driving a team of plough-oxen, and such-like drolleries. Grotesque and monstrous forms of all kinds abound, of course, and scenes of animal life are often depicted with great spirit.

The Ormesby Psalter at Oxford[1] belongs to the same group; a gift to Norwich Priory by one of the monks, Robert of Ormesby, a village about six miles north of

[1] Douce 366. See H. Shaw, *Illum. Ornaments*, 1833, No. 9; Cockerell, pl. 19; Michel, *Hist. de l'Art*, ii, pt. i, pl. iv.

ENGLISH ILLUMINATION AFTER 1300

Gorleston. Except for a few pages, it is much less richly decorated than the Perrins MS.; but those few pages are superb, especially the *Beatus vir*, in which the illumination covers the whole page, kneeling portraits of a monk (doubtless Robert of Ormesby himself) and bishop having been painted in on square panels over the few lines of text which were originally there. The plant-forms in the borders are exceptionally light and varied, cornflowers, bluebells, and other flowers appearing as well as the usual oak and ivy leaves.

Slightly later, perhaps, and representing East Anglian work at its greatest height of technical perfection, is the Psalter in Mr. Yates Thompson's collection,[1] begun for a member of the St. Omer family, of Mulbarton in Norfolk, but left unfinished by the fourteenth century illuminators, and completed about the beginning of the fifteenth century. Its *Beatus vir* page is indeed the *ne plus ultra* of this particular style of illumination, combining a rich, yet spacious and not overladen scheme of decoration with minute and exquisite delicacy in the spirited little figure-compositions, and with the utmost fertility in invention; the plant-forms are as varied as in the Ormesby Psalter, and bears, unicorns, stags, birds of all kinds, and tiny human figures are perched here and there on the stems, quite irrelevantly and yet with a perfect decorative fitness.

The Louterell Psalter[2] in the Lulworth Castle Library, made for Sir Geoffrey Louterell, of Irnham in Lincolnshire, about 1340, shows the East Anglian style already beginning to decay. It has historiated initials of a hard, brightly coloured, expressionless type; but its chief decoration is the marginal ornament, which is amazing in its mass, variety, and incoherence. Regardless of all sense of proportion or congruity, the illuminators have covered the margins with a mixture of studies of contemporary life, fabliaux, and gigantic, sometimes quaint,

---

[1] No. 58, described by Sir G. Warner in the *Catalogue*, ii, pp. 74–82. See too H. Y. Thompson, *Facsimiles from a Psalter*, 1900, and *Lecture on some Eng. Illum. MSS.*, 1902, pp. 23–5, pl. 31–6; Cockerell, pl. 15.

[2] *New Pal. Soc.*, pl. 41–3.

ILLUMINATED MANUSCRIPTS

but often merely hideous, grotesques. Many of the subjects, taken apart from their surroundings, are charming, ingenious, full of vivacity: such are the delightful series of scenes in a medieval kitchen, with pots boiling, and game on a spit before an open fire, tended by lightly clad and heated cooks; the Castle of Love, defended by ladies who throw roses from the battlements; the picture of Constantinople as a walled city; the ladies in a long, covered travelling-coach drawn by five horses; the portrait of Sir Geoffrey Louterell on horseback, taking leave of his wife and daughter-in-law, who hand up to him his helmet, shield, and lance. In fact, to the antiquary the book is a perfect treasure-house, though the beauty-lover must deplore its crude, ill-assorted designs and its garish, bizarre colouring.

About the middle of the century the East Anglian school, already decadent, seems to have died out as suddenly as it had sprung up; perhaps through the ravages of the Black Death, which devastated England in 1348-9, visiting Norfolk with especial severity. Whatever the cause, there is a great dearth of good English work from the middle until very near the end of the fourteenth century. During the greater part of the century, indeed, apart from the East Anglian group, Queen Mary's Psalter, and a few other choice books of the same period, English illumination is not so much beautiful as valuable and interesting for the wealth, vigour, and expressiveness of its illustrations of folk-lore, popular legend (sacred or profane), and contemporary life. In this category come such books as Roy. 10 E. iv, a copy of the Decretals of Gregory IX, written in Italy but illuminated in England, perhaps by the canons of S. Bartholomew's, Smithfield; its lower margins filled with rough but very lively and diverting coloured drawings, forming a vast medley of Bible-history and hagiography jostling up against less edifying literature, intermingled with fables, allegories, and sketches from everyday life—distracting, if not uninstructive, to the

ENGLISH ILLUMINATION AFTER 1300

student of Canon law.[1] Here too we must class the Taymouth Horae in Mr. Yates Thompson's collection,[2] with its delicious pictures of the sportswoman's exploits; the Carew-Poyntz Horae in the Fitzwilliam Museum at Cambridge,[3] with its long series of illustrations of the Mary-legends; and a Horae in the British Museum,[4] less copiously and much less finely illuminated than these, but interesting because of its unusual choice of subjects. Even the Psalter of Queen Philippa,[5] executed apparently between 1328 and 1340, graceful as its bordered pages are with their light sprays of foliage, is not of first-rate importance artistically; moreover, both the borders and the miniature-initials, with their backgrounds covered with gilt scroll-work, show strong traces of French influence, and cannot be regarded as characteristic English work of the time.

The progressive deterioration that went on during the latter half of the fourteenth century may be seen in such manuscripts as the Missal[6] of Nicholas Lytlington, Abbot of Westminster (1362-86), still preserved in Westminster Abbey, or the huge Wycliffite Bible[7] made for Thomas of Woodstock, Duke of Gloucester (d. 1397). The typical border has now become a framework of narrow rigid bars, sometimes broken midway and replaced by a sort of festoon of close-set foliage, but mostly diversified only by leafy bosses at the corners (a curious reversion to the tenth century Winchester style, as Sir G. Warner has remarked) and by short-stalked leaves or buds (usually in pairs or threes) and sprays of foliage thrown out at intervals. The total effect is heavy and dull, despite the plenteous use of gold.

[1] For a full list of subjects, etc., see the new *Catalogue of the Royal MSS.*
[2] No. 57. See *Cat.*, ii, pp. 50-74, and *Lecture on some Eng. Illum. MSS.*, pp. 20-3, pl. 14-30.
[3] No. 48. See M. R. James, *Cat. of Fitzwilliam MSS.*, 1895, pp. 100-20.
[4] Eg. 2781. See Warner, *Reprod.*, ii, 15; *Titus and Vespasian*, Roxburghe Club, 1905 (two coloured plates.)   [5] Harl. 2899. See Warner, *Reprod.*, i, 14.
[6] *Missale ad usum Eccl. Westmonast.*, ed. J. Wickham Legg, Hen. Bradshaw Soc., 1891-7.
[7] Eg. 617-18. See *Pal. Soc.*, i, 171; Kenyon, *Biblical MSS.*, pl. 24.

ILLUMINATED MANUSCRIPTS

Just before the end of the century, however, a new spirit was infused into English illumination, and the art revived and flourished for a short time in a style quite unlike that of the preceding period. This happy result is generally ascribed to the influence of Rhenish or Bohemian painters coming into the country with Anne of Bohemia, who married Richard II in 1382; a theory which is confirmed by Sir G. Warner's recent discovery [1] of Low-German inscriptions among the illuminations of one of the earliest and most splendid examples of this new style, the great Bible of Richard II. The work of the new school is characterized especially by great softness in the treatment of the face, the use of the pencil or pen being discarded in favour of pure brush-work; by a rich, warm, and harmonious colour-scheme (sadly wanting in the immediately preceding age); by the skilful use of architectural ornament; and by the introduction of new forms of foliage, in particular of light and feathery sprays putting forth curious spoon-shaped leaves and bell or trumpet-shaped flowers—frankly conventional, but producing a very decorative and pleasing effect. Another characteristic device is a white scroll with sinuated edges, resembling an elongated oak-leaf, which is wrapped festoon-wise round the upright shafts of pillars or initials.

The great Bible [2] just mentioned, a volume of enormous size, is supposed in default of evidence to have been made for the Royal Chapel; it is evidently of the time of Richard II, or Henry IV at latest, and its bulk and magnificence certainly suggest a royal patron. Every book has a large miniature-initial and full border, and the prologues have initials of equal size, either filled with scrolls of foliage or else enclosing pictures of S. Jerome at work among his books. The main characteristics of the decoration are those of the school in general, and it only remains to say a word about the treatment of land-

---

[1] See his description of Roy. 1 E. ix in the new *Cat. of Royal MSS.*

[2] Roy. 1 E. ix. See Thompson, *Eng. Illum. MSS.*, pp. 58-61, pl. 18, 19; Warner, *Illum. MSS.*, pl. 41-2, and *Reprod.*, iii, 27.

PLATE XXXIV

CUTTINGS FROM A MISSAL. ENGLISH, LATE XIVTH CENT.
BRIT. MUS. ADD. 29704

scape in the miniatures. This is now beginning tentatively to approach naturalism, so far as the ground on which the personages stand is concerned; but where sky should be, we still have gilded, tapestried or checkered backgrounds.

Another splendid work of the same school is a great Missal, of which nothing remains except a number of initials and border ornaments cut out by some former owner, and now filling two large volumes in the British Museum.[1] When complete the book must have been as stately as the Bible which it resembles so closely. Many of the initials are filled with foliate decoration; but there are also several which contain finely painted miniatures of the lives of saints, liturgical ceremonies, and other subjects more or less germane to the text.[2] In one of them a portrait of Richard II has been recognized; so it seems not unlikely that this book and the Bible were both made for him. Be that as it may, they are certainly magnificent specimens of the last period when illumination in this country approached greatness.

More gorgeous still is the gigantic Sherborne Missal[3] in the Duke of Northumberland's collection; of special interest, too, from the data which it supplies as to the circumstances of its production. Portraits of Richard Mitford, Bishop of Salisbury 1396–1407, and Robert Bruynyng, Abbot of Sherborne, in Dorsetshire, 1386–1415, recur in conjunction on page after page, proclaiming them the joint patrons of the book, and thus fixing its date within the limits of Mitford's episcopate. Nor is this all: more frequent still are the smaller figures of the scribe, John Whas, a Benedictine monk (doubtless of Sherborne Abbey), and the artist John Siferwas, a Dominican friar. The latter, one of the few illuminators whose names have come down to us in definite association

[1] Add. 29704–5. See Warner, *Reprod.*, i, 16.
[2] Pl. xxxiv shows S. Giles in one initial, a baptism in another.
[3] Described by Sir E. M. Thompson in the *Proceedings* of the Society of Antiquaries, xvi, 1896, pp. 226–30. Photographs of four pages are in the British Museum, MS. Facs. 64 (1).

ILLUMINATED MANUSCRIPTS

with particular works, also appears on the frontispiece of a Lectionary[1] in the British Museum, giving the volume to John, Lord Lovel (d. 1408), who had ordered it as an offering to Salisbury Cathedral. This book, now unfortunately in a very incomplete state, has decorations of a similar style to those in the Sherborne Missal, but far inferior in richness and variety. In both cases it is evident that Siferwas was the chief artist who planned and supervised the decoration, not the actual painter of the whole. It is not easy to do justice to the Sherborne Missal. Besides a great wealth of initial and border decoration, carefully executed in a style similar to that of Richard II's Bible and Missal, it has the margins enriched with scenes from Scripture, hagiography, and ecclesiastical history, and with many other subjects, including a delightful series of birds inscribed with their English names. Architectural canopies are frequently introduced; these are mostly of a highly ornate character, and greatly enhance the splendour of the pages.

The same manner appears again, though on a much more modest scale, in a charming miniature of the Annunciation contained in a Book of Hours in the British Museum.[2] The volume, which was executed about the end of the fourteenth century, presumably for a member of the Grandison family, is decorated throughout in the somewhat heavy, uninteresting style of what might be called the "unreformed" English illuminators of the time. But this frontispiece is plainly the work of an artist trained in the school which inspired John Siferwas. The colouring is soft and pleasing; especially gracious and charming are the cloaked figures of the patron and his wife who kneel in prayer on either side at the foot of the page. Mary and the angel are enclosed in an elaborately canopied tabernacle, from the sides and pedestal of which light sprays of foliage issue with delightful incongruity.

[1] Harl. 7026. See Warner, *Reprod.*, ii, 16.
[2] Roy. 2 A. xviii. See Thompson, pp. 61–4, pl. 20; Warner, *Reprod.*, i, 15.

ENGLISH ILLUMINATION AFTER 1300

This remarkable school left a permanent influence on English border-decoration, giving it a lightness of construction and variety of detail which it had needed sadly, and of which it retained some traces long after all other elements of good illuminative art had disappeared. In other respects the influence was shortlived. The first quarter of the fifteenth century saw the production of a few really fine manuscripts, foremost among which stands the admirable Horae of "Elysabeth the Quene" in Mr. Yates Thompson's collection.[1] But on the whole the art of illumination was on the down grade. Henry V's successful invasion of France introduced a taste for French illumination, then at its prime; and most of the fifteenth century Horae and other decorated books done for wealthy English patrons were the work of French artists or of mere copyists who imitated the foreign methods as best they could. Under Edward IV this fashion gave way to a similar enthusiasm for Flemish painting, and native art decayed and perished for lack of encouragement. The manuscripts of distinctively English character are chiefly interesting as illustrations of costume, like the famous Lydgate's Life of S. Edmund (Harl. 2278) presented to Henry VI in 1433; or as evincing a genuine depth of mystical devotion, like the Cottonian "Desert of Religion" (Faust. B. vi, pt. ii); rather than through their intrinsic merits as works of art.

[1] No. 59. See *Cat.*, ii, pp. 83-9, *Lecture*, pp. 26-7, pl. 38-42; *Pal. Soc.*, ii, 37.

CHAPTER XIV

FRENCH ILLUMINATION IN THE FOURTEENTH CENTURY

THE fourteenth century, in England so full of promise at the outset and so disappointing later on, was in France a period of steady advance, if not from good to better—for better of its kind than the Sainte Abbaye could scarcely be—at any rate from one good style to another. In the history of Western European miniature the year 1300 is a magical epoch, and marks the zenith of the early Gothic manner. But whilst the English painters after a few glorious decades fell away from their state of grace, their French fellow-craftsmen went on from strength to strength: preserving the excellent tradition they had inherited, yet continually vitalizing and developing it by the rejection of worn-out conventions and the introduction of new ideas, and progressing steadily towards a more perfect mastery of technique. This applies, of course, only to the best work of the century. It was an age of great activity in the production of illuminated manuscripts, good, bad, or indifferent; but we are not concerned here with the last two classes.

Researches among archives have revealed to us the names of many French illuminators (and of one " enlumineresse " at least) who worked in the fourteenth century.[1] But these discoveries, interesting as they are, are mostly tantalizing rather than informing; for while the painter's name and address are often recorded with the utmost precision, his actual work is rarely mentioned at all, still more rarely in such a way as to lead to its identification.

[1] See H. Martin, *Les Miniaturistes Français*, 1906, pp. 49-75, and *Les Peintres de MSS. et la Miniature en France* [1909], pp. 35-72.

FRENCH ILLUMINATION, 14TH CENT.

One or two names, however, stand out with such prominence that we are justified in regarding their owners as the leading illuminators of their respective times, though we need not therefore assume that they are to be credited personally, or even through their immediate pupils, with any and every piece of fine work that has survived from those times. Foremost among these are Jean Pucelle in the second quarter of the century, and André Beauneveu and Jacquemart de Hesdin at its close, each of whom has come to be definitely associated, on more or less secure foundation of actual evidence, with a well-marked distinctive style.

Of the miniaturists settled in Paris about the year 1300 the one esteemed most highly seems to have been Honoré, to whom the Breviary of Philippe le Bel (Bibl. Nat., lat. 1023),[1] executed in 1296, may probably be attributed. His son-in-law, Richard de Verdun, had been associated with him in 1292, and seems to have succeeded to his atelier by 1318, in which year Richard occurs as a painter of antiphoners for the Sainte Chapelle. One is strongly tempted to see more than a mere coincidence of local names between the latter artist and Mr. Yates Thompson's Verdun Breviary,[2] which, like its companion the Metz Pontifical in the same collection,[3] forms one of the most beautiful extant memorials of French early fourteenth century illumination. Of the two, which are plainly by the same hand, the Breviary is slightly the earlier, having been made for Marguerite de Bar, Abbess of S. Maur, at Verdun, 1291-1304; the Pontifical was made for her brother Renaud or Reinhold, Bishop of Metz 1302-16, probably towards the end of his episcopate, the last few miniatures in the book being more or

---

[1] Delisle, *Douze livres royaux*, No. vii.

[2] No. 31. See *Cat.*, i, pp. 142-78; H. Y. Thompson, *Illustrations of 100 MSS.*, vol. i, 1907, pl. 10. It is the first volume only, the second being in the Public Library at Verdun (No. 107).

[3] Formerly in the possession of Sir Thomas Brooke, who bequeathed it to his brother-collector. It was edited by the Rev. E. S. Dewick, and its illuminations reproduced (four in gold and colours), for the Roxburghe Club in 1902.

less unfinished, as though his death had interrupted its completion. Both books are copiously and beautifully decorated with historiated initials and with borders of a restrained and particularly pleasing type, consisting of slender cusped bars ending in foliage-stems, or sometimes in little human heads or grotesque forms, and supporting an immense variety of single figures or groups. These last are of the diverting character so dear to miniaturists at this period; inferior to none of their contemporaries in humour and invention, they far surpass most of them in the exquisite neatness of their execution and in the fine taste and sense of proportion with which they are fitted into the decorative scheme. The Pontifical is further enriched with a splendid series of half-page miniatures, which illustrate the text by representing with the minutest accuracy many of the rites and ceremonies in which a bishop is required to take the leading part. In the first nineteen pictures, for instance, the successive acts in the dedication of a church are shown in full detail: watching the relics in a tent the night before; the bishop knocking at the church-door and demanding admittance, tracing the Greek and Latin alphabets with his crosier on the floor of the nave,[1] etc. The delicately drawn figures stand out well against the diapered backgrounds; they still have the almost ascetic slenderness of early Gothic art, but its austere rigidity has now given place to a curious and distinctive sway of the body, not ungraceful, though somewhat artificial and suggestive of sentimentality. The faces, placid, smooth, and rounded, are of refined types, and are drawn with extraordinary delicacy.

In 1295 the Historia Scholastica of Petrus Comestor was translated into French by Guiart des Moulins, Canon of Aire in Artois; and this vernacular paraphrase of the Scriptures, known as the " Bible historiale," was in France almost as popular throughout the fourteenth century as the Vulgate had been in the thirteenth. One of the

[1] Pl. xxxv.

PLATE XXXV

METZ PONTIFICAL, 1302-16
LIBRARY OF SIR T. BROOKE, BART.

FRENCH ILLUMINATION, 14TH CENT.

earliest extant copies, written at Paris in 1317 by Jean de Papeleu, is now in the Arsenal Library (No. 5059).[1] Besides a frontispiece, representing Christ surrounded by angels, it has 176 illustrative miniatures on gold or diapered grounds. Good as these are, especially in depicting facial expression, they are not to be compared for delicate beauty with the paintings in the two manuscripts just mentioned; they are interesting, however, as typical of a very large class,[2] and also because of the preliminary sketches still visible in the margins opposite many of them. M. Martin has made a special study of such sketches, which occur in several other manuscripts, e.g. in Roy. 18 D. viii, a French Bible of about the same period; he sees in them the hand of the *chef d'atelier*, giving a rough working model for the assistant who paints the actual finished miniature—a theory which has much plausibility, especially in the case of works turned out in such numbers and with such virtual uniformity as these illustrated Bible-histories.

Another noteworthy Parisian production of the year 1317 is the Life of S. Denis, in Latin and French, composed by Yves, a monk of the famous abbey dedicated to that saint, and presented by the abbot to King Philip V. The manuscript, now in the Bibliothèque Nationale (fr. 2090-2), contains seventy-seven miniatures[3] (all but three full-page) of the lives and martyrdoms of S. Denis and his companions. These are all finely executed, on diapered or tapestried grounds, and were doubtless painted, not by a monk of S. Denis, but by one or more of the skilful lay "enlumineurs" of whom, as we have seen, there was an abundant supply in Paris at this time. There is a touch of

---

[1] Martin, *Peintres*, p. 58, fig. 12, *Miniaturistes*, p. 113, and *Cat. des MSS. de la Bibl. de l'Arsenal*, v, 1889, p. 29.

[2] A good, though hardly quite first-rate, representative is the well-known "Poitiers Bible" in the British Museum (Roy. 19 D. ii), so called because it was captured with its owner, John II, at the battle of Poitiers in 1356.

[3] Published in facsimile, with four more pages showing the initial and border decoration, by the Soc. de l'hist. de Paris, *Légende de Saint Denis*, ed. H. Martin, 1908. See too *New Pal. Soc.*, pl. 88-90.

ILLUMINATED MANUSCRIPTS

traditional formality in the purely hagiographical scenes; but the foregrounds are enlivened with a delightful series of pictures of everyday street and riverside life in the French capital, full of animation and assuredly a faithful representation of incidents witnessed daily by the artist: men bathing from boats, or fishing with rod or net; boats laden with merchandise, being towed along or unloaded; the streets above thronged with passers-by, on horse or foot, intent on pleasure or business—all depicted with a genial realism not commonly associated with the fourteenth century.

The name of Jean Pucelle first appears in 1319-24, in the accounts of a Paris confraternity, for whom he designed a seal. As a miniaturist, he can only be given three books with anything like certainty, viz. a Bible, completed in 1327, and now in the Bibliothèque Nationale (lat. 11935); the Belleville Breviary, also in the Bibl. Nat. (lat. 10483-4), which must have been finished before 1343; and a little book of Hours,[1] in Baroness Adolphe de Rothschild's collection, which M. Delisle has identified with the "Heures de Pucelle" mentioned in the inventories of the Duc de Berry's library. This last is perhaps, as M. Martin conjectures, the same book as the "bien petit livret d'oroisons . . . que Pucelle enlumina," between 1325 and 1328, for Charles IV to give his third wife Jeanne d'Evreux, who bequeathed it in 1370 to Charles V. At any rate, the fact that he received so important a commission proves his eminence among the miniaturists of his day; and the commemoration of his name more than forty years afterwards in Queen Jeanne's will, and still later in the Duc de Berry's inventories, is a very exceptional tribute to his reputation.

The Bible[2] of 1327 is very neatly written by a scribe named Robert de Billyng, and beautifully decorated with

---

[1] Delisle, *12 livres roy.*, pp. 67-75, and *Les Heures dites de Jean Pucelle*, 1910, reproducing the miniatures.

[2] See Martin, *Miniaturistes*, fig. 9; Delisle, *12 livres roy.*, pl. 14; *Exposition des Primitifs Français*, 1904, MSS., No. 23.

FRENCH ILLUMINATION, 14TH CENT.

pen-tracery in blue and red. Of illumination proper, however, it has but little, excellent and tasteful though that little is; and it owes its celebrity largely to the colophon, which not only gives the date of completion, but also states that Jehan Pucelle, Anciau de Cens, and Jaquet Maci "hont enluminé ce livre ci." The Belleville Breviary[1] contains some memoranda which seem to indicate that Pucelle was the *chef d'atelier* commissioned to execute the book, and that he employed Mahiet, Ancelet, and J. Chevrier to assist him as copyists or illuminators. Mahiet and Ancelet are perhaps variants of the names of his former collaborators Maci and Anciau; and it may be conjectured that their work consisted mainly of pen-work and other minor decoration, and that the finest miniatures were painted by Pucelle himself. At any rate, it is convenient, and need not be misleading, to give the name of "school of Pucelle" to the mid-fourteenth century style which is so admirably exemplified in the Belleville Breviary. This beautiful book has seventy-six small miniatures, not enclosed in the initials but set in the column immediately above them (a method which was now beginning to supplant the historiated initial), of the full width of the column of text and about one-third of its height; painted with exquisite minuteness and delicacy, the figures more softly rounded, the draperies more skilfully modelled by means of gradations of colour, than in the Metz Pontifical and its contemporaries. The border-frame is still slightly attached to the initial and miniature, but tends to become an entirely independent piece of ornament. It consists of narrow bars, cusped and knotted at the angles, surrounding the text on both sides and at the bottom; single leaves and sprays shoot out at intervals, and at the top the bars branch out into foliage-stems which nearly meet and complete the frame. Human figures, birds, insects, dragons, and grotesques are dispersed among the foliage, or used as terminals; they are

[1] Martin, *Miniaturistes*, fig. 10, *Peintres*, fig. 14, 15; Delisle, *12 livres roy.*, pp. 81-8, pl. 15-17.

ILLUMINATED MANUSCRIPTS

less freely employed, however, than in the earlier style, and the French border tends to rely more and more on graceful and symmetrical arrangements of conventional foliage, rather than on organic forms, for its effect. In the details of the foliage too there is little striving after either naturalism or variety, both so characteristic of contemporary English work; the three-lobed conventional "ivy-leaf" is used almost exclusively.

In the lower margins of several pages, between the text and the framing bar, are exquisite little scenes from Bible-history and allegorical representations of virtues and of the mysteries of the Church. The main idea in these, a contrast between the Old and New Dispensations, is treated more systematically in the Calendar-illustrations, which form an exceedingly interesting feature of the manuscript. Only the two pages for November and December remain, unfortunately; but the artist's meaning is set forth in an elaborate "exposition des ymages" at the beginning of the book, and the whole of this very curious series of subjects is preserved in a small group of contemporary and later manuscripts. One of the earliest of these is a beautiful Book of Hours, made about 1336-48 for Jeanne II, Queen of Navarre, daughter of Louis X of France; it is now in the collection of Mr. Yates Thompson,[1] who has reproduced its miniatures, together with the November page from the Belleville Breviary and two later manuscripts, the Duke of Berry's "Petites Heures" and "Grandes Heures." The same collector also possesses another member of the group in a Book of Hours made for Jeanne's daughter-in-law, Yolande de Flandre, about 1353.[2] Like the Belleville Breviary, these two Books of Hours are among the choicest surviving specimens of Parisian illumination of

[1] *Hours of Joan II, Queen of Navarre*, Roxburghe Club, 1899. Fully described as No. 75 in the *Catalogue*, ii, pp. 151–183, with the text of the Belleville "exposition" on pp. 365–8. See too *Pal. Soc.*, ii, 36; Burl. F.A. Club, No. 130, pl. 87.

[2] *Hours of Yolande of Flanders*, ed. S. C. Cockerell, 1905, with photogravure illustrations.

FRENCH ILLUMINATION, 14TH CENT.

the time; and both might be classed in the Pucelle school on general grounds of style, even without their remarkable agreement in the Calendar-designs.

The originator of this series, who may well have been Jean Pucelle himself, would seem to have aimed at proving that a high degree of artistic taste and skill was not incompatible with a love for theological symbolism; and he has achieved this so completely that his verbal explanations are, to say the least, a welcome adjunct to his designs. Each month is identified with one of the twelve apostles, with one of the twelve articles of the Creed, and with S. Paul's conversion or one of his Epistles; the whole year also symbolizes the gradual destruction of the Old Dispensation. At the top of each page is a battlemented gate, one of "les xij portes de Jérusalem de Paradis." From its battlements the Virgin Mary, "par quoi nous fu la porte ouverte," waves a banner emblazoned with a device illustrating one of the articles of the Creed. Below her is S. Paul, in January crouching beneath the Hand of God, "comment il fu ravi et apelé," in the other months preaching to attentive groups of Romans, Corinthians, etc. An arch springs from the right-hand side of the gateway, bearing the sun in a position which marks its meridian altitude for the successive months; below is the zodiacal sign, with a landscape sketch suggestive of the season (bare trunks and frost-bound earth in January, rain in February, budding shoots in March, and so on). At the foot of the page is a building, the Synagogue of the Old Testament, from which a prophet removes a stone, symbolizing a prophecy, and gives it to an apostle; in the latter's hands it turns into a scroll, inscribed with an article of the Creed corresponding with the device on the Virgin's banner. Thus the Synagogue, complete in January, crumbles away as the year advances, till in December it falls to the ground in ruins. The series apparently ended with a full-page design, in which the apostles are shown building the Church out of the spoils of the Synagogue;

ILLUMINATED MANUSCRIPTS

but this is no longer extant in the Belleville Breviary or the Yates Thompson MSS.

The Hours of Jeanne de Navarre also contain sixty-eight half-page miniatures and thirty-seven historiated initials, besides border and minor initial decoration on almost every page. The miniatures have the inevitable fourteenth century backgrounds of diaper, checker-work, or colour brocaded with gold scroll-work, and are nearly all enclosed in cusped quatrefoils within square frames of gold and colours. They are not all of equal fineness, but the best are unmistakably the work of a great artist. The soft, well-modelled figures are of a charming type, the colouring is light, bright, and delicate. One of the most interesting features of the book is the series of miniatures accompanying the Hours of S. Louis, an ancestor of Jeanne through both her parents, and therefore doubtless an object of her special devotion. Various scenes in the saint's life are depicted: his instruction as a child, under the watchful eye of his mother Blanche of Castile;[1] his journey to Rheims to be crowned; and so on, till we see him taking the cross on what was thought to be his death-bed.[2] Of the historiated initials, none is more charming than the first, in which Queen Jeanne kneels with a Prayer-book open before her, below a large miniature of the Trinity. The borders are mostly of the regulation bar-and-ivy-leaf type, but birds, butterflies, and other figures occur in a few of the margins: around the Coronation of the Virgin, for instance, are delightful half-length figures of angels playing musical instruments, with Queen Jeanne kneeling on a leaf; equally fascinating in a different way is the quaint group of peasants dancing to a bagpipe, on the Angel and Shepherds page.

The miniatures in the Hours of Yolande of Flanders have lost most of their colour through a Thames flood,

---

[1] Pl. xxxvi.

[2] It is noteworthy that the Hours of S. Louis are also contained in Baroness A. de Rothschild's "Heures de Pucelle."

PLATE XXXVI

HORAE OF JEANNE DE NAVARRE. FRENCH, CIRCA 1330-40
LIBRARY OF H. Y. THOMPSON ESQ.

FRENCH ILLUMINATION, 14TH CENT.

but the exquisite beauty of their design is still perceptible. Apart from its intrinsic merit, this book is interesting as an additional link between the Belleville Breviary and the Hours of Jeanne de Navarre, on the one hand, and the Rothschild "Heures de Pucelle" on the other. Allied to the first two through its Calendar-pictures, it has an equally rare feature in common with the third, viz. a double illustration of the Hours of the Virgin, each of the usual joyful subjects being contrasted with a scene from the Passion. This arrangement has already been noted in chapter xi, as occurring in the Nuremberg Hours; it is, however, very unusual.

The style which these manuscripts represent in its greatest perfection was followed, with more or less success, by French illuminators generally till well on in the latter half of the century. A good example of its application on a large scale may be seen in Roy. 17 E. vii,[1] a copy of the Bible Historiale written in 1357, and containing two half-page miniatures with full borders (one at the beginning of each volume) and eighty-seven smaller ones. In the main outlines of design this manuscript follows what we may call the Pucelle tradition; but it also exemplifies the vitality and continual growth which characterized French art all through the century, for already a change in technique has begun to show itself. The figures are no longer painted in full body-colour like the rest of the miniature, but are in *grisaille* or *camaïeu-gris*, a method of painting in monochrome, usually on a patterned or coloured ground, which soon became very popular with French miniaturists; and rightly so, for grisaille painting at its best is wonderfully effective, having all the combined sharpness and delicacy of cameo. The figures, very faintly shaded and modelled in a cold grey, seem as though moulded or carved in relief; and their pale, semi-lucent quality is enhanced by the splendidly brocaded and tessellated grounds of gold and bright colours against which they stand out. In the

[1] *New Pal. Soc.*, pl. 169.

ILLUMINATED MANUSCRIPTS

Breviary of Jeanne d'Evreux, at Chantilly,[1] we see the method employed on a minute scale. This little book, made about the middle of the century for Jeanne d'Evreux, widow (1328-70) of King Charles IV, contains 114 miniatures, in which the draperies are sometimes fully coloured, but the small, slender figures are delicately painted in grisaille on diapered, trellised or damasked backgrounds. Of somewhat later date, probably about 1370-80, are the two great volumes of S. Augustine's De Civitate Dei in the British Museum;[2] and they show a corresponding improvement in technique. The fine modelling of the grisaille figures, whether in the miniatures or disposed among the bars and foliage of the borders (as in vol i, f. 3), leaves little to be desired by the most exacting critic; and a perfect harmony is established between the figures and their setting, through the restraint observed in the patterned backgrounds, which are often over-emphasized in inferior work of the time, marring the effect of the compositions. A noteworthy advance is to be seen here, too, in the handling of landscape. This is still in a rudimentary condition: the picture is still set, as it were, against a screen covered with conventional patterns, and no attempt is made to represent the sky or distant effects. But the foreground is painted with great care, and with a serious effort in the direction of naturalism; especially in the Creation-scenes at the beginning of vol. ii.[3] Another good example of the grisaille work of this period may be seen in the Missal of S. Denis Abbey, now in the Victoria and Albert Museum at South Kensington. It has no large miniatures, the leaf before the Canon having been cut out; but this lack is atoned for by the exquisite loveliness of the small, delicately shaded figures in the lower margins and in the numerous histori-

---

[1] See the Chantilly *Catalogue*, i, pp. 48-51, pl. 4; Delisle, *12 livres roy.*, pp. 65-6, pl. 19, 20.

[2] Add. 15244-5. See Warner, *Illum. MSS.*, pl. 37, *Reprod.*, ii, 23, iii, 26; also Count A. de Laborde's monumental and sumptuously illustrated *Les MSS. à peintures de la Cité de Dieu de St. Augustin*, Soc. des Bibliophiles français, 1909.

[3] Pl. xxxvii.

PLATE XXXVII

S. AUGUSTINE DE CIVITATE DEI. FRENCH, LATE XIVTH CENT.
BRIT. MUS. ADD. 15245

FRENCH ILLUMINATION, 14TH CENT.

ated initials. The borders are of the usual ivy-leaf type, with well-drawn birds, butterflies, and grotesques in faintly tinted outline.

The history of French illumination in the fourteenth century is largely a catalogue of the library of John, Duke of Berry;[1] especially during the latter part, when he figures not only as collector but as patron. Born in 1345, he inherited from his father, King John II, that love for the fine arts which was traditional in the royal house of France; and his wealth and high position enabled him to gratify it without stint. His brother Charles V shared his taste to some extent, though there is little evidence of this in the pictorial record of his coronation, now in the British Museum.[2] This is a copy of the coronation service of the King and Queen of France, in Latin and French, made (as we learn from his autograph note) by his order in 1365, to serve at once as a memorial of his own coronation in the previous year, and as a guide for future occasions. Its thirty-eight miniatures are perfectly adapted to the latter purpose. Painted in gold and colours, on diapered, tessellated or damasked backgrounds, they are admirable as "diagrams to explain the coronation ritual," but have little significance as works of art, though there is unmistakable portraiture, albeit of a superficial kind, in the continually recurring face of Charles himself.

Among the many manuscripts which, though not made originally for the Duke of Berry, afterwards passed into his possession, there are two in the British Museum which deserve a word of mention, viz. Burney 275 and Harl. 2891, both dating from about the middle of the century. Burney 275 has an illustrious list of owners, having belonged successively to Pope Gregory XI (1370-8)

---

[1] The literature concerning him and his art treasures is extensive, but reference need only be made here to Delisle, "Les Livres d'Heures du duc de Berry," in *Gazette des Beaux-Arts*, 1884, i, pp. 97–110, 281–92, 391–405; and to Bastard, *Librairie de Jean de France, Duc de Berry*, 1834.

[2] Tib. B. viii, ff. 35–80. Reproduced in facsimile by the Henry Bradshaw Society, *Coronation Book of Charles V*, ed. E. S. Dewick, 1899. See too *Pal. Soc.*, i, 148; Warner, *Illum. MSS.*, pl. 36, *Reprod.*, i, 24.

ILLUMINATED MANUSCRIPTS

and the Antipope Clement VII (1378-94), the latter of whom gave it to the Duke of Berry. It contains the works of Priscian, Euclid, and Ptolemy, illustrated with delicious impersonations of the arts and sciences, and with borders in which finely executed animals and grotesques abound. Harl. 2891, a Missal of Paris use, seems to have been a gift from Itier de Martreuil, Bishop of Poitiers 1395-1405, to the Duke, who in his turn gave it to the Sainte Chapelle at Bourges. Besides two full-page miniatures, a Crucifixion and a Christ in Glory[1] (the former a very beautiful composition), prefixed to the Canon, it has a number of historiated initials, with borders of the earlier and more restrained type, all painted with great delicacy; the first page of the Temporale[2] is particularly charming, with an exquisite little miniature of the celebrant lifting up his soul to God—the usual subject, illustrating the introit "Ad te levavi animam meam," but treated with unusual felicity.

Appreciative as he was of the best productions of bygone generations of artists, the Duke of Berry did not neglect his own contemporaries; and we owe him an unspeakable debt of gratitude for his discerning munificence in encouraging the galaxy of brilliant illuminators which included André Beauneveu, Jacquemart de Hesdin, and above all Pol de Limbourg. The last-named belongs mainly to the fifteenth century, and must therefore be reserved for chapter xvi; Hesdin might with equal propriety be classed as late fourteenth or early fifteenth century; but most, if not all, of Beauneveu's work was done before 1400, and as he and Hesdin appear to have collaborated, it seems most convenient to mention them both here.

André Beauneveu[3] was primarily a sculptor and a painter in the ordinary sense, only incidentally a minia-

[1] Reproduced in the *Guide to Exhibited MSS.*, 1906.
[2] Warner, *Reprod.*, ii, 22.
[3] See Dehaisnes, *Hist. de l'Art dans la Flandre*, etc., 1886, pp. 242-57; Champeaux and Gauchery, *Travaux d'art exécutés pour Jean de France, duc de Berry*, 1894, pp. 92-8.

FRENCH ILLUMINATION, 14TH CENT.

turist. A native of Hainault, according to Froissart, who has given him a kind of immortality rare indeed among medieval artists, he occurs repeatedly from 1361 onwards in the municipal accounts of Valenciennes. In 1374 he received payment "pour ouvrage de peinture" (doubtless a wall-painting) which he made in the chamber of the Halle des Jurés; but the other entries refer mainly to his work as a sculptor. In this capacity he was already famous in 1364, when Charles V commissioned him to carve royal tombs for the basilica of S. Denis; and for several years afterwards he was busily engaged in carving statues and inspecting buildings at Ghent, Ypres, Cambrai, and elsewhere, for the Count of Flanders and others. We find him at Bourges in 1386, as salaried "ymagier" to the Duke of Berry; and Froissart mentions him, in terms of glowing eulogy, under the year 1390, as the Duke's director of sculptures and paintings ("maistre de ses oeuvres de taille et de peintures"). The exact date of his death is not known, but he is alluded to as "feu maistre André Beaunepveu" in an inventory[1] attested 16 October, 1403, but apparently drawn up in June, 1402.

Of his miniatures, only twenty-four pages,[2] prefixed to a Latin-French Psalter made for the Duke of Berry (Bibl. Nat., fr. 13091), have come down to us with documentary credentials. They represent the twelve apostles, each balanced by a prophet on the opposite page; the figures in grisaille, seated on faintly coloured thrones rich with architectural ornament; the backgrounds sometimes minutely diapered or tessellated, sometimes coloured reddish brown or very dark blue and covered with a pattern of oak-leaves or other foliage outlined in black. The figures, large in manner, with draperies softly and beautifully modelled, have all the solidity and statuesque-

---

[1] J. Guiffrey, *Inventaires de Jean duc de Berry*, ii, 1896, p. 119.
[2] Many of these have been reproduced, e.g. in Fond. E. Piot, *Mon. et Mém.*, i, p. 187, iii, pl. 6; *Le Manuscrit*, i, 1894, p. 51; Martin, *Peintres*, fig. 17, 18; Michel, *Hist. de l'Art*, iii, pt. i, p. 155.

ness that might be expected of a great sculptor; none of the tight neatness and flat effect that stamp the work of the trained miniaturist. The faces are full of character and individuality, and are obviously portraits of living models. The same qualities, displayed more tellingly on a larger scale, appear in two superb full-page miniatures[1] at the beginning of a Book of Hours in the Royal Library at Brussels (Nos. 11060-1). These two, on opposite pages, form a single composition, representing the Duke of Berry on his knees, between SS. Andrew and John the Baptist, before the Virgin and Child. The pose of the Virgin, enthroned like the prophets and apostles of the Psalter described above (fr. 13091); the handling of the draperies; the charming, unobtrusive backgrounds, of foliage behind the Duke and his patrons, of adoring angels behind the Virgin and Child; the fine expressive heads of the two saints, above all the masterly portrait of the Duke—all these seem to indicate Beauneveu's hand, though an eminent critic[2] has urged the claims of Jacquemart de Hesdin. Beauneveu has been credited on grounds of style with another work, which, though not strictly relevant to the history of illumination, is too interesting to be ignored: a series of exquisite silverpoint studies of the Madonna, a *bal masqué*, and other subjects, covering the boxwood panels of a little sketchbook in Mr. Pierpont Morgan's collection.[3]

Very little is known of Jacquemart de Hesdin's life.[4] Perhaps a pupil of Charles V's court painter Jean de Bruges, he was in the Duke of Berry's service at Bourges in 1384 and 1399; he seems to have been living in 1413, but probably died soon after. The inventories give him sole credit for the decoration of the Brussels Hours, and assign him a share (along with "autres ouvriers de Mon-

[1] Often reproduced, e.g. in Dehaisnes, pl. 8, 9; Michel, iii, i, pp. 156-7. For a description of the manuscript, with fine reproductions of all its miniatures, see Pol de Mont, *Musée des Enluminures*, fasc. i [1905].

[2] R. de Lasteyrie, in Fond. E. Piot, iii, pp. 71-119.

[3] Published by R. E. Fry in the *Burlington Magazine*, x, 1906, pp. 31-8.

[4] See Lasteyrie, as above; Champeaux and Gauchery, pp. 118-21.

FRENCH ILLUMINATION, 14TH CENT.

seigneur," who were doubtless under his direction) in that of the "Grandes Heures," now Bibl. Nat., lat. 919. But the former attribution, authoritative though it seems, is certainly inexact. The twenty large miniatures in the Brussels MS. are all framed in similar borders, of a graceful and unusual type; but the pictures themselves are plainly by several different hands. The first two, in particular, stand out strikingly from the rest, and are emphatically, as we have seen, in the Beauneveu manner; the third combines their subjects into a single picture, of greatly inferior execution and apparently the work of a copyist; while the remainder, varying in merit but sufficiently alike to have been all produced in the same atelier, are typical in style, with their full colouring and elaborate landscapes, of the first quarter of the fifteenth century. In fact, there is much to be said for M. Pol de Mont's theory that Beauneveu painted the first two pages and then left the book, which at a later date was completed by Jacquemart de Hesdin and his assistants.

Besides the "Grandes Heures," finished in 1409, Jacquemart is believed to have painted the best miniatures in the "Petites Heures" (Bibl. Nat., lat. 18014), finished in or before 1402, and also (except Beauneveu's prophets and apostles) in the Latin-French Psalter, fr. 13091. These show him to have been a painter of consummate skill. His work is more conventionally perfect than Beauneveu's, neater and crisper; but it lacks the sculptor's large conception of form. Distinct signs of primitive Italian influence are visible in his miniatures, as in those of most French painters of his time; notably in the landscape, now claiming more and more of the space hitherto given up to conventional patterns. Hardly less conventional itself, this landscape is at first of the type described in chapter iii as characteristic of Byzantine, and afterwards of early Italian art. We see the same flat-topped hillocks with smooth, steep, terraced slopes; but the aridity of the model is generally softened by the herbage, already prominent in French foregrounds, being continued up the hillsides, and the tops are often crowned by a clump of trees or a castle. On the whole, Jacquemart seems to have been an eclectic copyist of great expertness, rather than an original artist. As we have seen already, in choosing subjects to decorate the Calendars of his Books of Hours he had recourse to Jean Pucelle; and he reproduced almost every detail of the earlier artist's compositions with minute, almost slavish exactness. Only in the border-ornament is the divergence striking, and that not in Jacquemart's favour. His sense of proportion fails him here, perfect as his execution is; and he tends to overload his pages with intricate but monotonous convolutions of ivy-leaved sprays.

Before quitting the Duke of Berry's library for the present, we may notice two of his books now in the British Museum, not to be compared for beauty with those just mentioned, but useful as good examples of the average work of the third and last quarters of the fourteenth century. One is Lansd. 1175, the first volume of a French Bible, translated by Raoul de Presles for Charles V (1364–80). It is the only extant MS. containing the translator's dedicatory preface, and is probably the actual copy given to the king, many of whose books found their way into his brother's library. At all events, his portrait is unmistakable in the miniature which heads the preface and shows Raoul presenting his book to Charles. It is well written, by a scribe who signs himself Henri du Trevou, and adorned with neat little miniatures at the beginnings of the several books. The figures, whose chief fault is that their heads are too small, are in grisaille. The backgrounds are as usual checkered, tessellated, or damasked; landscapes of the type just described, with tufted hillocks, often occur. The other manuscript, commonly known as the Berry Bible, contains the Bible Historiale in two large volumes (Harl. 4381–2),[1] written about the end of the century. The first page of Genesis has an elaborate painting of the Trinity, with the

---

[1] Warner, *Illum. MSS.*, pl. 44, *Reprod.*, ii, 24.

FRENCH ILLUMINATION, 14TH CENT.

Virgin, SS. Peter and Paul, and the four Doctors of the Church, as well as a company of pagan philosophers (Plato, Aristotle, Seneca, etc.) and personifications of Dialectic and Arithmetic. The opening page of vol. ii is coarser in execution and less magnificent in design and colouring; it has only a large square enclosing four scenes from the life of Solomon, to illustrate the book of Proverbs. Smaller miniatures abound at the beginnings of books and chapters throughout both volumes, together with ivy-leaf borders and initials rich with burnished gold. The miniatures vary considerably: one or two are extremely good, especially the Nativity, at the beginning of S. Matthew, a really exquisite picture; but the majority are rather hard and flat in technique. In fact, the book is chiefly remarkable for the brilliancy of its colouring. This is particularly splendid in the miniatures whose grounds are of burnished gold or minute diaper, less effective where red, patterned with gold, is used instead.

The Songe du Vergier,[1] written by Philippe de Maizières for Charles V in 1378, is interesting for its frontispiece, which represents the author asleep in an orchard, while a clerk and a knight, the disputants in his dream, stand arguing, and the king sits in state between two charming queens, typifying Spiritual and Temporal Power, the subjects of the dispute. There is a striking contrast between the rudimentary landscape-painting and the mature, naturalistic treatment of the figures. Another curious frontispiece is that prefixed to the same writer's Epistle[2] to Richard II, composed in 1395-6 to promote peace and friendship between that monarch and the French King, Charles VI. In the upper half are the crowns of France and England on blue and red fields, with the Crown of Thorns between them on a black ground, all three under Gothic canopies and inscribed "Charles roy de France, Jesus roy de paix, Richart roy d'Angleterre." The space below is filled with the arms of the two coun-

---

[1] Brit. Mus., Roy. 19 C. iv. See *Pal. Soc.*, ii, 169.
[2] Roy. 20 B. vi. See Warner, *Reprod.*, i, 25.

ILLUMINATED MANUSCRIPTS

tries, the sacred monogram in gold written across the two divisions. On the opposite page is a large miniature of the author presenting his work to King Richard, together with initial and border ornament of the usual type. Like the miniatures of the Berry Bible, and of many contemporary manuscripts, these two pages are a blaze of brilliant colours.

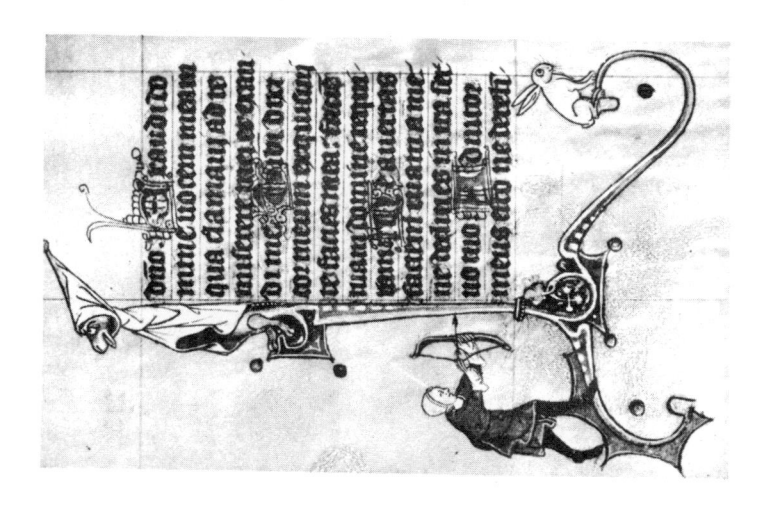

PLATE XXXVIII

HORAE, FLEMISH, CIRCA 1300
BRIT. MUS. STOWE 17

CHAPTER XV

ITALIAN ILLUMINATION IN THE FOURTEENTH CENTURY

AT the outset we might naturally have expected to find Italian illumination at its prime during the age of Giotto, Duccio, and their immediate followers. But as a matter of fact we find instead, among the manuscripts of the fourteenth century, a few frontispieces and other large pictures of supreme beauty, but hardly a single volume whose decoration as a whole will bear comparison with that of a representative French manuscript of the same period. That this is the case need not, however, surprise us very greatly. Closely as all branches of the art of painting must inevitably be allied, there is yet a certain divergence, indeed almost an antagonism, between the true aim of the book-decorator and that of the painter of frescoes or panels. The large, spacious manner which befits the latter requires modification even when applied to a full-page miniature, with its comparatively reduced scale, and is altogether inappropriate to the illumination of a page of text. Hence the ascendency of the great masters of early Italian painting led their disciples who practised miniature into the adoption of methods at variance with the strict canons of the minor art.

The fresco-like manner is seen at its best, naturally, in paintings which fill the page, without any writing to restrict the space and interfere with the design ; as in Mr. Yates Thompson's remarkable series[1] of miniatures of the life of Christ, painted about the beginning of the century, doubtless for inclusion in a Psalter or other

---

[1] No. 81, formerly Ashburnham, Appendix 72. See H. Y. Thompson, *Catalogue*, iii, pp. 45–9, *Illustrations*, ii, pl. 5–15 ; also *Pal. Soc.*, ii, 18.

ILLUMINATED MANUSCRIPTS

liturgical manuscript, of which, however, not a vestige remains. These pictures, thirty-eight in number, are painted on a deep blue ground and framed in plain narrow bands of blue and red, with no ornamentation beyond a little tracery in white on the inner side of the borders. The absence of conventional ornament is in keeping with the severity of the compositions, which are solemn, majestic, and thoroughly monumental in style. The grouping is well ordered and spacious, the gestures are leisurely and dignified, the faces expressive, with careful preservation of types; and one almost forgets such blemishes as the faulty proportions or the characteristically "Giottesque" representation of the hair as a series of laboriously emphasized wavy lines. The British Museum possesses a similar set of paintings (Add. 34309), detached in like manner from the manuscript for which they were made They seem contemporary with the Yates Thompson series, and are closely allied with it as to the subjects represented, some of which are unusual; both series include, for instance, a picture of Christ ascending the cross. The Museum paintings are greatly inferior, however, in feeling and execution, even when due allowance is made for their damaged condition. Most of the compositions are obviously of Byzantine descent, but the round table in the Last Supper seems to link the series to the German Psalters of the thirteenth century.

The illuminator of the verses[1] addressed by the town of Prato to its protector Robert of Anjou, King of Naples, about 1335–40, was evidently more at home in fresco-painting than in miniature. Large as the pages are, he almost always claims the whole of them for his designs, leaving the text to fit itself as best it can into the interstices left by his solid and gigantic figures. These are painted in a thick, rather viscid medium, generally without frames or background. On the best pages the work is very highly finished, face and hair especially

---

[1] Brit. Mus., Roy. 6 E. ix. See Warner, *Reprod.*, ii, 39, 40.

being treated with great care. The curious greyish pink flesh-tints, with a greenish tinge in the shadows, are characteristic of early Italian painting in general, and are found in most of the fourteenth century miniatures. Gold is used plentifully, and the colouring is strong, but with little attempt at gradation or modelling, so that the figures are flat and unshapely masses of colour rather than draped human beings.

The illustrated frontispiece lent itself readily to treatment in the large manner of the panel-painter. Such frontispieces were not confined to literary works, which in fact rarely contained them; but were prefixed to books of a kind from which modern ideas of congruity would banish all ornament: registers of wills, "matricole" (i.e. statutes and lists of members) of trade-guilds, municipal account-books, etc. The great majority of these are of no particular merit as works of art, though useful historically as fixed points,[1] date and locality being seldom stated with equal precision in other manuscripts. But there are one or two gems among them, especially the lovely Assumption of the Virgin[2] painted by Niccolò di Ser Sozzo on the first page of a Caleffo, or register of public documents, which was compiled at Siena in 1334-6, and is preserved in the Archivio di Stato of that city, where it is known as the Caleffo dell' Assunta. No other works by this great artist are known to exist; but he has fortunately signed this masterpiece (" Nicholaus ser sozzo de senis me pinxit "), which alone is enough to stamp him as one of the great Sienese painters of his time—and that the time of Simone Martini and the Lorenzetti. It is more than probable that in the next century Matteo di Giovanni, whose great altar-piece of

[1] A few examples may be named, more or less elaborately decorated at the beginning:—Brit. Mus., Add. 16532 (Bologna, 1334), 21965 (Perugia, 1368), 22497 (Perugia, before 1403); Vitelli e Paoli, *Facsimili paleografici*, Lat., pl. 20 (Florence, 1340); F. Carta, *Atlante pal.-art.*, 1899, pl. 58 (Venice, 1392), 59-60 (Bologna, 1394). Others will be mentioned farther on, in connection with Niccolò da Bologna.

[2] Pl. xxxix.

ILLUMINATED MANUSCRIPTS

the same subject is now in the National Gallery, was inspired by this beautiful miniature, which he must have had many opportunities of seeing. The frontispiece to Petrarch's Virgil, now in the Ambrosian Library, was painted by Simone Martini himself; and he has also been credited by some critics with the charming illuminations of the "Codice di S. Giorgio" in the Archives of S. Peter's at Rome, but this attribution is doubtful.[1]

The next best thing to a full page, for a painter who demands amplitude, is a large share in a page of exceptional size; and this was provided in generous measure for the illuminators charged with the decoration of the gigantic choir-books in which Italian chapter-libraries are so rich, and which form so important a feature in the history of Italian painting. The historiated initial, to the Northern illuminator at first a field for the congenial exercise of minute compression, afterwards so irksome through its restrictions that it was virtually abandoned in favour of the purely ornamental initial surmounted by a miniature in a separate frame, followed a different course of development in the hands of his Italian *confrère*. The letter itself, of elaborate design, rich in gold and bright colours and lavishly adorned with pendent decoration, claimed more and more of the page of a huge Gradual or Antiphoner, and framed a picture which in largeness of manner often rivalled the compositions of contemporary panel-painters. These splendid *Libri Corali* reached their full development before the end of the fourteenth century, as regards the main outlines of their decoration, though the finest examples now extant were mostly produced about a hundred years later. To be studied properly they must be visited in their native land.[2] Such enormous volumes do not lend themselves readily to transport overseas; and the single leaves or

---

[1] See Venturi, *Storia dell' Arte italiana*, v, pp. 621, 1018-30, fig. 786-91.

[2] A few examples are given by Venturi, iii, fig. 445-57, v, fig. 793-806, from Modena, Siena, and elsewhere. See too *Atl. pal.-art.*, pl. 51 (Asti Antiphoner, dated 1332).

PLATE XXXIX

NICCOLO DI SER SOZZO, 1334-6
SIENA, ARCHIVIO DI STATO. CALEFFO DELL' ASSUNTA

ITALIAN ILLUMINATION, 14TH CENT.

initials, cut out unscrupulously from their original setting, which abound in English libraries and art-collections,[1] public and private, are unsatisfactory for scientific purposes, however beautiful they may be in themselves. The British Museum is fortunate in possessing a handsome Gradual (Add. 18198)[2] made for some monastery near Florence, perhaps that of Vallombrosa, about the middle of the fourteenth century. It contains the Proprium and Commune Sanctorum, the former adorned at the principal feasts with large initials enclosing miniatures. These are painted in soft tints of blue, red, and other colours, on backgrounds of richly burnished gold. There is no border-ornament beyond a slight continuation of the leafy decoration of some of the initials. The initials to the less important feasts are mostly historiated with half-length figures of saints, painted on grounds of blue or lake with a little white tracery, and are not specially noteworthy; but many of the ordinary blue and red initials are surrounded with a most elaborate sort of lace-work design in red, white, and blue. Italian scribes or illuminators were particularly fond of this form of decoration, and practised it with amazing skill and excellent taste, especially in the fourteenth century. It is seen at its highest perfection of delicate intricacy in a late fourteenth century Missale Pontificis (Add. 21973), a book not otherwise remarkable artistically, though the painting of the Crucifixion, on a pale blue ground edged with white tracery, is by no means without merit. This filigree pen-work was sometimes extended from the initial to form a partial border, as in Add. 34247,[3] a Bolognese Book of Hours written near the end of the century.

Byzantine traditions were still strong in Italy at the

---

[1] Several volumes and portfolios in the British Museum are filled with cuttings of this kind, fourteenth to sixteenth centuries (Add. MSS. 18196–7, 21412, 32058, 35254); and many fine leaves are exhibited in the Victoria and Albert Museum.

[2] Warner, *Reprod.*, i, 46 (accidentally given the lettering which belongs to pl. 45).

[3] Warner, *Reprod.*, ii, 44.

ILLUMINATED MANUSCRIPTS

beginning of the fourteenth century, and appear plainly in much of the best illumination that was not really fresco or panel-painting on a small scale. Looking at the exquisite little figures which fill the margins of a Benedictine Breviary in the British Museum (Add. 15205-6),[1] we are forcibly reminded of the Theodore Psalter and the Simeon Metaphrastes. The small miniatures enclosed within initials are of course Byzantine in their iconography; this is all but inevitable in Italian art of the time. But the same influence is apparent here in the subdued colouring, the pose of the figures, the treatment of the faces. Among other interesting features of the book are the raised patterns of dots and lines with which the gold nimbi and backgrounds are covered.

Traces of Byzantine tradition may be seen again, combined with other influences, in the great Bible of the British Museum (Add. 18720)[2] and its twin-sister at Paris (Bibl. Nat., lat. 18),[3] where the figure-compositions and borders are not only effective in themselves, but are controlled by a nice sense of the due proportions between text and illumination—a rare quality in fourteenth century Italian manuscripts. Sig. Venturi assigns these two books, together with a similar Bible in the Vatican (Vat. lat. 20),[4] to a school of Bolognese miniaturists flourishing about the beginning of the fourteenth century. Whatever their provenance may be, about their excellence there can be no question. In the main outlines of its scheme of decoration, Add. 18720 follows the pattern of the normal thirteenth century French or English Bible: a series representing the Days of Creation set in a tall narrow frame at the beginning of Genesis, a similar frame containing a Jesse-tree prefixed to S. Matthew,

---

[1] Warner, *Reprod.*, ii, 38.
[2] Warner, *Illum. MSS.*, pl. 38, *Reprod.*, i, 43.
[3] Venturi, ii, fig. 345-50, v, fig. 774.
[4] Mr. Yates Thompson's Bentivoglio Bible (No. 4, *Cat.*, i, pp. 12-18, *Illustrations*, ii, pl. 16-21) has much in common with these manuscripts; it also seems allied to the Franciscan Bible (D. i. 13) at Turin. See *Atl. pal.-art.*, pl. 53.

ITALIAN ILLUMINATION, 14TH CENT.

and historiated initials to the other books. But the treatment is very different from that of the Northern miniaturists: the stately pose, the fine modelling of limbs and draperies, the soft, subdued, almost sombre colouring, the swarthy faces, with white high-lights and greenish shadows, all show close adherence to the best traditions of Italo-Byzantine art. The Genesis and Matthew pages have three additional scenes in the lower margin: the expulsion from Paradise, the sacrifices of Cain and Abel, and the murder of Abel on the former, the Annunciation, Nativity, and Presentation on the latter. The borders are of the light and pleasing type described at the end of chapter ix as characteristic of Italian fourteenth century illumination; less subdued in tint than the miniatures, they brighten up the pages most effectively. Human figures are sometimes employed as terminals or supports to the stems which form the framework; among these is a graceful youth, nude and exquisitely modelled, on the first page. At the foot of this page are also two Dominican friars, whose presence recalls the fact that Bologna was a great stronghold of that order.

The same well-adjusted balance between text and decoration is found in the British Museum Durandus (Add. 31032);[1] but this book has nothing like the large simplicity and majestic beauty of the great Bible. Borders and initials are very highly finished, but the multiplicity of minute details of ornament gives them a somewhat meaningless and finicking appearance. Detached gilt discs, a favourite device with Italian illuminators in the fourteenth and early fifteenth centuries, are used abundantly in the borders; but instead of enriching the decorative scheme they serve rather to enhance its triviality. The colour-effect would be somewhat pallid but for the brilliancy of the stippled gold grounds.

One might naturally expect to be confronted at every turn with evidences of the influence of Giotto; but as

[1] *Pal. Soc.*, i, 221; Warner, *Illum. MSS.*, pl. 39, *Reprod.*, ii, 41.

a matter of fact there are few manuscripts in which anything of the sort appears. One of these few is Add. 27428[1] in the British Museum, a volume containing Simone da Cascia's Lordene della Vita Cristiana (composed in 1333), followed by lives of saints in Italian. These last are illustrated with miniatures on gold grounds, in plain rectangular frames, set in the column of text and filling its whole width. The compositions are crowded, and appear still more so from the fact that the figures are of almost the full height of the picture, as though the artist had designed them without regard to the amount of space at his disposal. It would be a gross injustice to the great master to call these quaint, brilliantly coloured little paintings Giottesque; but there is a far-away suggestion of his manner in the clear-cut profiles, the well-defined types, the careful treatment of the hair.

A few words must be said about the great tomes of civil and canon law, the output of which must have been prodigious, to judge from the numbers still preserved. They were mostly written, no doubt, in the universities of Bologna and Padua, and were probably illuminated at the same time, as a rule, though some were sent out plain, to be decorated in their place of destination.[2] The illuminations in the vast majority of cases are singularly unattractive, being coarsely executed, with repulsive underhung faces. This ugly type of face is not peculiar to law-books, but recurs constantly in the inferior work of the North Italian schools in the first half of the century, e.g. in a copy of the Divina Commedia now in the British Museum (Eg. 943). After the middle of the century some improvement is visible, as in Add. 23923, a copy of the Decretals of Boniface VIII, written between 1370 and 1381, and illuminated in a style which Sig. Venturi considers distinctive of the school of Niccolò da

---

[1] *Pal. Soc.*, i, 247; Warner, *Reprod.*, i, 42.
[2] Roy. 10 E. iv, for instance, was illuminated in England. See above, p. 230.

ITALIAN ILLUMINATION, 14TH CENT.

Bologna. This prolific miniaturist,[1] who worked from 1349 to 1399, does not seem himself to have painted many law-books; his illuminations are to be found chiefly in choir-books, missals, and "matricole," and seem to be remarkable for his unusual habit of signing them rather than for their own superlative excellence. Of the many fourteenth century Italian law-books in the British Museum, the only one with real artistic significance is a fine two-volume copy of the Decretum (Add. 15274-5),[2] written in the latter part of the century. A large picture of the Pope in Council fills half the first page, which has also an initial enclosing a miniature of a scribe at work, and an elaborate and handsome border replete with a great variety of ornament. Each of the thirty-six chapters is preceded by a miniature illustrating its subject-matter, and begins with a large initial enclosing a single figure, usually legal or clerical. All these are well executed and very richly coloured, vermilion and deep blue prevailing.

The curious manuscript attributed to that shadowy person, Cybo the Monk of Hyères (Brit. Mus., Add. 27695, 28841),[3] has no very obvious relation to the main course of Italian illumination, but is too interesting to be passed over in silence. The Monk of Hyères was clearly an individualist, who owed as little to his predecessors as he bequeathed to his successors. His large miniatures, illustrating the text, a treatise on the Vices, are bold and expressive in design; but with their vivid colouring and aggressive checkered background they cannot be called beautiful. The conventions of figure-composition did not suit his genius, which was emphatically that of a naturalist; and he found a congenial exercise for his powers in covering the margins and line-endings of the text-pages with plants, insects, birds, and animals of various kinds,

---

[1] See Venturi, v, pp. 942, 1014-6; *Archivio Storico dell' Arte*, 1894, pp. 1-20; *L'Arte*, 1907, pp. 105-15.

[2] Warner, *Illum. MSS.*, pl. 40, *Reprod.*, ii, 42.

[3] *Pal. Soc.*, i, 149, 150.

ILLUMINATED MANUSCRIPTS

painted with the most marvellous fidelity to nature. All are wonderful, but his special predilection was evidently for insect life: his spiders, bees, grasshoppers, and stag-beetles seem to be positively starting out of the page. It is hard to find a parallel nearer to his date (end of the fourteenth century) than the Flemish miniaturists a hundred years later; and even their work seems tame and flat in comparison.

CHAPTER XVI

FRENCH ILLUMINATION AFTER 1400

BY the beginning of the fifteenth century the production of illuminated manuscripts had become in France almost a staple industry. Books of Hours, in particular, were produced in vast numbers, not only to the order of wealthy patrons, but also for booksellers to add to their stock and sell to any chance customer. Specimens of these "shop copies" may be seen in nearly every library in Europe, and form the nucleus of most private collections; being comparatively easy to acquire and at the same time pleasing to behold, despite the perfunctory nature of much of the miniature-painting, through the fidelity with which an excellent tradition in border-decoration was followed. This was founded on the "ivy-leaf" pattern which came into vogue early in the fourteenth century: modified by the gilding of the leaves and their diminution in size, by the increased intricacy of the stem-convolutions, and by the introduction of a few additional forms of foliate, floral, and other ornament, the type persisted with little variation until the second half of the fifteenth century, when it gave way to a much less tasteful style of border, with backgrounds partly or wholly gilt instead of the plain vellum. Another change for the worse began to come in about the same time, viz. the substitution of architectural frames of heavy Renaissance style, with much gilding, for the simple bands which had hitherto enclosed the large miniatures.

So much for the average work, which exists in such quantity as to demand some notice, and at the same time to render any attempt at detailed treatment impossible in a general sketch like the present. Of work of a higher class there is enough to fill many chapters, and only the salient points can be indicated here. The death of the Duke of Berry in 1416 marks the close of the first and greatest epoch, culminating (as indeed the whole art of illumination may be said to do) in the wonderful "Très Riches Heures," which Pol de Limbourg and his brothers were then engaged in painting for him. These artists did not long survive their patron; and the period which followed, though one of great luxuriance and brilliancy, producing a remarkable group of books among which the Bedford Hours holds a leading place, showed already the beginning of a decadence in point of taste. About the middle of the century flourished the great painter Jean Fouquet, and his influence survived among his disciples, notably the "egregius pictor Franciscus" who has been conjecturally identified with his son François, and later in the works of Jean Bourdichon, painter of the Hours of Anne of Brittany, and of his school, continuing until well on in the sixteenth century.

French illumination had reached a very high level by the end of the fourteenth century, as we saw in chapter xiv; and the opening years of the next century have bequeathed to us a great many manuscripts of such excellence that one only hesitates to call them first-rate because they are eclipsed by the superlative beauty of the few real masterpieces. An admirable sample of this class is the Boucicaut Hours,[1] in Madame Jacquemart-André's collection. This book, executed for the Maréchal de Boucicaut between 1396 and 1421, shows its transitional nature in the backgrounds, which in a few of the miniatures are filled with deep blue sky spangled with stars, a welcome relief from the somewhat wearisome checkered and brocaded patterns. The latter, appropriate enough as a setting for the comparatively flat, conventional treatment

---

[1] *Les Heures du maréchal de Boucicaut*, Soc. des Bibliophiles fr., 1889. See too Durrieu, "La peinture en France au début du xve siècle," in *Revue de l'art anc. et mod.*, xix, pp. 401-15, xx, pp. 21-35; and his "Jacques Coene," in *Les arts anc. de Flandre*, ii, pp. 5-22.

of figures and accessories seen in the miniatures of earlier date, match ill with the realism which begins to show itself in these pictures with their improved perspective and increasing attention to landscape. Still more striking is this incongruity in a splendid copy of the Livre de la Chasse of Gaston Phébus, Comte de Foix (Bibl. Nat., fr. 616), whose numerous and extremely interesting illustrations[1] quaintly combine these purely conventional backgrounds with a spirited and by no means unsuccessful attempt at naturalistic treatment of woodland hunting scenes. The various operations of the chase are depicted most clearly and in the fullest detail: questing for trails, setting snares, traps, and nets, etc., nothing is forgotten, not even the hunters' meal in a glade of the forest. The various species of game, and the corresponding breeds of dog, are all recognizable at a glance; and the whole of the foreground, vegetable as well as animal, shows a genuine and careful study of nature. But on reaching the tree-tops our artist almost invariably relapses into conventionalism, and gives us, instead of skies, backgrounds covered with the stereotyped lozengy, tessellated or brocaded patterns.

In many manuscripts of this period, however, these formal backgrounds are discarded altogether, and in their place we have a clear blue sky, very pale at the horizon, and deepening by careful gradation towards the top of the picture. Of this class are the Livre des Merveilles (Bibl. Nat., fr. 2810), the British Museum Statius (Burney 257), and the famous Terence of the Arsenal Library (No. 664). The first-named was apparently made for Philippe le Hardi, Duke of Burgundy (d. 1404), whose son, John the Fearless, gave it in 1413 to the Duke of Berry. It is a collection of Eastern travellers' tales, compiled from the narratives of Marco Polo, Mandeville, and others; and its 265 illustrations,[2] as might be expected, are interesting

---

[1] Published in reduced facsimile, ed. C. Couderc [1909]. For full-sized reproductions see W. A. and F. Baillie-Grohman, *The Master of Game*, 1904.

[2] *Livre des Merveilles*, ed. H. O[mont], 2 vols. [1907].

and amusing, presenting a most welcome variety of subject. The Arsenal Terence,[1] usually known as the "Térence des Ducs" from its first possessors, Louis, Duke of Guyenne and Dauphin (d. 1415), and John, Duke of Berry, is also very copiously illustrated; and its miniatures have a special value from the complete absence of any marvellous or symbolical element to interfere with the simpler aim of depicting actual life as the artists saw it. The faces are well and clearly drawn, the posing and grouping of the figures full of dramatic expressiveness, the costumes carefully painted. The Statius[2] is a less sumptuous manuscript, but belongs more or less to the same family; its figures are mostly in grisaille, very softly and delicately executed, with much grace and charm.

Among the many fine Books of Hours of this period, Lat. 1161 in the Bibliothèque Nationale is worthy of special mention. As in the Boucicaut Hours (with which this book, though on a smaller scale, has much in common), only a few of the miniatures have sky-backgrounds, the others having mostly a checkered pattern, or else purple or blue covered with gold filigree-work. The borders are graceful and varied, containing among other details of ornament (besides the inevitable ivy-leaf, which of course predominates) the long sinuated leaf entwined about a slender stem, which we noticed in some English manuscripts of the end of the fourteenth century; quatrefoils, birds, mermaid, and grotesque organist also occur. The miniatures are remarkable for their brilliant yet finely harmonized colours, the rich bright red and blue of the costumes contrasting effectively with the white or pale grey architecture. The best of them, perhaps, is the really beautiful half-page picture at the end, of the Virgin and Child adored by a lady whose guardian angel stands by her. The burial-scene in a monastic cemetery, prefixed to the Vigils of the Dead, is an impressive and

---

[1] H. Martin, *Le Térence des Ducs*, 1908, *Les Miniaturistes français*, 1906, fig. 29-32.

[2] Warner, *Reprod.*, iii, 28.

FRENCH ILLUMINATION AFTER 1400

interesting composition; but modern ideas of propriety are rudely jarred by the presence of a white dog, squatting just behind the celebrant, in the "Salve sancta parens" miniature (f. 192).

Closely allied to Lat. 1161 is a Horae in the British Museum (Add. 32454),[1] whose miniatures (above all, the splendid Coronation of the Virgin on f. 46), show the same brilliancy of colouring, and whose borders are even more varied, especially those which accompany the large miniatures. Some of the devices, e.g. putti springing from flowers, suggest the influence of Italian art; an influence unmistakably present in the decoration of another Horae in the same collection (Add. 29433).[2] This manuscript follows the liturgical use of Paris, and its minor decorations are thoroughly French in style, with diapered grounds to the small miniatures; but in the more elaborate pages there is a strong, sometimes even preponderating, admixture of the Italian element. These pages are very finely executed, and glow with burnished gold and bright colours. The borders are filled with various forms of natural or conventional foliage, partly painted on the plain vellum, partly against a ground of burnished gold; putti disport themselves among the leaves or grow Clytie-wise out of flowers, and birds, butterflies, rayed gilt discs, and detached flowers are disposed about the margins. All this gaiety produces sometimes a whimsical effect, as in the opening page of the Penitential Psalms: the miniature represents the damned being collected by devils from castle, city, and convent, and hurled down into hell, where they are devoured by Satan and tortured by his myrmidons; but instead of inspiring dread and horror, the whole picture gives an impression of light-hearted, hustling activity. There is a touch of the same bizarre humour in the fine miniature of the Annunciation: the Virgin and Gabriel are in opposite transepts of a Gothic church, while the

---

[1] Warner, *Reprod.*, ii, 25; Michel, *Hist. de l'Art.*, iii, i, fig. 96.
[2] Warner, i, 26.

space between them, in the nave, is occupied by a cat and dog fighting.

A very finished and beautiful example of this period is the Burgundy Breviary in the British Museum (Harl. 2897, Add. 35311).[1] Executed for John the Fearless, Duke of Burgundy (1404-19), and his wife Margaret of Bavaria, it was originally complete in one volume; but for convenience it was soon afterwards divided into two parts, and the Calendar and Psalter duplicated so as to complete the second part (now Harl. 2897), the miniatures in the second Psalter having evidently been copied, by a somewhat inferior hand, from those in the first, or at any rate from the same designs. The two volumes, after centuries of separation, were brought together again through the Rothschild bequest in 1899. Both volumes have suffered some mutilation, and the Rothschild MS. has now only two large miniatures, the Harleian but one. All three are of great beauty, and are specially remarkable for their luxuriant and yet harmonious colour-scheme. Particularly lovely is the blue, so characteristic of French illumination at this time; at once cold and brilliant, exquisitely transparent yet capable of forming a solid mass upon the page, its effect is always beautiful and satisfying, whether it be used in a pure or modified form, for skies, draperies, or ornament. The smaller miniatures are very numerous, and the best of these, though less imposing than the three large paintings, are no whit inferior in beauty and finish. One of the most charming is that of S. Anne teaching the Virgin to read;[2] the soft treatment of the face, the delicate gradations of colour, the fine modelling of the draperies, are here seen at their best, and so is the typical border-ornament of gilt ivy-leaves. More sumptuous and varied borders surround the three principal pages. The most splendid of these is at the beginning of the Psalter (Add. 35311, f. 8), with plaques of burnished and delicately patterned gold en-

---

[1] *Pal. Soc.*, i, 224-5; Warner, *Illum. MSS.*, pl. 45-6, *Reprod.*, i, 27, iii, 29-31.
[2] See Frontispiece.

FRENCH ILLUMINATION AFTER 1400

closing half-length figures of David, Goliath, and angel-musicians, and with exquisitely painted birds and flowers. Within the initial "B" on the same page is a wonderfully tender Madonna holding the Child closely to her and sheltering Him with her cloak. The border of the Ascension-day page (Harl. 2897, f. 188b) is more monotonous in design; its special interest lies in the graceful figure of a lady who sits on a daisy-studded lawn and holds the shields of arms of the Duke and Duchess —furnishing the sole evidence as to the history of the manuscript.

The books mentioned hitherto may serve to indicate the abundance and the great excellence of French illumination in the opening years of the fifteenth century; but they all—even the Burgundy Breviary—pale into insignificance beside the glory of the aptly named "Très Riches Heures," which Pol de Limbourg and his brothers Jehannequin and Hermann were painting for the Duke of Berry, when his death in 1416 brought their work to a premature end. This wonderful book, now in the Musée Condé at Chantilly,[1] was completed about 1485 by a miniaturist named Jean Colombe for Charles, Duke of Savoy, and his Duchess, Blanche de Montferrat; and the later illuminations, excellent examples of their period, only serve as a foil to the dazzling beauty of the pages painted by the Limbourg brothers. The latter begin with twelve full-page Calendar-pictures, the occupation-scenes in which were taken as models by Flemish illuminators at the end of the fifteenth century, e.g. in the Grimani Breviary and the Hennessy Hours. But while the later artists generally placed their compositions in landscapes of a distinctly Flemish character, Pol and his brothers paid a subtle compliment to their patron by introducing a fine series of paintings of his châteaux. Thus in March we see the fortress of Lusignan, with the dragon-fairy Mélusine flying to re-

[1] No. 1284. See the Chantilly *Catalogue*, i, pp. 59–71, pl. 5–8; Delisle, in *Gazette des Beaux-Arts*, 1884, i, pp. 401–4 (four plates); and above all Durrieu's two stately volumes, *Les Très Riches Heures de Jean, duc de Berry*, 1904.

join her husband Raymondin; the dainty and gracious betrothal-scene, which illustrates April, is placed just outside the walls of Dourdan; the May-day hunting-party rides through a wood above which the towers of Riom are visible. Moreover, the Duke himself is represented in the January picture, sitting in state at a banquet, conversing with an ecclesiastic, while groups of fashionably dressed courtiers stand about. Above each of these pictures, in a semicircle enclosed by a starry arch bearing the zodiacal signs for the month, is the chariot of the sun, drawn by winged steeds across the sky.

Landscape-painting is not confined to the Calendar, but is used when possible to enrich the scriptural and hagiographical scenes. The meeting of Mary and Elizabeth,[1] for instance, takes place in a region of bleak and craggy hills, with a stately pinnacled city in the distance. More specially appropriate is the illustration to the Mass of S. Michael—a fine picture of Mont S. Michel with its abbey buildings and with the waves breaking at the foot of the mount, the islet of Tombelaine in the offing, the Archangel and Satan fighting furiously in mid-air.

Masterly artists in every way, it is as colourists above all that the Limbourg brothers show their consummate powers. At once brilliant and delicate, clean without hardness, and infinitely varied without loss of unity, the colouring could hardly be surpassed in beauty; on vellum, at any rate, it assuredly never has been. Most of the pages glow with bright and joyous sunlight; but night-effects are attempted with great success in a few pictures, as in the dusky blue of the Gethsemane scene, where the soldiers fall prostrate before the divine majesty of Christ; or in the lurid darkness of hell, with the devils, and the lost souls whom they torture with every circumstance of medieval ingenuity, seen dimly in the smoky gloom.

Very little is known as to Pol and his brothers, beyond the fact that for the last few years of the Duke of Berry's life they were salaried members of his household. A

[1] Pl. xl.

PLATE XL

"TRES RICHES HEURES" OF JEAN DUC DE BERRY, D. 1416
BY PAUL DE LIMBOURG AND HIS BROTHERS. CHANTILLY, MUSÉE CONDÉ

FRENCH ILLUMINATION AFTER 1400

document dated 1 February, 1434, concerning a house at Bourges given by the Duke to Pol about 1409, shows that he had long been dead (his widow having married again and died, and her second husband having "longuement tenu et occupé" the said house), and implies by its silence that his two brothers were also dead. They must have had time, however, before 1416 if not after, to execute many other paintings besides those in the "Très Riches Heures"; among those which have been more or less confidently assigned to them, on grounds of style in default of documentary evidence, are the miniatures in the "Belles Heures" of the Duke of Berry, now in Baron Edmond de Rothschild's collection,[1] and a Crucifixion and a Majestas Domini in a Missal given to the church of S. Magloire at Paris in 1412 (Bibl. de l'Arsenal, No. 623).[2] Whether these attributions be well founded or not, it is clear that in the "Très Riches Heures" we have the supreme achievement of this remarkable band of brothers. In it, as in Add. 32454 and 29433, signs of Italian influence have been recognized; indeed, the miniature of the Purification (Durrieu, pl. 39) is all but identical in composition with Taddeo Gaddi's fresco of the Presentation of the Virgin, in the church of Santa Croce at Florence.[3]

We come next to a splendid group of manuscripts illuminated at Paris in or about the second quarter of the century, three of them for John, Duke of Bedford, uncle of Henry VI and Regent of France from 1422 until his death in 1435. The finest of these is his Book of Hours (Brit. Mus., Add. 18850),[4] commonly but incorrectly called the "Bedford Missal." It was probably made on the occasion of his marriage, in 1423, to Anne, daughter of John the Fearless, Duke of Burgundy; for it

---

[1] *Gazette des Beaux-Arts*, 1906, i, pp. 265–92.
[2] *Primitifs Français*, 1904, pt. ii, No. 222 (pl. opp. p. 61); Martin, *Peintres*, p. 75, fig. 20.
[3] M. Durrieu maintains, however (pp. 45–73), that not even this resemblance, striking though it is, affords any proof of direct Italian influence.
[4] *Pal. Soc.*, i, 172–3; Warner, *Illum. MSS.*, pl. 47, *Reprod.*, iii, 32–4.

ILLUMINATED MANUSCRIPTS

contains her portrait, arms, and motto as well as his, and it was given by her, with his consent, to the young King Henry on Christmas Eve, 1430. Its wealth of decoration is extraordinary, almost unique, in fact, though it falls far short of the "Très Riches Heures" in beauty. Every page of text has a full border of the same type as the most elaborate borders in the Burgundy Breviary, but more luxuriant, with columbines, violets, and other flowers combined with ivy-leaf and acanthus, and with brilliant little medallion-miniatures introduced. After the Calendar are four full-page paintings of scenes from Genesis, without borders; these are among the best pages in the book, especially the building of the Ark and the Tower of Babel, with their interesting details and the lively, natural action of the figures. Each of the large miniatures prefixed to the principal divisions of the text is accompanied by a series of vignettes connected with it in subject, usually placed in a richly ornate border of flowers, birds, and foliage, with little or none of the ivy-leaf pattern which forms the groundwork of the other borders. Thus the Lessons from the four Gospels have large pictures of the Evangelists writing, surrounded with vignettes representing incidents in their lives; at the Hours of the Dead, monks are seen chanting round a bier which stands in a stately Gothic choir, while the vignettes in the border illustrate the last rites of the Church.[1] But the Annunciation, prefixed to Matins of the Virgin, is completely framed by twelve scenes from Our Lady's life, which leave no space for any non-pictorial border-ornament. The two portrait-pages, near the end of the book (ff. 256b, 257b), are splendid. The Duke and Duchess, in magnificent attire, kneel before their respective patrons; their faces are very carefully painted in pure profile, and have every appearance of being authentic portraits of high value. The last miniature in the volume (f. 288b) is a fine full-page composition, illustrating the legend of the divine origin of the royal arms

[1] Pl. xli.

BEDFORD HOURS. FRENCH, CIRCA 1423

BRIT. MUS. ADD. 18850

FRENCH ILLUMINATION AFTER 1400

of France. On the whole, it is chiefly through its excessive sumptuousness that the Bedford Hours misses the very highest rank. Every page is lavishly flowered with brilliant colours and ingenious patterns, but the total effect is gorgeous rather than entirely satisfying; splendid and skilful as the painting is, it fails to achieve complete success through lack of restraint and simplicity of plan. In fact, a decline in artistic taste has already begun.

The Sarum Breviary in the Bibl. Nat. (lat. 17294)[1] was also made for the Duke of Bedford; its decoration is similar to that of his Hours, and was evidently the work of the same artists. Its date, however, is somewhat later, for it contains the arms of his second wife, Jacqueline of Luxembourg, whom he married in 1433. Another book begun for the same patron was the famous Pontifical of Jacques Jouvenel des Ursins, which was acquired by the city of Paris in 1861. Ten years later it perished in the fire at the Hôtel de Ville—a truly lamentable loss, to judge by Vallet de Viriville's description of the manuscript,[2] and by Le Roux de Lincy's coloured reproductions[3] of three of its miniatures containing views of old Paris.

The Sobieski Hours[4] (so called from having once belonged to John Sobieski, King of Poland), bequeathed by Cardinal Henry Stuart to George IV, and now in the Royal Library at Windsor, belongs to the same group. The precise circumstances of its origin are uncertain, but it seems probable that it was made for Margaret, sister of Anne, Duchess of Bedford, to signalize her marriage in 1423 to Arthur, Comte de Richemont. At any rate, it is clearly contemporary with the Bedford Hours and decorated to a large extent by the same artists. The best pages indeed are even superior to most of the work in that book: less overlaid with border-ornament, more

---

[1] *Primitifs Fr.*, ii, No. 106.
[2] *Gaz. des Beaux-Arts*, 1866, ii, pp. 471–88.
[3] *Paris et ses historiens*, 1867, pl. 4, 8, 10.
[4] *New Pal. Soc.*, pl. 94–6, 194–5; Burl. F.A. Club, No. 209, pl. 134.

delicate and harmonious in colouring. In fact, it may be regarded as a sort of connecting link between the comparatively restrained style of the Burgundy Breviary and "Très Riches Heures," on the one hand, and the florid sumptuousness of the Bedford books on the other. The Calendar preserves some traces of fourteenth century symbolism in its figures of prophets and apostles with scrolls, balancing each other at the foot of the page; but it also has, like the Bedford Hours, figures of saints in the margins opposite their respective days, not framed as in the Bedford Hours, but inserted in the borders. The large miniatures, many of which are interesting in subject as well as admirable in treatment, are mostly composite pictures, either divided into compartments or else representing several incidents continuously. Of the former, one of the most charming examples is the series of scenes from the life of the Virgin prefixed to her Hours; of the latter, the Mont S. Michel picture at the Memoria of S. Michael.

Of the same class, though on a much smaller scale, is a beautiful little Book of Hours in Mr. Yates Thompson's collection,[1] made for the famous Dunois, Bastard of Orleans, probably after his capture of Paris in 1436, for it is evidently the work of the brilliant school of Parisian illuminators who had enjoyed the patronage of the Duke of Bedford under the English *régime.* In its long series of admirable miniatures are some of uncommon design, especially the representations of the seven deadly sins which illustrate the Penitential Psalms; one of these, the picture of Idleness (f. 162), has a fine landscape background, which has been recognized as a careful copy from Jan van Eyck's well-known "Vierge au donateur" in the Louvre. Dunois himself is introduced in three of the miniatures, and these are perhaps the only authentic portraits of the great soldier in existence.

The same collection includes another Book of Hours [2]

[1] No. 11.   See *Catalogue*, i, pp. 49–57.
[2] No. 85.   See *Catalogue*, ii, pp. 238–64.

of this period, even more plentifully adorned with miniatures, though hardly of quite so high a level of artistic excellence; made for Admiral Prigent de Coëtivy (d. 1450), probably before 1445. In colouring the contrast between the two manuscripts is great, the Dunois book having all the rich brilliancy of its class, while most of the miniatures in the Coëtivy Hours are painted in what is practically a modification of grisaille, the draperies being left white, against backgrounds coloured in light tones.

Somewhat earlier is the Psalter of Henry VI,[1] which was probably a gift from his mother, Queen Catherine, on his coronation in 1430. It has nothing like the wealth of illustration with which the manuscripts just described abound; but its fifteen miniatures are all finely executed, and six of them have an added interest from the portraits of the young king which they contain—now kneeling before the Image of Pity or the Virgin and Child, now looking on at the combat between David and Goliath. The borders show the gilt ivy-leaf style at its best, and the church scenes, with nuns and friars singing the office, are admirable both for the display of architectural detail and for the soft and delicate treatment of the faces.

The first half of the fifteenth century was the flowering-time of French illumination in the proper sense of the term. An immense quantity was produced in the next fifty or sixty years, and some of this has considerable artistic merit; its special beauty, however, is that of pictures on a small scale, painted on vellum instead of wood or canvas, rather than that of manuscript pages fittingly adorned. The great master of the new school was Jean Fouquet, who, after receiving unstinted praise from his contemporaries and immediate successors, Italian as well as French (he is enshrined in the pages of Vasari), fell into neglect for nearly three centuries, but has been amply rehabilitated in recent years; on few

[1] Brit. Mus., Dom. A. xvii. See Warner, *Illum. MSS.*, pl. 48, *Reprod.*, i, 29.

ILLUMINATED MANUSCRIPTS

painters indeed, certainly on no other miniaturist, have such unremitting study and research been lavished.[1]

Born at Tours about 1410-20, he went to Rome while still a young man, and painted there, apparently between 1443 and 1447, a portrait of Pope Eugenius IV, on canvas, for the church of S. Maria sopra Minerva. He probably returned to France soon after, but nothing is actually known of his movements until 1461, when he was commissioned to paint the dead King Charles VII's portrait. From this time till his death, which took place between 1477 and 1481, his abode was at Tours, where he was engaged from time to time in designing the decorations for great civic displays. When Louis XI instituted the order of S. Michael, in 1469, Fouquet was charged with the execution of "certains tableaux . . . pour servir aux chevaliers de l'ordre"; these are not specified, but they doubtless included the frontispiece to the copy of the Statutes now in the Bibl. Nat. (fr. 19819),[2] which represents the royal founder presiding at a chapter. In 1474 he received payment "pour avoir tiré et peint sur parchemin" a portrait of Louis when that monarch was having his tomb prepared in advance; and in 1475 he was dignified with the title "Peintre du Roy." Contemporary records further show that he was commissioned to illuminate a Book of Hours for the Duchess of Orleans in 1472, and another for Philippe de Commines, apparently in or before 1474.

None of these works of Fouquet's is now known to exist, with the single exception of the frontispiece to the Statutes of the Order of S. Michael; and even that is not so precisely documented as could be wished. So this great painter would be a mere name to us, but for a note which François Robertet was happily inspired to insert, between 1488 and 1503, in a volume then belonging to

---

[1] The Fouquet literature is vast and scattered, but its results are very fully and carefully set forth by Durrieu, *Les Antiquités Judaïques et le peintre Jean Foucquet*, 1908. For a more succinct but useful summary, see G. Lafenestre, *Jehan Fouquet*, 1905.

[2] Durrieu, *Ant. Jud.*, pl. 19.

FRENCH ILLUMINATION AFTER 1400

his master Pierre de Bourbon, Sire de Beaujeu and Duc de Bourbon. This volume (now Bibl. Nat., fr. 247) contains the first half of a French translation of Josephus' Antiquities of the Jews and Jewish War, written originally for the Duc de Berry between 1403 and 1413; and the note states explicitly that its first three "ystoires" are by "l'enlumineur du duc Jehan de Berry," and the remaining nine (or rather, actually, eleven) are by the hand "d'un bon peintre et enlumineur du roi Loys XIe, Jehan Foucquet, natif de Tours." These "ystoires" are of large size and in perfect preservation, and sufficiently varied in subject to enable modern critics at once to endorse the verdict of his contemporaries and to form some idea of his distinctive characteristics; and his hand has consequently been recognized in other paintings, both miniatures and panels, the latter including some splendid portraits. The second volume of the Josephus, long given up as lost, reappeared in 1903 at Sotheby's sale-rooms, where it was bought by Mr. Yates Thompson. It then lacked twelve of its thirteen miniatures, but ten of the missing ones were discovered two years later by Sir G. Warner, in an album of detached leaves belonging to the Royal Library at Windsor; and thanks to King Edward's public-spirited generosity and that of Mr. Yates Thompson the volume, complete but for two leaves, has now rejoined its companion in the Paris Library, where it is numbered nouv. acq. fr. 21013. Its opening miniature is unmistakably by Fouquet; and the others, though much smaller, are in exactly the same manner, so that if (as some critics hold) they are not the master's own work, they must at any rate be assigned to a singularly faithful and skilful disciple.[1]

We need not follow those daring critics who see in certain manuscripts[2] the work of Fouquet in his youth,

[1] All the miniatures of both volumes, together with other examples of Fouquet's work, are reproduced by Durrieu, *Ant. Jud.*; for reduced facsimiles of the Josephus miniatures, see H. O[mont], *Antiquités et Guerre des Juifs de Josèphe* [1906].

[2] e.g. Brit. Mus., Add. 28785 (Warner, *Reprod.*, ii, 30), a Book of Hours whose interesting miniatures are specially admirable for their distant landscapes.

before his style had reached the maturity evident in the splendid paintings of the Josephus. The latter show plainly the hand of a great master in the plenitude of his powers; their large manner, moreover, bespeaks the "peintre" rather than the "enlumineur." In his faculty for handling landscape, his understanding of open-air effects, Fouquet rivals the great Flemish painters of his time; he resembles them too in the homely directness of his portraiture. From Italy he seems to have borrowed little directly beyond architectural details, in particular the twisted columns of S. Peter's; but there are suggestions of Italian influence in some of his figure-compositions. His pictures are admirably planned, with an unerring sense of balance and due proportion between the several parts. In battle-scenes and processions, especially, he excels in combining the total effect of serried crowds with life and individuality in the single figures. All these characteristics appear in other miniatures, along with more minute traits which stamp them as Fouquet's work beyond all question; among these are the illustrations of the Grandes Chroniques de France,[1] the Munich Boccace,[2] painted for Laurens Gyrard in or soon after 1458, and above all the Hours of Étienne Chevalier. The last-named manuscript, Fouquet's great masterpiece, was probably painted in or before 1461, since it contains a representation of Charles VII as one of the Magi. Étienne Chevalier, for whom it was made, as appears by his initials[3] or full name being introduced into most of the miniatures or ornamental initials, was a personage of great note under Charles VII and Louis XI, from about 1440 until his death in 1474. His portrait occurs twice

---

[1] Bibl. Nat., fr. 6465. Published in reduced facsimile by H. O[mont], *Grandes Chroniques de France* [1906].

[2] Munich, Hofbibl., Cod. gall. 369. See Durrieu, *Le Boccace de Munich, Reproduction des 91 miniatures*, 1909.

[3] The same "E C" device appears in a charming little Horae now in the British Museum (Add. 16997. See *Pal. Soc.*, ii, 116; Warner, *Illum. MSS.*, pl. 49, *Reprod.*, i, 30); a manuscript probably of slightly earlier date, and certainly not by Fouquet.

HORAE OF E. CHEVALIER, BY JEAN FOUQUET, MID. XVTH CENT.

CHANTILLY, MUSÉE CONDÉ

in the Hours: first, kneeling with his patron S. Stephen[1] before the Virgin and Child, in a splendid double-page picture at the beginning; and again in the Entombment, kneeling at the foot of the sepulchre.

Only forty-four detached leaves remain of this lovely Book of Hours; of these, forty are in the Musée Condé at Chantilly,[2] two in the Louvre,[3] one in the Bibliothèque Nationale,[4] and one in the British Museum.[5] Contrary to what might be expected, these are the most interesting as well as the most beautiful of Fouquet's extant miniatures. There is a touch of monotony in the battles, ceremonial processions, and murders with which the Jewish and French chronicles and the "Cas des nobles hommes et femmes" are illustrated; but here, well worn as the themes are, Fouquet has found ample scope in their presentment for his imagination and originality of design. In the Enthronement of the Virgin, for instance, his instinct for majestic composition and his skill in perspective are finely exemplified. We seem to be looking down the nave of a vast cathedral, built up not of stones but of saints and angels, rising tier on tier to the key of the vault. Far away in this living temple the Three Persons of the Trinity, all exactly alike, sit clothed in white on three Gothic canopied thrones; and the Virgin is seated on a fourth throne, placed like a bishop's at the side of the choir. The same conception appears, but with many variations in detail, in the Coronation of the Virgin,[6] where the Son descends from His place in the triple throne (here of Renaissance style) to place the crown on Mary's head. Sometimes Fouquet fills up his pages by inserting legendary scenes, as of the woman

---

[1] A panel-portrait of Chevalier, again supported by S. Stephen, was painted by Fouquet, probably about 1450, and is now in the Berlin Museum (*Primitifs Fr.*, i, No. 41, plate between pp. 24 and 25).

[2] Published by F. A. Gruyer, *Les Quarante Fouquet*, 1897.

[3] *Prim. Fr.*, i, Nos. 50, 50a.

[4] *Ibid.*, ii, No. 131 (nouv. acq. lat. 1416).

[5] Warner, *Reprod.*, iii, 35 (Add. 37421).

[6] Pl. xliii.

ILLUMINATED MANUSCRIPTS

forging the nails for the Crucifixion; or delights us with lifelike but irrelevant touches, such as the subsidiary group in the Visitation, a man drawing water from a well, under the deeply interested supervision of a little boy. Some of the subjects too are unusual: the curious "Mission of the Apostles" (Gruyer, pl. 20), for instance, or the beautiful picture of the angel's visit to Mary to announce her approaching death.

Fouquet's sons Louis and François were painters of some note; and it may be that the latter was the "egregius pictor Franciscus" who illustrated a huge "Cité de Dieu" (Bibl. Nat., fr. 18, 19)[1] for Charles de Gaucourt in or shortly before 1473, and whose hand has been recognized in other manuscripts of the time, notably in a Valerius Maximus made for Philippe de Commines about 1475, in two stately volumes (Brit. Mus., Harl. 4374-5).[2] Another large volume in the British Museum[3] has miniatures which may safely be referred to the same school, if not to the same artist. In all these the influence of Jean Fouquet is plainly discernible, in the composition, the pose of individual figures, the treatment of draperies, the frequent touches of gold to heighten effects; but the master's supreme genius is lacking, his pupil has not inherited his charm, refinement, and width of range, nor his consummate skill as a landscape-painter. That "Franciscus" was, however, an artist of considerable versatility is proved by the fact that besides these and other manuscripts of large size he also illustrated Books of Hours of the tiniest dimensions. Two such books, at least, are extant: one in Mr. Yates Thompson's collection,[4] executed for René II, Duke of Lorraine (1473-1508); the

---

[1] *Prim. Fr.*, ii, Nos. 141-2. Count A. de Laborde, *MSS. à peintures de la Cité de Dieu* (Soc. des Bibliophiles fr., 1909), pp. 397-416, pl. 47-56.

[2] Warner, *Valerius Maximus. Miniatures of the School of Jean Fouquet*, 1907; also *Illum. MSS.*, pl. 50, and *Reprod.*, ii, 33.

[3] Add. 35321, Boccace, Cas des malheureux nobles hommes et femmes; the subject of an illustrated article by Sir E. M. Thompson in the *Burlington Magazine*, vii, 1905, pp. 198-210. See too Warner, *Reprod.*, i, 33.

[4] Warner, *Valerius Maximus*, pp. 12, 15-17.

PLATE XLIII

HORAE, SCHOOL OF J. FOUQUET, FRENCH, CIRCA 1470

BRIT. MUS. EGERTON 2045

FRENCH ILLUMINATION AFTER 1400

other in the British Museum,[1] perhaps made for Louis de Luxembourg, Count of St. Pol (d. 1475). The latter has borders of the unpleasing type which came into vogue towards the end of the century, gilt triangular insertions alternating with the plain vellum as background for scrolls of foliage. But the miniatures are very finely painted, especially when one considers that the artist was accustomed to work on a much larger scale—a fact only recalled by an occasional tendency to make the heads too big for the bodies. The distant landscapes are excellent, and many of the compositions are interesting, notably the charming picture of the Virgin teaching the Child-Christ to read, and still more the frontispiece to Vespers of the Dead, with the mysterious symbolism of its nine crosses each bearing the crucified Saviour, and its twofold representation of the dead Christ in angels' arms below an empty cross.[2]

The work of Jean Fouquet and his school, like that of most Northern French illuminators in the latter half of the fifteenth century, shows strong affinities with Flemish art. In South-eastern France, on the other hand, there is often some admixture of Italian influence, especially in the border-ornament. There are hints of this in the Hours of René of Anjou (d. 1480);[3] and it is more pronounced in the Saluces Hours,[4] executed about 1450-60, probably for Amédée de Saluces. The former manuscript contains two miniatures, painted in a curious and somewhat uncouth style, which have been attributed to "le bon roi René" himself, but though his love for illumination is well known,[5] no certain evidence is forthcoming as to his practical proficiency in the art.

Illuminated manuscripts continued to be produced in France long after the introduction of printing, and much

---

[1] Eg. 2045. See Warner, *Val. Max.*, pp. 16-17, *Reprod.*, i, 31.
[2] For these two pages (ff. 216b, 280) see pl. xliii.
[3] Eg. 1070. See Warner, *Reprod.*, iii, 36-7.
[4] Add. 27697. See Pal. Soc., i, 253; Warner, *Illum. MSS.*, pl. 51, *Reprod.*, i, 32.
[5] See E. Chmelarz in the Vienna *Jahrbuch*, xi, 1890, pp. 116-39.

skill and labour were expended upon them. But the art may be said, without grave inaccuracy, to have finished its course by the end of the fifteenth century. It was no longer instinct with life and capable of natural development; and the great masters of painting ceased, with few exceptions, to devote their talents to it. Preeminent among the exceptions is the illuminator of the Hours of Anne of Brittany, Queen Consort of Charles VIII (1491-8) and of his successor Louis XII (1499-1514). This famous manuscript[1] was long attributed to Jean Poyet of Tours, on the strength of an entry in the Queen's accounts, recording a payment made to him in 1497 for illuminating "unes petites heures"; but since the discovery of a warrant, dated March 14, 1507, for the payment of six hundred crowns to Jean Bourdichon for having "richement et somptueusement historié et enlumyné une grans heures" for Anne's use, it has been generally identified, not with Poyet's "petites heures," but with the presumably larger and more sumptuous work of Bourdichon.[2] Like his rival Poyet, Bourdichon belonged to Tours, and was quite possibly a pupil of Fouquet, having been born in 1457. As early as 1478 he was commissioned to decorate the Royal Chapel at Plessis-lès-Tours, and from 1484 onwards he bore the title of "painctre du roy," apparently until his death in or shortly before 1521. Like Fouquet, he employed his artistic talents in various ways: he designed coins, lamps, and reliquaries, painted portraits, banners, and views of towns, as well as illuminating manuscripts. As in the case of Fouquet, too, we are dependent on a single manuscript for our knowledge of his actual work, and even of that, as we have seen, he has not been left in undisputed possession. M. Mâle has recognized his

[1] Bibl. Nat., lat. 9474. See H. O.[mont], *Heures d'Anne de Bretagne* [1907]; E. Mâle, in *Gaz. des Beaux-Arts*, 1902, i, pp. 185-203, 1904, ii, pp. 441-57; also F. de Mély, in *Gaz. des Beaux-Arts*, 1909, ii, pp. 177-96, 1910, ii, p. 173.

[2] It should be mentioned, however, that M. de Mély upholds the attribution to Poyet, though the weight of evidence seems against him.

FRENCH ILLUMINATION AFTER 1400

hand, however, in five other manuscripts now in French libraries; and a sixth, executed apparently for Jean Bourgeois soon after 1490, has been found in the University Library at Innsbruck.[1] All these show some lingering traces of Fouquet's influence, particularly the Innsbruck MS., which contains a miniature of David praying, clad in full armour, directly reminiscent of the corresponding picture in the Chevalier Hours (Brit. Mus., Add. 37421). The best of them is undoubtedly the Hours of Anne of Brittany, in its somewhat decadent way a veritable masterpiece. The groups are well planned, the landscapes and architectural ornaments are finely painted, but the faces, though not without a certain individuality, are sentimental, sleek, lacking in animation. Though not a great master, Bourdichon evidently had a numerous following; more or less feeble imitations of his manner abound in almost every large library,[2] the dying efforts of French illumination.

[1] See H. J. Hermann, " Ein unbekanntes Gebetbuch von Jean Bourdichon," in *Beiträge zur Kunstgeschichte, Franz Wickhoff gewidmet*, 1903, pp. 46–63.

[2] Samples may be seen in the Brit. Mus. MSS. Add. 18854 (executed in 1525 for François de Dinteville, Bishop of Auxerre), 18855, (early sixteenth century, contrasting unfavourably with two leaves from an exquisite Flemish calendar, of about the same period, inserted at the end of the volume), and 35254, T–V. The last, three leaves from a large Book of Hours, early sixteenth century, is decidedly the best of these; it is perhaps the work of one of Bourdichon's pupils.

CHAPTER XVII

THE ITALIAN RENAISSANCE

WE saw that in the fourteenth century Italy failed to reach in illumination a pre-eminence commensurate with that which she achieved in fresco and panel painting. Speaking broadly, the same may be said of the fifteenth century. In the first half she is eclipsed by the Franco-Flemish schools; and in the second, when her distinctive style had reached full maturity, even her most superb productions are rivalled, if not surpassed, by the more sober colouring and the minuter finish of the finest Flemish work of the same period. Her prime too was much briefer than her Northern rival's, her decay more rapid and complete; in all the mass of Italian sixteenth century illumination that exists there is little which gives the beholder anything like complete satisfaction by its beauty, which does not rather repel him by its tasteless exuberance of ornament and its ill-harmonized scheme of colour.

No great masterpieces have survived from the early decades of the fifteenth century, and there is no reason for supposing that any were produced; but the continuance and gradual development of the fourteenth century style often produced very pleasing results. A fair sample of the work of this period may be seen in the Hymnal of the Austin Hermits of Siena,[1] dated 1415, and decorated with large historiated initials and pendent borders. Compared with the fourteenth century Vallombrosa Gradual[2] which stands near it in the same show-

---

[1] Brit. Mus., Add. 30014. See Warner, *Reprod.*, i, 45 (accidentally given the lettering which belongs to pl. 46).

[2] Add. 18198. See above, p. 259.

THE ITALIAN RENAISSANCE

case at the British Museum, it marks a considerable advance; not so much in the miniatures (though these too show more elaboration of detail, more effort after minute finish) as in the borders. These are a modification of the old rod-and-acanthus design: the rods become less prominent and are usually curved, the leaves grow more freely and luxuriantly, and flowers and delicate sprays of foliage issue at the corners and extremities; human, grotesque, and other figures too are introduced—a monk praying, a woman carrying a basket on her head, a bird flying with food to its nestlings, etc. The most elaborate page is at Christmas (f. 51), where the initial encloses a miniature of the Nativity in a landscape of snow-clad hills, the Annunciation to the Shepherds is depicted in an interesting pastoral scene in the lower margin, and the borders are enriched with medallions of angel-musicians and half-length figures of David and John the Baptist. The miniature has a sky of stippled gold, and is surrounded with a square frame filled with a geometrical repeat-pattern. Throughout the volume, though the technique is not of the highest quality, the total effect is satisfying, sometimes even charming, through the simplicity and good taste of the compositions and ornament, and above all through the purity and brilliance of the colour-scheme, with its predominant gold and vermilion set off against paler tints and the plain vellum. The manuscript is full of exquisite lace-work initials in red and blue—another heritage from the preceding century.

This Hymnal is of special interest as being a complete manuscript, and one whose date and place of origin are known. The finest specimens of its class are mostly found (outside Italy, at all events) in single leaves or portions of leaves, ruthlessly cut out from choir-books to enrich collectors' albums. Among many such cuttings that have found their way to the British Museum are two large miniatures, which have evidently been taken from early fifteenth century Sienese choir-books. Both are

ILLUMINATED MANUSCRIPTS

resplendent with vermilion and burnished gold; and both are enclosed in tessellated frames, like the Nativity in the Hymnal. Characteristic too of the school are the largeness and simplicity of the compositions, and the serene, slightly sentimental facial types. One of these paintings[1] represents the Burial and Assumption of the Virgin, between two precipitous hills of the familiar primitive Italian type, against a vast expanse of gold background; the other[2] treats the subject of the Annunciation in a somewhat original way, Gabriel being half-hidden by the elaborately foliated "R" which encloses the picture. The Sienese school was exceptionally conservative, and these miniatures form an interesting link between the great masterpiece of Niccolò di Ser Sozzo and the illuminations painted by Sano di Pietro, after the middle of the fifteenth century, in choir-books still preserved in the cathedral at Siena.

Fra Angelico is sometimes said to have practised illumination, and he has actually been credited with the decoration of certain choir-books now exhibited in the Museo di S. Marco at Florence. But this attribution seems ill-founded,[3] though signs of his influence are obvious; and there is no real evidence that he painted on vellum at all. The history of Florentine illumination in the earlier part of the fifteenth century is obscure; and much the same may be said of Italian illumination generally during that period, until the Renaissance infused new life into the art. One of the first indications of the new movement was a revival of the style of script and decoration of the eleventh and twelfth centuries. This appears as early as 1433, in a copy of Justinus made at Verona;[4] still earlier at Florence, in a Valerius Flaccus written in

---

[1] Add. 37955, A.
[2] Add. 35254, C. See pl. xliv.
[3] See Langton Douglas, *Fra Angelico*, 1902, p. 159. For descriptions of the S. Marco MSS. see F. Rondoni, *Guida del R. Museo fiorentino di S. Marco*, 1872, and for plates, V. Marchese, *S. Marco, Convento dei Padri Predicatori in Firenze*, 1853.
[4] Brit. Mus., Add. 12012. See *Pal. Soc.*, i, 252.

PLATE XLIV

SINGLE LEAF, PERHAPS FROM A CHOIR BOOK. SIENESE, EARLY XVTH CENT
BRIT. MUS. ADD. **35254** C

THE ITALIAN RENAISSANCE

1429.[1] The script soon developed into the well-known "scrittura umanistica," whose exquisite neatness and precision made Italian calligraphers famous, and prepared the way for the triumphs of the early Italian printers; while the decorative scheme produced the borders which are so familiar to all students of late Italian illumination, and whose foundation is an interlaced scroll of white vine-tendrils. This scroll-work design was usually painted on grounds of alternating blue, green, and crimson, and set in a rectangular frame composed of narrow gold bands; and putti, birds, rabbits, and other animals were often introduced, together with medallions enclosed in wreaths of close-set foliage, and containing sometimes figure-compositions, sometimes heraldic or symbolical designs, sometimes busts copied from antique gems. This type of Renaissance work may be seen at its best in the sumptuous books written by Hippolytus Lunensis, a calligrapher who worked chiefly for Ferdinand of Aragon, King of Naples (1458–94), and who probably directed the illumination of the volumes to which his name is attached. Among these is a copy of "Joannis Scoti super libros Sententiarum quaestiones" in several bulky tomes, four of which are in the British Museum and one at Paris;[2] vol v. having on the opening page,[3] besides a full and elaborate border of this kind, a neatly executed miniature of a scribe at work, attached to the initial. The Ovid in Mr. Perrins's collection,[4] written by Hippolytus for Antonello Petrucci about 1480, combines the vine-tendril design with another style of Renaissance border, a scroll of thread-like stems with tiny leaves and large flowers on a plain vellum ground; and the artist cannot be congratulated on his juxtaposition of the two schemes, effective though each of them is when employed separately.

---

[1] Vitelli and Paoli, *Facsimili Paleografici*, Lat., tav. 48.
[2] Brit. Mus., Add. 15270–3; Bibl. Nat., lat. 3063. See Warner, *Reprod.*, iii, 38.
[3] Pl. xlv.
[4] Burl. F.A. Club, No. 186, pl. 124.

ILLUMINATED MANUSCRIPTS

This lack of simplicity and restraint, this tendency to spoil the decorative effect of a page by overloading it with ill-assorted ornaments, was a besetting sin of the Renaissance illuminators, and one which grew as time went on, after the accustomed manner of besetting sins. Early manuscripts are comparatively free from it, even to so late a date as 1457, when a Roman Missal[1] was executed, probably at or near Florence, for Sandra di Giovanni Cianchini da Gavignano, Abbess of Rosano in the diocese of Fiesole. This manuscript has no great intrinsic importance, but may be taken as marking the limit of persistence (outside Siena) of the Pre-Renaissance tradition. Its one full-page miniature, a Crucifixion prefixed to the Canon, is crude and unattractive; but the initial and border decorations are simple and effective, especially on the opening page of the Temporale (f. 7), where they form a pleasing harmony in pale blue, pale green, and burnished gold.

But more sophisticated tastes were coming in, together with a much wider range of decorative ideas and a great advance in technical skill. Despite the transitional character of this Missal, Italian illumination had already entered on its most brilliant period, and the next half-century witnessed the production of many splendid masterpieces. The florescence was general, and it is not easy to discriminate between the different local schools. The leading miniaturists undoubtedly moved about from place to place, fulfilling particular commissions; and though many of their names are preserved in records, there is still the old difficulty of identifying their work in actual extant manuscripts. Very few of them had the habit of signing their paintings; and the records, when they do specify individual manuscripts that are still in existence, often connect them with the names of several painters, giving no indication of the precise part performed by any one of them. It is tantalizing information of this kind that we are given, for instance, about the

[1] Brit. Mus., Add. 14802.

**SAMARITA
NVS ILLE
PIISSIM
VS SPOLIA**

tum cuidens hominem, & attrocrter saucratum miserationis affectu compatiens medicinam attulit efficacem qua curatis ipsius uulneribus ac plena reddita sanitate in sui principium a quo descenderet ab hierusalem descensurat, finaliter reducatur. Et ista saucii sanatione salubri, ac de ui reductione finali tanq de pedibus sedentis super solium excelsum magister in hoc opere finali determinat ut sicut ex primo & secundo claru it deum esse alpha tam in se entium omnia primum q omnium altero originale principium sic ex tertio, & quarto appareat ipsum esse & o tam in se finem ultimum q creature sue per seipsum in seipsum finaliter reductiuum. Hanc autem reductionem finalem precedit curatio semiplena, & plena curatio comitatur. Secundum hanc distinctione igitur potest diuidi quartus iste, dicendo q magister primo agit de homnis saucii curatione salubri. Secundo de hominis deum reductione finali. Curatur enim homo salubriter in susceptione deuota sacramentoru uicracum, & reducitur finaliter in perceptione iocunda premiorum celestium. Sacramenta enim disponunt, & preparant premia uero perficiunt & consumant. Vel potest dici q primo agit de curatione semiplena seu dispositiua, & secundo de curatione plena, seu perfectiua, & utraq diuisio redit in idem. Nam curatio semiplena fit per gratiam sacramentorum que sunt medicine salubres, plena curatio seu finalis reductio fit per collationem premiorum que sunt iocunde refectiones. In prima igitur parte agit de sacramentis per que curatur languidus a morbo culpe. In secunda de premiis per que liberatur a la gore pene. Et incipit secunda in principio distinctionis xlvii. Post hec &c. Prima diuiditur in duas primo nanq determinat de sacramento in generali secundo in speciali. Secunda in principio distinctione

SCOTUS, QUAESTIONES IN SENTENTIAS. ITALIAN, 1458-94

BRIT. MUS. ADD. 15273

great two-volume Bible of Borso d'Este, Lord of Ferrara, now in the library of the Archduke Francis Ferdinand of Austria-Este. Borso's accounts show that the decoration of this splendid book was begun in 1455 and completed in 1462, that the illuminator-in-chief was Taddeo Crivelli, and that his principal assistants were Franco Russi, Giorgio Tedesco, and Marco dell' Avogaro; but they leave much room for conjecture in the attribution to each artist of his share in the work.

The Borso Bible marks the highest achievement of the illuminators attached to the court of Ferrara, where the Este princes, especially Leonello (1441–50) and his successor Borso (1450–71), were liberal patrons of art.[1] It is, indeed, one of the most perfect and magnificent of all existing monuments of Italian illumination. For wealth of decoration it is almost without a rival, having something like a thousand miniatures. There is documentary evidence that the superb double-page illumination at the beginning of Genesis was painted by Taddeo Crivelli himself; and it amply justifies his reputation as one of the greatest illuminators of his time. The wide border which surrounds the three columns of text is filled with a great variety of decorative elements, but these are so well adjusted as to result in an admirable design, rich and yet harmonious and not overloaded. The two inner margins are comparatively simple, having a style of border very often found in Ferrarese manuscripts,[2] though not peculiar to them: consisting of flowers and discs, connected by a sort of network of filigree lines, representing the stems, which also enclose plaques painted with the Este arms and *imprese*. But decoration is freely lavished

---

[1] See H. J. Hermann, "Zur Geschichte der Miniaturmalerei am Hofe der Este in Ferrara," in the Vienna *Jahrbuch*, xxi, pp. 117–271 (copiously illustrated, especially from the Borso Bible); also G. Gruyer, *L'Art ferrarais*, 1897, ii, pp. 415–51; F. Carta, *Atl. pal.-art.*, pl. 92–7; *L'Arte*, 1900, pp. 341–73; 1910, pp. 353–61.

[2] e.g. in Brit. Mus., Add. 17294, a Ferrara Breviary made about 1472, apparently for Borso's successor, Ercole I, whose arms it contains, together with the " diamante" *impresa*: a beautifully written manuscript, but its decoration, though well executed, is not sumptuous or in any way remarkable.

ILLUMINATED MANUSCRIPTS

on the two broad outer bands, which, with the upper and lower margins, contain a series of Creation-scenes, placed in a gorgeous setting of Renaissance architectural and other ornament, putti, vases, doves, and conventional foliage. The Creation-scenes show much originality in composition, especially that in which the Almighty is putting the finishing touches to a lion under the interested surveillance of a horse. The animals and nude human figures are treated in a naturalistic and graceful manner, the putti are particularly charming; in the purely decorative work a fertile fancy is combined with excellent taste; the drawing is firm and delicate, the whole execution finely finished. Dr. Hermann has reproduced many other examples of what is apparently Taddeo's work, showing the same excellent qualities; the pages which he assigns to one or other of Taddeo's collaborators, though evidently painted by skilful craftsmen, are distinctly inferior, lacking the master's freedom, originality, and charm.

The Borso Bible is the only book in which we have anything like certainty that Taddeo Crivelli's work is to be found. But he is known to have been much in request from 1452 to 1476, illuminating choir-books for the Certosa at Pavia and the monasteries of S. Procolo and S. Petronio at Bologna; he died in or before 1479. His work at S. Petronio was continued, from 1477 to 1480, by Martino da Modena, son of his former collaborator Giorgio Tedesco. Martino also decorated service-books for Modena and Ferrara cathedrals, between 1480 and 1485, and he has been credited with a splendid Missal now in the Trivulzio collection at Milan. He seems to have had less aptitude than Taddeo for planning a sumptuous full-page design; but his treatment of the human face and figure, still more of landscape, is much more advanced. Elaborately painted landscape-backgrounds were now becoming a regular feature in Italian miniature; they are prominent, and sometimes quite beautiful, in the famous Breviary of Ercole I, most of which is now in the Austria-Este Library. Executed about 1502, this fine

THE ITALIAN RENAISSANCE

book already shows signs of decadent taste. The details of ornament, exquisitely painted though they be, are ill-distributed, now crowding up the borders with reckless profusion, now arranged in stiff and monotonous symmetry. The miniatures too are often hampered with incongruous details, and lacking in spaciousness of composition. The pages are gorgeous, magnificent; but few of them are satisfying. Among still later Este manuscripts the Officium of Alfonso I (*circa* 1505–10), in the Austria-Este Library, and the Missal of Cardinal Ippolito I (1503–20), in the University Library at Innsbruck, deserve mention for the fine pictures which both contain; but these are only the last flickerings of a moribund art.

Dr. Hermann's admirable survey of Ferrarese illumination, on which the above brief sketch is based, gives a fairly accurate idea of the course of development and decay of Renaissance illumination in any of the great centres of Italian painting. The names of patrons change —we have the Medicis at Florence, the Sforzas at Milan, and so on; so do the names of artists, where these are known at all. There are great varieties of style, due to the special circumstances of a local school or the individual genius of a great master. But the general trend is much the same everywhere, though its course cannot as a rule be followed step by step for lack of material, or of precise data with regard to the abundant material which exists. One of the few exceptions is the Venetian school, whose successive stages are shown by the Ducali in almost uninterrupted continuity down even to the eighteenth century.[1] Strictly speaking, the Ducale was the covenant which the Doge made with the Venetian people on his election; but the term is also applied in a more general sense to ducal commissions and other documents, and even to congratulatory addresses offered to a Doge. The decoration of the earlier Ducali was usually confined to a figure-initial with pendent border-ornament, and had

[1] Holmes and Madden's Catalogue of Ducali (Brit. Mus., Add. 20758) ranges from 1367 to 1718.

ILLUMINATED MANUSCRIPTS

little artistic significance;[1] but it became more elaborate about the middle of the fifteenth century, and began to be fairly representative of Venetian illumination. The earliest Ducale in the British Museum, the covenant of Cristoforo Mauro, 1462,[2] has on the first page three illuminated initials, besides a full border of flowers, rayed discs, and filigree-stems, with numerous small figures of birds, foxes, etc., painted on the plain vellum (like the Ferrarese borders described above), and enclosing medallions of apes, lions, and other animals, with the Mauro arms within a wreath supported by putti in the lower margin. The principal initial contains (or rather, is replaced by) a miniature of the Doge adoring the enthroned Madonna and Child between S. Mark and S. Bernardino; finely painted, for the most part in subdued colours, but lit up by the deep crimson of the Doge's robe. Venetian illumination is seen at its best in this early Renaissance phase, preserving due balance between text, ornament, and figure-composition. The full-page frontispiece which usually adorns the later Ducali[3] is more imposing, with its gorgeous colouring and florid design, but is much less satisfying as a work of art; lacking as it does the essential character of miniature, it quickly degenerates into a poor imitation of panel-painting on a reduced scale.

Florence, the great home of all the arts, produced a large number of illuminated manuscripts during the Renaissance period; but comparatively few of these approach the first rank. There are two manuscripts in the British Museum which contain the Medici arms, and were perhaps made for Lorenzo the Magnificent himself, to whose time (1469-92) they seem to belong; but they cannot be called better than mediocre. One of them is a

---

[1] See L. Testi, *Storia della Pittura Veneziana*, i, 1909, pp. 503, 512-15.

[2] Add. 15816. See Warner, *Reprod.*, i, 48.

[3] There are many of these in the British Museum, including a volume (Add. 20916) filled with detached frontispieces, late fifteenth century to 1620. Of the rest, the following may be noted as fair samples of their respective periods:—Add. 21463 (1486, see Warner, i, 49), 18000 (1521), 21414 (*c.* 1530), 17373 (1554), and King's 156 (1568).

THE ITALIAN RENAISSANCE

Breviary (Add. 25697), the other a Petrarch (Harl. 5761);[1] both are very small books, and are chiefly worth notice for the border-ornament, which is characteristically Florentine, painted on the plain vellum, and differing chiefly from the North Italian border, already described, in its profusion of rayed gilt discs. The Petrarch also has tiny vignette miniatures at the foot of the pages, representing the Triumphs in a sketchy, but skilful and effective manner. Another type of border, not peculiar to Florence, but often found also in Milanese and other illuminations of the end of the fifteenth century, appears in Add. 33997, a Horae made in Florence, after 1472,[2] for a lady named Smeralda, consisting mainly of arabesques in dead gold on blue, green, or crimson grounds, enclosed in a rectangular frame. The colouring in this manuscript is brilliant, but somewhat hard; one of the most pleasing features in the book is the half-length portrait of a fair-haired girl (evidently the lady Smeralda), which appears on almost all the illuminated pages. Both styles of border are used in the decoration of Add. 29735,[3] a Breviary of the great Franciscan convent of S. Croce, written towards the end of the century (certainly after April 14, 1482, the Calendar citing a decree of that date, instituting the Feast of S. Bonaventura). The more sumptuous style, with grounds of crimson, blue, and green, occurs only on the opening page of the Temporale (f. 7): the most elaborate page in the book, the lower border filled with a miniature of the Annunciation, the arabesques at the sides interrupted by half-length figures of saints set in richly jewelled medallions. The long narrow picture of the Annunciation is very carefully painted; it has some resemblance in manner to Lorenzo di Credi's panels, especially in the sentimental figures of the kneeling Gabriel and his attendant angels. Borders of the lighter and more graceful type, with

---

[1] Warner, ii, 48.
[2] Having the Translation of S. Bernardino in the Calendar.
[3] *Pal. Soc.*, i, 227; *Guide to Exhibited MSS.*, 1906, p. 139; Warner, ii, 50.

figure-initials, abound throughout the volume; and there is an interesting miniature, at the Invention of the Cross (f. 127b), of the miracle whereby the true cross was recognized.

To be seen at its best, however, Florentine illumination should be studied in the work of Attavante; or in such books as the beautiful little Horae of Lorenzo the Magnificent, formerly Libri MS. 1874 in the Ashburnham Library,[1] but now restored to the Laurentian Library at Florence. The latter volume, like its companion, the "Liber Precatorius" in the Munich Library (Cimel. 42),[2] was written in 1485 by the famous scribe Antonio Sinibaldi. Its little miniatures are surrounded with very lovely borders, in which tiny but wonderfully lifelike amorini uphold festoons and vases of fruit and flowers, amidst a well-ordered medley of medallions, cherubs, birds, sphinxes, etc., and the characteristic scroll of foliage, flowers, and rayed gilt discs. All this sounds crowded, especially when one considers that the whole page measures only six inches by four; and yet, painted on the plain white vellum, it produces a light and charming effect.

Attavante degli Attavanti, the most famous of the Florentine miniaturists, had the useful habit of signing his work, much of which has survived. Mr. Bradley[3] enumerates no less than thirty-one manuscripts certainly or probably illuminated by him. Born in 1452, he had already established his reputation by 1483, when he was commissioned by Thomas James, Bishop of Dol, to decorate a Missal which is now in the treasury of Lyons Cathedral;[4] and in the next few years he illustrated several volumes for that great book-lover Mathias Corvinus, King of Hungary (d. 1490). One of these, a

[1] *Pal. Soc.*, ii, 19.
[2] L. von Kobell, *Kunstvolle Miniaturen*, p. 88.
[3] *Dict. of Miniaturists*, i, pp. 74–80. See too P. d'Ancona, in Thieme and Becker's *Allgemeines Lexikon der bildenden Künstler*, ii, 1908, pp. 214–16.
[4] Described, with illustrations, by E. Bertaux and G. Birot in *Revue de l'Art Anc. et Mod.*, xx, pp. 129–46.

THE ITALIAN RENAISSANCE

Missal executed in 1485-7, and now in the Royal Library at Brussels,[1] may be taken as representing his style at its best. It is splendidly decorated throughout, especially the great double-page paintings prefixed to the Temporale and the Canon (ff. 8b-9, 193b-4), the latter including a fine picture of the Crucifixion set in the foreground of a Tuscan landscape. It is in the accessories, however, rather than the large figure-compositions, that Attavante finds the most congenial scope for his powers: he delights in gorgeous colouring and rich and varied ornament; his pages glow with crimson, blue, and gold, his borders are filled with a bewildering wealth of "humanistic" decoration—copies or imitations of Classical friezes, cameos, and coins; arabesques, putti, pearls, and rubies; all painted with great skill, against grounds of brilliant hues. In fact, his work is typical of Renaissance illumination at its height, with its florid taste and dexterous technique.

Many of Attavante's contemporaries are chiefly known as illuminators of choir-books. Pre-eminent among these are Girolamo da Cremona and Liberale da Verona, both of whom did some of their finest work of this kind at Siena, the former from 1468 to 1473, the latter from 1470 to 1476.[2] The conventional ornament, in the books illuminated by these two masters, is often heavy, commonplace, even perfunctory, and was perhaps done by their assistants; but the miniatures enclosed in the large initials are always interesting and finely finished, and sometimes exquisite, e.g. Liberale's illustration of the parable of the Labourers in the Vineyard.[3] A fine North Italian choir-book, apparently made for a church dedicated to SS. Cosmas and Damian, was recently acquired

---

[1] No. 9008. See J. van den Gheyn, *Cat. des MSS. de la Bibl. Roy. de Belgique*, i, 1901, pp. 277-9; E. Müntz, *Hist. de l'Art pendant la Renaissance*, ii, 1891, p. 221, and in *Gazette Archéol.*, 1883, pp. 116-20. For another, but inferior, example of Attavante's work, the Martianus Capella at Venice, see A. Perini, *Facsimile delle miniature di Attavante Fiorentino*, 1878.

[2] Bradley, *Dict. of Min.*; Crowe and Cavalcaselle, *Hist. of Painting in N. Italy.*   [3] Pl. xlvi.

ILLUMINATED MANUSCRIPTS

by the Society of Antiquaries.[1] Besides the large historiated initials, it has at the beginning a half-page miniature of that favourite episode in the legend of the two physician-saints, the miracle of the Ethiopian's leg. A sixteenth century inscription, signed "Frater Jacobus de Mantua," attributes the illuminations to Andrea and Francesco Mantegna. This attribution cannot be accepted, though it may indicate a Mantuan origin. Both borders and miniatures have a strong resemblance to the work of the neighbouring school of Ferrara about 1460–70.

Most important of all the local schools, perhaps, is the Milanese,[2] a superb monument of which is preserved at the British Museum in the Sforza Book of Hours.[3] Executed for Bona of Savoy, widow of Galeazzo Maria Sforza, Duke of Milan (d. 1476), probably about 1490, this famous book seems to have been given by her to her daughter Bianca Maria, who married the Emperor Maximilian I in 1493; and thus to have descended to Charles V, who succeeded Maximilian in 1519. At all events, in 1519–20 several pages were inserted to make good the then imperfections of the manuscript. The illuminations on these inserted pages are Flemish, and will be noticed in the next chapter; here it need only be said that they include a portrait of Charles V, dated 1520. The imperfections have been conjecturally accounted for by the supposition that the book was originally intended as a wedding-gift to Bianca Maria as the bride of John Corvinus, natural son of King Mathias, and that the pages which contained direct allusions to this abortive marriage-project were removed when Bianca's hand was transferred to the Emperor. Be this as it may, the book is fully

---

[1] *New Pal. Soc.*, pl. 171–3.

[2] See G. Mongeri, "L'arte del minio nel ducato di Milano," in *Archivio Storico Lombardo*, 1885, pp. 330–56, 528–57, 759–96.

[3] Add. 34294. See *Pal. Soc.*, ii, 204–5; Warner, *Illum. MSS.*, pl. 58–9, *Reprod.*, iii, 42–3, and above all his fully illustrated monograph, *The Sforza Book of Hours*, 1894.

PLATE XLVI

LIBERALE DA VERONA, CIRCA 1475
SIENA, LIBRERIA PICCOLOMINI. GRADUAL

THE ITALIAN RENAISSANCE

worthy, even in its unfinished or mutilated condition, either of an Empress or of the daughter-in-law of so impassioned a lover of Italian art as Mathias Corvinus. Its forty-eight full-page miniatures and numerous frame-borders vary in merit, as well as in style, and are plainly the work of several hands; but the great majority of them represent Milanese illumination at its highest pitch of excellence. They are painted in the sharp, vivid manner of the Lombard school; as crisp as medals, as brilliant as enamels, they yet avoid hardness, and their saints and angels have all the tense, ardent spirituality of expression which the great North Italian masters knew so well how to convey. The contrast between them and the Flemish insertions, as to colouring and style, is very striking and instructive, but is not detrimental to either; each school has its own special qualities, and each is admirably represented here.

The forty-eight Italian miniatures include three Evangelist-portraits, ten scenes from the Passion, the Death and Assumption of the Virgin, and a long and interesting series of saints. In this last series are many of the most beautiful compositions in the book; it is difficult to make a selection, but among the best, unquestionably, are the two S. Catherines and SS. Clare, Bernardino, Albert of Trapani, and Gregory.[1] The borders are painted with the same brilliancy as the miniatures, and are designed with equal freedom and originality, with regard to details of conventional ornament as well as figure-compositions. The conventional ornament is all of the Renaissance Classical type, but is varied with amazing fertility of invention. The figure-compositions include angel-musicians[2] (an extremely interesting and charming series), saints whimsically depicted as putti, a putto teaching a dog to beg, etc.

None of the illuminations are signed, and no document has been discovered which helps to identify the

[1] Pl. xlvii.   [2] Pl. xlviii.

ILLUMINATED MANUSCRIPTS

artists, with the doubtful exception of a letter from an otherwise unknown "presbiter Johannes Petrus Biragus, miniator," concerning an "officiol imperfecto" which he had in hand for Duchess Bona. Even if, as is by no means certain, this "officiol" is the Museum Sforza Book, Birago cannot be supposed to have painted the whole of it himself. Other names have been suggested, viz. Antonio da Monza and Ambrogio de Predis. The former, a Franciscan friar, illuminated a Missal for Pope Alexander VI (1492–1503), whereof one leaf remains in the Albertina Museum at Vienna, containing a miniature[1] of the Descent of the Holy Spirit; a fine painting, and clearly allied to some of the miniatures in the Sforza Book, though the resemblance is hardly close enough to form secure foundation for an attribution. Ambrogio de Predis is best known through his association with Leonardo da Vinci; but Dr. Müller-Walde attributes to him some of the miniatures in a Donatus made for Maximilian Sforza, now in the Trivulziana; and if this attribution be correct, there seems little doubt that he must also be credited with the Passion-series, at any rate, in the Sforza Book. The British Museum is fortunate in possessing two more fine examples of Milanese borders of this period, in the printed *Sforziada* (Milan, 1490)[2] and a grant of lands[3] from Ludovico Sforza to his wife Beatrice d'Este, dated 1494. These are in the same style as the Sforza Book borders, though on a larger scale, and are specially interesting for the splendid medal-like portraits of Ludovico and Beatrice, and of Ludovico's father Francesco Sforza-Visconti. They have not led so far, however, to a satisfactory solution of the question of the artists' identity.

If Ambrogio de Predis really painted the miniatures which Dr. Müller-Walde has ascribed to him, then he must be acknowledged to rank still higher as a miniaturist than as a panel-painter, and to outshine completely his

---

[1] Reproduced in *Arch. Stor. Lomb.*, 1885, p. 769.
[2] Warner, *Sforza Book*, p. xxvii, pl. lxi–lxv, *Illum. MSS.*, pl. 60.
[3] Add. 21413. *Sforza Book*, p. xxxii.

PLATE XLVII

SFORZA BOOK OF HOURS. MILANESE, CIRCA 1490

BRIT. MUS., ADD. 34294

THE ITALIAN RENAISSANCE

deaf-mute brother Cristoforo,[1] who is only known in the former capacity. Cristoforo's extant works are: (1) the Borromeo Hours in the Ambrosian Library;[2] (2) Lives of SS. Joachim and Anna, etc., in the Royal Library at Turin (Cod. 14434); (3) Missal, in the church of the Madonna del Monte sopra Varese; (4) a detached leaf, in the Wallace Collection. All these are signed, and all but the first are dated, viz. Nos. 2 and 3, 1476, and No. 4, 147.. (the last digit is illegible, but the miniature was evidently painted in the lifetime of Galeazzo Maria Sforza, and so not later than 1476). Thus Cristoforo represents an earlier phase of Milanese illumination than the masterpieces which we have been considering. He adopts the full Renaissance style of ornament, filling his frame-borders with festoons, arabesques, vases, pearls, and precious stones, cameos and medallions, as well as birds and innumerable putti; but his figure-drawing and perspective are poor, and his colouring, though deep and brilliant, is ill-harmonized and unpleasing in effect. The Calendar-pictures in the Borromeo Hours are one of the most interesting features of his work; filling the lower margins and part of the sides of each page (a plan often followed in the later French Horae), and containing some curious illustrations of contemporary life.

The materials probably do not exist for writing a complete and orderly history of Central and South Italian illumination. The court of Rome doubtless attracted, or from time to time hired the services of, the best illuminators from all parts of Italy; we have seen, for instance, that the Lombard Antonio da Monza worked for Alexander VI. But there is no evidence of the existence of what could properly be called a Roman school of miniature. The Neapolitan school is equally elusive. There

---

[1] The relationship between them, together with many other facts concerning them and their three brothers, has been ascertained through the researches of Dr. Biscaro, published in *Arch. Stor. Lomb.*, 1910, pp. 132, 223–6. For other notices of Cristoforo, with illustrations, see Vienna *Jahrbuch*, xxi, p. 214, and *Rassegna d'Arte*, i, 1901, p. 28; see too *Arch. Stor. Lomb.*, 1885, pp. 344–7.

[2] Published in heliotype by L. Beltrami, *Il libro d'ore Borromeo*, 1896.

ILLUMINATED MANUSCRIPTS

is a great mixture of styles in the Psalter[1] executed in 1442 for Alfonso of Aragon, King of Naples 1442-58; it looks in great part like a clumsy imitation of French work of earlier date, and was probably done by Spanish artists. Alfonso's natural son and successor Ferdinand, King of Naples 1458-94, appears more definitely as a patron of Italian art. Besides the volumes prepared for him by Hippolytus Lunensis (above, p. 289), the British Museum possesses a copy of S. Augustine's Commentary on the Psalms, written for him in 1480, in four large volumes,[2] by a scribe named Rudolfo Brancalupo. There is nothing very distinctive about its decoration, which consists mainly, like that of countless other manuscripts of the time, of gold initials with pendent borders of interlaced white vine-tendrils on coloured grounds; but the third volume has an elaborately bordered first page of text, in full Renaissance style (putti, architecture, etc.), preceded by a well-designed title-page. A word may be said here about these late Italian title-pages, which are among the most pleasing features of Renaissance illumination, being usually characterized by a good taste checking that delight in ornament which so often ran riot elsewhere. One of the most charming examples is in Add. 15246,[3] another manuscript connected with the Neapolitan court: a copy of S. Augustine's De Civitate Dei made for Don Iñigo Davalos, Count of Monte Odorisio and Grand Chamberlain of Naples under King Ferdinand, d. 1484. The title, written in plain Roman capitals, is encircled by a garland, which again is surrounded by a scroll-work design of foliage, flowers, and rayed gilt discs, with the patron's arms and with numerous putti disporting themselves among the branches; the total effect is delightful, combining symmetry, lightness, and grace. All the decoration of this volume is admirable, especially the first page of text, with its miniature-initial and its

---

[1] Brit. Mus., Add. 28962. *Pal. Soc.*, i, 226.
[2] Add. 14779-14782.
[3] Warner, *Reprod.*, iii, 39, 40. See too *Illum. MSS.*, pl. 57.

PLATE XLVIII

SFORZA BOOK OF HOURS. MILANESE, CIRCA 1490

BRIT. MUS., ADD. 34294

THE ITALIAN RENAISSANCE

highly ornate, yet light and pleasing, full border. It would be difficult, however, to point out any definite feature which stamps it as Neapolitan and differentiates it from the best Ferrarese or Venetian or Florentine work of the same period. The same may be said, *mutatis mutandis*, about a smaller and more mediocre manuscript of the same period, Add. 28271; a Horae of Rome use, made for a patron whose name began with C (f. 159), and whose arms (per bend, azure and or, over all a leopard rampant argent) are on the first page. It lacks the Calendar, but the Litany points distinctly to Sicily or the extreme south of Italy—a localization which could not easily have been inferred from the decoration, unless perhaps through a certain coarseness in the miniatures, especially in the facial types. There is more distinctiveness, on the other hand, in Add. 21120,[1] a copy, evidently made for the translator himself, of Prince Charles of Viana's Spanish translation of Aristotle's Ethics. This manuscript, which has no miniatures but is elaborately adorned with initials and borders, is generally supposed to have been made in Sicily during the Prince's residence there (1458-9). But there is no direct evidence of this; and a Spanish origin seems not only to be indicated by the language and what little is known of the history of the volume, but to be confirmed by the resemblance in style between its decoration and that of a fragmentary Toledo Missal recently acquired by the British Museum.[2] The borders are a modification of the familiar branch-work type, with putti, birds, and human figures interspersed somewhat stiffly; they are chiefly distinguished from those found in undoubtedly Italian manuscripts by the greater thickness of the curving stems. The initials are mostly gold, filled with conventional foliage, and have the marked peculiarity of being made to appear as if cut out of the solid.

[1] *Pal. Soc.*, ii, 157; *New Pal. Soc.*, pl. 145-6; Warner, *Illum. MSS.*, pl. 56, *Reprod.*, i, 47.
[2] Add. 38037.

ILLUMINATED MANUSCRIPTS

Not much need be added to what has already been said about sixteenth century illumination. Its quantity is considerable, both in the great choir-books which were still required for use in monastic and other churches, and in smaller volumes made to gratify the sumptuous tastes of princes and prelates. But its quality is decadent, its vitality is ebbing rapidly, and it has no real significance in the history of painting. Great masters of panel-painting condescended at times to practise the art: Perugino, for instance, painted one of the miniatures in the Albani Horae.[1] But among the specialists in illumination the names which stand out most prominently are those of Giulio Clovio and his disciple Apollonio de' Bonfratelli. Giulio Clovio,[2] though reckoned among Italian painters, was actually a Croatian, born at Grizane in 1498; but he came to Italy in 1516, and remained there almost continuously until his death in 1578, working now at Perugia, now at Rome, now at Florence. He formed his style largely on that of his friend Giulio Romano, the pupil of Raphael; but he also felt the influence of Michelangelo, and effete imitations of that great master's sibyls and athletes often appear in his miniatures. Giulio Clovio is a typical master of the decadence; fond of weak suave forms, cheap sentiment, and soft broken colours. His work, though often technically good, never rises above an insipid elegance. He is best known in England by two works of his middle period, both done for his patron Cardinal Marino Grimani: the Commentary on S. Paul's Epistle to the Romans, in the Soane Museum, and a Book of Hours in the British Museum (Add. 20927). The Soane MS. has a large frontispiece of the Conversion of S. Paul, painted in Clovio's characteristic style, weak and affected, but beau-

---

[1] *Pal. Soc.*, ii, 38. The plate is from another page, signed by Amico [Aspertini] of Bologna, on which the picture combines great brilliancy in execution with confused and overcrowded composition, while the border is a mere incoherent medley of disconnected and incongruous ornaments.

[2] J. W. Bradley, *Life and Works of Giorgio Giulio Clovio*, 1891.

THE ITALIAN RENAISSANCE

tifully finished. The Horae is a much smaller book, containing several full-page illuminations. These have frame-borders of the amazingly miscellaneous character so loved by the late Renaissance illuminators: satyrs, pieces of armour, birds, nude athletes, scriptural scenes, jostling one another on the gilded and coloured grounds. Many of the miniatures are exquisitely painted, soft and delicate; occasionally vigorous too, as in the vignette of David beheading Goliath, which forms part of the admirable frontispiece to the Penitential Psalms (f. 91b). But Clovio's usual weaknesses peep out continually, especially in the larger compositions: his mawkish sentiment, want of dignity, and florid taste. His actual output does full credit to his industry; but he has also been made responsible for an immense number of paintings in which modern critics see rather the work of his pupils or imitators. Such are the Victories of Charles V, in the British Museum (Add. 33733); a large miniature of the Crucifixion, in the Musée Condé at Chantilly: and a host of other pictures. The Chantilly Crucifixion is really by Apollonio de' Bonfratelli, as appears plainly on comparing it with his signed miniatures, cut out from a manuscript executed in 1564 for Pope Pius IV, and preserved in the Rogers Album at the British Museum (Add. 21412, ff. 36-44); especially with the Crucifixion and Pietà (ff. 42, 43). Apollonio has many of his master's affectations; but he composes in a larger, freer manner, and adopts a deeper and more brilliant colour-scheme. His conception of the human form too is essentially different; instead of Giulio's slender and often absurdly elongated figures he prefers a more robust type, and gives us thickset, clumsy, yet vital and actual men and women. He cannot be called a great artist, but his work is not without merit, and he may fitly be taken as the last representative of Italian illuminators.

CHAPTER XVIII

FLEMISH ILLUMINATION AFTER 1300

THE materials for the history of Flemish illumination in the fourteenth century are as distressingly scarce as those for the fifteenth are embarrassingly plenteous. We have an abundance of manuscripts executed in the near neighbourhood of the year 1300; some of these have been noticed at the end of chapter xi, notably Stowe 17 and the Sneyd MS., which might with equal propriety have been placed at the beginning of the present chapter. In all of them a close affinity to contemporary East Anglian and Northern French work is apparent. French influence predominates in some, e.g. in the little Breviary[1] of the Dominican convent of Val-Duchesse, at Auderghem near Brussels, whose miniatures, with their daintily swaying, white-faced figures painted against diapered or burnished gold grounds, and their use of black pen-lines to indicate all details of drapery and features, have little to distinguish them from French illuminations of the time, except the characteristic Flemish dark blue. In others, it is the resemblance to the East Anglian manuscripts, noticed in chapter xiii, which catches the eye. This shows itself not only in the love for grotesques and caricatures, so prominent in Stowe 17 and many other manuscripts, such as Add. 30029 and 29253, both from Blandigny Abbey near Ghent, or the slightly later S. Omer Horae, Add. 36684 (*circa* 1320), formerly in Ruskin's library; but also in the whole decorative scheme, and sometimes in the larger compositions. Thus the Crucifixion in a Cambrai Missal,[2] now

[1] Brit. Mus., Harl. 2449.
[2] No. 149. See A. Durieux, *Les miniatures des MSS. de la Bibl. de Cambrai*, 1861, pl. 7.

FLEMISH ILLUMINATION AFTER 1300

preserved in the Public Library of that place, might almost pass as the work of the Gorleston or Norwich school; and the same may be said about the ornamentation of the two-volume Bible[1] in the same library. It is difficult to fix the "scientific frontier" between France and Flanders for the purposes of art history. Perhaps Cambrai ought strictly to be regarded as French; undoubtedly Soissons and Laon must be, and yet these places too provide examples of just the same type of miniature and ornament.[2] South-eastwards too the influence spread at any rate as far as Trèves, where it appears plainly in the border-decoration of a "Kopialbuch" written for Archbishop Baldwin, now in the Archives at Coblenz.[3]

The difficulty of distinguishing Flemish from French illumination in the second half of the fourteenth century is increased by the fact that many of the best Flemish miniaturists are known to have worked in France, for the king and for great nobles such as the Duke of Berry. Their work, so far as it can be identified with any approach to certainty, was usually of a high order, as we saw when dealing with André Beauneveu and Jacquemart de Hesdin.[4] Their native land seems to have been content with a less refined form of art, if we may judge by such books as the "Kuerbouc" of Ypres,[5] dated 1363, and copiously adorned with marginal figures, almost invariably of grotesque character; or by the illustrations of the "Biblia Pauperum" and "Speculum Humanae Salvationis," most of which are worthless artistically, though of great interest from an iconographical point of view. The majority of the extant manuscripts of

---

[1] No. 327. Durieux, pl. 8.

[2] See E. Fleury, *Les MSS. à miniatures de la Bibl. de Soissons*, 1865, and his similar volume for Laon, 1863.

[3] A. Chroust, *Mon. Pal. Denkmäler der Schreibkunst des Mittelalters*, Abth. i. ser. ii, Lief. vi (1911), Taf. 7.

[4] See chapter xiv.

[5] M. Verkest, "La satire dans le 'Kuerbouc' d'Ypres," in *Les Arts anciens de Flandre* (Bruges, 1904, etc.), pp. 95–107.

these two closely allied compositions[1] are German rather than Flemish in origin; and many of them, being on paper, do not come within the scope of the present volume. One of the few exceptions is King's MS. 5[2] in the British Museum, a finely illuminated copy of the "Biblia Pauperum" on vellum, executed by Flemish or Rhenish artists about the year 1400. As now bound up, it consists of thirty-one long narrow pages, each page having in the centre a scene from the life of Christ, accompanied by four half-length figures of prophets bearing scrolls, and flanked by two Old Testament scenes by which it is supposed to have been foreshadowed. The parallelism is sometimes curiously far-fetched, as when the widow of Zarephath gathering sticks is made to typify Christ carrying the cross. But this manuscript does not differ from other copies of the work in the choice of subjects; it is the finished excellence of their treatment which distinguishes it above its fellows. The backgrounds of the pictures are either gilded or diapered in the old style, the landscape-painting which was later to constitute one of the chief glories of Flemish art not having yet been developed. Touches of naïve absurdity still occur in some of the compositions, e.g. where Michal lets down David from a window in full view of Saul; but the flat treatment of the figure has now given way to careful modelling by means of skilful and delicate gradations of colour. The range of colours is not wide, but is generally used with felicity, a favourite tint being a particularly soft and pleasing violet. In the faces a distinct striving after individual types is noticeable, especially in the grave, intensely pathetic Christ.

Among the earliest attempts to represent the figures in their natural setting, instead of placing them against a conventional background, is a series of twenty-eight

---

[1] For their bibliography, etc., see W. L. Schreiber, *Biblia Pauperum*, 1903; J. Lutz and P. Perdrizet, *Speculum Humanae Salvationis*, 1907-9.

[2] Fully described, with illustrations, by Sir E. M. Thompson in *Bibliographica*, iii, 1897, pp. 385-406.

MANDEVILLE'S TRAVELS. FLEMISH, EARLY XVTH CENT
BRIT. MUS., ADD. 24189

FLEMISH ILLUMINATION AFTER 1300

full-page miniatures, without text, illustrating the travels of Sir John Mandeville.[1] Executed early in the fifteenth century, probably at or near Liége, these delightful pictures are almost entirely in monochrome. The whole page is tinted a pale milky green, on which the outlines are drawn in ink, and delicately shaded with washes of pale grey, with occasional touches of opaque white. Faces and hands are faintly tinted, sea and sky are blue, sometimes patterned in white, and gold is used for crowns, nimbi, and other accessories; otherwise the only colouring is in the foliage, usually a sombre green. The pictures are filled almost to the limit of their frame-lines with buildings or landscapes, the latter sometimes of quite an elaborate description, as in the representation of pilgrims visiting Aristotle's tomb;[2] and despite the rudimentary perspective, resembling that of a bird's-eye view, the artist goes far towards achieving his aim of making us see the actual scene which he has in his mind. The figures, though often faulty, and out of all proportion to the tiny buildings which surround them, are spirited and expressive; and the architecture is drawn with characteristically Flemish attention to detail. In fact, with its firm yet delicate draughtsmanship, its freedom from conventionality, this series constitutes a veritable masterpiece.

To the same period belong the first additions to that ill-fated book known as the Turin Hours, whose history has been worked out so fully by M. Durrieu.[3] Begun in or after 1404 for the famous Duke of Berry, it was for some reason left unfinished, and was given by him, before 1413, to his keeper of jewels, Robinet d'Estampes. The latter had entered it in his inventories, even in its incomplete state, as "unes très belles heures de Nostre

---

[1] Brit. Mus., Add. 24189, reproduced for the Roxburghe Club, *The Buke of John Maundevill*, ed. G. F. Warner, 1889. See too *Pal. Soc.*, ii, 154-5; Warner, *Reprod.*, i, 36.
[2] Pl. xlix.
[3] *Heures de Turin*, 1902, reproducing the forty-five illuminated pages then at Turin and in the Louvre; "Les 'très belles heures de N. D.' du duc Jean de Berry," in *Revue Archéol.*, ser. iv, vol. xvi, 1910, pp. 30-51, 246-79.

ILLUMINATED MANUSCRIPTS

Dame"; and the epithet is amply justified by what remains of the original work, which is worthy to rank almost among the finest productions of the Duke of Berry's artists. The greater part of this is now in Baron Maurice de Rothschild's collection at Paris. The remainder seems very soon to have been detached, and to have passed into the possession of William IV of Bavaria, Count of Hainault and Holland (d. 1417). A new Calendar was prefixed to this part, showing a Netherlandish origin by the preponderance of local saints as well as by the style of its decorations; and many of the uncompleted pages were now filled up with miniatures by Flemish artists. Some of these are superb, displaying a remarkable advance in perspective and in all the problems of landscape-painting, especially the picture which contains Count William's portrait, a sea-shore piece, with a long line of breakers along the coast (*Heures de Turin*, pl. 37); and that of SS. Martha and Julian in a small sailing-boat, guiding the sailors into harbour (pl. 30), with its masterly treatment of the choppy sea, the boat and its occupants, and the distant wooded hills. This portion of the manuscript was afterwards split up again; some fragments are now in the Louvre, others in the Trivulzio Collection at Milan, but the greater part (including the two admirable pages just mentioned) perished in the disastrous fire of January 1904, which wrought such havoc among the treasures of the Turin Library.

These miniatures are enough to show that the art had already been brought to a high state of perfection; and for the next hundred years Flemish illuminators not only held their ground against their French and Italian fellow-craftsmen, but ultimately eclipsed them completely, maintaining great excellence, and even continuing to improve, especially in the delicacy of their handling of landscape and portraiture, long after their rivals had sunk into tasteless decadence. This remarkable fact is largely due, it may not unreasonably be supposed, to the propensity of

FLEMISH ILLUMINATION AFTER 1300

Flemish art in general throughout this period—the time of the great masters of early Flemish painting, from the Van Eycks to Gerard David, Quentin Metsys, and Mabuse —for methods peculiarly appropriate to miniature. Indeed, David is known to have painted miniatures as well as panels;[1] and there is no antecedent improbability in the supposition that Memlinc did so too, though the many attributions of miniatures to him are quite unsupported by evidence. It is probably safer, however, to assign the resemblance to his work, often noticed in illuminations of the late fifteenth and early sixteenth centuries, to direct imitation. Most of these illuminations were done at Bruges, the scene of Memlinc's career as a great painter, and also the home of a flourishing guild of illuminators, whose chapel was presented in 1478 with an altar-piece painted by him for Willem Vrelant, a distinguished member of the guild.[2] What, then, is more likely than that younger members should have sought inspiration for their miniatures in Memlinc's panels, aptly suited as these were in so many ways to their special needs?

Among the many illuminators who are known to have worked for, or in the time of, Philip the Good, Duke of Burgundy (1419-67), and his successor, Charles the Bold (1467-77), Willem Vrelant is one of the few whose names are definitely associated with extant manuscripts. From 1454 until his death in 1480-1 his name occurs in the accounts of the illuminators' guild at Bruges; but the only certain examples of his work are the miniatures in vol. ii of the "Histoire du Haynaut" (Brussels, Bibl. Roy., 9242-4), for which he was paid in 1467-8; and even these cannot all be assigned with confidence to his hand, though doubtless all were painted under his direction. Taking these as basis, critics have been led to attribute many other fine miniatures to his school, notably those

---

[1] See W. H. J. Weale, *Gerard David*, 1895, p. 47; also his chapter on "The Miniature Painters and Illuminators of Bruges, 1457-1523," in *The Hours of Albert of Brandenburg*, ed. F. S. Ellis [1883], pp. 9-16.

[2] Weale, *Hans Memlinc*, 1907, pp. 10, 20-3.

ILLUMINATED MANUSCRIPTS

in the "Chroniques de Jherusalem" and the romance of Girard de Roussillon at Vienna, both executed for Philip the Good about 1450;[1] and the "Histoire du bon roi Alexandre" in the Dutuit Collection at Paris.[2] M. Durrieu also sees his hand in the Breviary of Philip the Good (Brussels, 9511, 9026); but the illuminations in this book are of a less finished character, and are probably to be referred to a somewhat earlier date, though they may conceivably have been done in the atelier where Vrelant learnt his craft.[3] The other manuscripts prove him and his assistants to have thoroughly mastered the art of depicting the operations of war: in the representation of beleaguered cities especially they excelled, showing the scaling-ladders, catapults, and other siege engines in full detail, and combining the realistic and the picturesque with great success. There is a certain stiffness and artificiality about the grouping and posing of figures, both in battle-scenes and in other pictures: but the landscape-painting has now reached a pitch of excellence not surpassed until the beginning of the next century, combining softness, sense of distance, and atmosphere, with a marvellous rendering of detail.

Other miniaturists of the same period, and more or less of the same school, are Jean le Tavernier of Oudenarde, who illustrated the "Conquêtes de Charlemagne" (Brussels, 9066–8)[4] in 1458 for Philip the Good; and Loyset Liédet, who worked at Hesdin and Bruges from 1460 to 1478, becoming a member of the guild of illuminators at the latter place in 1469. Several of Liédet's works are extant, at Brussels, Paris, and elsewhere. His illustrations to the "Histoire de Charles Martel" (Brussels, 6–9), made in 1463–5 for Philip the

---

[1] See A. Schestag, "Die Chronik von Jerusalem," in the Vienna *Jahrbuch*, xx, 1899, pp. 195–216.

[2] Durrieu, "L'histoire du bon roi Alexandre" in *Rev. de l'art anc. et mod.*, xiii, 1903, pp. 49–64, 103–21; F. de Mély, "Les signatures des primitifs," in *Gaz. des Beaux-Arts*, 1910, ii, pp. 173–94.

[3] See J. van den Gheyn, *Le Bréviaire de Philippe le Bon*, 1909.

[4] *New Pal. Soc.*, pl. 44.

FLEMISH ILLUMINATION AFTER 1300

Good, have been published,[1] and show him to have been, if not a great or original artist, at least a highly accomplished craftsman. Another great name is that of Simon Marmion of Valenciennes, called " prince d'enlumineure " by a contemporary poet;[2] and fitly, if the splendid miniatures of the Grandes Chroniques at St. Petersburg,[3] painted for Philip the Good about 1456, are actually, as M. Reinach supposes, the work of him and his assistants. The best of these are unquestionably by a great master, who rivalled Jean Fouquet in his power of giving individuality and character to the personages of a group.[4]

Besides fully illuminated pictures, this period has bequeathed to us many fine examples of painting *en grisaille*. Among the most perfect are the illustrations to the two volumes of Mielot's Miracles de Nostre Dame at Paris.[5] The first volume was completed at the Hague in 1456; the second is evidently somewhat later, and represents a more advanced stage of the art: architecture, landscape, and figure-composition being all handled with the utmost delicacy and finish. A replica of vol. ii, as regards text and subjects, made apparently about the beginning of Charles the Bold's reign, is in the Bodleian.[6] Its seventy miniatures, in bluish grey shaded from white to nearly black, are spirited, humorous, and quaintly expressive, but are not to be compared for artistic merit with those of the Paris counterpart.

The alliance between Edward IV and Charles the Bold, consolidated by the marriage of Charles with Edward's sister Margaret in 1468, was followed by a

---

[1] *Histoire de Charles Martel*, ed. J. van den Gheyn, 1910.
[2] See E. Gilliat-Smith, *The Story of Bruges*, 1909, p. 372.
[3] S. Reinach, *Un MS. de la Bibl. de Philippe le Bon à St. Pétersbourg* (Fond. E. Piot, *Mon. et Mém.*, vol. xi), 1904.
[4] See especially pl. 1, the dedication-picture.
[5] Bibl. Nat., fr. 9198-9. Published in facsimile, slightly reduced, by H O[mont], *Miracles de Notre Dame* [1906].
[6] Douce 374, reproduced for the Roxburghe Club, *Miracles de Nostre Dame*, ed. G. F. Warner, 1885.

corresponding change in English taste; and French illumination began to be supplanted by Flemish in the esteem of the nobility of this country. The king himself led the fashion, adding to his library a large collection of huge tomes written and illuminated in the Low Countries, especially at Bruges and Ghent. One of these, a Josephus, is in the Soane Museum; but the great majority are now in the British Museum, having been transferred thither with the rest of the old Royal Library.[1] They consist mainly of copies of the Bible Historiale and of histories, romances, and philosophical works in French. None of them can be called quite first-class in point of artistic merit, but they serve as useful examples of the style most in vogue towards the end of the fifteenth century. The miniatures, filling half the page or more, are very large, and their technique resembles that of scene-painting; looked at from a distance they are effective and not unpleasing, but a close inspection reveals in many cases an almost repulsive coarseness of execution. Among the best are those in 18 E. iii and iv (Valerius Maximus, dated 1479), 15 E. ii and iii (Livre des propriétéz des choses, written at Bruges in 1482),[2] and 19 E. v (Romuleon, a compilation of Roman history). 16 G. iii (Vita Christi, written by D. Aubert at Ghent in 1479) may also be mentioned in connection with these manuscripts, though its miniatures are on a much smaller scale; they are attributed by M. Durrieu[3] to Alexander Bennink, and are certainly by an artist of some distinction and individuality. The borders in these books are practically always of the same type, consisting of a scroll of conventional foliage, mixed with sprays of leaves, fruit, and flowers treated more naturalistically, and sometimes varied by the introduction of angels, birds, or insects; the ground of the border-frame is usually left white, but is occasionally covered with a thin wash of colour.

[1] A few specimens are exhibited in the Saloon and the Grenville Room. See *Guide*, 1906, pp. 82, 140–1.
[2] Warner, *Reprod.*, i, 38.   [3] *Gaz. des Beaux-Arts*, 1891, i, p. 364.

FLEMISH ILLUMINATION AFTER 1300

Towards the end of the century the demand for these colossal tomes declined; and Flemish illumination in its last and most attractive phase, from about 1490 to 1530, is found mainly in devotional books intended for private use—or private enjoyment, it would perhaps be more correct to say—especially Breviaries and Books of Hours. In technical skill the best miniaturists had now reached the utmost heights attainable in the art, and their rendering of landscape leaves little to be desired by the most exacting critics; while their close relations with the great painters saved them from the decadence into which their French and Italian fellow-craftsmen fell, and gave their compositions something of the sincerity and homely simplicity, combined with dignity and intense spirituality, which give such character to the masterpieces of Memlinc and his contemporaries. The development of border-decoration was less satisfactory. The continuous scrolls of conventional foliage, painted on the plain margins of the vellum page, had served their turn, and a new style of border came into fashion. This, though more in harmony with the passionate fidelity to nature which inspired the landscape and *genre* painting of the miniatures, cannot be called an entire success as a decorative scheme; it has even been compared, flippantly yet not inaptly, to a modern seedsman's illustrated catalogue. The miniature-pages are now framed in broad rectangular bands of dead gold, or less commonly of pale grey, purple, or other monochrome; and these bands are covered with flowers (singly or in short sprays), fruits, birds, snails, butterflies, bees, and other insects, painted with consummate skill and most scrupulous accuracy. Each in itself is delightful, but as an *ensemble* the scheme is somewhat incoherent and unmeaning, and tends rather to distract attention from the picture, instead of forming an appropriate setting for it. Despite these strictures, however, one cannot refuse a tribute of admiration to these illustrations from natural history. The objects selected are beautiful in themselves (carnations, pansies, corn-

ILLUMINATED MANUSCRIPTS

flowers, and columbines are the favourite flowers, wild strawberries the favourite fruit), and colour and form alike are reproduced almost faultlessly; the illusion of solidity is enhanced by the device of making the objects cast shadows on the background, as though slightly raised above it.

Good examples of these naturalistic borders may be seen in Add. 25698 at the British Museum, an interesting fragment consisting of eleven leaves from a prayer-book of unknown origin, but apparently made about 1492-3 and connected with the military order of S. George (founded by the Emperor Frederick III in 1469, and extended by his successor Maximilian), and with a project of Maximilian's, in which that order was meant to play an important part, for an international crusade against the Turks. This seems plainly alluded to on f. 3, where Frederick and Maximilian, with the Kings of England, France, and Spain, and the Archduke Philip of Austria, are kneeling before the altar of S. George;[1] and on f. 11, an anticipatory picture of the knights of the order defeating the Turks in battle. Other miniatures, similar in plan to that on f. 3, show the Pope and prelates invoking S. Peter (f. 4), monks and friars invoking the Holy Ghost (f. 10), and all sorts and conditions of the laity invoking Christ (f. 8)—all, probably, with the same object of ensuring victory against the Turk. On another page (f. 5) we see the deathbed of some great lady, whose name apparently began with M :[2] a friar holds a crucifix before her eyes, and props up the candle in her feeble hands, while Michael and the devil fight for her soul, and she is cheered by a vision of the Virgin and Child; the picture is completed by two clerics praying by the bedside, and a richly dressed indifferent group chatting near the door. Another subject (f. 9) is the Lenten

---

[1] Warner, *Reprod.*, ii, 37.

[2] One is tempted to identify her with Mary of Burgundy (d. 1482), or with Margaret of York, widow of Charles the Bold (d. 1503); but there are chronological or other objections to either conjecture.

PLATE L

LEAF FROM A BOOK OF HOURS, FLEMISH, CIRCA 1492

BRIT. MUS., ADD. 25698

FLEMISH ILLUMINATION AFTER 1300

Penance,[1] a priest shriving one penitent while others kneel before the altar with its veiled Calvary. Another (f. 2) is the Elevation of the Host, in a church whose sanctuary is raised high above the nave, with a flight of steps on either side and a crypt underneath.[2] This composition was copied faithfully, down to the minutest detail, including the kneeling figures in the nave, by the illuminator of the Hours of Floris van Egmond, Count of Buren and Knight of the Golden Fleece (1505-39), and Margaret van Bergen his wife;[3] but the copyist was a greatly inferior artist, and his work lacks the charming softness and grace of the original. One more page must be mentioned before we leave this fascinating fragment, viz. f. 1, which represents simply a Flemish countryside: a village by a river, animals grazing in the fields, trees and low hills misty on the horizon. This is one of the few instances to be found, in illuminated manuscripts, of landscape painting for its own sake, not as the setting of a subject-picture.

Two manuscripts of a secular character deserve some notice, both executed about the year 1500, and both now in the British Museum. One of these[4] contains the poems of Charles, Duke of Orleans, and was evidently made for Henry VII or his son Arthur, Prince of Wales. It has six large miniatures, of varying degrees of merit, and none of them quite representative of Flemish art at its best. The artists were perhaps brought into England for the purpose, or attached permanently to Henry's court. At all events, the work seems to have been done in this country, for it closely resembles that of a manuscript written for Henry at Sheen in 1496 (Roy. 19 C. viii), and one of the best miniatures is a quaint but thoroughly realistic picture of the Tower of London (where the poet-

[1] Pl. l.
[2] This unusual construction recalls the Church of Jerusalem at Bruges, but the details are somewhat different.
[3] Add. 35319, f. 33b.
[4] Roy. 16 F. ii. See Warner, *Illum. MSS.*, pl. 54.

ILLUMINATED MANUSCRIPTS

duke spent most of his captivity, from 1415 to 1440), with the Thames, Traitor's Gate, London Bridge, and the City. It is curious to see in this picture the persistent survival of the "continuous" method: Charles appears at once writing at a table, in his prison-chamber in the White Tower; looking out of a window; and giving a letter to a messenger. The second manuscript[1] is a copy of the Roman de la Rose: a very sumptuous volume, with four large and eighty-eight small miniatures. There is a quaint artificial elegance (French rather than Flemish in spirit) about the large garden-scenes; but the great merit of the book consists in the admirable figure-drawing and characterization shown in many of the smaller pictures. The text seems to have been transcribed from one of the early printed editions[2]—a curious inversion of the usual order of things.

The well-known "Isabella Book" of the British Museum[3] is a Breviary of Spanish Dominican use, illuminated by Flemish artists (probably working in Spain, where the text was evidently written), and given to Queen Isabella in or about 1497 by Francisco de Roias. Besides numerous borders, and over one hundred small miniatures, it contains forty-five half-page pictures, which taken as a whole exemplify most admirably the work of this period. The technique has not yet reached the summit of its perfection, that combination of firm outline with extreme delicacy and softness, which distinguishes the Hennessy Hours and a few other books of slightly later date; but many of the compositions are very beautiful, especially the Adoration of the Magi (f. 41), the Nativity (f. 29), the Apocalyptic vision of S. John (f. 309), and the lovely S. Barbara (f. 297), in all of which the influence of Memlinc and his disciples is plainly dis-

---

[1] Harl. 4425. See Warner, *Reprod.*, iii, 47.

[2] See F. W. Bourdillon, *Early Editions of the Roman de la Rose*, 1906, pp. 12, 28.

[3] Add. 18851. See *Pal. Soc.*, i, 174–5; Warner, *Illum. MSS.*, pl. 53, *Reprod.*, iii, 45–6.

FLEMISH ILLUMINATION AFTER 1300

cernible. The borders are of three kinds: 1st, the nearly obsolete Franco-Flemish scroll-work; 2nd, the naturalistic style described above; 3rd, striped repeat-patterns, apparently copied from brocaded stuffs. This last style occurs also, it may be noted, on some of the pages of an interesting little Book of Hours[1] of the same period, which contains portraits of Isabella's daughter Joan and the latter's husband Philip the Fair. The Calendar-illustrations in the Isabella Book are of a type often followed about this time. There are no separate miniatures, but the whole text for each month is inlaid, as it were, in a picture of an appropriate occupation. One of the subjects newly introduced into the cycle is worth noting, for it forms a striking feature in the Calendar-pictures produced by the Bruges miniaturists during the next decade or two: for May, a boating pleasure-party on a river.

Still more famous is the Grimani Breviary, preserved in S. Mark's Library at Venice.[2] Many conflicting and misleading statements have been published by various ill-informed writers concerning the age of this book, the names of its illuminators, and even its actual contents. For the last kind of misstatement the facsimile reproduction, with Dr. Coggiola's detailed description, leaves now no shred of excuse. In the absence of documentary evidence, critics will always claim freedom to attribute the miniatures according to their several tastes; but one may perhaps venture to deprecate the repeated and confident attributions of particular miniatures to Memlinc,[3] who probably had no hand in the work at all. As to the date, a *terminus ad quem* is furnished by Cardinal Domenico

[1] Add 17280. See Warner, *Reprod.*, i, 37. In Add. 18852 the Museum possesses another book associated with the unfortunate Joan: an exquisite little Horae with many charming miniatures, containing her portrait on ff. 26 and 288.

[2] See F. Zanotto, *Facsimile delle miniature contenute nel Breviario Grimani*, 1862; F. Ongania, *A Glance at the Grimani Breviary*, 1903; and the complete reproduction, largely in colour, edited by S. Morpurgo and S. de Vries, with introduction by G. Coggiola, *Le Bréviaire Grimani*, 1904–10. A succinct but useful account of the manuscript, with illustrations, is in Weale's *G. David*, pp. 55–68.

[3] As in Ongania's publication, *passim*.

ILLUMINATED MANUSCRIPTS

Grimani's mention of the book in his first will, dated 5 October, 1520. He had bought it from Antonio Siciliano; farther back its history has not been carried. The text of the Calendar, however, shows plainly that it was intended for the Italian market (whether actually written in Italy or not), and that it was certainly not begun before 1481, probably not before 1490. The advanced technique, especially in the handling of trees, suggests a still later date, say about 1510. Splendid monument as it is of the illuminator's art, its pre-eminence in fame above all its contemporaries is due to the extent of its decorations rather than to their intrinsic superiority in point of beauty. With its 831 leaves of ample size, containing forty-nine full-page miniatures, besides the Calendar-pictures and minor decorations, it stands almost alone in its class. The twelve full-page miniatures which illustrate the Calendar agree most remarkably with the corresponding series in the "Très Riches Heures," not only in subject and main outlines of composition, but in such details as the device of the Sun-God in his chariot, set in a semicircle at the top of each page; even the backgrounds are reminiscent of the earlier work, though no longer containing precise representations of the Duke of Berry's castles. In short, there is no room for doubt as to the parentage of these designs; and it must be admitted that they suffer badly by comparison with the originals—one seeks here vainly for the exquisite dainty grace of the Limbourg brothers' painting. The Adoration of the Magi, again, is almost identical with that in the Isabella Book; but here it is not easy to say which is the original—if either, for very likely both are derived from some lost panel, perhaps by David, some of whose pictures are known to have inspired the artists of the Grimani Breviary. Other compositions also occur in a Book of Hours, now in the British Museum,[1] which

---

[1] Add. 35313. See Warner, *Reprod.*, ii, 36. A possible allusion to the death of Mary of Burgundy (1482) has been seen in the design prefixed to Vigils of the Dead, three skeletons with darts attacking a lady in the hunting-field.

FLEMISH ILLUMINATION AFTER 1300

is probably of somewhat earlier date, and certainly of greatly inferior execution: notably the Annunciation, Nativity, and Augustus with the Sibyl. Originality of design, however, is the last thing to be expected of a miniaturist at this period, with a few rare exceptions. As to execution, the various styles discernible in the Grimani Breviary differ widely, from the comparative coarseness of some of the Calendar-scenes to the charming softness of the picture of S. Mary Magdalene. The book is, in fact, not one work of art but many—a gallery of little masters. Of the cognate manuscripts, those best worth notice are Mr. Pierpont Morgan's Breviary;[1] the Hours of Albert of Brandenburg;[2] three manuscripts at Munich;[3] and Maximilian's Prayer-book[4] and the Hortulus Animae[5] at Vienna.

The Flemish additions to the Sforza Book[6] were made during the years 1519-21, by artists working for the Emperor Charles V, whose portrait, with date 1520, is on one of the pages, painted in gold within a medallion. The border-decoration of this page (the first of the Penitential Psalms) is a close imitation of the work of the original Milanese artists. But the sixteen inserted full-page miniatures are thoroughly Flemish in conception, design, and colouring, and are among the finest extant examples of the school. Differences of style suggest that more than one artist was employed; but an exceedingly high level of merit is maintained throughout, and it is difficult to make a selection. Especially striking are the Adoration of the Magi and the Presentation, with their masterly portraiture, simple yet effective grouping, and skilful, characteristically minute and careful treatment of architecture and costume; the "O intemerata," with its

---

[1] See *Burl. Mag.*, Mar. 1907, pp. 400-5.
[2] Ed. F. S. Ellis [1883].
[3] See Kobell, pp. 90-1.
[4] See Vienna *Jahrbuch*, vii, pp. 201-6.
[5] *Ibid.*, ix, pp. 429-45; *Hortulus Animae, facsimile reproductions* (partly in colour), 1907, etc.
[6] See above, p. 298.

ILLUMINATED MANUSCRIPTS

placid, dreamy Madonna and the delightful group of angel-musicians; and loveliest of all, perhaps, the "Salve Regina," with its beautiful soft colouring and large, gracious manner.

Finally, a group of manuscripts must be mentioned whose most complete representatives are the Hennessy Hours[1] at Brussels and the "Golf Book"[2] in the British Museum. It is clear that they all emanate from the same school; and the resemblance of the Calvary in the Hennessy Hours to that painted in 1530 by Simon Bennink, eldest son of Alexander, in a Missal at Dixmude[3] has led to the association of his name with the whole group. The Hennessy Hours contains twenty-seven full-page miniatures, including a full Calendar series, portraits of the Evangelists, scenes of the Passion, and other subjects; besides many pages with interesting marginal decoration. The "Golf Book" is more fragmentary; it consists of thirty leaves, and has only twenty-one full-page miniatures, viz. S. Boniface, eight Passion scenes, and a Calendar series. The kinship between these two books is obvious, especially in the Passion pictures, many of which are identical in almost every detail (including the Calvary, a subject whose pathos is rendered with wonderful intensity). The Calendar subjects do not always agree, though the style is always similar; but when the two manuscripts have the same subject, as in the delightful May scene[4] of a boating-party passing one of the gates of Bruges, the June tournament, or the exquisitely homely August picture of the harvest-labourers taking their midday meal in the cornfield, the agreement is as close as in the Passion series. The same, or very nearly the same, cycle of subjects occurs in many other Flemish manuscripts of this period,

---

[1] J. Destrée, *Les Heures de N. D. dites de Hennessy*, 1895; *Musée des Enluminures*, fasc. 4–6.

[2] Add. 24098. See *Pal. Soc.*, ii, 135–6; Warner, *Reprod.*, iii, 49.

[3] Reproduced in *Burl. Mag.*, Feb. 1906, p. 357, illustrating an article by Mr. Weale, whose researches prove that Simon Bennink was born at Ghent in 1483–4, went to Bruges in 1508, settled there permanently in 1517, and died in 1561.   [4] Pl. li.

PLATE LI

HORAE ("GOLF BOOK"). FLEMISH, EARLY XVITH CENT.
BRIT. MUS. ADD. **24098**

FLEMISH ILLUMINATION AFTER 1300

e.g. in Eg. 1147 in the British Museum; but nowhere else is it treated in so finished and delicate a manner, except in a dismembered manuscript of which two leaves are in the British Museum[1] and two more in the Salting Collection at South Kensington;[2] in this fragment the execution is finer still, and could hardly be surpassed in any form of landscape-painting. One very interesting feature of the "Golf Book" is the representation of popular games and pastimes in little miniatures at the foot of the pages; it is from this that its sobriquet is derived, the September page showing a party of men playing golf. In these exquisite pictures, and in those of the Sforza Book, Flemish miniature-painting reaches its culminating point; it would be an unprofitable as well as ungracious task to carry its history farther.

[1] Add. 18855, ff. 108, 109. See Warner, *Reprod.*, iii, 50.
[2] Burl. F.A. Club, No. 231, pl. 144.

NOTE

ON THE VARIOUS KINDS OF LITURGICAL ILLUMINATED MANUSCRIPTS

TO purists in terminology the common habit of speaking of all illuminated manuscripts as missals is an abomination; and there are many lovers of illumination who, without being in the least pedantic, have a laudable desire to call things by their right names, but who lack time or opportunity or inclination to become deeply versed in the mysteries of liturgiology. To such persons the following remarks may, it is hoped, be of some service. They must bear in mind, however, that no attempt is made here to cover the whole field of liturgical manuscripts, or even to deal exhaustively with any one of the classes mentioned. The variations due to difference in age, locality, and circumstances are endless; and the many volumes that have been written, and remain to be written, about them could not possibly be summarized in a few pages. My present aim is merely to point out to the beginner in the study of illumination the salient features by which he may recognize the several classes of manuscripts which are likely to come most frequently under his notice. These are all of a liturgical character; Biblical manuscripts form a class apart, and the other non-liturgical books which will come his way (whether religious or secular) are comparatively few, and neither require, nor from their diversity lend themselves readily to, a formal classification.

There are six classes of manuscripts to be considered, viz. Missals, Breviaries, Psalters, Graduals, Antiphoners, and Books of Hours. This is by no means a complete list of the liturgical books of the medieval Latin

LITURGICAL MANUSCRIPTS

Church, but it comprises those in which illuminations are most commonly found. As to date, the manuscripts range, roughly speaking, from the eleventh century to the sixteenth; but illuminated Breviaries and Books of Hours of earlier date than the latter part of the thirteenth century are, to say the least, extremely rare; and so are Psalters of later date than the middle of the fourteenth. The Calendar of festivals, which forms an integral part of most of these books, often contains entries which give valuable indications of date and provenance; but great care must be taken to ascertain whether they are in the original hand or later additions, and not to infer more from them than is warranted. It is not always safe, for instance, to take the presence of a saint's name as proof of a date subsequent to his canonization.[1]

The Missal, or Mass-book, is the book used by the celebrating priest at the altar, and corresponds in large measure to the earlier Sacramentary. Its normal contents are: (1) Calendar. (2) Temporale, or Proper of Time, containing the variable parts (introit, collect, epistle, gradual, gospel, offertory, secret and post-communion) of the Mass for every Sunday and week-day throughout the year, beginning with the first Sunday in Advent. This is sometimes headed "Incipit ordo missalis secundum consuetudinem ecclesie Sarum" (or whatever the special use may be), but more often simply "Dom. i. in aduentu Domini. Ad missam officium" (or "introitus"). (3) Ordinary (unchanging introductory part, including the Gloria and Credo), Prefaces for various days (always beginning "Vere dignum et justum est," and often set to music), and Canon of the Mass. These are usually placed in the middle of the Temporale, just before Easter. The Canon is the most solemn part of the Mass, including the consecration. It begins with the prayer "Te igitur, clementissime Pater," and is almost always immediately preceded by a full-page miniature of the

---
[1] S. Anselm (d. 1109) was not canonized until 1494, but his name occurs in English Calendars written centuries earlier.

Crucifixion. (4) Sanctorale, or Proper of Saints: the introits, collects, etc., for saints' days throughout the year, generally beginning with S. Andrew (Nov. 30). (5) Common of Saints: introits, etc., for saints not individually provided for, e.g. for one apostle, for many martyrs, etc. (6) Votive Masses, for special occasions; followed by various prayers, and sometimes by the services forming what is commonly called the Manual, viz. Baptism, Marriage, Visitation of the Sick, Burial, etc.

As a general rule, the Missal has but little illumination beyond the Crucifixion-picture at the Canon; and that little is confined to historiated initials at the principal divisions. A favourite subject is the priest lifting up his soul to God, illustrating the first introit of the Temporale, "Ad te levavi animam meam." A few magnificently decorated Missals do exist; but they are quite exceptional, and were probably never intended for actual use.

The Breviary contains the office, i.e. the services to be said or sung every day by the clergy at the canonical hours (Matins, Lauds, Prime, Tierce, Sext, None, Vespers, Compline). These services consist mainly of psalms, interspersed with antiphons, verses, and responses, together with a few hymns and prayers. At matins there are also three, nine or twelve lessons, taken from Scripture, patristic homilies, or lives of saints: three lessons on minor festivals, nine on major (except in monasteries of the Benedictine Order and its off-shoots, which have twelve). The normal arrangement is as follows:—(1) Calendar; (2) Psalter; (3) Temporale, beginning at Advent, as in the Missal; (4) Sanctorale; (5) Common of Saints; (6) Hours of the Virgin, Office of the Dead, and other special services. Finely illuminated Breviaries are not common, the book being as a rule required for constant practical use. The nature of its contents, however, provides unlimited opportunities for illustration; and these are freely used in such manuscripts as the Breviary of John the Fearless, the Isabella Book, and the Grimani Breviary.

LITURGICAL MANUSCRIPTS

The Psalter contains the 150 Psalms, usually preceded by a Calendar and followed by the Te Deum and other Canticles, a Litany of Saints, and prayers; often too by Vigils of the Dead. Illuminated Psalters occur as early as the eighth century, and from the eleventh to the beginning of the fourteenth they form by far the most numerous class of illuminated manuscripts. Several pages at the beginning are filled in some copies, especially in the thirteenth century, with scenes from the life of Christ. The initial "B" of Psalm i is always lavishly decorated, and so are the initial letters of the principal divisions of the Psalter. These divisions vary with country and date; in the majority of thirteenth and fourteenth century manuscripts they occur at Psalms xxvi ("Dominus illuminatio mea," usually illustrated by a miniature of David looking up to God and pointing to his eyes, enclosed within the "D"), xxxviii ("Dixi custodiam"; David pointing to his lips), lii ("Dixit insipiens"; a fool with club and ball, either alone or before King David), lxviii ("Salvum me fac"; David up to his waist in water, appealing to God for help; or sometimes Jonah and the whale), lxxx ("Exultate Deo"; David playing on bells), xcvii ("Cantate Domino"; choristers singing), cix ("Dixit Dominus"; the Father and Son enthroned, the Dove hovering between them). The more sumptuous copies have a great wealth of additional illustration, from scriptural, hagiographical, and other sources.

Graduals and Antiphoners, classed together as Libri Corali by Italian bibliographers, contain the choral parts of the Mass and Office respectively. Thus the Gradual answers to the Missal, the Antiphoner to the Breviary. The former derives its name from the Gradual in the Mass, a short passage from the Psalms to be said or sung immediately after the Epistle; the latter from the antiphons which make up a large part of its contents. They are enormous volumes, having the text with full musical setting, and being designed each to serve for several choristers. They have no full-page miniatures, but their

ILLUMINATED MANUSCRIPTS

principal initials enclose pictures as large as the page of an average-sized book. The finest are of the fourteenth and fifteenth centuries, and were produced in Italy.

The Book of Hours is hardly liturgical in the strictest sense, being intended for private devotional use, and usually containing some non-liturgical matter. But it would be absurd to omit it from this list, seeing how immensely it outnumbers all other classes of illuminated manuscripts. Its contents vary greatly, both in matter and arrangement, but almost always include the following nucleus :—(1) Calendar ; (2) Four Lessons, one from each Gospel, viz. the opening verses of S. John (" In principio erat verbum," etc.), the Annunciation from S. Luke, the Adoration of the Magi from S. Matthew, and the conclusion of S. Mark. These are called " Cursus Evangelii " by some modern writers, " Sequences of the Gospels " by others; but neither title occurs in the manuscripts. (3) Two prayers to the Virgin, beginning " Obsecro te," and " O intemerata"; (4) Hours or Office of the Virgin. It is from this section, generally the longest in the volume, that the name " Book of Hours " is taken. The opening words of Matins are " Domine labia mea aperies"; the other Hours begin " Deus in adjutorium meum intende," except Compline, which begins " Converte nos Deus salutaris noster." (5) Hours of the Cross, and of the Holy Ghost, usually in a very condensed form ; (6) The Seven Penitential Psalms (" Domine ne in furore tuo," etc.), followed by Litany and prayers ; (7) Memorials of Saints (in English Horae these are introduced into Lauds of the Virgin); (8) Vigils, or Office, of the Dead ; consisting of Vespers (called " Placebo," from its opening word, in old English literature) and Matins (" Dirige "). (9) English Horae usually have also the Commendation of Souls, beginning " Beati immaculati." Additions to the above, too many and too various to be enumerated here, are frequently found, especially in French Horae of the fifteenth century, e.g. Hours of S. Catherine, Mass of the Trinity, etc.

LITURGICAL MANUSCRIPTS

Illuminated Books of Hours occur before the end of the thirteenth century, and by the end of the fourteenth they had become extremely popular. Their normal decoration includes the following full or half-page miniatures (apart from Calendar-illustrations, borders, and initials):— At the Gospel-lessons, portraits of the Evangelists. At Matins of the Virgin, the Annunciation, sometimes with a portrait of the owner adoring the Virgin; Lauds, the Visitation; Prime, the Nativity; Tierce, Angel and Shepherds; Sext, Adoration of the Magi; None, Presentation in the Temple; Vespers, Flight into Egypt; Compline, Coronation of the Virgin. Hours of the Cross; the Crucifixion. Hours of the Holy Ghost; Pentecost. Penitential Psalms; David kneeling, or sometimes Bathsheba, sometimes the Death Angel. Memorials of Saints; miniatures of the several saints commemorated. Vigils of the Dead; Raising of Lazarus, or sometimes a Burial, or sometimes the Three Living and Three Dead; but most commonly the interior of a church, with monks chanting round a bier. Commendation of Souls; the Day of Judgment, with the dead rising from their graves.

SELECT BIBLIOGRAPHY

THE following list contains, for the most part, only those publications which the present writer has found specially useful, and which ought to be consulted by all serious students of the several branches of the art of illumination with which they deal. It may be supplemented to some extent by reference to the footnotes on the foregoing pages.

I. PERIODICALS

Archivio Storico dell'Arte. Rome, 1888, etc.; continued from 1898 as *L'Arte.*
Les Arts anciens de Flandre. Bruges, 1904, etc.
Burlington Magazine. London, 1902, etc.
Fondation Eugène Piot. Monuments et Mémoires. Paris, 1894, etc. (Acad. des Inscr. et Belles-Lettres).
Gazette des Beaux-Arts. Paris, 1859, etc.
Jahrbuch der kunsthistorischen Sammlungen des allerhöchsten Kaiserhauses. Vienna, 1883, etc. Cited below as *Jahrb.*
Revue de l'Art ancien et moderne. Paris, 1897, etc.

II. GENERAL WORKS

BASTARD, COUNT A. DE. *Peintures et ornements des MSS.* 1832-69.
BRADLEY, J. W. *Dictionary of Miniaturists.* 1887-9.
CHROUST, A. *Monumenta Palaeographica. Denkmäler der Schreibkunst des Mittelalters.* 1899, etc.
GARRUCCI, R. *Storia della Arte cristiana.* 1872-81.
KRAUS, F. X. *Geschichte der christlichen Kunst.* 1896-1900.
MICHEL, A. *Histoire de l'Art.* 1905, etc. (sections on miniature by G. Millet, P. Leprieur, A. Haseloff, and P. Durrieu).
NEW PALAEOGRAPHICAL SOCIETY. *Facsimiles of ancient MSS., etc.,* ed. E. M. Thompson, G. F. Warner, and F. G. Kenyon. 1903, etc.
PALAEOGRAPHICAL SOCIETY. *Facsimiles of MSS. and Inscriptions,* ed. E. A. Bond, E. M. Thompson, and G. F. Warner. 1873-94.
SHAW, H. *Illuminated Ornaments.* 1833.
THIEME, U., and BECKER, F. *Allgemeines Lexikon der bildenden Künstler.* 1907, etc.
VENTURI, A. *Storia dell' Arte italiana.* 1901, etc.

ILLUMINATED MANUSCRIPTS

III. CATALOGUES, ETC., OF SINGLE COLLECTIONS OR EXHIBITIONS

Ancona, P. d'. *La miniatura ferrarese nel fondo urbinate della Vaticana* (*L'Arte*, 1910, pp. 353–61).

Beissel, S. *Vaticanische Miniaturen. Miniatures choisies de la bibl. du Vatican.* 1893.

British Museum. *Catalogue of Ancient MSS.*, by E. M. Thompson and G. F. Warner. 1881–4.
—— *Guide to Exhibited MSS.* 1906.
—— v. Kenyon, F. G., and Warner, Sir G. F.

Burlington Fine Arts Club. *Exhibition of Illuminated MSS. Catalogue* [by S. C. Cockerell]. 1908. Illustrated edition [1909].

Carta, F. *Codici corali e libri a stampa miniati della Bibl. Naz. di Milano.* 1895.

Carta, F., Cipolla, C., and Frati, C. *Atlante paleografico-artistico* [Turin Exhibition, 1898]. 1899.

Chantilly, Musée Condé. *Cabinet des Livres. MSS.* [illustrated Catalogue by the Duc d'Aumale]. 1900.

Dorez, L. *Les MSS. à peintures de la bibl. de Lord Leicester.* 1908.

Durieux, A. *Les miniatures des MSS. de la bibl. de Cambrai.* 1861.

Fleury, E. *Les MSS. à miniatures de la bibl. de Laon.* 1863 ; — *de Soissons.* 1865.

Hermanin, F. *Le miniature ferraresi della bibl. Vaticana* (*L'Arte*, 1900, pp. 341–73).

James, M. R. *Catalogue of the Fitzwilliam MSS.* 1895 ; — *of the MSS. at Pembroke College, Cambridge.* 1905 ; — *at Trinity College, Cambridge.* 1900–4 ; — and of many other collections at Cambridge and elsewhere, especially Morgan, J. P., and Thompson, H. Y., *q.v.*

Kenyon, F. G. *Facsimiles of Biblical MSS. in the British Museum.* 1900.

Kershaw, S. W. *Art Treasures of the Lambeth Library.* 1873.

Kobell, L. von. *Kunstvolle Miniaturen* [from Munich MSS. 1890].

Marchese, V. *S. Marco, Convento dei Padri Predicatori in Firenze.* 1853.

Morgan, J. Pierpont. *Catalogue of MSS. of* [by M. R. James. Many plates in gold and colours]. 1906.

Muñoz, A. *L'art byzantin à l'exposition de Grottaferrata.* 1906.
—— *I codici greci miniati delle minori bibliotheche di Roma.* 1905.

Oechelhäuser, A. von. *Die Miniaturen der Universitäts-Bibliothek zu Heidelberg.* 1887–95.

Omont, H. *Facsimilés des miniatures des MSS. grecs de la Bibl. Nat.* Paris, 1902.

Primitifs Français, Exposition des. *Catalogue.* 1904.

Rondoni, F. *Guida del R. Museo fiorentino di S. Marco.* 1872.

SELECT BIBLIOGRAPHY

TAEGGI, O. P. *Le Miniature nei codici cassinesi.* 1887, etc.
—— *Paleografia artistica di Montecassino.* 1876.
THOMPSON, SIR E. M. [Notes on an exhibition of English illuminated MSS.] (Soc. of Antiquaries, *Proceedings*, 2nd ser., xvi, pp. 213–32). 1896.
THOMPSON, H. YATES. *Catalogue of MSS. of*, by M. R. James and others. 1898–1907.
—— *Illustrations of 100 MSS.* 1907–8.
—— *Lecture on some English illuminated MSS.* 1902.
VALERI, F. M. *La collezione delle miniature dell' Archivio di Stato in Bologna* (*Archivio Storico dell' Arte*, 1894, pp. 1–20).
WARNER, SIR G. F. *British Museum. Reproductions from illuminated MSS.* 1907–8.
—— *Illuminated MSS. in the Brit. Mus.* [60 plates in gold and colours]. 1899–1903.

IV. REPRODUCTIONS OF, OR MONOGRAPHS ON, PARTICULAR MSS.

ABBOTT, T. K. *Celtic Ornaments from the Book of Kells.* 1895.
ALBANI, CARD. A. *Menologium Graecorum.* 1727.
BAILLIE-GROHMAN, W. A. and F. *The Master of Game.* 1904.
BASTARD, COUNT A. DE. *Peintures de la Bible de Charles le Chauve.* 1883.
BEISSEL, S. *Die Bilder der Hs. des Kaisers Otto im Münster zu Aachen.* 1886.
—— *Des hl. Bernward Evangelienbuch im Dome zu Hildesheim.* 1891.
BELTRAMI, L. *Il Libro d' Ore Borromeo, alla Bibl. Ambros., miniato da Cristoforo Preda.* 1896.
BERTAUX, E., and BIROT, G. *Le Missel de Thomas James, Évêque de Dol* [by Attavante] (*Revue de l'Art anc. et mod.*, xx, pp. 129–46). 1906.
BETHE, E. *Terentius. Cod. Ambros. H. 75 inf. phototypice depictus* (De Vries, *Codd. Gr. et Lat.*, viii). 1903.
BIRCH, W. DE G. *Liber Vitae.* Hampshire Record Soc., 1892.
—— *Memorials of St. Guthlac.* 1881.
—— *On two Anglo-Saxon MSS.* (Roy. Soc. of Lit., *Transactions*, new ser., xi, pt. iii). 1876.
—— *The Utrecht Psalter.* 1876.
BOUCICAUT. *Heures du Maréchal de Boucicaut.* Soc. des Bibliophiles fr., 1889.
CARYSFORT, WILLIAM, EARL OF. *Pageants of Richard Beauchamp, Earl of Warwick.* Roxb. Club, 1908.
CERIANI, A. M. *Homeri Iliadis pictae fragmenta Ambrosiana phototypice edita.* 1905.
CHMELARZ, E. *Das ältere Gebetbuch des K. Maximilian I* (*Jahrb.*, vii, pp. 201–6). 1888.
—— *König René der Gute und die Hs. seines Romanes " Cuer d'Amours Espris"* (*ib.*, xi, pp. 116–39). 1890.

ILLUMINATED MANUSCRIPTS

CHMELARZ, E. *Ein Verwandter des Breviarium Grimani* (*ib.*, ix, pp. 429-45). 1889.
COCKERELL, S. C. *The Gorleston Psalter.* 1907.
—— *Hours of Yolande of Flanders.* 1905.
—— *Psalter and Hours of Isabelle of France.* 1905.
COUDERC, C. *Livre de la Chasse* [1909].
COXE, H. O. *The Apocalypse of S. John the Divine.* Roxb. Club, 1876.
DELISLE, L. *Les Heures dites de Jean Pucelle.* 1910.
DELISLE, L., and MEYER, P. *L'Apocalypse en français.* Soc. des anc. textes fr., 1901.
DESTRÉE, J. *Les Heures de N. D. dites de Hennessy.* 1895 ;—
—— [same title. Full reproduction of the miniatures, without letterpress] (*Musée des Enluminures*, fasc. 4-6) [1907].
DE VRIES, S. *Codices Graeci et Latini photographice depicti.* *v.* Bethe, E., Omont, H., and Premerstein, A. von.
—— *v.* Grimani Breviary.
DEWICK, E. S. *Coronation Book of Charles V.* Henry Bradshaw Soc., 1899.
—— *Metz Pontifical.* Roxb. Club, 1902.
DIEZ, E. *Die Miniaturen des Wiener Dioskurides* (*Byzantinische Denkmäler*, iii, pp. 1-69). 1903.
DÖRNHÖFFER, F. *Hortulus Animae* [reproduction in colours]. 1907, etc.
DURRIEU, COUNT P. *Les Antiquités Judaïques et le peintre Jean Foucquet.* 1908.
—— *Les Belles Heures de Jean de France, duc de Berry* (*Gaz. des Beaux-Arts*, 1906, i, pp. 265-92).
—— *Le Boccace de Munich.* 1909.
—— *Heures de Turin.* 1902.
—— *L'histoire du bon roi Alexandre* (*Revue de l'Art anc. et mod.*, xiii, pp. 49-64, 103-21). 1903.
—— *L'origine du manuscrit célèbre dit le Psautier d'Utrecht.* 1895.
—— *Les 'très belles heures de N.D.' du duc Jean de Berry* (*Revue Archéol.*, ser. iv, xvi, pp. 30-51, 246-79). 1910.
—— *Les Très Riches Heures de Jean, duc de Berry.* 1904.
ELLIS, F. S. *The Hours of Albert of Brandenburg* [1883].
ELLIS, SIR H. *Caedmon's Paraphrase* (*Archaeologia*, xxiv, pp. 329-4). 1832.
FORBES-LEITH, W. *Gospel Book of St. Margaret.* 1896.
—— *Life of St. Cuthbert.* 1888.
GAGE, J. *St. Aethelwold's Benedictional and the "Benedictionarius Roberti Archiepiscopi"* (*Archaeologia*, xxiv, pp. 1-136). 1832.
GASQUET, F. A., and BISHOP, E. *The Bosworth Psalter.* 1908.
GEBHARDT, O. VON. *The Miniatures of the Ashburnham Pentateuch.* 1883.
GEBHARDT, O. VON, and HARNACK, A. *Evangeliorum Codex graecus purpureus Rossanensis.* 1880.
GOLDSCHMIDT, A. *Der Albani-Psalter in Hildesheim.* 1895.
—— *Das Evangeliar im Rathaus zu Goslar.* 1910.

SELECT BIBLIOGRAPHY

GOODWIN, J. *Evangelia Augustini Gregoriana* (Cambridge Ant. Soc., No. 13). 1847.

GRIMANI BREVIARY. *Le Bréviaire Grimani*, ed. S. Morpurgo and S. De Vries, with introd. by C. Coggiola [full reproduction, mostly in colours]. 1904-10.

—— *v*. Ongania, F., and Zanotto, F.

GRUYER, F. A. *Les Quarante Fouquet.* 1897.

HARTEL, W. RITTER VON, and WICKHOFF, F. *Die Wiener Genesis.* 1895.

HASELOFF, A. *Codex purpureus Rossanensis.* 1898 (and *v*. Muñoz, A.).

—— *Der Psalter Erzbischof Egberts von Trier, Codex Gertrudianus.* 1901.

HERMANN, H. J. *Ein unbekanntes Gebetbuch von Jean Bourdichon* (*Beiträge zur Kunstgeschichte, Franz Wickhoff gewidmet*, pp. 46-63). 1903.

HERRADE DE LANDSBERG. *Hortus Deliciarum.* [reproductions in colour]. 1877.

—— *Hortus Deliciarum*, ed. G. Keller. 1901.

JAMES, M. R. *Description of an illuminated MS. of the thirteenth century.* 1904.

—— *The Trinity College Apocalypse.* Roxb. Club, 1910.

JANITSCHEK, H. *Die Trierer Ada-Handschrift.* 1889.

KRAUS, F. X. *Die Miniaturen des Codex Egberti.* 1884.

MAI, CARD. A. *Picturae antiquissimae, bellum Iliacum repraesantes.* 1819.

—— *Homeri Iliados picturae.* 1835.

MARTIN, H. *Légende de St. Denis.* Soc. de l' hist. de Paris, 1908.

—— *Psautier de St. Louis et de Blanche de Castille* [1909].

—— *Le Térence des Ducs.* 1908.

MÉLY, F. DE. *Les Heures d'Anne de Bretagne* (*Gaz. des Beaux-Arts*, 1909, ii, pp. 177-96).

—— *Les signatures des Primitifs. L'histoire du bon roi Alexandre* (*ib.*, 1910, ii, pp. 173-94).

MONT, P. DE. *Un livre d'heures du duc Jean de Berry* (*Musée des Enluminures*, fasc. i) [1905].

MUGNIER, F. *Les MSS. à miniatures de la maison de Savoie.* 1894. [Many plates from Breviary of Marie de Savoie, Chambéry MS. 4, and Hours of Duke Louis, Bibl. Nat., lat. 9473].

MUÑOZ, A. *Il Codice Purpureo di Rossano e il Frammento Sinopense.* 1907. Reviewed by A. Haseloff in *L'Arte*, 1907, pp. 466-72.

MÜNTZ, E. *Le Missel de Mathias Corvin* [by Attavante] (*Gaz. Archéol.*, 1883, pp. 116-20).

NOLHAC, P. DE. *Le Virgile du Vatican* (*Notices et Extraits*, xxxv, pt. ii, pp. 683-791). 1897.

OMONT, H. *Antiquités et Guerre des Juifs de Josèphe* [1906].

—— *Comédies de Térence* [1907].

—— *Grandes Chroniques de France* [1906].

—— *Heures d'Anne de Bretagne* [1907].

—— *Livre des Merveilles* [1907]

ILLUMINATED MANUSCRIPTS

OMONT, H. *Livre d'heures de Henri II* [1906].
—— *Miniatures du Psautier de S. Louis de l'Univ. de Leyde* (De Vries, *Codd. Gr. et Lat.*, suppl. ii). 1902.
—— *Miracles de Notre Dame* [1906].
—— *Notice sur un très ancien MS. grec* [Cod. Sinop.] (*Not. et Extr.*, xxxvi, ii, pp. 599–675). 1901.
—— *Psautier illustré* [1906].
—— *Peintures d'un MS. grec* [Cod. Sinop.] (*Fond. E. Piot*, vii, pp. 175–85, pl. 16–19). 1900.
—— *Psautier de St. Louis* [1902].
—— *Vie et Histoire de St. Louis* [1906].
ONGANIA, F. *A Glance at the Grimani Breviary.* 1903.
PERINI, A. *Facsimile delle miniature di Attavante Fiorentino.* 1878.
PREMERSTEIN, A. VON. *Anicia Juliana im Wiener Dioskorides-Kodex* (*Jahrb.*, xxiv, pp. 105–24). 1903.
—— *Dioscurides, Codex Aniciae Julianae* (De Vries, *Codd. Gr. et Lat.*, x). 1906.
QUARITCH, B. *Description of a Book of Hours, illuminated probably by H. Memling and G. David.* 1905.
REINACH, S. *Un MS. de la bibl. de Philippe le Bon à St. Pétersbourg* (*Fond. E. Piot*, xi). 1904.
ROBINSON, S. F. H. *Celtic Illuminative Art in the Gospel Books of Durrow, Lindisfarne, and Kells.* 1908.
SCHESTAG, A. *Die Chronik von Jerusalem* (*Jahrb.*, xx, pp. 195–216). 1899.
SCHULTZE, V. *Die Quedlinburger Itala-miniaturen.* 1898.
SIMKHOVITCH, V. G. *A predecessor of the Grimani Breviary* (*Burl. Mag.*, Mar. 1907, pp. 400–5).
SPRINGER, A. *Die Psalterillustrationen im frühen Mittelalter* (*Abhandlungen der phil.-hist. Cl. der k. sächs. Gesellsch. der Wissensch.*, viii, pp. 228–94). 1883. [Utrecht Psalter]
STRZYGOWSKI, J. *Der Bilderkreis des gr. Physiologus*, etc. 1899.
—— *Die Calenderbilder des Chronographen vom Jahre 354.* 1888.
—— *Das Etschmiadzin-Evangeliar.* 1891.
STUART, J. *Book of Deer.* Spalding Club, 1869.
THOMPSON, Sir E. M. *A contemporary account of the fall of Richard II* (*Burl. Mag.*, v, pp. 160–72, 267–70). 1904.
—— *Pageants of Richard Beauchamp, Earl of Warwick* (*ib.*, i, pp. 151–64). 1903.
—— *A Rothschild MS. in the Brit. Mus.* (*ib.*, vii, pp. 198–210). 1905.
—— *On a MS. of the Biblia Pauperum* (*Bibliographica*, iii, pp. 385–406). 1897.
THOMPSON, H. YATES. *Facsimiles from a Psalter.* 1900.
—— *Les Heures de Savoie. Facsimiles of 52 pages*, with a notice by Dom P. Blanchard. 1910.
—— *Hours of Joan II, Queen of Navarre.* Roxb. Club, 1899.

SELECT BIBLIOGRAPHY

TIKKANEN, J. J. *Le rappresentazioni della Genesi in S. Marco a Venezia* (*Arch. Stor. dell' Arte*, i, pp. 212–23, 257–67, 348-63). 1888–9. [Cotton Genesis]
—— *Die Genesismosaiken von S. Marco in Venedig* (*Acta Societatis Scientiarum Fennicae*, xvii, pp. 205–357). 1891. [Expanded version of above]
USPENSKY, T. *L'Octateuque du Sérail à Constantinople.* 1907.
UTRECHT PSALTER. *Autotype Facsimile.* Pal. Soc., 1874.
—— *Reports on the age of the MS.*, by E. A. Bond and others. 1874.
—— *v.* Birch, W. de G., Durrieu, P., and Springer, A.
VAN DEN GHEYN, J. *Le Bréviaire de Philippe le Bon.* 1909.
—— *Histoire de Charles Martel.* 1910.
—— *Le Psautier de Peterborough* (*Musée des Enluminures*, fasc. 2–3) [1907].
VATICAN LIBRARY. *Codices e Vaticanis selecti phototypice expressi* (i, *Fragmenta et picturae Vergiliana Cod. Vat. 3225*, 1899 ; ii, *Picturae Cod. Vat. 3867*, 1902 ; v, *Il rotulo di Giosuè*, 1905 ; viii, *Il Menologio di Basilio II*, 1907 ; x, *Le miniature della topografia cristiana di Cosma Indicopleuste*, 1908).
—— *Collezione Paleografica Vaticana* (i, *Miniature della Bibbia Cod. Vat. Reg. gr. 1 e del Salterio Cod. Vat. Pal. gr. 381*). 1905.
VERKEST, M. *La satire dans le "Kuerbouc" d'Ypres* (*Les Arts anc. de Flandre*, 1904, etc., i, pp. 95–107).
WARNER, SIR G. F. *Buke of John Maundevill.* Roxb. Club, 1889.
—— *Miracles de Nostre Dame.* Roxb. Club, 1885.
—— *Sforza Book of Hours.* 1894.
—— *Valerius Maximus. Miniatures of the school of Jean Fouquet.* 1907.
WARNER, SIR G. F., and WILSON, H. A. *Benedictional of S. Aethelwold.* Roxb. Club, 1910.
WESTLAKE, N. H. J., and PURDUE, W. *Illustrations of O. T. hist. in Qu. Mary's Psalter.* 1865.
WESTWOOD, J. O. *Bible of the Monastery of St. Paul near Rome.* 1876.
WILSON, H. A. *Benedictional of Abp. Robert.* Henry Bradshaw Soc., 1903.
—— *Missal of Robert of Jumièges.* H. B. Soc., 1896.
—— *v.* Warner, Sir G. F.
WICKHOFF, F. *Die Ornamente eines altchristl. Cod. der Hofbibl.* (*Jahrb.*, xiv, pp. 196–213). 1893.
—— *v.* Hartel, W. Ritter von.
ZANOTTO, F. *Facsimile delle miniature contenute nel Breviario Grimani.* 1862.

V. MISCELLANEOUS

BASTARD, COUNT A. DE. *Librairie de Jean de France, Duc de Berry.* 1834.
BEISSEL, S. *Der hl. Bernward von Hildesheim als Künstler, etc.* 1895.
BERTAUX, É. *L'art dans l'Italie méridionale*, i, 1904.

ILLUMINATED MANUSCRIPTS

BISCARO, G. *Intorno a Cristoforo Preda (Archivio Storico Lombardo*, 1910, pp. 223-6).

BRADLEY, J. W. *Life and Works of Giorgio Giulio Clovio.* 1891.

BROCKHAUS, H. *Die Kunst in den Athos-Klöstern.* 1891.

BRUUN, J. A. *Celtic Illuminated MSS.* 1897.

CIACCIO, L. *Appunti intorno alla miniatura bolognese del sec. xiv* (*L'Arte*, x, pp. 105-15). 1907.

CIPOLLA, C. *Codici Bobbiesi.* 1907.

CONSTANTINOPLE, INSTITUT ARCHÉOL. RUSSE. *Bulletin*, vol. xii, Album [Octateuch MSS.]. 1907.

DEHAISNES, M. LE CHANOINE. *Histoire de l'Art dans la Flandre, l'Artois et le Hainaut.* 1886.

DELISLE, L. *Les Livres d'Heures du duc de Berry* (*Gaz. des Beaux-Arts*, 1884, i, pp. 97-110, 281-92, 391-405).

—— *Livres d'images* (*Hist. Litt. de la France*, xxxi, pp. 213-85). 1893.

—— *Mélanges de Paléographie et de Bibliographie.* 1880.

—— *Mémoire sur d'anciens sacramentaires* (*Mém. de l'Acad. des Inscr. et Belles-Lettres*, xxxii, i). 1886.

—— *Notice de douze livres royaux.* 1902.

DIEHL, C. *Justinien.* 1901.

DURRIEU, COUNT P. *Un dessin du Musée du Louvre, attribué à André Beauneveu* (*Fond. E. Piot*, i, pp. 179-202). 1894.

—— *Jacques Coene, peintre de Bruges* (*Les Arts anc. de Flandre*, ii, pp. 5-22). 1906.

—— *Les miniatures d'André Beauneveu* (*Le Manuscrit*, i, pp. 52-6, 84-95). 1894.

—— *La peinture en France au début du xve siècle* (*Revue de l'art anc. et mod.*, xix, pp. 401-15, xx, pp. 21-35). 1906.

FOWLER, J. *On mediaeval representations of the months and seasons* (*Archaeologia*, xliv, pp. 137-224). 1873.

GILBERT, J. T. *National MSS. of Ireland*, pt. i. 1874. [Coloured plates]

GRUYER, G. *L'Art ferrarais.* 1897.

HASELOFF, A. *Les Psautiers de St. Louis* (*Mém. de la Soc. Nat. des Antiquaires de France*, lix, pp. 18-42). 1900.

—— *Eine thüringisch-sächsische Malerschule des 13. Jahrhunderts.* 1897.

HERMANN, H. J. *Miniaturhss. aus der Bibl. des Herzogs Andrea Matteo III Acquaviva* (*Jahrb.*, xix, pp. 147-216). 1898.

—— *Zur Geschichte der Miniaturmalerei am Hofe der Este in Ferrara* (*ib.*, xxi, pp. 117-271). 1900.

JANITSCHEK, H. *Geschichte der deutschen Malerei.* 1890.

KALLAB, W. *Die toscanische Landschaftsmalerei im xiv und xv Jahrhundert* (*Jahrb.*, xxi, pp. 1-90). 1900.

SELECT BIBLIOGRAPHY

KELLER, F.   *Bilder in den irischen MSS. der schweiz. Bibliotheken* (*Mittheil. der Antiq. Gesellsch. in Zürich*, vii, Heft 3, pp. 61-97). 1851. Transl. by W. Reeves, *Ulster Journ. of Archaeol.*, viii, pp. 210-30, 291-308. 1860.

KONDAKOFF, N. P.   *Histoire de l'Art byzantin*. 1886-91.

LABORDE, COUNT A. DE.   *Les MSS. à peintures de la Cité de Dieu.* Soc. des Bibliophiles fr., 1909.

LAFENESTRE, G.   *Jehan Fouquet.* 1905.

LASTEYRIE, R. DE.   *Les miniatures d'André Beauneveu et de Jacquemart de Hesdin* (*Fond. E. Piot*, iii, pp. 71-119). 1896.

LATIL, A. M.   *Le Miniature nei Rotoli dell' Exultet.* 1899, etc.

LUTZ, J., and PERDRIZET, P.   *Speculum Humanae Salvationis.* 1907-9.

MÂLE, E.   *Jean Bourdichon et son atelier* (*Gaz. des Beaux-Arts*, 1904, ii, pp. 441-57).

——— *Trois oeuvres nouvelles de Jean Bourdichon* (*ib.*, 1902, i, pp. 185-203).

MARTIN, H.   *Les Miniaturistes français.* 1906.

——— *Les Peintres de MSS. et la Miniature en France.* [1909]

MILLER, K.   *Die Weltkarte des Beatus* (*Die ältesten Weltkarten*, Heft i). 1895.

MONGERI, P.   *L' arte del minio nel ducato di Milano* (*Archivio Storico Lombardo*, 1885, pp. 330-56, 528-57, 759-96).

B., L.   *Miniature Sforzesche di Cristoforo Preda* (*Rassegna d'Arte*, i, pp. 28-9). 1901.

PROU, M.   *Dessins du xie siècle et peintures du xiiie siècle* (*Revue de l'art chrétien*, 1890, pp. 122-8).

RIEGL, A.   *Die mittelalterliche Kalenderillustration* (*Mittheil. des Instituts für oesterr. Geschichtsforschung*, x, pp. 1-74). 1889.

RUSHFORTH, G. McN.   *The "Descent into Hell" in Byzantine Art* (*Papers of the British School at Rome*, i, pp. 114-19). 1902.

SCHREIBER, W. L.   *Biblia Pauperum.* 1903.

STETTINER, R.   *Die illustrierten Prudentius-Handschriften.* 1895. Same title, vol. i (200 plates). 1905.

STOKES, M.   *Early Christian Art in Ireland.* 1887.

SWARZENSKI, G.   *Die Regensburger Buchmalerei des X und XI Jahrhunderts.* 1901.

TESTI, L.   *Storia della Pittura veneziana*, i, 1909.

THOMPSON, SIR E. M.   *English Illuminated MSS.* 1895.

TIKKANEN, J. J.   *Die Psalterillustration im Mittelalter.* 1895.

VALLET DE VIRIVILLE, A.   *Notice de quelques MSS. précieux* (*Gaz. des Beaux-Arts*, 1866, i, pp. 453-66, ii, pp. 275-85, 471-88).

VITELLI E PAOLI.   *Facsimili paleografici.* n.d.

VITZTHUM, GRAF G.   *Die Pariser Miniaturmalerei von der Zeit des hl. Ludwig bis zu Philipp von Valois.* 1907.

ILLUMINATED MANUSCRIPTS

Vöge, W.   *Eine deutsche Malerschule um die Wende des ersten Jahrtausends.* 1891.

Weale, W. H. J.   *Gerard David.*   1895.

—— *Simon Binnink, miniaturist* (*Burl. Mag.*, viii, pp. 355–7).   1906.

Westwood, J. O.   *Facsimiles of the Miniatures and Ornaments of Anglo-Saxon and Irish MSS.*   1868.

—— *On peculiarities in Irish MSS.* (*Archaeol. Journ.*, vii., pp. 17–25).   1850.

—— *Palaeographia Sacra Pictoria.*   1843–5.

INDEX

MANUSCRIPTS

Abbeville: No. 1 (Cod. Aur.), 101
Aix-la-Chapelle, Cathedral: Gospel-books, 92, 148
Arras: No.1045 (S.Vaast Lectionary),105
Austria-Este, Archduke Francis Ferdinand of: Borso Bible, 291; Breviary and Officium of Ercole I, 292–3

Bamberg: A. 1.5 (Alcuin-Bible), 95
Bari: Exultet Roll, 166
Berlin, Royal Library: Eneidt (germ. fol. 282), 156; Itala, 16
Boulogne, Bibl. Municip.: No. 20 (S. Omer Psalter), 110
Bristol, Baptist College: Cotton Genesis, 17
Brussels, Royal Library: Apocalypse (B. 282), 217; Berry Hours (11060–1), 250; Breviary of Philip the Good (9511, 9026), 312; Conquêtes de Charlemagne(9066–8),312; Gospels of S. Victor-in-Santem (18723), 92; Hennessy Hours, 322; Histoire de Charles Martel (6–9), 312; Histoire du Haynaut (9242–4), 311; Missal of Mathias Corvinus (9008), 297; Peterborough Psalter (9961–2), 224

Cambrai, Public Library: Nos. 149, 327 (Missal and Bible), 306–7
Cambridge, Corpus Christi College: No. 286 (S. Augustine's Gospels), 160
— Fitzwilliam Museum: No. 48 (Carew-Poyntz Horae), 231
— Pembroke College: No. 120 (Bury St. Edmund's Gospels), 136
— St. John's College: C. 9 (Irish Psalter), 82
— Trinity College: Apocalypse (R. 16.2), 214; Eadwin Psalter, 110; Winchester Gospels (B. 10.4), 128

Cambridge, University Library: Ii. vi. 32 (Book of Deer), 83; Ll. i. 10 (Bp. Aethelwald's Prayer-book), 85
Chantilly, Musée Condé: Breviary of Jeanne d'Evreux, 246; Crucifixion (A. de' Bonfratelli), 305; Hours of É. Chevalier, 280, pl. xlii; Ingeburge Psalter, 193; Registrum Gregorii, 150; Très Riches Heures, 271, pl. xl
Cividale: Cod. Gertrud., 147, pl. xix
Coblenz, Archives: Trèves "Kopialbuch," 307
Constantinople, Seraglio: Octateuch, 48

Darmstadt: No. 1948 (Gero Gospels), 145
Devonshire, Duke of: Benedictional of S. Aethelwold, 126
Douai, Public Library: No. 171 (Psalter), 226
Dublin, Trinity College: Book of Armagh, 81; of Dimma, 72; of Durrow, 71; of Kells, 76, pl. vii; of Mulling, 81; Psalter of Ricemarch, 83
Durham, Cathedral Library: Pudsey Bible, 138; Cassiodorus (B. ii. 30), 85; Gospels (A. ii. 17), 85

Épernay: No. 1722 (Ebbo Gospels), 104
Etschmiadzin: Gospels, 34

Florence: Rabula Gospels, 32; Reichenau Sacramentary, 146

Gaeta, Cathedral: Exultet Rolls, 167
Gotha: Echternach Gospels, 149

Heidelberg, University Library: Sacramentary (Sal. ix^b), 145

341

ILLUMINATED MANUSCRIPTS

Hildesheim, Cathedral: Bible, Gospels, and Sacramentary of S. Bernward, 151
— S. Godehard's Church: S. Alban's Psalter, 136
Holford, Sir G. L.: Passion of S. Edmund, 135
Holkham, Lord Leicester's Library: Weingarten Missals, 207

Innsbruck, University Library: Missal of Card. Ippolito I d'Este, 293; Prayer-book of J. Bourgeois, 285
Ivrea, Chapter Library: Sacramentary of S. Warmund, 162

Jacquemart-André, Madame: Boucicaut Hours, 266

Leyden, University Library: Psalter of S. Louis, 141
Lichfield, Cathedral Library: Gospels of S. Chad, 75
London, British Museum: Additional MSS. 4949, 64; 5111, 30; 9350, 168; 10546 (Alcuin-Bible), 95, pl. xi; 11662, 4; 11695, 210; 11838, 62; 11870 (Metaphrastes), 54, pl. v; 12012, 288; 14779-82, 302; 14788-90 (Louvain Bible), 158; 14802, 290; 15205-6, 260; 15244-5, 246, pl. xxxvii; 15246, 302; 15270-3, 289, pl. xlv; 15274-5, 263; 15816, 294; 16532, 257; 16605, 157; 16949, 203; 16997, 280; 17280, 319; 17294, 291; 17333, 218; 17341, 199, pl. xxvi; 17373, 294; 17687, 208; 17737-8 (Floreffe Bible), 159; 17742, 194; 17868, 197; 18000, 294; 18144, 208; 18196-7, 259; 18198, 259; 18633, 218; 18719, 200; 18720 (Bologna Bible), 260; 18850 (Bedford Hours), 273, pl. xli; 18851 (Isabella Book), 318; 18852, 319; 18854, 285; 18855, 285, 323; 18859, 164; 19352 (Theodore Psalter), 49; 19899, 205; 20916, 294; 20927 (G. Clovio), 304; 21120, 303; 21412 (Rogers Album), 259; 21413 (Sforza deed), 300; 21414, 294; 21463, 294; 21965, 257; 21973, 259; 22493, 218; 22497, 257; 22736, 64; 22740, 64; 23923, 262; 24098 (" Golf Book "), 322, pl. li; 24189, 309, pl. xlix; 24199, 111; 24683, 205; 24686 (Tenison Psalter), 190, pl. xxiv; 25600, 210; 25697, 295; 25698, 316, pl. l; 27428, 262; 27695, 263; 27697 (Saluces Hours), 283; 28106-7 (Stavelot Bible), 157; 28162 (Somme le Roi), 201, pl. xxviii; 28271, 303; 28785, 279; 28815, 64; 28841, 263; 28962, 302; 29253, 306; 29433, 269; 29704-5, 233, pl. xxxiv; 29735 (S. Croce Breviary), 295; 30014 Siena Hymnal), 286; 30029, 306; 30337 (Exultet Roll), 167, pl. xx.; 30844-6, 30850, 30853 (Silos MSS.), 210; 31032, 261; 32058, 259; 32454, 269; 33733 (Victories of Charles V), 305; 33997, 295; 34247, 259; 34294 (Sforza Book), 298, pl. xlvii, xlviii; 34309, 256; 34890 (Grimbald Gospels), 131, pl. xv; 35030, 47; 35085, 196; 35166, 214; 35254, 259, 285, 288, pl. xliv; 35311 (Burgundy Breviary), 270; 35313, 320; 35319, 317; 35321, 282; 36684, 306; 36928, 47; 37421 (J. Fouquet), 281; 37517 (Bosworth Psalter), 129; 37768 (Lothaire Psalter), 104; 37955A, 288; 38037 (Toledo Missal), 303
London, British Museum: Arundel MSS. 60, 132; 83 (E. Anglian Psalter), 224, pl. xxxiii; 155, 129; 157, 176; 547, 65
— — — Burney MSS. 3, 182; 19, 64, pl. iv; 20, 64; 257, 267; 275, 247
— — — Cotton MSS. Calig. A. xv, 120; Claud. B. iv (Aelfric's Hexateuch), 120; Claud. D. vi, 185; Cleop. C. viii, 112; Dom. A. xvii (Psalter of Hen. VI), 277; Faust. B. vi, pt. ii, 235; Galba A. xviii (Athelstan's Psalter), 122; Jul. A. vi, 113; Nero C. iv, 137; Nero D. i, 185; Nero D. iv (Lindisfarne Gospels), 73, pl. viii; Otho B. vi (Cotton Genesis), 17; Tib. A. ii (Athel-

342

INDEX

stan's Gospels), 144; Tib. B. v, 114; Tib. B. viii (Charles V's Coronation-book), 247; Tib. C. vi, 119, pl. xiv; Tit. D. xvi, 112; Tit. D. xxvii, 117; Vesp. A. i (Psalter of S. Augustine's, Canterbury), 85; Vesp. A. viii (King Edgar's charter), 125; Vitell. F. xi, 81

London, British Museum: Egerton MSS. 617-8 (Wycliffite Bible), 231; 768 (Franco-Saxon Gospels), 105; 809, 153; 943, 262; 1070 (Hours of René of Anjou), 283; 1139 (Melissenda Psalter), 57, pl. vi; 1147, 323; 1151, 188; 2045 (S. Pol Hours), 283, pl. xliii; 2781, 231

— — — Harley MSS. 76 (Bury S. Edmund's Gospels), 130; 603 (copy of Utrecht Psalter), 115; 928, 188; 1023, 82; 1526-7 (Moralized Bible), 200; 1802 (Maelbrigt Gospels), 82; 1810, 58; 2278 (Lydgate's Life of S. Edmund), 235; 2449 (Val-Duchesse Breviary), 306; 2788 (Cod. Aur.), 100, pl. ix; 2798-9 (Arnstein Bible), 154; 2800-2 (Arnstein Passionale), 155; 2803-4 (Worms Bible), 154; 2891, 247; 2897 (Burgundy Breviary), 270, frontispiece; 2899 (Qu. Philippa's Psalter), 231; 2904, 116; 2930, 205; 3045, 155; 4374-5 (Valerius Maximus), 282; 4381-2 (Berry Bible), 252; 4425 (Roman de la Rose), 318; 4751, 187; 4986, 186; 5102, 141; 5761 (Medici Petrarch), 295; 5790 (Greek Gospels of Card. F. Gonzaga), 65; 7026 (Lovel Lectionary), 234; 7183, 168

— — — Harley Roll Y. 6 (Guthlac Roll), 140, pl. xvii

— — — King's MSS. 5 (Biblia Pauperum), 308; 156 (Ducale), 294

— — — Lansdowne MSS. 420, 179; 1175 (Bible of Charles V), 252

— — — Royal MSS. 1 D. i (Bible of William of Devon), 183, pl. xxiii; 1 D. ix (Canute's Gospels), 130; 1 D x, 176, pl. xxi; 1 E. vi, 87; 1 E. ix (Bible of Richard II), 232; 2 A. iii, 205; 2 A. xviii. (Grandison Hours), 234; 2 A. xxii (Westminster Psalter), 141; 2 B. ii, 197; 2 B. iii, 204, pl. xxix; 2 B. vii (Qu. Mary's Psalter), 221, pl. xxxi-ii; 3 D. vi, 190; 6 E. ix (Prato verses), 256; 10 E. iv, 230; 14 C. vii (Matthew Paris), 185; 15 D. ii (E. Anglian Apocalypse), 217; 15 E. ii-iii, 314; 16 F. ii (Charles, Duke of Orleans), 317; 169. iii (D. Aubert, Vita Christi), 314; 17 E. vii, 245; 18 D. viii, 239; 18 E. iii-iv, 314; 19 B. xv, 217; 19 C. iv (Songe du Vergier), 253; 19 C. viii, 317; 19 D. ii (Poitiers Bible), 239; 19 E. v (Romuleon), 314; 20 B vi (Epistle to Richard II), 253

London, British Museum: Sloane MS. 1977 (Treatise on Surgery), 195, pl. xxvii

— — — Stowe MSS. 12 (Norwich Breviary), 227; 17 (Maestricht Hours), 205, pl. xxxviii; 944 (Newminster Liber Vitae), 117, pl. xiii

— Lambeth Archiepiscopal Library: Apocalypse (209), 215; Mac Durnan Gospels, 80

— Soane Museum: Giulio Clovio, 304; Josephus of Edw. IV, 314

— Society of Antiquaries: Mantuan (?) Choir-book, 298; Peterborough Psalter (59), 180, pl. xxii

— Victoria and Albert Museum, South Kensington: Flemish Calendar-pictures (Salting collection), 323; Italian Choir-books, 259; S. Denis Missal, 246

— Wallace Collection: C. de Predis, 301

— Westminster Abbey. Lytlington Missal, 231

Lulworth Castle Library: Louterell Psalter, 229-30

Lyons Cathedral: Attavante Missal, 296

Manchester, John Rylands Library: Lat. 8 (Beatus on the Apocalypse), 211

Milan, Ambrosian Library: Borromeo Hours (C. de Predis), 301; Greek Gospels (B. 56 Sup.), 65; Greek Psalter (54), 46; Iliad, 8; Petrarch's Virgil (S. Martini), 258; Terence (H. 75 inf.), 12

ILLUMINATED MANUSCRIPTS

Milan, Trivulzio Collection: Donatus of Maximilian Sforza (Ambr. de Predis?), 300; Missal (Martino da Modena?), 292; Turin Hours, 310
Monte Cassino: No 73 (S. Gregory's Moralia), 164; 99 (Homilies), 164; 175 (Commentary on Rule of S. Benedict), 163
Morgan, J. Pierpont, Esq.: Flemish Breviary, 321; Huntingfield Psalter, 141; Windmill Psalter, 220; Worksop Bestiary (107), 187
Mount Athos, Pantocrator: 49 (Psalter), 46
— — Vatopedi: 515 (Octateuch), 48; 609 (Psalter), 46
Munich, Hofbibl: Cim. 54 (Uta-codex), 153; Cim. 55 (Cod. Aur. of S. Emmeran), 98; Cim. 57 (Bamberg Lectionary), 150; Cim. 58 (Bamberg Gospels), 149; Cod. gall. 369 (Boccace, J. Fouquet), 280
— Schatzkammer: Prayer-book of Charles the Bald, 98

Nuremberg, Stadtbibl: Solger in 4°, No. 4 (Hours of King Charles), 200

Oxford, Bodleian Library: Auct. D. 4. 17 (Apocalypse), 213; Bodl. 270b (Moralized Bible), 200; Bodl. 579 (Leofric Missal), 116; Douce 180 (Apocalypse), 216, pl. xxx; Douce 366 (Ormesby Psalter), 228; Douce 374 (Miracles de N. D.), 313; Junius 11 (Caedmon), 118; Lat. Liturg. f. 5 (S. Margaret's Gospel-book), 133; Rawlinson B. 484 (leaf from Athelstan's Psalter), 123; Rushworth Gospels (Mac Regol), 79

Padua, Cathedral: Epistolar, 170; Gospel-book, 169
Paris, Bibl. de l'Arsenal: No. 623 (S. Magloire Missal), 273; 664 (Térence des Ducs), 267; 1186 (Psalter of Blanche of Castile), 193; 5059 (Papeleu Bible), 239
— Bibl. de Ste. Geneviève: Canterbury Bible, 139
— Bibl. Nationale: Coislin 79 (Chrysostom of Nicephorus Botaniates), 41

Paris, Bibl. Nationale: Fonds français, 18–9 (Cité de Dieu), 282; 247 (Fouquet, Josephus), 279; 403 (Apocalypse), 213; 616 (Livre de la Chasse), 267; 2090-2 (Légende de St. Denis), 239; 2810 (Livre des Merveilles), 267; 6465 (Fouquet, Grandes Chroniques), 280; 9198-9 (Miracles de N. D.), 313; 9350 (after Cotton Genesis), 17; 13091 (Duke of Berry's Lat.-Fr. Psalter), 249; 19819 (Fouquet, Order of S. Michael), 278
— — Fonds grec., 139 (Psalter), 42; 510 (Greg. Naz.), 40; 1208 (Homilies of Jacobus), 56
— — Fonds latin, 1 (Vivian Bible), 96; 2 (2nd Bible of Charles the Bald), 105; 18 (Bologna Bible), 260; 257 (Gospels of Francois II), 105; 265 (Blois Gospels), 104; 266 (Lothaire Gospels), 97; 919 (Duke of Berry's "Grandes Heures"), 251; 1023 (Breviary of Philippe le Bel), 237; 1150 (Moralized Bible), 200; 1152 (Psalter of Charles the Bald), 98; 1161 (Hours), 268; 3063 (Scotus of Ferd. of Aragon), 289; 8846, anc. Suppl. lat. 1194 (Tripartite Psalter), 110; 8850 (Soissons Cod. Aur.), 103, pl. x; 9383, 9388 (Gospel-books), 104; 9428 (Drogo Sacramentary), 103; 9474 (Hours of Anne of Brittany), 284; 10483-4 (Belleville Breviary), 240; 10525 (Little Psalter of S. Louis), 198; 11935 (Billyng Bible), 240; 12048 (Gellone Sacramentary), 89; 17294 (Breviary of John, Duke of Bedford), 275; 17326 (Ste. Chapelle Lectionary), 199; 18014 (Duke of Berry's "Petites Heures"), 251
— — Nouv. acq. fr., 1098 (Vie de St. Denys), 195; 21013 (Fouquet, Josephus), 279
— — Nouv. acq. lat., 1203, anc. 1993 (Godescalc Gospel-book), 100; 1359 (Chronicle of S. Martin des Champs), 4; 1416 (Fouquet, Hours of É. Chevalier), 281; 2334 (Ashburnham Pentateuch), 161

INDEX

Paris, Bibl. Nationale: Suppl. gr. 1286 (Cod. Sinop.), 29
— Collection Dutuit: Hist. du bon roi Alexandre, 312
— Musée du Louvre. Fouquet, Hours of É. Chevalier, 281; Turin Hours, 310
Perrins, C. W. Dyson, Esq.: Gorleston Psalter, 226; Ovid, 289

Rome, Archives of S. Peter's: Codice di S. Giorgio, 258
— Barberini Library: Calendar of Filocalus, 3
— S. Paul's: Bible, 98
— Vatican Library: Pal. gr. 381 (Psalter), 47; 431 (Joshua Roll), 42
— — — Pal. lat. 1071 (Fred. II, De arte venandi cum avibus), 172
— — — Reg. gr. 1 (Bible), 47; Reg. lat. 438 (Calendar-pictures), 113
— — — Urbino-Vat. gr. 2 (Gospels), 60
— — — Vat. gr. 394 (Climacus), 56; 666 (Alexius Comnenus), 41; 699 (Cosmas Indicopleustes), 40; 746-7 (Octateuchs), 48; 1162 (Homilies of Jacobus), 56; 1291 (Ptolemy), 39; 1613 (Menology of Basil II), 52; 2138 (Evangelistarium). 65
— — — Vat. lat. 20 (Bologna Bible), 260; 1202 (Life of S. Benedict), 164; 3225 (Vatican Virgil), 5, pl. ii; 3867 (Virgil, Codex Romanus), 10; 3868 (Terence), 12
Rossano, Cathedral: Greek Gospels (Cod. Rossan.) 22, pl. iii
Rothschild, Baroness Adolphe de: Heures de Pucelle, 240
— Baron Edmond de: Duke of Berry's "Belles Heures," 273
— Baron Maurice de: Duke of Berry's "Très belles heures," 309
Rouen, Public Library: Benedictional of Abp. Robert, 127; Missal of Robert of Jumièges, 128
Rutland, Duke of: Psalter, 188

S. Gall: No 51 (Irish Gospel-book), 84
St. Petersburg: Grandes Chroniques, 313
Siena, Archivio di Stato: Caleffo dell' Assunta, 257, pl. xxxix

Siena, Libreria Piccolomini: Choirbooks, 297, pl. xlvi
Smyrna: Octateuch, 48

Thompson, H. Yates, Esq.: Albani Hours, 304; Apocalypse, (55), 215; Beatus on the Apocalypse (97), 210; Beaupré Antiphoner (83), 207; Bentivoglio Bible (4), 260; Carrow Psalter (52), 181; Coëtivy Hours (85), 276; Dunois Hours (11), 276; Gallican Missal (69), 157; Hours of "Elysabeth the Quene" (59), 235; of Jeanne de Navarre (75), 242, pl. xxxvi; of René II, Duke of Lorraine, 282; of Yolande de Flandre, 242; Life of Christ (81, formerly Ashb. App. 72), 255; Life of S. Cuthbert, 140; Martyrology (8), 164; Metz Pontifical (formerly Sir T. Brooke's), 237, pl. xxxv; St. Omer Psalter (58), 229; Sainte Abbaye (40), 202; Taymouth Hours (57), 231; Verdun Breviary (31), 237
Trèves, City Library: Ada Gospels (22), 101; Cod. Egberti, 147, pl. xviii
Turin, National Library: Franciscan Bible (D. i. 13), 260; Turin Hours, 310
— Royal Library: Lives of SS. Joachim and Anna (14434), 301

Utrecht, University Library: Utrecht Psalter, 106, pl. xii

Varese, Church of the Madonna del Monte sopra: Missal (C. de Predis), 301
Venice, S. Mark's: Grimani Breviary, 319; Iliad (454), 13
Verdun, Public Library: Breviary (107), 237
Verona: Psalter, 161
Vienna, Albertina Museum: Leaf from Missal of Alex. VI (A. da Monza), 300
— Imperial Library: No. 847 (Euseb. Canons, etc.), 30; 1907 (Maximilian's Prayer-book), 321; 2533 (Chron. de Jherus.), 312; 2549 (G. de Roussillon), 312; 2706 (Hortulus Animae), 312; 3416 (Calendar of Filocalus), 5

ILLUMINATED MANUSCRIPTS

Vienna, Imperial Library: Med. gr. 1 (Dioscorides), 34
— — — Theol. gr. 31 (Vienna Genesis), 20
— Schatzkammer: Gospel-book of Charlemagne, 92

Winchester, Chapter Library: Bible, 138, pl. xvi
Windsor, Royal Library: Sobieski Hours, 275
Zurich, Cantonal Library: No. 1 (Alcuin-Bible), 95

SCRIBES AND ILLUMINATORS

Aelfwin, Abbot of Newminster, 117
Aldred, 73
Alighieri, Giovanni, 13
Ancelet, al. Anciau de Cens, 241
Aspertini, Amico, 304
Attavanti, Attavante degli, 296
Aubert, D., 314
Avogaro, Marco dell', 291

Basilius, 58
Beauneveu, André, 237, 248-51, 307
Bede, 85
Bennink, Alexander, 314, 322
— Simon, 322
Berengarius, 98
Billyng, Robert de, 240
Biragus, Johannes Petrus, 300
Blachernae, Michael and Simeon of, 52
Bologna, Niccolò da, 257, 262
Bonfratelli, Apollonio de', 304
Bourdichon, Jean, 266, 284
Brancalupo, Rudolfo, 302

Chevrier, J., 241
Clovio, Giulio, 304
Coene, Jacques, 266
Colombe, Jean, 271
Columba, S., 71
Cremona, Girolamo da, 297
Crivelli, Taddeo, 291
Cybo, Monk of Hyères, 263

David, Gerard, 311
Devon, William of, 183, pl. xxiii
Dimma, Mac Nathi, 72

Eadfrith, Bp. of Lindisfarne, 73, pl. viii
Ernestus, 158

Fouquet, François, 266, 282
— Jean, 266, 277-85, 313, pl. xlii

Fouquet, Louis, 282
Franciscus, "egregius pictor," 266, 282, pl. xliii

Gaibana, Giovanni di, 171
Geroldus, clerk of Amiens, 194
Goderannus, 158
Godescalc, 100
Guntbald the Deacon, 151

Heribertus, 147
Hesdin, Jacquemart de, 237, 248, 250-2, 307
Hippolytus Lunensis, 289, 302
Honoré, 237

John, Cretan priest, 65

Keraldus, 147

Leo, 164
Liédet, Loyset, 312
Limbourg, Pol de, and his brothers, 248, 266, 271-3, 320, pl. xl
Liuthard, 98

Mac Durnan, Maelbrigte, 80
Mac Regol, 79
Maci, Jaquet, 241
Maelbrigt hua Maeluanaigh, 82
Mahiet, 241
Manerius, of Canterbury, 139
Mantegna, Andrea and Francesco, 298
Marmion, Simon, 313
Martini, Simone, 258
Memlinc, Hans, 311, 319
Michael the Little, 53
Modena, Martino da, 292
Monza, Antonio da, 300
Mulling, S., 81

346

INDEX

Niccolò di Ser Sozzo, 257, 288, pl. xxxix

Pantoleon, 53
Papeleu, Jean de, 239
Paris, Matthew, 185-6
Pedro, Prior of Silos, 210
Perugino, 304
Poyet, Jean, 284
Predis, Ambrogio de, 300
— Cristoforo de, 301
Pucelle, Jean, 237, 240-5, 252

Rabula the Calligrapher, 32
Ricemarch, Bp. of S. David's, 83

Russi, Franco, 291

Sano di Pietro, 288
Siferwas, John, 233

Trevou, Henri du, 252
Tavernier, Jean le, 312
Tedesco, Giorgio, 291-2
Theodore, Arch-priest of Caesarea, 49

Verona, Liberale da, 297, pl. xlvi
Vrelant, Willem, 311

Whas, John, 233

GENERAL

Ada Gospels, school of, 99-103
Adonis, death of, 45
Aelfgyfu, 117
Aelfric's Hexateuch, 120
Aelfwin, Abbot of Newminster, Winchester, 117-8
Aethelgar, Abbot of Newminster, 127
Aethelwald, Bp. of Lindisfarne, Prayerbook of, 85
Aethelwold, S., 124; Benedictional of, 126
Aix-la-Chapelle, 90, 92-3, 143; Ottonian Gospels at, 148-50
Albani Horae, 304
Albert of Brandenburg, Hours of, 321
Alcuin, 91, 94; Alcuin-Bibles, 94-7, 149, pl. xi
Alexander VI, 300-1
Alexandria, 2, 14
Alexius Comnenus, portraits of, 41, 60
Alfonso of Aragon, King of Naples, Psalter of, 302
Alfred the Great, 122
Alphonso, son of Edw. I, 190
Amiens, 194
Angelico, Fra, 288
Ani, Book of the Dead of, 1
Animal-lore, fabulous, 186-7, 222
Anne of Bohemia, 232
— of Brittany, Hours of, 266, 284-5
— of Burgundy, Duchess of Bedford, 273-5
Antiphoners, 327. v. Choir-books

Annunciation, early instance of divided form, 33
Apocalypse, illustrations of, 96, 209-19, pl. xi, xxx
Arabic Gospel, in portrait of S. Matthew, 64
Aratea, 13
Archippus, hermit, legend of, 53-4, pl. v
Aristotle, Ethics, 303; tomb of, 309, pl. xlix
Armagh, Book of, 81
Arnstein Abbey, Bible, etc., from, 154-5
Arthur, Prince of Wales, 317
Arundel Psalter, E. Anglian, 26, 224-7, pl. xxxiii
Ashburnham House, fire at, 17
— Pentateuch, 161
Ashridge College, 191
Assumption of the Virgin, notable Italian paintings of, 137, 257-8, 299, pl. xxxix
Asti Antiphoner, 258
Athelstan's Gospels, 144-5; Psalter, 122-3
Augustine, S., Commentary on the Psalms, 302; De Civitate Dei, 246, 282, 302, pl. xxxvii

Backgrounds, architectural, 198; diapered, 140; patterned, 146, 151; punctured gold, 227; striped, 96, 146, 152, 211; transitional, 266-8

347

ILLUMINATED MANUSCRIPTS

Bamberg Gospels, 149-50; Lectionary, 150-1
Bar, Marguerite de, Abbess of S. Maur at Verdun, 237
— Renaud de, Bp. of Metz, 237
Bari Exultet Roll, 166
Basil I, the Macedonian, 36, 38; portrait of, 40-1
— II, Menology of, 52-5
Bavarian schools, 143, 152-3
Beatus on the Apocalypse, 209-12
Beaupré Antiphoner, 207
Bedford, John, Duke of, Hours of ("Bedford Missal"), 273-5, pl. xli; Breviary and Pontifical of, 275
Belleville Breviary, 240-5
Belton, wall-paintings at, 225
Benedict, S., 130, 163; Life of, 164
Benedictional of Abp. Robert, 127; of S. Aethelwold, 126
Bentivoglio Bible, 260
Berengaudus on the Apocalypse, 215
Bergen, Margaret van, Countess of Buren, Hours of, 317
Bernward, S., Bp. of Hildesheim, 143, 151-2
Berry, John, Duke of, 240, 247-54, 266-8, 271-3, 279, 307, 309-10, 320; his "Belles Heures," 273; Bibles, 252; "Grandes Heures," 242, 251; "Petites Heures," 242, 251; Psalter, 249, 251; "Très Belles Heures," 309; "Très Riches Heures," 266, 271-4, 276, 320, pl. xl
Bestiaries, 34, 186-7
Bible Historiale, 238-9, 245, 252, 314
— Moralized, 199-200
Bibles, 11th and 12th centt., huge, 138, 154, 157-8; 13th cent., mostly small, 175, 181-4, 196-7; 14th cent., Italian, 260-1
Biblia Pauperum, 307-8
Billfrith, 73
Blachernæ, miniaturists of, 52-3
Black Death, 230
Blackfriars, London, 190
Blanche of Castile, 244; Psalter of, 193-4
Blandigny Abbey, near Ghent, 306
Blois Gospels, 104
Bobbio MSS., 83, 86, 162
Boccace, 280, 282

Bologna, illumination at, 170, 172, 259-62, 292
Book of the Dead, 1
Borders, various styles of, 28, 125, 128-33, 171-2, 175-6, 189, 231, 241, 287, 289, 291, 295, 303-5, 314-6, 319
Borromeo Hours, 301
Borso Bible, 291
Bosworth Psalter, 129
Boucicaut Hours, 266, 268
Bourbon, Pierre, Duc de, 279
Bourgeois, Jean, 285
Bourges, 248-250, 273
Braybrooke Psalter. v. Gorleston
Breviaries, 326
Bridget, S., 77
Bruges, 311-4, 317, 322
— Jean de, 250
Bruynyng, Robert, Abbot of Sherborne, 233
Burgundy, Dukes of. Philippe le Hardi, 267. John the Fearless, 267; Breviary of, 270-1, 276, 326, frontispiece. Philip the Good, 311-3; Breviary of, 312. Charles the Bold, 311, 313
Bury S. Edmund's, MSS. from, 111, 131, 135-7
Byzantine illumination, 14-5, 36-65
Byzantium, 14, 19, 36. v. Constantinople

Caedmon, 118-9
Calendar of Filocalus, 3-5
— illustrations, 4, 39, 113-5, 177, 204-5, 242-5, 271-2, 276, 319-23
Cambrai, 249, 306-7
Canterbury, 109, 139, 184; MSS. from Christ Church, 110, 120, 129-30, 144; from S. Augustine's, 85-6 (Psalter), 115, 120, 160 (Gospels), 182-3 (Bible), 215
Canute, 117, 130
Capua, MSS. written at, 65, 163
Cardeña, S. Pedro de, MS. from, 210
Carew-Poyntz Horae, 231
Carolingian illumination, 88-105
Carrow Psalter, 181
Cascia, Simone da, 262
Cassiodorus, Commentary on the Psalms, 85
Celtic illumination, 66-87

INDEX

Chad, S., Gospels of, 75-6
Charlemagne, 88-94, 100-2
Charles the Bald, 96-8, 105
— the Fat, 98
— the Simple, 123
— V, Emperor, 298; portrait of, 321; Victories of, 305
— IV, King of France, 240
— V, King of France, 240, 249, 252-3; Coronation-book of, 247
— VI, King of France, 253
— VII, King of France, 278, 280
Chester, 179
Chevalier, Étienne, Hours of, 280-2
Chicksand nunnery, 224
Choir-books, 258-9, 286-8, 297-8, 304, 327-8
Chroniques de Jherusalem, 312
Cingal, 75
Clement VII, Antipope, 248
Clementia, Domicella, 207
Clermont in Auvergne, 196
Codex Egberti, 147-50, pl. xviii
— Gertrudianus, 147, pl. xix
— Romanus (Virgil, Cod. Vat. lat. 3867), 2, 5, 10-12
— Rossanensis, 19, 22-31, 33, 37, 39-40, 51, 61-2, pl. iii
— Sinopensis, 19, 28-30, 149
Codices Aurei, 100-3
Coëtivy Hours, 276-7
Commines, Philippe de, 278, 282
Communion, representations of, 25-6, 33, 51, pl. iii
Conquêtes de Charlemagne, 312
Constantinople, 2, 20, 23, 35, 44, 49, 52, 61. *v.* Byzantium
Constantius II, 4
— Gallus Caesar, 4
"Continuous" method, 21, 25, 41, 141, 318
Copies and repetitions, 3-5, 17, 45-9, 56, 110, 114-5, 150, 198, 270, 273, 276, 313, 317, 320-3; danger of relying on, 4
Corbie, school of, 92, 98-9
Coronation, Byzantine, 46, 48, 51
— book of Charles V, 247
Corvinus, John, 298
— Mathias, King of Hungary, 296-9; Missal of, 297
Cosmas and Damian, SS., 297-8
— Indicopleustes, 39-40

Cotton, Sir Robert, 17, 106
Credi, Lorenzo di, 295
Croyland abbey, 140
Crucifixion, earliest appearance of, in illumination, 32; various representations of, 41, 51, 116-7, 132, 180, 305, 322; grotesque, 82, 84-5; symbolical, 152-3, 194, 225-6, 283 (nine Crucifixes, two dead Christs); Christ ascending the cross, 256; legend of nails for, 281-2; pl. xxii, xxiii, xliii
Cunigunde, S., 150
Cuthbert, S., 73; Life of, 140, 195

Daniel, commentary on, 210
Danish raids, effect of, on English art, 122, 124
Dante, Divina Commedia, 262
Davalos, Don Iñigo, 302
David as Byzantine Emperor, 46; as Orpheus, 39, 44-7; as prophet-witness, 24, 30, 51
Deathbed scene, 316
Decretals of Boniface VIII, 262; of Gregory IX, 230
Decretum, 263
Dedication of a church, 238, pl. xxxv
Deer, Book of, 83
Denis, S., Life of, 195, 239-40
Desert of Religion, 235
Desiderius, Abbot of Monte Cassino, 164, 167
Dimma, Book of, 72
Dinteville, François de, Bp. of Auxerre, 285
Dioscorides, 34-5, 186
Diptychs, consular, imitated, 35, 46
Dixmude Missal, 322
Donatus, 300
"Donor" picture, early instance of, 98
Douai Psalter. *v.* Gorleston
Dourdan, view of, 272
Drogo, Sacramentary of, 103, 153
Ducali, Venetian, 293-4
Duccio, 171, 255
Dunois Hours, 276-7
Dunstan, S., 124, 129
Durandus, 261
Durham, 85, 135, 138, 140, 175
— Book (Lindisfarne Gospels), 62-3, 66, 70, 73-6, 79, 84, 86, pl. viii
Durrow, Book of, 71-2, 80, 84, 89

ILLUMINATED MANUSCRIPTS

Eadwin Psalter, 110
Early Christian illumination, 14–35
East Anglian school, 217–8, 223–30
— Winch, 225
Ebbo Gospels, 104, 108–9
Echternach Gospels, 149
Edgar, King, 124; charter of, 124–5
Edmund, Earl of Cornwall, 191
— S., Passion of (Holford MS.), 135–7, 179; Lydgate's Life of, 235
Edward IV, patron of Flemish art, 235, 313–4
— VII, 279
Egbert, Abp. of Trèves, 143, 147–8, 150
Egmond, Floris van, Count of Buren, Hours of, 317
Egypt, skins used for writing in, 1
Egyptian influence on Celtic art, 78
— papyri, illumination of, 1
"Elysabeth the Quene," Hours of, 235
Eneidt, 156
English illumination, 7th and 8th cent., 72–5, 84–7; 9th–12th cent., 106–21 (outline-drawings), 122–42; 13th cent., 174–91; after 1300, 220–35
Eormenilda, S., 179
Estampes, Robinet d', 309
Este, House of, 291–3; Alfonso I, 293; Beatrice, 300; Borso, 291; Ercole I, 291–2; Ippolito I, Cardinal, 293; Leonello, 291
Ethilwald, Lindisfarne Gospels bound by, 73
Etschmiadzin Gospel-book, 34, 91
Euclid, 248
Eudocia, Empress, portrait of, with her sons, 40–1
Eugenius IV, portrait of, 278
Eumenes II, King of Pergamum, 1
Eusebian Canons, decoration of, 23, 28, 30–3, 60, 74, 87, 90–105 *passim*, 128, 130, pl. ix
Evangelists, emblems of, first appearance of, 62–3; in Celtic MSS., 71–84 *passim*, pl. vii; Merovingian, 89
— portraits of, early Christian, 28; Byzantine, 61–4; Celtic, 70–84 *passim;* Carolingian, 90–4, 98, 100–3
Exeter Cathedral, 116
Exultet Rolls, 164–7

350

Falconry, illustrations of, 172
Ferdinand of Aragon, King of Naples, 289, 302
Ferrara, Aeneid formerly at, 13; school of, 291–3
Filocalus, Calendar of, 3–5
Fitton, Alice, 225
Flanders, Count of, 249
Flann, King, 71
Flemish illumination, A.D. 900–1200, 156–9; 13th cent., 203–7; after A.D. 1300, 306–23
Fleury, 124
Floreffe Bible, 144, 159
Florence, 259, 273, 293, 304; school of, 288, 294–7; S. Marco, 169, 288; Breviary of S. Croce, 295–6
Fortescue, Sir John, 17
Fountain of Life, 34, 91, 94, 100, 103, pl. x
Francis, S., 199, 204
Franco-Saxon school, 92, 105
François II, Gospels of, 105
Frederick II, De arte venandi cum avibus, 172
— III, 316
French illumination, A.D. 900–1200, 143, 156–7; 13th cent., 174, 192–203; 14th cent., 236–54; after A.D. 1400, 265–85
Froissart, 249
Frontispieces, 13, 28, 31, 125, 151, 163, 257–8, 294. *v.* Title-pages
Fugger, Ulrich, 43

Gaddi, Taddeo, 273
Gaston Phébus, Comte de Foix, Livre de la Chasse, 267
Gaucourt, Charles de, 282
Gavignano, Sandra di Giovanni Cianchini da, Abbess of Rosano, 290
Gellone Sacramentary, 89
Genesis, Cotton, 17–19; Vienna, 19–22, 161
Geoffrey, Abbot of S. Alban's, 136
George IV, 275
— S., Order of, 316
German illumination, A.D. 900–1200, 143–56; after A.D. 1200, 207–8, 307–8
Gero Gospels, 145–6
Gertrude, owner of Cod. Gertrud., 147

INDEX

Ghent, 249, 322; Missal of S. Bavon's, 203; Vita Christi, etc., written at, 314
Giotto, 26, 255, 261
Giraldus Cambrensis, 77
Girard de Roussillon, romance of, 312
Godescalc, school of, 99–103
Gold, MSS. written in, 19, 23, 29, 125. *v.* Codices Aurei
Golf Book, 322–3, pl. li
Gonzaga, Card. Francesco, 65
Gorleston, 225–9, 307; Psalters (Braybrooke and Douai) from, 226–8
Gothic style in illumination, 135, 174, 236
Graduals, 327. *v.* Choir-books
Grandes Chroniques, 280, 313
Grandison Hours, 234
Greek artists imported to Monte Cassino, 164
Greenfield nunnery, 217
Gregory V, 148
— XI, 247
— Nazianzen, S., Sermons, 40–2
Grimani Breviary, 271, 319–21, 326
— Card. Domenico, 319–20
— — Marino, 304
Grimbald Gospels, 131–2, pl. xv
Grisaille, 245–6, 249, 277, 313
Grizane, 304
Guiart des Moulins, 238
Guthlac Roll, 121, 140, pl. xvii
Guyenne, Louis, Duke of, 268
Gyrard, Laurens, 280

Hague, The, 313
Hainault, 249
— and Holland, William IV of Bavaria, Count of, 310
Harrowing of Hell, various representations of, 59–60, 119, 139, 167, pl. vi, xvi, xx
Hautvillers, 104, 109
Head-pieces, Byzantine, 55–6, pl. v
Heidelberg Sacramentary, 145–6, 153
Helena, S., portrait of, 41
Hennessy Hours, 271, 318, 322
Henry II, Emperor, 143, 150
— II, King of England, 138
— V, 235
— VI, 235, 273–4; Psalter of, 277

Henry VII, 317
— VIII, 17
— of Blois, Bp. of Winchester, 137
Herbals, 34, 186–7
Herrad von Landsperg, 155
Hesdin, 312
Hildesheim, school of, 143, 151–2
Histoire de Charles Martel, 312–3
— du bon roi Alexandre, 312
— du Haynaut, 311
Holkham MSS., 207
Homer, 3. *v.* Iliad
Hortulus Animae, 321
Hortus Deliciarum, 144, 155–6
Hours, Books of, 328–9; early, 188; French, 15th cent., 265
Howard, Sir William, 225
Hugh, S., Prior of Witham, 138
Hunting, illustrations of, 227, 267
Huntingfield Psalter, 141

Iconoclastic Controversy, 20, 36; depicted, 51–2
Iliad, Ambrosian, 2–3, 8–12; Marcian, 13
Incarnation, symbolical representation of, 152
Ingeburge Psalter, 193
Initials, decorative: Byzantine, 64–5; Celtic and Hiberno-Saxon, 69–87 *passim*, pl. viii; Lombardic, Merovingian, and Visigothic, 65, 88, 209–12; Carolingian, 91–109 *passim*; English, 127–42 *passim*, 183 (pen-work), 189, 220–1 (pen-work), 232–3; German, 144–55, pl. xix; French, 57, 195, 240–1 (pen-tracery); Flemish, 157–9, 203; Italian, 162–9, 259 (pen lace-work), 287 (do.)
— historiated: early examples of, 102, 104, 110, 130, 133, 153–5; decline of, in France, 241; development of, in Italy, 258–9, 286–8, 297–8; pl. xvi, xxvi, xxxii, xxxiv, xxxv, xxxvii, xxxix, xliv–vi
Instructions to artist, written across field of pictures, 17
Isabella Book, 318–20, 326
Isabelle of France, Psalter of, 198–9
Isidore, 186
Itala, Quedlinburg, 16–7, 148

351

ILLUMINATED MANUSCRIPTS

Italian illumination before A.D. 1300, 160–73; 14th cent., 255–64; after A.D. 1400, 286–305
Italo-Byzantine paintings in a Winchester MS., 137

Jacobus, Homilies of, 56
Jacqueline of Luxembourg, Duchess of Bedford, 275
James, Thomas, Bp. of Dol, 296
Jeanne d'Evreux, 240; Breviary of, 246
— II, Queen of Navarre, Hours of, 242–5, pl. xxxvi
Jerome, S., Commentary on Daniel, 210; sumptuous MSS. decried by, 19
Jerusalem, entry into, traditional iconography of, 26–7
Joan of Castile, Hours of, 319
John, Abbot of Capua, 163
— Comnenus, portrait of, 60
— II, King of France, 239, 247
— S., dictating his Gospel, 54, 63
Jordan, personified, 22, 59, 126
Josephus, 279–80, 314
Joshua Roll, 42–4
Jouvenel des Ursins, Jacques, Pontifical of, 275
Joyful and dolorous mysteries contrasted, 201, 245
Juliana Anicia, portrait of, 35
Jumièges, Robert of, Missal of, 128
Justinus, 288

Kells, Book of, 66, 68–9, 74, 76–80, 84, pl. vii
Kildare, 77

Landscape-painting, naturalistic, in the Vatican Virgil, 6–8, pl. ii; peculiar Italo-Byzantine tradition of, 53–4, 251, 288; gradual development of French, 251–3, 267, 271–2, 276–85 *passim*, pl. xxxvii, xl; Italian, 292, 297; Flemish, 308–23 *passim*, pl. xlix, li; English, 225, 227, 232–3
Laon, 307
Laurent, Frère, 202
Law-books, illumination of, 230, 262–3
Lazarus, raising of, 26–7, 59
Leo the Patrician, 47
Leofric Missal, 116–7
Liége, 309

Lindeseye, Robert de, Abbot of Peterborough, 180
Lindisfarne Gospels. *v.* Durham Book
Line-endings, 178–9, 221
Livre de la Chasse, 267
— des Merveilles, 267
— des propriétéz des choses, 314
Livres de lestat de lame, 203
Lombardic illumination, 88–9; initials, 65
London, Tower of, depicted, 317–8
Longchamp Abbey, 198
Lorenzetti, the, 257
Lorraine, René II, Duke of, 282
Lothaire, Emperor, Gospels of, 95, 97; Psalter of, 104
Louis VIII, 194
— IX, S., 192, 199; Psalters of, 193–4, 198–9; scenes in the life of, 244
— XI, 278–80
Louterell Psalter, 229–30
Lovel, John, Lord, Lectionary of, 234
Lumière as Lais, 217
Lusignan, view of, 271
Lydgate, Life of S. Edmund, 235
Lyle, Robert de, 224–5
Lytlington, Nicholas, Abbot of Westminster, 231

Mabuse, 311
Mac Durnan, Maelbrigte, Gospels of, 80–1
Mac Regol, Gospels of, 79
Madan, F., 133
Maelbrigt hua Maeluanaigh, Gospels of, 82
Maestricht Psalters and Hours, 205–6
Maizières, Philippe de, 253
Malcolm Canmore, 134
Mandeville, Travels of, 267, 309, pl. xlix
Mandrake, legend of, 35, 186
Mantua, Fr. Jacobus de, 298
Marco Polo, 267
Margaret of Bavaria, Duchess of Burgundy, 270–1
— of Burgundy, Countess of Richemont, 275
— of Scotland, S., Gospel-book of, 133–4
— of York, Duchess of Burgundy, 313, 316
Martial, 2

INDEX

Martreuil, Itier de, Bp. of Poitiers, 248
Mary of Burgundy, death of, 316, 320
— I, Queen of England, Psalter of, 121, 217, 221–3, 230, pl. xxxi–ii
Matilda, widow of Henry the Fowler, 144
Matteo di Giovanni, 257
Matthew, S., portrait of, with Arabic exemplar, 64
Mauro, Cristoforo, Ducale of, 294
Maximilian I, 298, 316; Prayer-book of, 321
Medici, House of, 293–4; Lorenzo de', 294, 296 (Hours of)
Melissenda, Queen of Jerusalem, Psalter of, 57–61, pl. vi
Mélusine, 271
Memlinc, Hans, 311, 315, 318–9
Menology of Basil II, 52–5
Merovingian illumination, 88–9
Metaphrastes, Simeon, 52, 54–7, 63, 260, pl. v
Metsys, Quentin, 311
Metz Pontifical, 237–8, 241, pl. xxxv
— school of, 92, 99–104
Michael, Abbot of the Studium, 49
— S., fighting with devil, 272, 316; rescuing hermit, 53–4, pl. v; Order of, 278
Michelangelo, 304
Mielot, Miracles de N. D., 313
Milan, school of, 293, 298–301
Missals, 324–6
Mitford, Richard, Bp. of Salisbury, 233
Modena, choir-books at, 258, 292
Mont S. Michel, 272, 276
Monte Cassino, school of, 163–7
Montferrat, Blanche de, Duchess of Savoy, 271
Mozarabic MSS., 210
Mulbarton, 229
Mulling, Book of, 81
Mundford, 224

Nantes, 197
Naples, 5, 160; mosaics at, 62; school of (?), 301–3
Nativity, typical Byzantine representation of, 53
Natural history, illustrations of, 263–4, 315–6. v. Bestiaries, Falconry, Herbals, Woodland
Newminster. v. Winchester.

Nicephorus Botaniates, portraits of, 41–2
— Patriarch, 51
Nimbus, in Classical MSS., 10, 12; cruciferous, 27; rectangular, for living persons, 162
Noah's wife, legend of, 222
Norfolk, 224–5, 229–30
Norman Conquest, 121
Norwich, 227–8, 307; Breviary of, 227
Nuremberg Hours, 200–1, 245

Oath-book, 144
Octateuch MSS, 48–9
Offas, Lives of the Two, 185–6
Olaf, S., scenes from the legend of, 181
Old and New Dispensations, symbolically contrasted, 181, 194, 242–4, 276
Organ, early painting of, 189
Orleans, Charles, Duke of, 317–8
— Duchess of, 278
Ormesby Psalter, 228–9
Otto I, the Great, 123, 143–4
— II, 143, 150
— III, 148–51; apotheosis of, 149
Ottonian illumination, 143 seq.
Outline-drawings, 1, 12, 106–21, 140, 184–6, 212–7, 221–2, etc.
Ovid, 289
Oxford, 176

Pachomius, S., 120–1, 130
Padua, 26, 170–1, 262; Gospel and Epistle-books of, 169–71
Papyri, illuminated, 1
Parco, Abbey of S. Mary de, MSS. from, 158–9
Paris, illumination at, 192–5, 198–9, 237, 239–42, 273–6; liturgical use of, 248, 269; scenes of everyday life in, 240; views of, 275; Hôtel de Ville, fire at, 275; Sainte Chapelle MSS., 193–4, 199, 237; S. Magloire's Missal, 273; University, 175, 192
— Matthew, 185–6
Parma, 170
— Roger of, Treatise on Surgery, 195
Paul the Deacon, Commentary on the Rule of S. Benedict, 163
Pavia, 292
Peiresc, illuminations copied for, 3, 17

353

ILLUMINATED MANUSCRIPTS

Pen-work initial and border ornament, 183, 220, 259, 287
Perugia, 304
Peterborough Psalter, at Brussels, 224; London, 180-1, pl. xxii
Petrarch, 258, 295
Petrucci, Antonello, 289
Petrus Comestor, Historia Scholastica, 190-1, 238
Philip Augustus, 192-3, 199
— III, 202
— the Fair, Archduke of Austria, 316, 319
Philippa, Queen, Psalter of, 231
Philippe le Bel, Breviary of, 237
Philippi, 17
Physiologus, 186
Pius IV, 305
Plessis-lès-Tours, 284
Pliny, 34, 186
Poitiers Bible, 239
Pontano, Gioviano, 5
Prato MS., 256
Presles, Raoul de, 252
Priming, in Byzantine MSS., 47, 49
Priscian, 248
Prochorus, S., writing down S. John's Gospel, 54, 63
Prophets and apostles, in pairs, 243, 249, 276
— figures of, in Gospel scenes, 24, 29, 51
Prudentius, Psychomachia, 111-3
Psalters, 327; illustration of, 44-52, 109, etc.; popularity of, 12th-14th cent., 140, 176, 193, etc.
Ptolemy, 39, 248
Pudsey Bible, 138
Purple vellum, MSS. on, 19-29, 102

Quedlinburg Itala, 16-7, 148

Rabanus, De Laudibus S. Crucis, 155
Rabula Gospels, 31-4, 41
Raphael, 6, 304
Ratisbon, school of, 143, 152-3
Ravenna, 56, 90; mosaics, 7, 15, 22, 37, 126, 148
Raymondin, 272
Registrum Gregorii, 150
Reichenau, school of, 143-51 *passim*
René of Anjou 283

Rheims, 197; school of, 92, 104-5, 108-9, 143, 145
Ricemarch, Psalter of, 83
Richard II, Bible and Missal of, 232-4, pl. xxxiv; Epistle to, 253-4
Rigan, 186
Riom, view of, 272
Robert of Anjou, King of Naples, 256
— of Normandy, Abp. of Rouen, Missal of (?), 127
Robertet, François, 278
Rogers Album, 305
Roias, Francisco de, 318
Roman de la Rose, 318
Romano, Giulio, 304
Rome, 2, 14, 85, 90-1, 137, 160, 278, 304; MS. written at, 65; school of (?), 301; mosaics of S. Maria Maggiore, 43; Bible of S. Paul's, 98-9; twisted columns of S. Peter's, 101, 103, 280
Romuleon, 314
Rosano, Abbess of, 290
Rushworth Gospels. *v.* Mac Regol, Gospels of
Rutland Psalter, 188-90

Sacramentaries, 325. *v.* Drogo, Gellone, Heidelberg, Warmund
S. Alban's, MSS. executed at, 136-7, 140, 184-6, 214
— Denis, abbey of, 11, 239, 249; Franco-Saxon school of, 92, 105; Missal of, 246-7; Vie de S. Denis, executed at, 195
— Gall, Celtic MSS. at, 83-4
— Omer, Hours of, 306; Psalter of S. Bertin's abbey, 110, 156
— Omer family, Psalter of, 229
— Pol, Louis de Luxembourg, Count of, Hours of, 283
— Vaast, Gospel-lectionary of, 105
— Victor-in-Santem, Gospels of, 92
Sainte Abbaye, 202-3, 236
Salisbury Cathedral, 234
Saluces Hours, 283
Savoy, Charles, Duke of, 271
Scala Paradisi, 56-7
Script, Greek: capitals, 42; uncials, 8, 17, 19; Slavonic uncials, 65; minuscules, 42, 44

INDEX

Script, Latin: rustic capitals, 6, 10, 107, 109; uncials, 16; cursive, 17; half-uncials, 74; Irish, 67; minuscules, Merovingian and Caroline, 91; Lombardic, 165; Visigothic, 210; 13th cent. Bible-hand, 175, 182, 196; "scrittura umanistica," 289
Scotus, Joannes, 289
Sforza, Bianca Maria, 298; Bona, 298, 300; Galeazzo Maria, 301; Ludovico, 300; Maximilian, 300
— Book of Hours, 298-300, 321-2, pl. xlvii-viii
— Visconti, Francesco, 300
Sforziada, 300
Shaftesbury, 137
Sheen, MS. written at, 317
Sherborne Missal, 233-4
Siciliano, Antonio, 320
Sicily, 303
Siena, school of, 257-8, 286-8, 290, 297, pl. xxxix, xliv, xlvi
Silos abbey, MSS. from, 210-2
Silver, MSS. written in, 19, 20, 23
Sketchbook, artist's, 250
Sketches, preliminary, in margins, 239
Smeralda, Hours of, 295
Smithfield, S. Bartholomew's, 230
Sneyd MS., 206, 306
Sobieski Hours, 275-6
Soissons, 307; Gospels of S. Medard's, 103, pl. x
Somme le Roi, 201-3, pl. xxviii
Songe du Vergier, 253
Spanish illumination, 209-12, 302-3
Speculum Humanae Salvationis, 307-8
Stained glass medallions, 140, 180
Statius, 267-8
Stavelot abbey, MSS. from, 157-8
Strassburg, 155
Stuart, Card. Henry, 275
Surgical and medical MSS., 195-6, pl. xxvii
Susa, mosaic-portrait of Virgil at, 11
Syrian illumination, 31-4; influence of, on Carolingian art, 91, 100

Tail-pieces, 211-2
Taymouth Horae, 231
Teano, 163
Teilo, S., 75
Tenison Psalter, 190-1, pl. xxiv

Terence, MSS. of, 12-3, 110; "Térence des Ducs," 267-8
Theobald, Abbot of Monte Cassino, 164
Theodore, Abbot of the Studium, 51
— Psalter, 49-52, 54, 65, 260
Theophano, wife of Otto II, 143, 149, 151
Thomas of Canterbury, S., 176, 180; miniatures of the murder of, 141, 181, 184; of a miracle of the Virgin to, 184
— of Woodstock, Duke of Gloucester, Bible of, 231
Three living and three dead, 205, 225; variant of, 320
Title-pages, 31, 161, 302. v. Frontispieces
Toledo Missal, 303
Tombelaine, 272
Tours, 278-9; school of, Carolingian, 92, 94-9, 143; late French, 277-85
Trefoil-arched canopy, early use of, 181, 197, pl. xxv
Trèves, 143, 149; Gospel-lectionary of S. Maximin's, 153; "Kopialbuch" of Abp. Baldwin, 307
Troyes, 139
Turin Hours, 309-10

Ussher, Abp., 77
Uta-codex, 152-3
Utrecht Psalter, 92, 104, 106-11; copies of, 110, 115

Val-Dieu monastery, 219
Val-Duchesse Breviary, 306
Valenciennes, 249
Valentine, Calendar of Filocalus made for, 4
Valerius Flaccus, 288
— Maximus, 282, 314
Vallombrosa Gradual, 259, 286
Van Eyck, Jan, his "Vierge au donateur" copied, 276
Vatican Virgil (Cod. Vat. lat. 3225), 5-10, 12, 16-9, 21, 148, pl. ii
Veldegke, Heinrich von, 156
Vellum, earliest use of, 1
Venice, school of, 293-4
Verdun Breviary, 237
— Richard de, 237
Verona, 162, 288; early Psalter at, 161

355

ILLUMINATED MANUSCRIPTS

Viana, Domicella de, 207
— Prince Charles of, 303
Vinci, Leonardo da, 300
Virgil, MSS. of, 2, 13, 258. *v.* Codex Romanus, Vatican Virgil
— portraits of, 2, 11
Visigothic illumination, 88–9, 209–12
Vivian Bible, 96–7, 99

Waermund, 186
Warmund, S., Sacramentary of, 162–3
Weingarten Missals, 207
Werburga, S., 179
Westminster, 135; Missal, 231; Psalter, 141–2, 176–7
Wickhampton, wall-paintings at, 225
Winchester, school of, 106–39 *passim*, 151, 176, 231; Bible, 137–9, 158, pl. xvi; Psalters, 116, 127, 137–8; Newminster Foundation-charter, 124–5; Gospels, 128–9; Liber Vitae, 117–8, pl. xiii; Office-book, 117; Psalter, 132–3
Windmill Psalter, 220–1
Witham Priory, 138
Woodland scenes, 225, 227, 267
Worms Bible, 144, 154–5, 158
Worksop Bestiary, 187
Wycliffite Bible, 231

Yolande de Flandre, Hours of, 242–5
Ypres, 249; "Kuerbouc" of, 307
Yves, monk of S. Denis, 239

Zagba, MS. written at, 32